THE GOOD DOCTOR GUIDE

THE GOOD DOCTOR GUIDE

(Third Edition)

A Unique Directory of Recommended Medical Specialists

CATHERINE VASSALLO

SIMON & SCHUSTER

A VIACOM COMPANY

Important Note
The book has been researched and compiled in unusually difficult
circumstances imposed by medical regulations concerning publicity.
In particular, these regulations have prevented the doctors named in this book
from being able to check their own entries. Despite this, every effort has been
made to ensure the accuracy of all entries and neither the author nor the
publisher can accept responsibility for any errors of fact.

The Good Doctor Guide is not a comprehensive work and the omission of
a particular doctor's name is in no way an adverse reflection on that doctor's
skill, actual or implied.

First published in Great Britain by Simon & Schuster Ltd, 1997
A Viacom Company

Simon & Schuster Ltd
West Garden Place
Kendal Street
London W2 2AQ

Simon & Schuster of Australia Pty Ltd
Sydney

A CIP catalogue record for this book is available
from the British Library

ISBN 0-684-81781-0

Typeset by Hewer Text Composition Services, Edinburgh
Printed and bound in Great Britain by Butler & Tanner Ltd, Frome and London

FOR CLIVE and NICOLA
whose constant help and encouragement made this possible

ACKNOWLEDGEMENTS

With many thanks to:

Martin and Catherine Page for allowing me to take over as editor; Papà, for his help and advice; Ian Francis for his patience and time; and Catherine Reed, for putting it all together.

CONTENTS

SCOTLAND

• Edinburgh

• Glasgow

• Newcastle

NORTHERN
AND
YORKSHIRE

NORTH
WEST

TRENT

• Manchester

WEST
MIDLANDS

• Birmingham

Norwich •

ANGLIA &
OXFORD

WALES ·

Cardiff •

• Bristol

LONDON &
SOUTH EAST

• London

SOUTH AND
WEST

• Southampton

INTRODUCTION

The Good Doctor Guide is a listing of 1000 of the best doctors in England, Scotland and Wales. The guide is divided into 37 areas of medical expertise and is designed for patients who want to choose a top specialist for a second opinion or to perform a major operation.

London is a world-renowned centre of excellence for medicine and surgery. However, the 'bureaucracy' of the medical establishment often prevents patients from finding out who the best doctors are in any particular field. For example, not every orthopaedic surgeon can be an expert on knee surgery with a track record of hundreds of successful operations. Your GP can give you some guidance, but may have a limited knowledge of specialists in certain fields or be restricted to using local hospitals. This guide simply provides another source of information to help in the process of choosing a specialist doctor or hospital unit.

The majority of doctors included in this book work for both the private and public sectors. Selection was based on nominations from over 500 specialist doctors, who were asked the following questions:

1. To which of your colleagues would you refer a close relative and for what?
2. To which of your colleagues would you turn for a second opinion, when you wanted to discuss the diagnosis of one of your own patients?

Each doctor receiving the requisite number of nominations in a particular field of medicine was selected for the guide. The nominations were then ratified by an advisory body of top consultants.

It is important to note that no such selection could include every outstanding doctor in the country. Some extremely eminent doctors do not appear in this book because they devote so much of their time to research and teaching that they see few patients.

Medical Bureaucracy

The UK health sector is in a process of continual change, driven by a delicate balancing act between quality of service and cost. One of the most important elements of service is choice, and the objective of *The Good Doctor Guide* is to help those patients who need a specialist doctor to make an informed choice.

The last two editions of *The Good Doctor Guide* were not welcomed by the General Medical Council (GMC), which viewed it as an underhand way for consultants to unlawfully advertise their skills. It is against GMC regulations for specialists to nominate themselves for a publication of this type and the GMC even views a doctor checking his own entry as contravening its regulations. This restrictive policy has been enforced for years. However, in the era of the Patients' Charter, clinical audits and an ever improving flow of information, the GMC's view looks increasingly outdated.

In the United States of America, peer reviews by government health organisations and private insurance schemes, keep a constant check on health care standards. Details of individual doctors who have been excluded from the Medicare programme and fined are published monthly in a consumer health letter.

In the UK, mandatory clinical audits are carried out in every hospital, listing morbidity and mortality rates. It is a huge cost to the taxpayer but the results are seldomly made public, and never in a manner which identifies individual doctors and their performance. There also exists a system of distinction awards where doctors are given a 'bonus' type payment as recognition for outstanding professional work of national or international significance. Awards are paid in addition to the doctors' salary with an A+ award-holder receiving £49,820 and a C award-holder receiving £10,490. The estimated total cost of these awards last year was around £70 million, including administration and actual payments. For the first time since its implementation in 1948, this list will be made public in January 1997. In addition, some hospitals, under pressure from private patients, are at last producing their own list of consultants and area of speciality.

The medical establishment is at last beginning to shed some of its secrecy and make it easier for British patients to choose which doctor they wish to consult, a right Americans and most EC citizens have always taken for granted. Although the choice of a doctor is ultimately up to the patient, in most cases individuals should seek advice from their GP. NHS patients have to be referred in all cases but private patients can contact specialists direct.

This referral process has recently changed with the introduction of fundholding, following the 1989 white paper 'Working for Patients'. It is the process whereby GP practices are allocated budgets to pay directly for hospitals and other referrals. The main rationale for fundholding was the financial leverage it afforded GPs who can now, for the first time, stipulate – within their purchasing contracts – certain minimum standards regarding services and waiting times. If the hospital does not agree to the fundholder's requirements, GPs could potentially take their contracts to another hospital.

The advantages for patients are mainly in the areas of convenience and speed of secondary referral and treatment. The downside for individual patients is that the question of money now becomes a contributing factor in any referral. A fundholding GP can, in theory, refer you to any NHS consultant of your choice. In practice, they may have entered into their own contracts for treatment with particular hospitals and consultants for reasons to do with quality of care, price and accessibility. They may not wish to refer you outside these contracts. In theory, under the patients' charter you are given the right to be 'referred to a consultant acceptable to you, when your GP thinks it is necessary, and to be referred for a second opinion if you and your GP agree this is desirable'. The interpretation of this section is somewhat vague, although if you find a doctor unacceptable you can insist on seeing a specialist of your choice.

Similar problems exist for non-fund-holding GPs in that a GP will be constrained by contracts agreed by the District Health Authority (DHA). Although the DHA can permit extra-contractual referrals, money for these is in short supply. Once again, if as an NHS patient you want to see a particular specialist, it is your right, so be assertive.

How to Use the Good Doctor Guide

The guide is divided into 37 sections, based on medical specialities. Within each section doctors are listed alphabetically with details of their qualifications and particular special interests (subspecialities). Each section is subdivided into six geographic regions as outlined by the map on page xi.

To help identify which section you should be using, Index 1 is a list of doctors included in the guide, while Index 2 provides a list of major medical conditions.

There are four appendices. Appendix 1 is a list of specialist medical units which can be used in conjunction with the list of doctors for that particular speciality. Appendix 2 is a quick reference list of hospitals with telephone numbers and addresses. Appendix 3 provides an explanation of doctors' degrees and qualifications; and Appendix 4 is a glossary of technical medical terms used throughout the book.

ALLERGISTS AND CLINICAL IMMUNOLOGISTS

See also Chest Physicians

These doctors offer diagnosis of allergic disorders including: immunologically mediated diseases such as post viral fatigue syndrome, vasculitis and immunodeficiencies, food, drug and insect allergies as well as problems related to organ transplant and immune system cancers.

Many allergies such as asthma and eczema are now being treated by respiratory (Chest) Physicians and dermatologists. HIV/AIDS which is treated by immunologists is also dealt with in a separate section.

LONDON AND THE SOUTH EAST

GRIFFIN, Professor George E.

Special interests:	**Intestinal immunity; HIV and the intestine**
NHS:	Honorary Consultant Physician and
	Professor of Infectious Diseases
	Division of Communicable Diseases
	St George's Hospital
	Blackshaw Road
	London SW17 0QT
Tel:	0181 672 9944
Fax:	0181 725 5827
Private:	Refer to address and number above
First Qualified:	1974 – London
Major Degrees:	PhD, FRCP, FRCP Ed
Academic:	Professor of Infectious Diseases
	St George's Hospital Medical School
Specialist Training:	Hammersmith Hospital, London
USA:	Honorary Professor of Medicine, Michigan University
	Harkness Fellow, Harvard University, Boston

1

PEPYS, Professor Mark B.

Special interests:	**Amyloidosis**
NHS:	Immunological Medicine Unit
	Royal Postgraduate Medical School
	Hammersmith Hospital
	Du Cane Road
	London W12 0NN
Tel:	0181 740 3261
Fax:	0181 749 7478
Private:	Refer to address and number above
First Qualified:	1968 – Cambridge
Major Degrees:	MD, PhD, FRCP, FRCPath
Academic:	Professor of Clinical Immunology, London University
Specialist Training:	Cambridge and Royal Free Hospital, London
Distinctions:	Previously President, British Allergists and International Association Allergy and Clinical Immunology

PINCHING, Professor Anthony J.

Special interests:	**Immunology including HIV/AIDS**
NHS:	Professor of Immunology
	St Bartholomew's Hospital
	West Smithfield
	London EC1A 7BE
Tel:	0171 601 8428
Fax:	0171 600 3839
Private:	Refer to address and number above
First Qualified:	1973 – Oxford
Major Degrees:	FRCP
Academic:	Professor of Immunology, St Bartholomew's Medical School, London
Specialist Training:	Royal Postgraduate Medical School and St Mary's Hospital, London

WEBSTER, Dr Anthony D. B.

NHS:	Honorary Consultant in Clinical Immunology
	Royal Free Hospital Medical School
	Pond Street
	London NW3 2QG
Tel:	0171 794 0500 Ext. 4519 or 0171 830 2141
Fax:	0171 830 2224
Private:	Refer to address and number above
First Qualified:	1964 – Cambridge
Major Degrees:	MD, FRCP
Distinctions:	Senior Scientist MRC Head Immunodeficiency Research Group

NORTH WEST REGION

MANCHESTER

PEARSON, Dr David J.

Special interests:	**Identifies external causes of allergic reactions affecting multiple organ systems; food allergies; asthma**
NHS:	Honorary Consultant Physician
	Withington Hospital
	West Didsbury
	Manchester M20 2LR
Tel:	0161 445 8111
Fax:	0161 434 5194
Private:	Refer to address and number above
First Qualified:	1968 – London
Major Degrees:	PhD, FRCP
Academic:	Senior Lecturer, Manchester University
	Research fellow, Manchester University

SOUTH AND WEST REGION

SOUTHAMPTON

WARNER, Professor John O.

Special interests:	**Paediatric allergies**
NHS:	Professor of Child Health
	Southampton General Hospital
	Tremona Road
	Southampton SO16 6YD
Tel:	01703 796160
Fax:	01703 796378
Private:	Refer to address and number above
First Qualified:	1968 – Sheffield
Major Degrees:	MD, FRCP
Academic:	Professor of Child Health, Southampton University
Specialist Training:	Great Ormond Street Hospital for Children, London
Distinctions:	Previously Secretary, British Society of Allergy and Immunology

SCOTLAND

EDINBURGH

FERGUSON, Professor Anne

Special interests:	**Gastrointestinal immunology**
NHS:	Consultant Physician
	Gastrointestinal Unit
	Western General Hospital
	Crewe Road
	Edinburgh EH4 2XU
Tel:	0131 537 1000
Fax:	0131 537 1007
Private:	Refer to address and number above
First Qualified:	1964 – Glasgow
Major Degrees:	PhD, FRCP Ed, FRCPath
Academic:	Professor of Gastroenterology, Edinburgh University
Specialist Training:	Royal Infirmary, Glasgow

ARTERIAL AND VASCULAR SURGEONS

These surgeons treat blood vessel ailments of the heart, lungs and brain. The surgeons generally specialise in either arterial disease or venous disease. Arterial surgeons treat disease of the arteries. The commonest disorders in veins is varicose veins. About one third of all deaths in Britain are due to failure of an artery either in the brain (stroke) or the heart muscle (coronary thrombosis).

LONDON AND THE SOUTH EAST

BASKERVILLE, Mr Paul A.

Special interests:	**Varicose veins; carotid artery disease**
NHS:	Consultant Surgeon
	King's College Hospital
	Denmark Hill, London SE5 9RS
Tel:	0171 346 3339
Private:	3 Upper Harley Street
	London NW1 2PR
Tel:	0171 935 5843
Fax:	0171 224 0080
First Qualified:	1974 – Oxford
Major Degrees:	MA (vide infra), DM, FRCS
Specialist Training:	St Bartholomew's and St Thomas' Hospitals, London

BISHOP, Mr Christopher C. R.

Special interests:	**Carotid artery surgery; aortic aneurysm surgery; varicose vein surgery**
NHS:	Consultant Surgeon
	The Middlesex Hospital
	Mortimer Street, London W1N 8AA
Tel:	0171 636 8333
Fax:	0171 637 5541
Private:	149 Harley Street
	London W1 2DE
Tel:	0171 235 6086
Fax:	0171 235 6052
First Qualified:	1978 – Cambridge
Major Degrees:	MChir, FRCS
Specialist Training:	St Thomas' Hospital, London, and
	Scripps Clinic, La Jolla, California
USA:	See 'Specialist Training' above

CROFT, Mr Rodney J.

Special interests:	**General and vascular surgery; aneurysms; carotid artery surgery**
NHS:	Consultant General and Vascular Surgeon
	North Middlesex Hospital
	Sterling Road
	Edmonton, London N18 1QX
Tel:	0181 887 2000 Ext. 401
Fax:	0181 887 4219
Private:	144 Harley Street
	London W1N 1AH
Tel:	0171 935 0023
Fax:	0171 935 5972
First Qualified:	1969 – Cambridge
Major Degrees:	FRCS, FSCS, MChir
Academic:	Clinical Sub-Dean and Honorary Senior Lecturer
	Royal Free Hospital Medical School, London
Specialist Training:	The Middlesex and Central Middlesex Hospitals, London
Distinctions:	Examiner and recognised teacher, London University
USA:	Fellow, American College of Surgeons

GREENHALGH, Professor Roger M.

Special interests:	**Vascular surgery**
NHS:	Charing Cross Hospital
	Fulham Palace Road
	London W6 8RF
Tel:	0181 846 7316
Fax:	0181 846 7330
Private:	Refer to address and number above
First Qualified:	1966 – Cambridge
Major Degrees:	MD, FRCS
Academic:	Professor of Surgery, Charing Cross and Westminster, London
Specialist Training:	St Bartholomew's Hospital, London
Distinctions:	Councillor: Association of Surgeons of Great Britain and Ireland
	European Society for Vascular Surgery
	Honorary member, Vascular Societies USA, Canada, Germany
	Previously Moyniham Fellow, Association of Surgeons of Great Britain and Ireland, Hunterian Professor, Royal College of Surgeons
USA:	Visiting Professor, Harvard, Mayo Clinic; Baylor College of Medicine, Dallas & UCLA

HAMILTON, Mr George

Special interests:	**Renal vascular surgery**
NHS:	Consultant Surgeon
	Royal Free Hospital
	Pond Street
	London NW3 2QG
Tel:	0171 794 0550 Ext. 3072
Fax:	0171 431 4528
Private:	6 Devonshire Place
	London W1M 1HH
Tel:	0171 486 9319
Fax:	0171 431 4528
First Qualified:	1971 – Glasgow
Major Degrees:	FRCS
Specialist Training:	Royal Free Hospital, London
USA:	Previously Clinical and Research Fellow in Vascular Surgery, Massachusetts General Hospital, Harvard Medical School, Boston
	Attending Surgeons Association and Staff member, Spaulding Rehabilitation Hospital, Boston

HOBBS, Mr John T.

Special interests:	**Treatment of peripheral vascular disorders with an emphasis on venous disorders**
NHS:	No NHS work
Private:	4 Upper Wimpole Street
	London W1M 7TD
Tel:	0171 323 2830
Fax:	0171 224 2930
First Qualified:	1954 – London
Major Degrees:	MD, FRCS
Academic:	Senior Lecturer, St Mary's and St George's Hospitals, London
Specialist Training:	St Mary's Hospital, London, and Birmingham
USA:	Previously Research Fellow in Surgery
	Harvard Medical School, Boston

JAMIESON, Mr Crawford William

Special interests:	**Vascular surgery**
NHS:	Consultant Surgeon
	St Thomas' Hospital
	Lambeth Palace Road
	London SE1 7EH
Tel:	0171 928 9292 Ext. 2716
Fax:	0171 261 0358
Private:	The Consulting Rooms
	York House
	199 Westminster Bridge Road
	London SE1 7UT
Tel:	0171 928 3013
Fax:	0171 938 6794
First Qualified:	1960 – London (with Honours)
Major Degrees:	MS, FRCS
Academic:	Honorary Senior Lecturer, Royal Postgraduate Medical School Hammersmith, London
Distinctions:	Previously Hunterian Professor, Royal College of Surgeons
USA:	Wellcome Research Fellow in Surgery Tulane University, New Orleans

MANSFIELD, Professor Averil O.

Special interests:	**Head and neck vascular surgery**
NHS:	Consultant Vascular Surgeon
	St Mary's Hospital
	Praed Street
	London W2 1NY
Tel:	0171 725 6666 or 0171 725 1068
Fax:	0171 725 6200
Private:	Lindo Wing, St Mary's Hospital
Tel:	0171 402 9491
Fax:	0171 706 2193
First Qualified:	1960 – Liverpool
Major Degrees:	ChM, FRCS
Academic:	Professor of Vascular Surgery, St Mary's, London
Specialist Training:	Liverpool
Distinctions:	Chairman, Court of Examiners, Royal College of Surgeons

NICOLAIDES, Professor Andreas N.

Special interests:	**Noninvasive cardiovascular investigations; carotid bifurcation disease; prevention of stroke**
NHS and Academic:	Professor of Vascular Surgery St Mary's Hospital Praed Street London W2 1NY
Tel:	0171 725 6666 or 0171 725 6243
Fax:	0171 725 6200
Private:	Refer to address and number above
First Qualified:	1962 – London
Major Degrees:	MS, FRCS
Specialist Training:	King's College Hospital, London
Distinctions:	Jacksonian Prize, Royal College of Surgeons

SCURR, Mr John H.

NHS:	Consultant Surgeon Middlesex Hospital Mortimer Street London W1N 8AA
Tel:	0171 380 9414
Fax:	0171 380 9413
Private:	The Lister Hospital Chelsea Bridge Road London SW1W 8RH
Tel:	0171 730 9563
Fax:	0171 259 9938
First Qualified:	1972 – London (with Honours)
Major Degrees:	FRCS
Academic:	Senior Lecturer, The Middlesex Hospital, London
Specialist Training:	Westminster Hospital, London

TAYLOR, Mr Peter R.

Special interests:	**Aortic aneurysms and arterial bypass procedures for peripheral vascular disease**
NHS:	Consultant Vascular Surgeon Guy's Hospital St Thomas Street London SE1 9RT
Tel:	0171 955 5000
Fax:	0171 403 0212
Private:	Refer to address above
Tel:	0171 403 3893
First Qualified:	1979 – Cambridge
Major Degrees:	MChir, FRCS
Academic:	Senior Lecturer in Vascular Surgery, Guy's Hospital, London
Specialist Training:	Guy's Hospital, London

WOLFE, Mr John H. N.

Special interests:	**Vascular surgery; thoraco-abdominal aneurysm repair**
NHS:	Consultant Vascular Surgeon
	St Mary's Hospital
	Praed Street
	London W2 1NY
Tel:	0171 725 6072
Fax:	0171 725 6200
Private:	66 Harley Street
	London W1N 1AE
Tel:	0171 580 5030
Fax:	0171 631 5314
First Qualified:	1981 – London
Major Degrees:	MS, FRCS
Specialist Training:	St Thomas' Hospital, London
Distinctions:	Previously Hunterian Professor, Royal College of Surgeons
USA:	Previously Research Fellow, Harvard University, Boston

NORTH WEST REGION

LIVERPOOL

HARRIS, Mr Peter Lyon

Special interests:	**Vascular surgery: aortic aneurysms; carotid artery disease; critical limb ischaemia; minimally invasive vascular surgery**
NHS:	Royal Liverpool University Hospital
	Prescot Street
	Liverpool L7 8XP
Tel:	0151 706 3447
Fax:	0151 706 5827
Private:	88 Rodney Street
	Liverpool L1 9AR
Tel:	0151 709 0669
First Qualified:	1967 – Manchester
Major Degrees:	MD, FRCS
Academic:	Previously Secretary, Vascular Surgical Society of Great Britain and Ireland
Distinctions:	President, European Board of Vascular Surgery

MANCHESTER

CHARLESWORTH, Mr David

Special interests:	**Vascular surgery**
NHS:	Consultant Surgeon
	Withington Hospital
	West Didsbury
	Manchester M20 2LR
Tel:	0161 447 4423
Private:	Alexandra Hospital
	Mill Lane
	Cheadle SK8 2PX
Tel:	01565 650619
Fax:	01565 654813
First Qualified:	1959 – Manchester
Major Degrees:	MD, FRCS
Academic:	Reader in Surgery, University Hospital of South Manchester
Distinctions:	Chairman, Regional Higher Surgical Training Committee
	Previously Director, North West Regional Health Authority Regional Centre for Vascular Surgery
	Previously President, Vascular Surgical Society of Great Britain and Ireland

NORTHERN AND YORKSHIRE REGION

NEWCASTLE

LAMBERT, Mr David

Special interests:	**Arterial and venous surgery**
NHS:	Consultant Vascular Surgeon
	Royal Victoria Infirmary
	Queen Victoria Road
	Newcastle upon Tyne NE1 4LP
Tel:	0191 227 5134
Fax:	0191 232 5278
Private:	Newcastle Nuffield Hospital
	Clayton Road
	Jesmond, Newcastle upon Tyne NE2 1JP
Tel:	0191 281 6131
First Qualified:	1977 – Newcastle
Major Degrees:	MD, FRCS
Academic:	Clinical Lecturer in Surgery, Newcastle University
Specialist Training:	St Mary's Hospital, London, and Leicester Royal Infirmary

SOUTH AND WEST REGION

BOURNEMOUTH

DARKE, Mr Simon G.

Special interests:	**Venous disease**
NHS:	Consultant Vascular and General Surgeon
	Royal Bournemouth Hospital
	Castle Lane East, Bournemouth BH7 7DW
Tel:	01202 704601
Fax:	01202 704623
Private:	The Oaks
	6 Leicester Road
	Branksome, Poole BH13 6BZ
Tel:	01202 761870
Fax:	01202 752353
First Qualified:	1965 – London
Major Degrees:	MS, FRCS
Academic:	Honorary Lecturer, Southampton University
Distinctions:	Previously Secretary and President 1995–6, Vascular Surgical Society of GB & I; Previously Treasurer and Trustee of the European Society for Vascular Surgery

SCOTLAND

EDINBURGH

RUCKLEY, Professor Charles Vaughan

Special interests:	**Vascular surgery: carotid surgery, aneurysm surgery and all aspects of the management venous disease**
NHS:	Consultant Surgeon
	Royal Infirmary
	Lauriston Place
	Edinburgh EH3 9YW
Tel:	0131 536 3924
Fax:	0131 536 3937
Private:	Refer to address above
Tel:	0131 667 8678
First Qualified:	1959 – Edinburgh
Major Degrees:	FRCP Ed, ChM, FRCS Ed
Academic:	Professor Vascular Surgery, Edinburgh University
Specialist Training:	Edinburgh
Distinctions:	Previously President, Vascular Surgical Society of Great Britain and Ireland
USA:	Previously Research Fellow, University of Colorado Medical Centre

CARDIOLOGISTS

Cardiologists treat heart, lung and blood vessel disorders and also hypertension. Some do interventional procedures such as angioplasty (widening of the arteries). For surgery, patients are normally sent to Cardiothoracic or thoracic surgeons (please refer to these sections).

Cardiovascular disease is the cause of almost 50% of deaths in the UK, accounting for 300,000 deaths a year. In addition 1.9 million people are estimated to suffer from angina. Coronary heart disease (CHD) is the single largest cause of death. One in three men, and one in four women, die from CHD, although death rates have been falling in the UK since the late 70s. Three per cent of all hospital admissions are from CHD costing the NHS £917 million pounds a year. The death rates from CHD in Scotland and Northern Ireland are the highest in the world. (See appendix 1(ii) for a list of specialist cardiac units).

LONDON AND THE SOUTH EAST

BALCON, Dr Raphael

Special interests:	**Cardiac catheterisation and angioplasty**
NHS:	Consultant Cardiologist
	The London Chest Hospital
	Bonner Road
	London E2 9IQ
Tel:	0181 980 4433
Fax:	0181 983 2278
Private:	22 Upper Wimpole Street
	London WIM 7TA
Tel:	0171 486 8963
Fax:	0171 486 7918
First Qualified:	1960 – London
Major Degrees:	MD, FRCP
Academic:	Senior Lecturer, Cardiothoracic Institute, London
Specialist Training:	King's College and National Heart Hospitals, London
Distinctions:	Councillor, British Cardiac Society
USA:	Previously Fellow in Cardiology
	Wayne State University, Detroit

BANIM, Dr Seamus

Special interests:	**Coronary angioplasty, stenting and mitral valvuloplasty**
NHS:	Consultant Cardiologist
	St Bartholomew's Hospital
	West Smithfield
	London ECIA 7BE
Tel:	0171 601 7804
Fax:	0171 600 3866
Private:	62 Wimpole Street
	London WIM 7DE
Tel:	0171 486 1813
Fax:	0171 224 3282
First Qualified:	1967 – Dublin
Major Degrees:	FRCP
Specialist Training:	Royal Postgraduate Medical School, Royal Brompton and London Chest Hospitals, London

BUCKNALL, Dr Cliff

Special interests:	**Management of angina and rhythm disturbance (coronary angioplasty, radiofrequency ablation and complex pacing)**
NHS:	Consultant Cardiologist and Clinical Director of Cardiology
	Guy's Hospital
	St Thomas Street
	London SE1 9RT
Tel:	0171 955 4930
Fax:	0171 378 7881
Private:	Suite 302, Emblem House
	London Bridge Hospital
	27 Tooley Street
	London SE1 2PR
Tel:	0171 403 7503
Fax:	0171 378 7881
First Qualified:	1979 – London
Major Degrees:	MD, FRCP
Academic:	Honorary Senior Lecturer, Guy's and St Thomas' Medical School, London
Specialist Training:	Guy's and King's College Hospitals, London

COLTART, Dr John

Special interests:	**Coronary angiography; angioplasty; medical treatment of ischaemic heart disease and lipid abnormalities; pacemaker insertions**
NHS:	Consultant Cardiologist
	St Thomas' Hospital
	Lambeth Palace Road
	London SE1 7EH
Tel:	0171 928 9292 Ext. 2708
Fax:	0171 922 8079
Private:	15 Upper Wimpole Street
	London W1M 7TB
Tel:	0171 486 5787
Fax:	0171 486 5470
First Qualified:	1967 – London
Major Degrees:	MD, FRCP, FESC
Specialist Training:	Royal Postgraduate Medical School, London
Distinctions:	Buckson Browne Medal of Harvian Society
	Brackenbury Fellow
USA:	Fellow, American College of Cardiology

CURRY, Dr Paul V. L.

Special interests:	**Electro-myocardial physiology; coronary stent insertions**
NHS:	No NHS work
Private:	Emblem House
	London Bridge Hospital
	27 Tooley Street
	London SE1 2PR
Tel:	0171 403 0824
Fax:	0171 403 2306
First Qualified:	1969 – London (with Honours)
Major Degrees:	MD, FRCP
Specialist Training:	Royal Brompton Hospital and Royal Postgraduate Medical School, London
Distinctions:	Goulstonian Lecturer, Royal College of Physicians

DAVIES, Dr Wyn

Special interests:	**Rhythm disturbances of the heart**
NHS:	Consultant Cardiologist
	St Mary's Hospital
	Praed Street
	London W2 1NY
Tel:	0171 725 6666
Fax:	0171 725 1763
Private:	Refer to address and number above

DAWSON, Dr J. Rex

Special interests: **Interventional management of coronary artery disease; valvular disease**

NHS: Consultant Cardiologist
St Bartholomew's Hospital
West Smithfield
London EC1A 7BE

Tel: 0171 601 8289
Fax: 0171 601 8288

Private: 149 Harley Street
London W1N 2DE

Tel: 0171 935 6846
Fax: 0171 486 4578
First Qualified: 1975 – Birmingham
Major Degrees: FRCP
Specialist Training: St Thomas', Royal Brompton and St George's Hospitals, London

EVANS, Dr Tom

Special interests: **Arrhythmias; valve disease; ischaemic heart disease**

NHS: Consultant Cardiologist
Royal Free Hospital
Pond Street
London NW3 2QG

Tel: 0171 794 0500 Ext. 3140
Fax: 0171 830 2857
Private: Refer to address and number above
First Qualified: 1968 – Liverpool (with Honours)
Major Degrees: FRCP
Specialist Training: King's College Hospital and Royal Postgraduate Medical School, London

USA: Fellow, American College of Cardiology

FOX, Dr Kim M.

Special interests: **Ischaemic heart disease; interventional cardiology**

NHS: Consultant Cardiologist
Royal Brompton Hospital
Sydney Street, London SW3 6NB

Tel: 0171 352 8121
Fax: 0171 351 8099

Private: 81 Harley Street
London W1N 1DE

Tel: 0171 486 4617
Fax: 0171 935 0896
First Qualified: 1971 – St Andrews
Major Degrees: MD, FRCP
Specialist Training: Royal Postgraduate Medical School, London
Distinctions: Editor, European Heart Journal

GIBSON, Dr Derek G.

Special interests:	**Echocardiography**
NHS:	Consultant Cardiologist
	Royal Brompton Hospital
	Sydney Street
	London SW3 6NB
Tel:	0171 352 8121 or 0171 351 8636
Fax:	0171 351 8629
Private:	Refer to address and number above
First Qualified:	1961 – Cambridge
Major Degrees:	FRCP
Specialist Training:	St Bartholomew's Hospital, London
Distinctions:	Previously, Strickland–Goodall Lecturer and
	Sir Thomas Lewis Lecturer, British Cardiac Society
USA:	Previously Laennec Lecturer, American Heart Association

GILL, Dr Jaswinder Singh

Special interests:	**Electrophysiology**
NHS:	Consultant Cardiologist
	Guy's Hospital
	St Thomas Street
	London SE1 9RT
Tel:	0171 955 5000 Ext. 3557
Fax:	0171 955 4941
Private:	Guy's Nuffield House
	Guy's Hospital
	London SE1 9RT
Tel:	0171 955 4257
First Qualified:	1979 – Cambridge
Major Degrees:	MRCP, MD
Academic:	Honorary Senior Lecturer, United Medical and Dental Schools, London
Specialist Training:	St George's Hospital Medical School, London
Distinctions:	Fellow, American College of Cardiology
	Faculty Member, North American Society of Pacing and Electrophysiology
USA:	See 'Distinctions' above

JEWITT, Dr David E.

Special interests:	**Interventional cardiology; angioplasty; stenting; valvuloplasty; clinical cardiology**
NHS:	Director, Cardiac Unit
	King's College Hospital
	Denmark Hill
	London SE5 9RS
Tel:	0171 346 3379
Fax:	0171 346 3489
Private:	Cromwell Hospital
	Cromwell Road
	London SW5 OTU
Tel:	0171 370 4233
Fax:	0171 244 6678
First Qualified:	1962 – London (with Honours and university medal)
Major Degrees:	FRCP
Academic:	Previously Consultant Cardiac Physician and Senior Lecturer, Royal Postgraduate Medical School, London
Specialist Training:	King's College Hospital and Royal Postgraduate Medical School, London

McDONALD, Dr Alastair H.

NHS:	Consultant Cardiologist
	Royal London Hospital
	Whitechapel Road
	London E1 1BB
Tel:	0171 377 7000
Fax:	0171 601 8288
Private:	Refer to address and number above
First Qualified:	1962 – Edinburgh
Major Degrees:	FRCP
Academic:	Senior Lecturer in Cardiology, London Hospital
Specialist Training:	Edinburgh, National Heart Hospital and Royal London Hospital

McKENNA, Professor William J.

Special interests:	**Cardiomyopathies**
NHS:	Honorary Consultant Cardiologist
	St George's Hospital
	Blackshaw Road
	London SW17 0QT
Tel:	0181 725 5911
Fax:	0181 682 0944
Private:	Refer to address and number above
First Qualified:	1969 BA – Yale, USA; 1974 MD – McGill, Canada
Major Degrees:	FRCP, FESC
Academic:	Professor Cardiac Medicine, St George's Hospital, London
Specialist Training:	Royal Postgraduate Medical School, London, and Royal Victoria Hospital, Montreal, Canada
USA:	Fellow, American College of Cardiology

NATHAN, Dr Anthony

Special interests:	**Coronary artery disease, arrhythmias, especially catheter ablation of accessory pathways and implantable defibrillators**
NHS:	Consultant Cardiologist
	St Bartholomew's Hospital
	West Smithfield
	London EC1A 7BE
Tel:	0171 601 8708
Fax:	0171 601 7170
Private:	BUPA Hospital
	Heathbourne Road
	Bushey, Herts WD2 1RD
Tel:	0181 420 4471
Fax:	0181 420 4472
and:	62 Wimpole Street
	London W1M 7DE
Tel:	0171 487 3887
First Qualified:	1975 – London
Major Degrees:	MD, FRCP, FESC
Specialist Training:	Royal Brompton and St Bartholomew's Hospitals, London
Distinctions:	Founding Fellow, European Society of Cardiologists
USA:	Fellow, American College of Cardiology

OAKLEY, Dr Celia M.

Special interests:	**Heart disease in pregnancy; cardiomyopathies; infective endocarditis; adult congenital heart disease**
NHS:	Consultant Cardiologist Hammersmith Hospital Du Cane Road London W12 0NN
Tel:	0181 740 3141
Fax:	0181 740 8373
Private:	Refer to address and number above
First Qualified:	1954 – London (with Honours)
Major Degrees:	MD, FRCP
Academic:	Professor of Cardiology, Royal Postgraduate Medical School, London
Specialist Training:	Royal Brompton Hospital and Royal Postgraduate Medical School, London
USA:	Fellow, American College of Cardiology

OLDERSHAW, Dr Paul J.

Special interests:	**Echocardiography and all aspects of ischaemic heart disease including impaired ventricular function**
NHS:	Consultant Cardiologist Royal Brompton Hospital Sydney Street London SW3 6NP
Tel:	0171 351 8121
Fax:	0171 351 8473
Private:	81 Harley Street London W1
Tel:	0171 351 8632
Fax:	0171 351 8629
First Qualified:	1974 – Cambridge
Major Degrees:	MD, FRCP
Specialist Training:	St George's and Royal Brompton Hospitals, London

RICKARDS, Dr Anthony F.

Special interests:	**Cardiac catheterisation; coronary angioplasty; coronary stents/lasers; cardiac pacing**
NHS:	Consultant Cardiologist
	Royal Brompton Hospital
	Sydney Street
	London SW3 6NP
Tel:	0171 351 8705
Fax:	0171 351 8743
e-mail:	a.rickards@ucl.ac.uk
Private:	The Heart Hospital
	47 Wimpole St
	London WIM 7DG
Tel:	0171 573 8899
Fax:	0171 573 8898
First Qualified:	1968 – London
Major Degrees:	FRCP
Academic:	Previously Vice Dean, Cardiothoracic Institute, London
Specialist Training:	The Middlesex and National Heart Hospitals, London
Distinctions:	Previously Secretary, British Cardiac Society
Europe:	Fellow, American College of Cardiologists
	Founding Fellow, European Society of Cardiology

ROWLAND, Dr Edward

Special interests:	**Management of cardiac arrhythmias; pacing and catheter ablation; electrophysiology**
NHS:	Honorary Consultant Cardiologist
	Cardiological Services
	St George's Hospital Medical School
	Cranmer Terrace
	London SW17 0RE
Tel:	0181 725 2922
Fax:	0181 767 7141
Private:	47 Wimpole Street
	London W1M 7DG
Tel:	0171 573 8899
Fax:	0171 573 8898
First Qualified:	1974 – London
Major Degrees:	MD, FESC
Academic:	Senior Lecturer, St George's Hospital Medical School, London
	Lecturer, National Heart and Lung Institute, London
Specialist Training:	Royal Postgraduate Medical School, London
USA:	Fellow, American College of Cardiology

SEVER, Professor Peter S.

Special interests:	**Hypertension**
NHS:	Director, Peart-Rose Clinic
	St Mary's Hospital
	Praed Street
	London W2 1NY
Tel:	0171 725 1521
Fax:	0171 725 1340
e-mail:	P.Sever@ic.ac.uk
Private:	Refer to address and number above
First Qualified:	1968 – Cambridge
Major Degrees:	FRCP
Academic:	Professor of Clinical Pharmacology and Therapy, St Mary's Hospital Medical School and Imperial College of Science Technology and Medicine, London
Specialist Training:	St Mary's Hospital, London
Distinctions:	Previously President, British Hypertension Society

SHINEBOURNE, Dr Elliot A.

Special interests:	**Heart disorders in children**
NHS:	Consultant Paediatric Cardiologist
	Royal Brompton Hospital
	Sydney Street
	London SW3 6NP
Tel:	0171 352 8121
Fax:	0171 351 8099
Private:	Private Consulting Rooms
	Royal Brompton Hospital
	Sydney Street
	London SW3 6NP
Tel:	0171 352 6468
Fax:	0171 351 8541
First Qualified:	1970 – London
Major Degrees:	MD, FRCP
Academic:	Senior Lecturer, Heart and Lung Institute, London
Specialist Training:	St Bartholomew's and National Heart Hospitals, London
USA:	Previously American Heart Association Travelling Fellow in Cardiovascular Medicine

SIGWART, Dr Ulrich

Special interests:	**Invasive cardiology; interventional cardiology**
NHS:	Director, Department of Invasive Cardiology
	Consultant Physician
	Royal Brompton Hospital
	Sydney Street
	London SW3 6NP
Tel:	0171 351 8615
Fax:	0171 351 8614
Private:	47 Wimpole Street
	London WIM 7DG
Tel:	0171 573 8899
Fax:	0171 573 8898
First Qualified:	1967 – Freiburg, Germany
Major Degrees:	MD, FRCP, FESC
Academic:	Professor of Medicine, Universities of Düsseldorf and Lausanne; Recognised teacher, University of London
Specialist Training:	Boston University, Tufts University, Baylor College of Medicine, Houston, University of Zurich
Distinctions:	Assistant Editor, Journal of Interventional Cardiology
	Editor, Handbook of Cardiovascular Interventions
	Editor, Endovascular Stents
	Founding Fellow, European Society of Cardiology
USA:	Fellow, American College of Cardiology and see 'Specialist Training' above

SOMERVILLE, Dr Jane

Special interests:	**Women's heart disease; adolescents and adults with congenital heart disease**
NHS:	Consultant Cardiologist
	Grown-up Congenital Heart Unit
	Royal Brompton Hospital
	Sydney Street
	London SW3 6NP
Tel:	0171 262 2144
Fax:	0171 351 8473
Private:	Refer to address and number above
First Qualified:	1955 – London
Major Degrees:	MD, FRCP
Academic:	Senior Lecturer, Cardiothoracic Institute, London, and Lecturer in Paediatric Cardiology, University of Turin, Italy
Specialist Training:	National Heart Hospital, London
USA:	Fellow, American College of Cardiology

SPURRELL, Dr Roworth A. J.

Special interests:	**Cardiac cathetherisation; angioplasty**
NHS:	Consultant in Charge of Cardiology
	St Bartholomew's Hospital
	West Smithfield
	London EC1A 7BE
Tel:	0171 601 8888 Ext. 7800
Fax:	0171 601 7899
Private:	10 Upper Wimpole Street
	London W1M 7TD
Tel:	0171 935 3955
Fax:	0171 935 1637
First Qualified:	1960 – London
Major Degrees:	MD, FRCP
Specialist Training:	Guy's, St George's and National Heart Hospitals, London
USA:	Fellow, American College of Cardiology

SUTTON, Dr Richard

Special interests:	**Pacing**
NHS:	Consultant Cardiologist
	Royal Brompton Hospital
	Sydney Street
	London SW3 6NP
Tel:	0171 352 8619
Fax:	0171 352 8625
Private:	149 Harley Street
	London W1N 1HG
Tel:	0171 935 4444
Fax:	0171 935 6718
First Qualified:	1964 – London
Major Degrees:	DSc, FRCP
Academic:	Recognised teacher, London University
Specialist Training:	National Heart Hospital, London
Distinctions:	President, British Pacing Electrophysiology Group 1990–95
USA:	Previously Research Fellow in Cardiology, University of North Carolina. Twice awarded the Governors' Award of the American College of Cardiology

SWANTON, Dr R. Howard

Special interests:	**Clinical cardiology; angioplasty**
NHS:	Consultant Cardiologist
	The Middlesex Hospital
	Mortimer Street
	London WIN 8AA
Tel:	0171 380 9055
Fax:	0171 380 9415
Private:	The Harley Street Clinic Consulting Rooms
	81 Harley Street
	London W1N 1DE
Tel:	0171 486 7416
Fax:	0171 487 2569
First Qualified:	1970 – Cambridge
Major Degrees:	MD, FRCP
Specialist Training:	St Thomas' and National Heart Hospitals, London

---

WEBB-PEPLOE, Dr Michael Murray, OBE

Special interests:	**Interventional cardiology; laser angioplasty; intra-vascular ultrasound**
NHS:	Consultant in Charge
	Department of Cardiology
	St Thomas' Hospital
	Lambeth Palace Road
	London SE1 7EH
Tel:	0171 928 9292 Ext. 3097
Fax:	0171 922 8079
Private:	York House
	199 Westminster Bridge Road
	London SE1 7UT
Tel:	0171 261 9877
Fax:	0171 922 8301
First Qualified:	1961 – Cambridge
Major Degrees:	FRCP
Specialist Training:	Royal Brompton, National Heart and Royal Postgraduate Medical School Hospitals, London
Distinctions:	Civilian Consultant in Cardiology to the Army, OBE
USA:	Fellow, Nuffield Foundation
	Research Associate, Mayo Clinic, Rochester, Minnesota

ANGLIA AND OXFORD REGION

CAMBRIDGE

PETCH, Dr Michael C.

Special interests:	**Clinical cardiology**
NHS:	Consultant Cardiologist
	Papworth Hospital
	Papworth Everard
	Cambridge CN3 8RE
Tel:	01480 830541 Ext. 4351
Fax:	01480 831083
Private:	Refer to address and number above
First Qualified:	1965 – Cambridge and London
Major Degrees:	MD, FRCP, FESC
Academic:	Associate Lecturer, Cambridge University
Specialist Training:	National Heart Hospital, London
USA:	Fellow, American College of Cardiology

OXFORD

FORFAR, Dr John Colin

Special interests:	**Authority on hormonal aspects and drug treatments of heart disease; arrhythmias**
NHS:	Consultant Physician and Cardiologist
	Department of Cardiology
	John Radcliffe Hospital
	Headington
	Oxford OX3 9DU
Tel:	01865 220326
Private:	Refer to address and number above
First Qualified:	1975 – Oxford
Major Degrees:	PhD, MD, FRCP
Academic:	Previously Reader in Cardiovascular Medicine and Fellow, Oxford University
Specialist Training:	John Radcliffe Hospital, Oxford, and Royal Infirmary, Edinburgh

SLOUGH

BLACKWOOD, Dr Roger Arthur

Special interests:	**Clinical and noninvasive cardiology**
NHS:	Consultant Cardiologist
	Wexham Park Hospital
	Wexham
	Slough SL2 4HL
Tel:	01753 525369
Fax:	01753 691083
Private:	Thames Valley Nuffield Hospital
	Slough
	Berks SL3 6NH
Tel:	01753 662241
Fax:	01494 817132
First Qualified:	1970 – Oxford
Major Degrees:	FRCP
Specialist Training:	Radcliffe Infirmary, Oxford, and Johannesburg

NORTH WEST REGION

MANCHESTER

BENNETT, Dr David H.

Special interests:	**Angina; angioplasty and arrhythmias**
NHS:	Consultant Cardiologist
	Regional Cardiac Centre
	Wythenshawe Hospital
	Southmore Road
	Manchester M23 9LT
Tel:	0161 946 2388
Fax:	0161 946 2389
Private:	Alexandra Hospital
	Mill Lane
	Cheadle
	Cheshire SK8 2PX
Tel:	0161 428 3656
Fax:	0161 946 2389
First Qualified:	1978 – Manchester
Major Degrees:	MD, FRCP

BROOKS, Dr Nicholas Hugh

Special interests:	**Coronary disease and coronary angioplasty; heart failure and heart transplantation; valve disease**
NHS:	Consultant Cardiologist
Wythenshawe Hospital
Southmore Road
Manchester M23 9LT
Tel:	0161 946 2388
Fax:	0161 946 2389
Private:	Alexandra Hospital
Mill Lane
Cheadle
Cheshire SK8 2PX
Tel:	0161 428 3656
Fax:	0161 491 3867
and:	Fernleigh Consulting Centre
77 Alderley Road
Wilmslow SK9 1PA
Tel:	01625 536488
First Qualified:	1970 – London (with Honours)
Major Degrees:	MD, FRCP
Academic:	Clinical Lecturer, University of Manchester, 1984 – present
Previously Clinical Lecturer, Cardiothoracic Institute, London
Specialist Training:	St Bartholomew's, St George's and London Chest Hospitals, London
Distinctions:	Assistant Secretary, British Cardiac Society (1994–6)
Secretary, British Cardiac Society

NORTHERN AND YORKSHIRE REGION

HULL

CAPLIN, Dr John L.

Special interests:	**Nuclear cardiology; grown-up congenital heart disease; interventional cardiology**
NHS:	Department of Cardiology
	Hull Royal Infirmary
	Anlaby Road
	Hull HU3 2JZ
Tel:	01482 674902
Fax:	01482 321128
Private:	Nuffield Hospital
	81 Westbourne Avenue
	Hull HU5 3HP
Tel:	01482 342327
Fax:	01482 470133
First Qualified:	1976 – London
Major Degrees:	MD, FRCP

LEEDS

PERRINS, Dr E. John

Special interests:	**Interventional cardiology**
NHS:	Consultant Cardiologist
	Department of Cardiology
	General Infirmary
	Great George Street
	Leeds LS1 3EX
Tel:	01132 437174
Fax:	01132 460596
Private:	Refer to address and number above
First Qualified:	1975 – Leeds (with Honours)
Major Degrees:	MD, FRCP
Distinctions:	Previously President, Society of Cardiology Technicians
	Secretary, British Pacing group
USA:	Fellow, American College of Cardiology

SOUTH AND WEST REGION

PLYMOUTH

MARSHALL, Dr Andrew

NHS:	Consultant Cardiologist
	Department of Cardiology
	Derriford Hospital
	Plymouth PL6 8DH
Tel:	01752 777111 Ext. 52661
Fax:	01752 781220
Private:	Plymouth Nuffield Hospital
	Derriford Road
	Plymouth PL6 8BG
Tel:	01752 773343
Fax:	01752 773343
First Qualified:	1967 – London
Major Degrees:	MD, FRCP
Academic:	Honorary Senior Lecturer, Plymouth Postgraduate Medical School, University of Plymouth
Distinctions:	Chairman, South West Cardiologists

SOUTHAMPTON

DAWKINS, Dr Keith D.

Special interests:	**Interventional cardiology; coronary angioplasty; intracoronary stenting**
NHS:	Southampton General Hospital
	Tremona Road
	Southampton SO16 6YD
Tel:	01703 696242
Fax:	01703 796352
Private:	Refer to address and number above
First Qualified:	1975 – London
Major Degrees:	MD, FRCP
Specialist Training:	Royal Brompton and St George's Hospital, London
Distinctions:	Clinical Director, Wessex Cardiothoracic Unit
USA:	Research Fellow, Stanford University, California
	Fellow, American College of Cardiology

SIMPSON, Dr Iain

Special interests:	**Coronary ultrasound particularly echocardiography, transoesophageal echocardiography and colour flow doppler mapping; coronary intervention and medical information technology**
NHS:	Consultant Cardiologist
	Wessex Regional Cardiac Unit
	Southampton General Hospital
	Tremona Road
	Southampton SO16 6YD
Tel:	01703 796648
Fax:	01703 796352
Private:	Chalybeate Hospital
	Tremona Road
	Southampton SO16 6UQ
Tel:	01703 764333
Fax:	01703 511551
First Qualified:	1980 – Glasgow
Major Degrees:	MD, FRCP
Academic:	Previously British–American Fellow
	California University, San Diego
Specialist Training:	Royal Brompton, National Heart and Lung and St George's Hospitals, London
Distinctions:	Editorial Board Member, Heart
USA:	Fellow, American College of Cardiology

TRENT REGION

SHEFFIELD

CUMBERLAND, Professor David C.

Special interests:	**Interventional cardiology**
NHS:	Professor of Interventional Cardiology
	Northern General Hospital
	Herries Road
	Sheffield S5 7AU
Tel:	0114 243 4343
Fax:	0114 256 2366
Private:	Refer to address and number above
First Qualified:	1967 – Edinburgh
Major Degrees:	FRCP Ed, FRCS, FRCR
Academic:	Professor of Interventional Cardiology
	University of Sheffield
Specialist Training:	Chalmers and City Hospitals, Edinburgh
USA:	Fellow, American College of Cardiology

OAKLEY, Dr George David Gastineau

Special interests:	**Ischaemic heart disease**
NHS:	Consultant Cardiologist
	Cardiothoracic Unit
	Northern General Hospital
	Herries Road
	Sheffield S5 7AU
Tel:	0114 243 4343
Fax:	0114 256 2366
Private:	Refer to address and number above
First Qualified:	1973 – Cambridge
Major Degrees:	MD, FRCP
Academic:	Honorary Clinical Lecturer, Sheffield University
Specialist Training:	North General Hospital, Sheffield; Royal Postgraduate Medical School, London; City General Hospital and North Staffordshire Royal Infirmary, Stoke on Trent

WEST MIDLANDS

BIRMINGHAM

BULLER, Dr Nigel Pearson

Special interests:	**Management of angina including cardiac catheterisation; coronary artery angioplasty**
NHS:	Queen Elizabeth Hospital
	Edgbaston
	Birmingham B15 2TH
Tel:	0121 627 2538
Fax:	0121 414 1045
Private:	Nuffield Hospital and Priory Hospital
	22 Somerset Road
	Edgbaston
	Birmingham
	B15 2QQ
Tel:	0121 627 2538
Fax:	0121 414 1045
First Qualified:	1980 – London
Major Degrees:	MRCP
Academic:	Honorary Senior Lecturer, Birmingham University
Specialist Training:	Royal Brompton Hospital, London and Harefield, Middlesex

SCOTLAND

EDINBURGH

BOON, Dr Nicholas A.

Special interests:	**Cardiomyopathies and HIV-related heart disease**
NHS:	Consultant Cardiologist
	Royal Infirmary
	1 Lauriston Place
	Edinburgh EH3 9YW
Tel:	0131 536 2004
Fax:	0131 536 2021
Private:	Refer to address and number above
First Qualified:	1975 – Cambridge
Major Degrees:	MD, FRCP Ed
Academic:	Previously Lecturer in Cardiovascular Medicine
	John Radcliffe Hospital, Oxford
Distinctions:	Councillor, British Cardiac Society

FOX, Professor Keith A. A.

Special interests:	**Cardiomyoplasty pioneeer, transplanting muscle from patient's own body instead of a complete heart from another**
NHS:	Honorary Consultant Cardiologist
	Royal Infirmary
	1 Lauriston Place
	Edinburgh EH3 9YQ
Tel:	0131 536 1000
Fax:	0131 536 2021
Private:	Refer to address and number above
First Qualified:	1974 – Edinburgh
Major Degrees:	FRCS, FRCP
Academic:	Professor of Cardiology
Distinctions:	Member, editorial board, Cardiology in Practice
USA:	Previously Assistant Professor, Washington University, Missouri

MILLER, Dr Hugh C.

Special interests:	**Arrythmias; electrophysiology**
NHS:	Consultant Cardiologist
	Royal Infirmary
	1 Lauriston Place
	Edinburgh EH3 9YW
Tel:	0131 536 2002
Fax:	0131 536 2021
Private:	Refer to address and number above
First Qualified:	1966 – Edinburgh
Major Degrees:	FRCP Ed
Academic:	MRC Research Fellow, Edinburgh University
Specialist Training:	Brompton Hospital, London
USA:	Research Fellow, Duke University, North Carolina, Durham

---

SHAW, Dr Thomas R. D.

Special interests:	**Interventional cardiology, particularly valvuloplasty**
NHS:	Consultant Cardiologist
	Western General Hospital
	Crewe Road
	Edinburgh EH4 2XU
Tel:	0131 537 1843
Fax:	0131 537 1005
Private:	Refer to address above
Tel:	0131 334 0363
Fax:	0131 537 1005
First Qualified:	1969 – Glasgow
Major Degrees:	MD, FRCP, FESC

CARDIOTHORACIC SURGEONS

(Heart Surgeons)

Cardiothoracic surgeons specialise in all surgeries relating to congenital and acquired defects of the heart, great vessels and lungs, oesophagus and diaphragm. Patients normally see a cardiologist first, who refers them to a cardiothoracic surgeon if surgery is required. They usually work with experts in related fields such as immunology and postoperative critical care. Operations include coronary artery bypass graft, valve surgery including repair and replacement as well as transplants. (See appendix 1(ii) for a list of specialist cardiac units).

LONDON AND THE SOUTH EAST

ANDERSON, Mr David Robert

Special interests:	**Congenital defects; neonatal correction**
NHS:	Consultant Cardiac Surgeon
	Department of Cardiac Surgery
	Guy's Hospital
	St Thomas Street
	London SE1 9RT
Tel:	0171 955 4065
Fax:	0171 955 4858
Private:	Guy's Nuffield House
	London SE1 1YR
Tel:	0171 955 4752
Fax:	0171 955 4858
First Qualified:	1979 – Cambridge
Major Degrees:	FRCS, FRCS Ed
Academic:	Senior Lecturer, Guy's Hospital
Specialist Training:	Guy's and St George's Hospitals, London, and Birmingham Children's Hospital
Distinctions:	Previously Hunterian Professor, Royal College of Surgeons
USA:	Research Fellow, Pennsylvania University
	Research Fellow, Wayne State University, Michigan

de LEVAL, Mr Marc R.

Special interests:	**Doyen of children's heart surgery**
NHS:	Consultant Cardiothoracic Surgeon
	Great Ormond Street Hospital for Children
	Great Ormond Street
	London WC1N 3JH
Tel:	0171 404 4383
Fax:	0171 831 4931
Private:	Refer to address and number above
First Qualified:	1966 – Liege, Belgium
Major Degrees:	MD, FRCS

DESAI, Mr Jatin B.

Special interests:	**Coronary bypass with arterial conduits; mitral valve repair**
NHS:	Consultant Cardiothoracic Surgeon
	King's College Hospital
	Denmark Hill
	London SE5 9RS
Tel:	0171 346 3191
Fax:	0171 346 3433
Private:	Emblem House
	London Bridge Hospital
	Tooley Street
	London SE1 2PR
Tel:	0171 346 3191
Fax:	0171 346 3433
First Qualified:	1975 – Glasgow
Major Degrees:	FRCS, FRCS Ed
Specialist Training:	Hammersmith, The Middlesex and St Mary's Hospitals, London, and Harefield Hospital, Middlesex
USA:	Barnes Hospital, St Louis, Missouri

DEVERALL, Mr Philip B.

Special interests:	**Patients of all ages; congenital heart disease, valve heart disease and all types of degenerative disease of the structures of the heart with particular emphasis on coronary vascular disease and disease of the major blood vessels within the thorax**
NHS:	Consultant Cardiothoracic Surgeon Guy's Hospital St Thomas Street London SE1 9RT
Tel:	0171 955 4339
Fax:	0171 922 8079
Private:	21 Upper Wimpole Street London WIM 7TA
Tel:	0171 486 7753
Fax:	0171 935 4416
First Qualified:	1960 – London
Major Degrees:	FRCS
Academic:	Lecturer in Surgery, Guy's Hospital, London
Specialist Training:	Great Ormond Street Hospital for Children, London
USA:	Cardiovascular Research Fellow, Alabama University

EDMONDSON, Mr Stephen J.

Special interests:	**Surgery of coronary heart disease; cardiac arrhythmias**
NHS:	Consultant Cardiothoracic Surgeon St Bartholomew's Hospital West Smithfield London ECIA 7BE
Tel:	0171 601 7137
Fax:	0171 601 7899
Private:	69 Harley Street London W1N 1DE
Tel:	0171 935 6375
Fax:	0171 224 3823
First Qualified:	1974 – London (with Honours)
Major Degrees:	FRCS, FRCP
Specialist Training:	St Bartholomew's and Hammersmith Hospitals, London

LEWIS, Mr C. Terence

Special interests:	**General thoracic surgery and oesophageal surgery**
NHS:	Consultant Cardiothoracic Surgeon
	St Bartholomew's Hospital
	West Smithfield
	London EC1A 7BE
Tel:	0171 601 7118
Fax:	0171 601 7117
Private:	149 Harley Street
	London W1N 2DE
Tel:	0171 935 6397
Fax:	0171 486 4578
First Qualified:	1968 – London
Major Degrees:	FRCS
Specialist Training:	Royal Brompton, National Heart and Royal London Hospitals, London

LINCOLN, Mr J. Christopher

Special interests:	**Paediatric**
NHS:	Consultant Cardiothoracic Surgeon
	Royal Brompton Hospital
	Sydney Street
	London SW3 6NP
Tel:	0171 351 8251
Fax:	0171 351 8099
Private:	38 Devonshire Street
	London W1N 1LD
Tel:	0171 935 7529
Fax:	0171 351 8214
First Qualified:	1959 – Dublin
Major Degrees:	FRCS Ed, FRCS
Academic:	Senior Lecturer in Paediatric Surgery
	Heart and Lung Institute, London
Specialist Training:	Great Ormond Street Hospital for Children and Westminster Hospital, London
Distinctions:	Previously Hunterian Professor, Royal College of Surgeons
USA:	Previously Clinical and Research Fellow, Harvard Medical School and Massachusetts General Hospital

PARKER, Mr D. John

NHS:	Consultant Cardiac Surgeon
	St George's Hospital
	Blackshaw Road
	London SW17 0QT
Tel:	0181 672 1255
Fax:	0181 725 2049
Private:	6 Upper Wimpole Street
	London W1 7TD
Tel:	0171 935 1590
Fax:	0171 224 2075
First Qualified:	1962 – St Andrews
Major Degrees:	FRCS, FRCP
Academic:	Senior Lecturer, Heart and Lung Institute, London
Specialist Training:	Dundee Royal Infirmary and National Heart Hospital, London

REES, Mr Gareth M.

NHS:	Consultant Cardiothoracic Surgeon
	St Bartholomew's Hospital
	West Smithfield
	London EC1 7BE
Tel:	0171 601 7134
Fax:	0171 600 4197
Private:	10 Upper Wimpole Street
	London W1M 7TD
Tel:	0171 487 3598
Fax:	0171 935 1637
First Qualified:	1960 – London (with Honours)
Major Degrees:	FRCP, FRCS
Academic:	Recognized teacher, University of London
Specialist Training:	Royal Brompton and National Heart Hospitals, London
USA:	Previously Research Fellow in Cardiac Surgery, University of Oregon at Portland. Worked with Dr Albert Starr on the origin and development of bypass surgery

SHABBO, Mr Fikrat P.

NHS:	Consultant Cardiothoracic Surgeon
	St Thomas' Hospital
	Lambeth Palace Road
	London SE1 7EH
Tel:	0171 928 9292 Ext. 2905
Fax:	0171 922 8005
Private:	Refer to address and number above
Major Degrees:	FRCS
Specialist Training:	National Heart and St Bartholomew's Hospitals, London

SHORE, Mr Darryl

NHS:	Consultant Cardiothoracic Surgeon
	Royal Brompton Hospital
	Sydney Street
	London SW3 6NP
Tel:	0171 351 8561
Fax:	0171 351 8562
Private:	Refer to address and number above
First Qualified:	1971 – Sheffield
Major Degrees:	FRCS

SMITH, Mr Peter L. C.

Special interests:	**Redo coronary artery surgery; valve surgery for endocarditis**
NHS:	Consultant Cardiothoracic Surgeon
	Hammersmith Hospital
	Du Cane Road
	London W12 0HS
Tel:	0181 740 3125
Fax:	0181 740 7019
Private:	Refer to address and number above
First Qualified:	1975 – London
Major Degrees:	MRCP, FRCS
Specialist Training:	Royal Brompton, The Middlesex and Hammersmith Hospitals, London, and Harefield Hospital, Middlesex
Distinctions:	Previously Hunterian Professor, Royal College of Surgeons
	Member of the Court of Examiners, Royal College of Surgeons

STANBRIDGE, Mr Rex D. L.

NHS:	Consultant Cardiothoracic Surgeon St Mary's Hospital Praed Street London W2 1NY
Tel:	0171 725 6038
Fax:	0171 725 1341
Private:	Refer to address and number above
First Qualified:	1971 – London
Major Degrees:	FRCS
Academic:	Senior Lecturer, Royal Postgraduate Medical School, London
Specialist Training:	Great Ormond Street Hospital for Children, Hammersmith and The Middlesex Hospitals, London, and Harefield Hospital, Middlesex
USA:	Research Fellow, Cardiac Surgery, Alabama University, Birmingham

TREASURE, Professor Tom

NHS:	Consultant Cardiothoracic Surgeon St George's Hospital Blackshaw Road London SW17 0QT
Tel:	0181 767 9859
Fax:	0181 725 3548
Private:	19 Wimpole Street London W1M 7AD
Tel:	0171 637 9050
Fax:	0171 637 2789
First Qualified:	1970 – London
Major Degrees:	MS, MD, FRCS
Specialist Training:	Royal Brompton and National Heart, Guy's and St Thomas' Hospitals, London

VENN, Mr Graham E.

Special interests:	**Ischaemic heart disease and reconstructive surgery of the mitral valve**
NHS:	Clinical Director of Cardiothoracic Services
	Consultant Cardiothoracic Surgeon
	St Thomas' Hospital
	Lambeth Palace Road
	London SE1 7EH
Tel:	0171 261 9401
Fax:	0171 261 9401
Private:	Suite 203, Emblem House
	London Bridge Hospital
	27 Tooley Street
	London SE1 2PR
Tel:	0171 378 6566
Fax:	0171 378 8156
First Qualified:	1977 – London
Major Degrees:	FRCS Ed, FRCS
Academic:	Director of Cardiac Surgical Research, Rayne Institute, St Thomas' Hospital, London
	Honorary Senior Lecturer, Cardiothoracic Surgery, London University
Specialist Training:	The Middlesex, Hammersmith, and Brompton Hospitals, London, and Harefield Hospital, Middlesex
Distinctions:	Previously Hunterian Professor, Royal College of Surgeons
USA:	Fellow, International College of Surgeons, Chicago

WALESBY, Mr Robin K.

Special interests:	**Adult cardiac and thoracic surgery**
NHS:	Consultant Cardiothoracic Surgeon
	London Chest Hospital
	Bonner Road
	Bethnal Green
	London E2 9JX
Tel:	0181 983 2323
Fax:	0181 983 2331
and:	St Bartholomew's Hospital
	West Smithfield
	London EC1 7BE
Tel:	0171 601 7119
and:	Royal Free Hospital
	Pond Street
	London NW3 2QG
Tel:	0171 794 0500 Ext. 4652
Fax:	0171 830 2198
Private:	81 Harley Street
	London W1N 1DE
Tel:	0171 486 4617
Fax:	0171 935 0896
First Qualified:	1970 – London
Major Degrees:	FRCS
Specialist Training:	Great Ormond Street Hospital for Children and Hammersmith Hospitals, London, and Harefield Hospital, Middlesex

---

WILLIAMS, Mr Bryn T.

Special interests:	**High risks groups of coronary artery surgery**
NHS:	No NHS work
	Ex-Consultant Cardiothoracic Surgeon at St Thomas' Hospital
Private:	Suite 204, Emblem House
	London Bridge Hospital
	27 Tooley Street, London SE1 2PR
Tel:	0171 403 2150
Fax:	0171 403 4329
First Qualified:	1962 – Birmingham
Major Degrees:	FRCS
Distinctions:	Consultant Cardiothoracic Surgeon to the Army
USA:	Fellow in Surgical Research, New York University, Buffalo

---

WOOD, Mr Alan J.

NHS:	Consultant Cardiothoracic Surgeon
	St Bartholomew's Hospital
	West Smithfield
	London EC1 7BE
Tel:	0171 601 7119
Fax:	0171 601 7117
and:	London Chest Hospital
	Bonner Road
	London E2 9JX
Tel:	0181 983 2323
Private:	London Independent Hospital
	Beaumont Square
	London E1 4NL
Tel:	0171 790 0990 Ext. 2262
Fax:	0171 265 9032
First Qualified:	1975 – London
Major Degrees:	FRCS
Specialist Training:	St Bartholomew's Hospital, London

WRIGHT, Mr John E. C.

NHS:	Consultant Cardiothoracic Surgeon
	London Chest Hospital
	Bonner Road
	London E2 9JX
Tel:	0171 983 2322
Fax:	0171 983 2331
Private:	22 Upper Wimpole Street
	London W1M 7TA
Tel:	0171 486 8961
Fax:	0171 486 7918
First Qualified:	1958 – London
Major Degrees:	FRCS
Specialist Training:	National Heart Hospital, London
USA:	Previously Harvard Research Fellow
	Massachusetts General Hospitals, Boston

YACOUB, Professor Sir Magdi H.

Special interests:	**Heart transplants**
NHS:	Professor of Cardiac Surgery
	Royal Brompton and National Heart Hospitals
	Fulham Road
	London SW3 6HP
Tel:	0171 351 8533
Fax:	0171 351 8229
Private:	Old Court Hospital
	19 Montpelier Road
	London W5 2QT
Tel:	0181 998 2848
Fax:	0181 566 9414
First Qualified:	1966 – London
Major Degrees:	FRCS, FRCP
Academic:	Professor of Cardiac Surgery, Royal Brompton and National Heart Hospitals
USA:	Department of Cardiothoracic Surgery Chicago University

YOUNG, Mr Christopher

Special interests:	**Aortic surgery**
NHS:	Consultant Cardiac and Thoracic Surgeon
	St Thomas' Hospital
	Lambeth Palace Road
	London SE1 7EH
Tel:	0171 928 9292 Ext. 2030
Fax:	0171 922 8005
Private:	Consulting Rooms
	York House
	199 Westminster Bridge Road
	London SE1 7UT
Tel:	0171 922 8077
Fax:	0171 922 8005
First Qualified:	1980 – Sheffield
Major Degrees:	MD, FRCS
Academic:	Honorary Senior Lecturer, London University
Specialist Training:	Hospital for Sick Children and St Thomas' Hospitals, London
Distinctions:	Previously British Heart Foundation Junior Research Fellow

ANGLIA AND OXFORD REGION

CAMBRIDGE

WALLWORK, Mr John

Special interests:	**Transplantation of heart and lungs; cardiac surgery in the elderly**
NHS:	Consultant Cardiothoracic Surgeon and Director of Transplant Services Papworth Hospital Papworth Everard Cambridge CB3 8RE
Tel:	01480 830541
Fax:	01480 831281
Private:	Refer to address and number above
First Qualified:	1970 – Edinburgh
Major Degrees:	MA, FRCS Ed
Academic:	Associate Lecturer, Edinburgh University Director of Transplant Unit
Specialist Training:	Stanford University, California
USA:	Association of Cardiothoracic Surgeons and see 'Specialist Training' above

NORTH WEST REGION

MANCHESTER

JONES, Mr Mark T.

Special interests:	**General adult cardiac and thoracic surgery**
NHS:	Consultant Cardiothoracic Surgeon Wythenshaw Hospital Southmoor Road Wythenshaw, Manchester M23 9LT
Tel:	0161 946 2513
Fax:	0161 946 2530
Private:	Consulting Suite Alexandra Hospital Mill Lane, Cheadle SK8 2PX
Tel:	0161 428 3656
Fax:	0161 491 3867
First Qualified:	1977 – Manchester
Major Degrees:	FRCS
Specialist Training:	Manchester University, London University and Toronto University, Ontario, Canada
Distinctions:	Douglas Prize, Manchester University

NORTHERN AND YORKSHIRE REGION

NEWCASTLE

HILTON, Mr Colin John

Special interests:	**Cardiopulmonary transplantation; surgical treatment of cardiac arrhythmias**
NHS:	Consultant Cardiothoracic Surgeon Freeman Hospital Freeman Road Newcastle upon Tyne NE7 7DN
Tel:	0191 284 3111 Ext. 26587
Fax:	0191 223 1175
Private:	8 Westfield Grove Gosforth Newcastle upon Tyne NE3 4YA
Tel:	0191 284 7394
Fax:	0191 284 7394
First Qualified:	1968 – Newcastle
Major Degrees:	FRCS
Academic:	Honorary Clinical Lecturer, Newcastle University Medical School
Specialist Training:	St Bartholomew's Hospital, London, Harefield Hospital, Middlesex, and Papworth Hospital, Cambridge
USA:	Research Fellow, Brown University, Providence, Rhode Island

SOUTH AND WEST REGION

BRISTOL

HUTTER, Mr Jonathan A.

Special interests:	**Coronary artery and adult cardiac surgery**
NHS:	Consultant Cardiac Surgeon
	Bristol Royal Infirmary
	Maudlin Street
	Bristol BS2 8HW
Tel:	0117 928 3835/6
Fax:	0117 928 3871
Private:	BUPA Glen Hospital
	Redland Road
	Bristol BS6 7JJ
Tel:	0117 973 2562
Fax:	0117 974 3203
First Qualified:	1976 – London
Major Degrees:	FRCS
Academic:	Senior Transplant Fellow, Papworth Hospital, Cambridge
Specialist Training:	Guy's and St Thomas' Hospitals, London

WEST MIDLANDS

BIRMINGHAM

BONSER, Mr Robert Stuart

Special interests:	**Coronary artery surgery; thoracic aortic surgery; transplantation and Marfan's Syndrome**
NHS:	Consultant Cardiothoracic Surgeon
	Queen Elizabeth Hospital
	Edgbaston
	Birmingham B15 2TH
Tel:	0121 627 2559
Fax:	0121 627 2542
Private:	Priory Hospital
	Priory Road
	Edgbaston
	Birmingham B5 7UG
Tel:	0121 440 2323
Fax:	0121 446 5686
First Qualified:	1977 – Wales
Major Degrees:	FRCS
Academic:	Honorary Senior Lecturer, Queen Elizabeth Hospital, Birmingham
Specialist Training:	Royal Brompton and National Heart Hospitals, London
USA:	British Heart Foundation in America
	Fellow, Heart Association Reciprocal, Minnesota University

CHEST PHYSICIANS

(Respiratory Physicians)

These doctors treat lung and airway disease, including cancer, pneumonia, emphysema, asthma, tuberculosis and sleep-related breathing disorders.

LONDON AND THE SOUTH EAST

BARNES, Professor Peter J.

Special interests:	**Asthma, especially asthma that is difficult to control**
NHS:	Consultant Physican National Heart and Lung Institute Dovehouse Street London SW3 6LY
Tel:	0171 351 8174
Fax:	0171 351 5675
e-mail:	p.j.barnes@ic.ac.uk
Private:	Refer to address and number above
First Qualified:	1972 – Oxford
Major Degrees:	DM, DSc, FRCP
Academic:	Professor of Thoracic Medicine, National Heart and Lung Institute, London
Specialist Training:	Royal Postgraduate Medical School, London

BATEMAN, Dr Nigel T.

Special interests:	**Lung infections in HIV disease**
NHS:	Consultant Physician St Thomas' Hospital Lambeth Palace Road London SE1 7EH
Tel:	0171 928 9292 Ext. 2251
Fax:	0171 922 8206
Private:	York House 199 Westminster Bridge Road London SE1 7UT
Tel:	0171 928 5485
Fax:	0171 928 3748
First Qualified:	1969 – Oxford
Major Degrees:	FRCP
Academic:	Honorary Senior Lecturer, United Medical and Dental Schools, London

COLE, Professor Peter John

Special interests:	**Recurrent chronic respiratory (upper and lower) tract infections; bronchiectasis**
NHS:	Host Defence Unit
	National Heart and Lung Institute
	Imperial College
	Emmanuel Kaye Building
	Manresa Road, London SW3 6LR
Tel:	0171 351 8326
Fax:	0171 351 8338
and:	Honorary Consultant Physician
	Royal Brompton Hospital
	Fulham Road
	London SW3 6HP
Tel:	0171 352 8121
Private:	Refer to address and number above
First Qualified:	1967 – London
Major Degrees:	FRCP, FRCPath
Academic:	Previously Senior Lecturer and Reader, Thoracic Medicine, Cardiothoracic Institute and Brompton Hospital
	Visiting worker, Department of Immunology, The Middlesex Hospital, London
	Cytogenetics Research, University of Western Ontario, London, Canada
	Visiting Professor, University of Alberta, Calgary, Canada
Specialist Training:	The Middlesex, Northwick Park and Brompton Hospitals, London
Distinctions:	Member, Scientific Staff of MRC at Clinical Research Centre
	Previously President, Clinical Immunology and Allergy Section, Royal Society of Medicine
	Royal Society Soiree Presentation 1990
	HC Roscoe Fellowship, British Medical Association
USA:	Previously Visiting Professor, Royal Society of Medicine to the USA

COLLINS, Dr John V.

NHS:	Consultant Physician
	Royal Brompton Hospital
	Sydney Street
	London SW3 6NP
Tel:	0171 352 8121
Fax:	0171 351 8085
Private:	Royal Brompton Hospital
	Private Rooms
	Sydney Wing
	Sydney Street
	London SW3 6NP
Tel:	0171 351 8030
First Qualified:	1966 – London
Major Degrees:	MD, FRCP
Specialist Training:	St Bartholomew's, Westminster, Royal Brompton and National Heart Hospitals, London

COSTELLO, Dr John

Special interests:	**Asthma; intensive care; general respiratory medicine**
NHS:	Director, Respiratory Department
	King's College Hospital
	Denmark Hill
	London SE5 9RS
Tel:	0171 737 4233
Fax:	0171 346 3589
Private:	Cromwell Hospital
	Cromwell Road
	London SW5 OTU
Tel:	0171 370 4233
First Qualified:	1968 – Dublin
Major Degrees:	MD, FRCP
Academic:	Senior Lecturer, King's College Hospital, London
Specialist Training:	Royal Infirmary, Edinburgh and Royal Brompton and Hammersmith Hospitals, London
USA:	Previously Assistant Professor in Medicine University of California

DAVIES, Professor Robert J.

Special interests:	**Allergies**
NHS:	Consultant Physician, Respiratory Medicine
	St Bartholomew's Hospital
	West Smithfield
	London EC1A 7BE
Tel:	0171 601 8436
Fax:	0171 601 7899
Private:	Refer to address and number above
First Qualified:	1968 – Cambridge
Major Degrees:	MD, FRCP
Academic:	Professor of Respiratory Medicine, St Bartholomew's, London
Specialist Training:	St Thomas' and Royal Brompton Hospitals, London
Distinctions:	President of the British and Executive of the International Association of Allergy and Clinical Immunology
	Editor, Journal of Respiratory Medicine
	Author, *Allergy: The Facts*
USA:	Previously Medical Fellow, Tulane University, New Orleans
	Fellow, American Academy of Allergy and Immunology

EMPEY, Dr Duncan W.

Special interests:	**Cystic fibrosis**
NHS:	Consultant Physician
	Royal London Hospital
	Whitechapel, London E1 1BB
Tel:	0171 377 7339
Fax:	0171 377 7396
Private:	18 Upper Wimpole Street
	London W1
Tel:	0171 935 2977
Fax:	0171 935 2740
First Qualified:	1969 – London
Major Degrees:	FRCP
Specialist Training:	Royal London and Royal Brompton Hospitals, London
Distinctions:	Co-Director, East London Tuberculosis Centre
	Editor, British Journal of Diseases of the Chest
	Executive Committee, European Society of Clinical Respiratory Physiology
USA:	Previously Fellow, Cardiovascular Research Institute, University of California, San Francisco

EVANS, Dr Timothy W.

Special interests:	**Intensive care**
NHS and Academic:	Consultant Physician and Reader in Critical Care
	Royal Brompton Hospital
	Sydney Street
	London SW3 6NP
Tel:	0171 351 8523
Fax:	0171 351 8524
Private:	Refer to address and number above
First Qualified:	1979 – Oxford
Major Degrees:	MRCP, MD, FRCP
Specialist Training:	Royal Brompton Hospital, London
Distinctions:	Previously Doverdale Fellow, Royal Brompton and National Heart Hospitals, London
USA:	Previously Fellow, University of California Medical Center, San Francisco

GEDDES, Dr Duncan M.

Special interests:	**Cystic fibrosis; asthma; broncoscopy**
NHS:	Consultant Physician
	Royal Brompton Hospital
	Sydney Street
	London SW3 6NP
Tel:	0171 352 8121
Fax:	0171 351 8473
Private:	Royal Brompton Hospital
	Private Consulting Rooms
	Sydney Street, London SW3 6NP
Tel:	0171 351 8182
Fax:	0171 351 8999
and:	Princess Grace Hospital
	42/52 Nottingham Place
	London WIM 3FD
Tel:	0171 486 1234
First Qualified:	1971 – Cambridge (with Honours)
Major Degrees:	MD, FRCP

GREEN, Dr Malcolm

Special interests:	**Asthma; general respiratory medicine; infections; respiratory muscles**
NHS:	Consultant Physician
	Royal Brompton Hospital
	Sydney Street
	London SW3 6NP
Tel:	0171 351 8058
Fax:	0171 351 8939
Private:	Lister Hospital
	Chelsea Bridge Road
	London SW1W 8RH
Tel:	0171 376 4985
Fax:	0171 351 8939
First Qualified:	1965 – Oxford
Major Degrees:	DM, FRCP
Academic:	Director, British Postgraduate Medical Federation
	Previously Dean, National Heart and Lung Institute
	Previously Consultant in Charge, Department of Respiratory Medicine, St Bartholomew's Hospital, London
Specialist Training:	St Thomas', Westminster and Royal Brompton Hospitals, London
Distinctions:	Founder and President, British Lung Foundation
USA:	Radcliffe Fellow, Harvard Medical School, Boston

HETZEL, Dr Martin Roger

Special interests:	**Asthma; lung cancer; tuberculosis; tracheal tumours**
NHS:	Consultant Physician in Respiratory and General Medicine
	Respiratory Medicine Department
	Bristol Royal Infirmary
	Bristol BS2 8HW
Tel:	0117 928 3485/2620
Fax:	0117 928 2921
Private:	Longwood House
	The Bath Clinic
	Claverton Down Road
	Bath BA2 7BR
Tel:	01225 835 555 Ext. 261
Fax:	01223 835 900
First Qualified:	1970 – London
Major Degrees:	MD, FRCP
Academic:	Honorary Senior Lecturer, Faculty of Clinical Science, University College London
	Clinical Tutor, Whittington Hospital, London
Specialist Training:	Royal Brompton Hospital and Cardiothoracic Institute, London
Distinctions:	Thoracic Society Prize

MITCHELL, Dr David Mackenzie

Special interests:	**Asthma and allergies; tuberculosis and sarcoidosis; pulmonary infections**
NHS:	Consultant Physician
	Chest and Allergy Clinic
	St Mary's Hospital
	Praed Street
	London W2 1NY
Tel:	0171 725 1082
Fax:	0171 725 1613
Private:	55 Harley Street
	London W1N 1DD
Tel:	0171 725 1082
Fax:	0171 725 1613
First Qualified:	1973 – Cambridge and London
Major Degrees:	MD, FRCP
Academic:	Previously Honorary Senior Lecturer, St Mary's Hospital Medical School, London
Specialist Training:	Royal Brompton and London Chest Hospitals, London

MOORE-GILLON, Dr John C.

Special interests:	**Asthma; lung cancer; tuberculosis**
NHS:	Consultant Physician, Respiratory Medicine
	St Bartholomew's Hospital
	West Smithfield
	London EC1A 7BE
Tel:	0171 601 8441
Fax:	0171 601 8444
Private:	Refer to address and number above
First Qualified:	1976 – Cambridge
Major Degrees:	MD, FRCP
Academic:	Honorary Senior Lecturer in Respiratory Medicine St Bartholomew's, London
Specialist Training:	Royal Brompton and London Chest Hospitals, London

SCADDING, Dr Glenys K.

Special interests:	**Medical management of otitis media with effusion; chronic rhinosinusitis and the combination of asthma and rhinitis (especially with aspirin-sensitive patients)**
NHS:	Consultant Rhinologist
	The Royal National Throat, Nose and Ear Hospital
	Gray's Inn Road
	London WC1X 8DA
Tel:	0171 915 1310
Fax:	0171 833 9480
Private:	Refer to address and number above
First Qualified:	1973 – Cambridge
Major Degrees:	MD, FRCP
Specialist Training:	The Middlesex and Royal Brompton Hospitals, London

SPIRO, Dr Stephen G.

Special interests:	**Diagnosis and treatment of lung cancer; asthma; sleep-disordered breathing**
NHS:	Consultant Chest Physician
	The Middlesex Hospital
	Mortimer Street
	London W1M 8AA
Tel:	0171 380 9004
Fax:	0171 637 5809
Private:	Private Consulting Rooms
	University College Hospital
	25 Grafton Way
	London WC1 6AU
Tel:	0171 387 9709
Fax:	0171 380 9816
First Qualified:	1967 – Manchester
Major Degrees:	MD, FRCP
Academic:	Honorary Senior Lecturer, University College and Middlesex School of Medicine, London
Specialist Training:	Royal Free Hospital and Royal Postgraduate Medical School, London
Distinctions:	Editor, Thorax (Journal, British Thoracic Society) President-elect European Respiratory Society
USA:	Previously Senior Research Fellow in Respiratory Diseases, University of Washington, Seattle

ANGLIA AND OXFORD REGION

CAMBRIDGE

HIGENBOTTAM, Professor Timothy W.

Special interests:	**Heart/lung transplantation; pulmonary hypertension**
NHS:	Professor of Respiratory Medicine
	Section of Respiratory Medicine
	Floor F Medical School
	University of Sheffield
	Beech Hill Road
	Sheffield S10 2RX
Tel:	0114 271 3897
Fax:	0114 271 3904
Private:	No private work
First Qualified:	1971 – London
Major Degrees:	MD, FRCP
Academic:	Professor of Resipratory Medicine, Sheffield University
Specialist Training:	Papworth Hospital, Cambridge
USA:	Fellow, American College of Chest Physicians

STARK, Dr John E.

NHS:	Consultant Thoracic Physician
	Addenbrooke's Hospital
	Hills Road
	Cambridge CB2 2QQ
Tel:	01223 245151
Fax:	01223 216953
Private:	Refer to address and number above
First Qualified:	1958 – Cambridge
Major Degrees:	MD, FRCP
Academic:	Associate Postgraduate Dean, Cambridge University
	Formerly Senior Lecturer, St Bartholomew's Hospital, London
Distinctions:	Honorary Consultant, St Bartholomew's Hospital, London
USA:	Fellow, Webb–Waring Institute, Denver, Colorado

NORTH WEST REGION

BLACKBURN

ORMEROD, Dr Lawrence P.

Special interests:	**Tuberculosis; asthma**
NHS:	Consultant Chest Physician
	Chest Clinic
	Blackburn Royal Infirmary
	Walton Road, Blackburn, Lancashire BB2 3LR
Tel:	01254 294338
Fax:	01254 294423
Private:	Sherwood Rooms
	Beardwood Hospital
	Preston New Road
	Blackburn, Lancashire BB2 7AE
Tel:	01254 581311
Fax:	01254 691874
First Qualified:	1974 – Manchester
Major Degrees:	MD, FRCP
Specialist Training:	Manchester and Birmingham
Distinctions:	Chairman, Joint Tuberculosis Committee, British Thoracic Society

LIVERPOOL

CALVERLEY, Professor Peter M. A.

Special interests:	**Diagnosis and treatment of chronic airways diseases; sleep-related breathing disorders; applied respiratory physiology**
NHS:	Honorary Consultant Physician
	Fazakerley Hospital
	Lower Lane, Liverpool L7 7AL
Tel:	0151 529 3845
Fax:	0151 529 2873
Private:	No private work
First Qualified:	1973 – Edinburgh
Major Degrees:	FRCP, FRCP Ed
Academic:	Professor of Medicine, Pulmonary Rehabilitation, Liverpool University
Specialist Training:	Royal Infirmary and City Hospitals, Edinburgh
Distinctions:	Chairman, Committee Grants Committee, British Lung Foundation
	Croom Lecturer, Royal College of Physicians, Edinburgh
USA and Canada:	Visiting MRC fellow, Meakins–Christie Laboratories, McGill University, Montreal, Canada

DAVIES, Dr Peter

Special interests:	**Mycobacterial diseases including tuberculosis**
NHS:	Consultant Chest Physician
	Cardiothoracic Centre Liverpool NHS Trust
	Thomas Drive
	Liverpool L14 3PE
Tel:	0151 228 1616 Ext. 5453
Fax:	0151 220 8573
Private:	Refer to address and number above
First Qualified:	1973 – Oxford
Major Degrees:	DM, FRCP
Academic:	Lecturer, Kenyatta Hospital, Nairobi
Specialist Training:	University of Wales

EARIS, Dr John

NHS:	Consultant Respiratory Physician
	Fazakerley Hospital
	Lower Lane
	Liverpool L7 7AL
Tel:	0151 529 3845
Fax:	0151 529 2873
Private:	Refer to address and number above
First Qualified:	1970 – London
Major Degrees:	MD, FRCP
Academic:	Clinical Lecturer, Liverpool University
Specialist Training:	Broadgreen and Walton Hospitals, Liverpool, and
	Hope Hospital, Manchester

EVANS, Dr Christopher Charles

Special interests:	**General chest problems of uncertain diagnosis**
NHS:	Cardiothoracic Centre
	Thomas Drive
	Liverpool L14 3PE
Tel:	0151 228 1616
Fax:	0151 220 8573
Private:	Refer to address and number above
First Qualified:	1964 – Liverpool
Major Degrees:	MD, FRCP
Academic:	Clinical Lecturer (Medicine), Liverpool University
Specialist Training:	Cardiothoracic Unit, Broadgreen Hospital, Liverpool
Distinctions:	Wellcome – Swedish Travelling Fellow
	Uppsala University, Sweden

MANCHESTER

WOODCOCK, Dr Ashley

Special interests:	**Asthma; sleep disorders; transplantation**
NHS:	Consultant Respiratory Physician
	North West Lung Centre
	Wythenshaw Hospital
	Southmoor Road
	Manchester M23 9LT
Tel:	0161 946 2398
Fax:	0161 946 2398
Private:	The Beeches Consulting Centre
	Mill Lane
	Cheadle, Cheshire SK8 2PY
Tel:	0161 428 4185
Fax:	0161 428 1692
First Qualified:	1975 – Manchester (with Honours)
Major Degrees:	MD, FRCP
Academic:	Honorary Senior Lecturer, Manchester University
Specialist Training:	Royal Brompton Hospital, London
Distinctions:	Chairman, Clinical Assembly
	Executive Member, European Respiratory Society
	Formerly, Member Executive: British Thoracic Society;
	Specialist Physician, Brunei, Southeast Asia

WOODHEAD, Dr Mark Andrew

Special interests:	**Respiratory infection**
NHS:	Consultant Physician in Respiratory and General Medicine
	Manchester Royal Infirmary
	Oxford Road
	Manchester M13 9WL
Tel:	0161 276 4322
Fax:	0161 276 4989
Private:	BUPA Hospital
	Russell Road
	Whalley Range
	Manchester M16 8AJ
Tel:	0161 226 0112
First Qualified:	1979 – London
Major Degrees:	DM, MRCP
Specialist Training:	City Hospital and University Hospitals, Nottingham

NORTHERN AND YORKSHIRE REGION

NEWCASTLE

BREWIS, Dr R. Alastair L.

Special interests:	**Asthma**
NHS:	Consultant Physician and Medical Director
	Royal Victoria Infirmary
	Queen Victoria Road
	Newcastle NE1 4LP
Tel:	0191 232 5131
Fax:	0191 261 8505
Private:	Refer to address and number above
First Qualified:	1960 – Durham
Major Degrees:	MD, FRCP
Academic:	Senior Lecturer, Newcastle University
Specialist Training:	Charing Cross and Royal Brompton Hospitals, London, and Newcastle

GIBSON, Professor G. John

Special interests:	**General respiratory disease**
NHS:	Consultant Physician
	Regional Cardiothoracic Centre
	Freeman Hospital
	High Heaton
	Newcastle upon Tyne NE7 7DN
Tel:	0191 284 3111
Fax:	0191 213 1575
Private:	Refer to address and number above
First Qualified:	1968 – London
Major Degrees:	MD, FRCP
Academic:	Professor in Respiratory Medicine, Newcastle University
Specialist Training:	Hammersmith and Guy's Hospitals, London, and St Joseph's Hospital, McMaster University, Hamilton, Canada

TRENT REGION

NOTTINGHAM

JOHNSTON, Dr Ian D. A.

Special interests:	**Interstitial lung disease including fibrosing alveolitis, lung cancer, asthma; medico-legal aspects of respiratory medicine**
NHS:	Consultant Physician in General and Respiratory Medicine University Hospital Queen's Medical Centre Nottingham NG7 2UH
Tel:	0115 970 9155
Fax:	0115 942 4554
Private:	The Convent Hospital 748 Mansfield Road Woodthorpe Nottingham NG5 3FZ
Tel:	0115 9209209
Fax:	0115 9673005
First Qualified:	1975 – Cambridge and London (with Honours)
Major Degrees:	MD, FRCP
Academic:	Previously Clinical Sub-Dean, Nottingham University Medical School Clinical Research Fellow, St George's Hospital, London
Specialist Training:	Brompton, St George's, Whittington and The Middlesex Hospitals, London
Distinctions:	Allen and Hanbury/Hospital Doctor Respiratory Team of the Year 1994/5

STOKE ON TRENT

PROWSE, Dr Keith

Special interests:	**Sleep-related breathing disorders; occupational lung disease**
NHS:	Consultant Physician and Medical Director
	North Staffordshire Hospital
	City General
	Newcastle Road
	Stoke on Trent ST4 6QG
Tel:	01782 718329
Fax:	01782 718323
Private:	540 Etruria Road
	Basford
	Stoke on Trent
Tel:	01782 614419
Fax:	01782 630270
First Qualified:	1962 – Birmingham
Major Degrees:	MD, FRCP
Academic:	Senior Clinical Lecturer, Department of Postgraduate Medicine, Keele University
	Formerly, INSERM research Fellow, Nancy, France and Previously Senior Lecturer in Medicine, Department of Postgraduate Medicine, Keele University
Specialist Training:	Birmingham
Distinctions:	Executive Chairman of British Thoracic Society and President-elect

WEST MIDLANDS

BIRMINGHAM

AYRES, Dr Jonathan Geoffrey

Special interests:	**Asthma**
NHS:	Consultant in Respiratory Medicine
	Department of Respiratory Medicine
	Birmingham Heartlands Hosptial
	Brodesley Green East
	Birmingham B9 5SS
Tel:	0121 766 6611
Fax:	0121 773 6897
Private:	Refer to address and number above
First Qualified:	1974 – London
Major Degrees:	FRCP
Academic:	Honorary Senior Lecturer, Birmingham University
Specialist Training:	East Birmingham Hospital

STABLEFORTH, Dr David Edward

Special interests:	**Cystic fibrosis**
NHS:	Consultant Physician
	Birmingham Heartlands Hospital
	Brodesley Green East
	Birmingham B9 5ST
Tel:	0121 772 4311
Private:	Solihull Parkway Hospital
	Dawson Parkway
	Solihull, West Midlands B91 2PP
Tel:	0121 704 1451
Fax:	0121 711 1080
First Qualified:	1966 – Cambridge and London
Major Degrees:	FRCP
Academic:	Honorary Senior Clinical Lecturer
	Birmingham University
Specialist Training:	Royal Brompton Hospital, London
Distinctions:	President, Midland Thoracic Society

SCOTLAND

EDINBURGH

DOUGLAS, Dr Neil James

Special interests:	**Sleep apnoea**
NHS:	Professor of Respiratory and Sleep Medicine
	Respiratory Medicine Unit
	Royal Infirmary
	Lauriston Place
	Edinburgh EH3 9YW
Tel:	0131 536 3252
Fax:	0131 536 3255
Private:	Scottish National Sleep Laboratory
	Royal Infirmary
	Lauriston Place
	Edinburgh EH3 9YW
Tel:	0131 536 2355
Fax:	0131 536 2362
First Qualified:	1973 – Edinburgh
Major Degrees:	MD, FRCP
Academic:	Professor of Respiratory and Sleep Medicine
	Edinburgh University
Specialist Training:	Edinburgh University
Distinctions:	Director, Scottish National Sleep Laboratory
	Dean, Royal College of Physicians, Edinburgh
USA:	Previously Fellow, Cardiovascular/Pulmonary Research
	Laboratories, Colorado University, Denver

GLASGOW

PATON, Dr James Y.

Special interests:	**Breathing difficulties in children**
NHS:	Honorary Consultant Paediatrician
	Royal Hospital for Sick Children
	Yorkhill
	Glasgow G3 8SJ
Tel:	0141 201 0000
Fax:	0141 209 0387
Private:	Refer to address and number above
First Qualified:	1977 – Glasgow (with Honours)
Major Degrees:	MD, MRCP, DCH
Academic:	Senior Lecturer, Royal Hospital for Sick Children, Glasgow
Specialist Training:	Royal Hospital for Sick Children, Glasgow
USA:	MRC Travelling Fellow Children's Hospital, Los Angeles

CLINICAL ONCOLOGISTS

(Radiotherapists)

Clinical oncologists are medical specialists skilled in all non-surgical forms of cancer treatment. A clinical oncologist is the modern term for radiotherapist, oncologist and/or radiation oncologist. They constitute the largest body of specialists with a full-time commitment to cancer work. A clinical oncologist's work includes the use of treatments such as radiotherapy, brachytherapy and chemotherapy.

Radiotherapy involves the use of high-energy X-rays to kill cancer cells. It is aimed at a particular part or parts of the body in order to destroy cancer cells. Cancer cells are more receptive than normal cells and are consequently destroyed more quickly. Chemotherapy is the use of systemic drugs to kill cancer cells dispersed throughout the body. The drugs are administered orally or intravenously. Chemotherapy is given to destroy or control cancer cells, particularly cells which might be difficult to detect in the body.

Some types of cancer require the insertion into or near to the tumour of radioactive materials capable of destroying cancers locally. These techniques, known as brachytherapy, are sometimes used in conjunction with external beam irradiation. For some patients with various types of leukaemia and other bone marrow and lymphatic diseases, total body irradiation followed by bone marrow transplantation is an important new technique.

LONDON AND THE SOUTH EAST

ARNOTT, Dr Sidney J.

Special interests:	**Tumours of the gastrointestinal tract**
NHS:	Consultant Radiotherapist Oncologist
	St Bartholomew's Hospital
	West Smithfield
	London EC1A 7BE
Tel:	0171 601 8353
Fax:	0171 601 8364
Private:	53 Harley Street
	London W1N 1BD
Tel:	0171 323 4331
Fax:	0171 636 4596
First Qualified:	1962 – Edinburgh
Major Degrees:	FRCS Ed, FRCR
Academic:	Previously Senior Lecturer in Radiotherapy, Edinburgh University
Specialist Training:	Edinburgh

COLTART, Dr R. Stewart

NHS:	Consultant Clinical Oncologist
	Kent and Canterbury Hospital
	Ethelbert Road
	Canterbury
	Kent CT1 3NG
Tel:	01227 766877 Ext. 4563
Fax:	01227 783012
Private:	Refer to address and number above
First Qualified:	1976 – London
Major Degrees:	FRCR
Specialist Training:	Cardiff

COULTER, Dr Carmel

Special interests:	**Breast and gynaecological cancer**
NHS:	Consultant Clinical Oncologist
	St Mary's Hospital
	Praed Street
	London W2 1NY
Tel:	0171 725 1132
Fax:	0171 725 1840
Private:	108 Harley Street
	London W1
Tel:	0171 224 1120
Fax:	0171 436 2945
and:	King Edward VII Hospital For Officers,
	Beaumont Street
	London W1N 2AA
Tel:	0171 486 4411
Fax:	0171 935 6770
First Qualified:	1970 – London
Major Degrees:	FRCP, FRCR
Specialist Training:	St Bartholomew's Hospital, London

DEARNALEY, Dr David Paul

Special interests:	**Urological cancers**
NHS:	Honorary Consultant and Head of Urology Department
	Institute of Cancer Research
	Royal Marsden Hospital
	Downs Road
	Sutton, Surrey SM2 5PT
Tel:	0181 642 6011 Ext. 3271
Fax:	0181 643 8809
Private:	Refer to address and number above
First Qualified:	1976 – Cambridge
Major Degrees:	MD, FRCP, FRCR
Academic:	Senior Lecturer and Vice-Dean, Institute of Cancer Research, London
Specialist Training:	Royal Marsden Hospitals, London and Surrey

DEUTSCH, Dr George

Special interests:	**Breast, head and neck, and colorectal cancer**
NHS:	Consultant in Clinical Oncology
	Sussex Oncology Centre
	Royal Sussex County Hospital
	Eastern Road
	Brighton BN2 5BE
Tel:	01273 696955 Ext. 4328
Fax:	01273 623312
Private:	55 New Church
	Hove, Sussex
Tel:	01273 720217
Fax:	01273 220919
First Qualified:	1967 – London
Major Degrees:	FRCP, FRCR
Specialist Training:	Middlesex Hospital, London, and Mount Vernon Hospital, Middlesex

DOBBS, Dr H. Jane

Special interests:	**Breast Cancer; prostate cancer**
NHS:	Consultant Radiotherapist
	St Thomas' Hospital
	Lambeth Palace Road
	London SE1 7EH
Tel:	0171 922 8030 Ext. 2044
Fax:	0171 928 9968
Private:	Consultant Rooms
	The Sloane Hospital
	125 Albemarle Road
	Beckenham, Kent
Tel:	0181 466 6911
Fax:	0181 313 9547
First Qualified:	1975 – Cambridge, London
Major Degrees:	FRCP, FRCR
Academic:	Teacher, London University
	Previously Senior Lecturer, Royal Marsden Hospital, London
Specialist Training:	Royal Marsden Hospital, London

GODLEE, Dr J. Nicholas

Special interests:	**Bone cancer; brain tumours**
NHS:	Retired from the NHS
Private:	Consultant in Radiotherapy and Oncology
	Private Patients Wing
	University College Hospital
	25 Grafton Way
	London WC1E 6DB
Tel:	0171 383 7911
Fax:	0171 380 9816
First Qualified:	1955 – Cambridge
Major Degrees:	FRCR
Specialist Training:	Royal Marsden Hospital, London
Distinctions:	Former Director, Radiotherapy and Oncology
	Department, University College, London
USA:	Previously Research Associate, Stanford Medical Centre, California

HANHAM, Dr Iain W. F.

Special interests:	**Cancer of the head and neck**
NHS:	Consultant Radiotherapist and Physician in Medical Oncology
	Charing Cross Hospital
	Fulham Palace Road
	London W6 8RF
Tel:	0181 746 8000 or 0181 746 8427
Fax:	0181 846 1603
Private:	Cromwell Hospital
	Cromwell Road
	London SW5 OTU
Tel:	0171 370 4233 Ext. 5024
Fax:	0171 370 5750
First Qualified:	1962 – Cambridge
Major Degrees:	FRCP, FRCR
Academic:	Approved teacher in Medicine, London University
Specialist Training:	Westminster Hospital, London
Distinctions:	Civilian Consultant Radiotherapist and Clinical Oncologist to the Royal Air Force

HODSON, Dr Neil J.

Special interests:	**Urological cancers**
NHS:	Consultant in Clinical Oncology
	Sussex Oncology Centre
	The Sussex County Hospital
	Eastern Road
	Brighton BN2 5BE
Tel:	01273 696955 Ext. 4600
Fax:	01273 623312
Private:	Refer to address and number above
First Qualified:	1970 – Bristol (with Honours)
Major Degrees:	FRCR
Academic:	Senior Lecturer and Research Fellow, Royal Marsden Hospital, London
Specialist Training:	Royal Marsden Hospital, London, and Bristol Royal Infirmary

HORWICH, Professor Alan

Special interests:	**Urological cancers; Hodgkin's disease**
NHS:	Consultant Clinical Oncologist
	Royal Marsden Hospital
	Downs Road
	Sutton, Surrey SM2 5PT
Tel:	0181 642 6011 Ext. 3269
Fax:	0181 643 8809
Private:	Refer to adress and number above
First Qualified:	1971 – London
Major Degrees:	PhD, FRCR, FRCP
Academic:	Professor of Radiotherapy and Oncology, Institute of Cancer Research, London
Specialist Training:	Royal Marsden Hospital, London
USA:	Previously Fellow in Medical Oncology, Harvard Medical School

KEEN, Dr Colin

Special interests:	**Breast cancer; prostate and bladder cancer**
NHS:	Clinical Director in Oncology
	Mid Kent Oncology Centre
	Maidstone Hospital
	Maidstone, Kent ME16 9QQ
Tel:	01622 729000 Ext. 5014
Fax:	01622 721303
Private:	Refer to address and number above
First Qualified:	1958 – London
Major Degrees:	FRCPC, FRCR
Specialist Training:	Princess Margaret Hospital, Toronto, Canada, and Queensland Radium Institute, Brisbane, Australia
USA and Canada:	See 'Specialist Training' above

LAMBERT, Dr Joanna

Special interests:	**Gynaecological cancer**
NHS:	Consultant Clinical Oncologist
	Hammersmith Hospital
	Du Cane Road
	London W12 0HS.
Tel:	0181 743 2030 Ext. 3059
Fax:	0181 740 3169 or 01494 431671
Private:	Refer to address and number above
Major Degrees:	MD, FRCR

LAWTON, Dr Patricia Ann

NHS:	Consultant Clinical Oncologist
	Mount Vernon Centre for Cancer Treatment
	Mount Vernon Hospital
	Rickmansworth Road
	Northwood
	Middlesex HA6 2RN
Tel:	01923 826111 Ext. 4313
Fax:	01923 835803
Private:	Refer to address and number above
First Qualified:	1983 – London
Major Degrees:	FRCR
Specialist Training:	Midddlesex and Hammersmith Hospitals, London, and Mount Vernon Hospital, Middlesex
Distinctions:	Previously Clinical Research Fellow, Mount Vernon Hospital, Middlesex

MacDONALD, Dr Elizabeth Anne

Special interests:	**Breast cancer; lymphomas; children's brain tumours**
NHS:	Consultant Clinical Oncologist
	Radiotherapy Department
	Guy's Hospital
	London SE1 9RT
Tel:	0171 955 4407
Fax:	0171 955 4828
Private:	Radiotherapy Department
	Cromwell Hospital
	Cromwell Road
	London SW5 0TU
Tel:	0171 370 4233 Ext. 5024
Fax:	0171 370 4063
First Qualified:	1969 – London
Major Degrees:	DMRT, MA (Medical Law and Ethics), FRCR
Academic:	Previously Clinical Tutor, Hammersmith Hospital, London
Specialist Training:	Westminster and Charing Cross Hospitals, London
Distinctions:	Previously Consultant, Nice Cancer Centre, France
	Founder, London Paediatric Neuro-oncology Forum
USA:	Clinical Researcher, Northern California Oncology Group, Stanford University

MANTELL, Dr Brian S.

Special interests:	**Head and neck, brain and pituitary, lung, oesophagus, benign disease skin; HIV**
NHS:	Consultant Radiotherapist and Oncologist
	Royal London Hospital
	Whitechapel Road
	London E1 1BB
Tel:	0171 377 7000 Ext. 7681 or 0171 377 7683
Fax:	0171 377 7689
Private:	Refer to adddress and number above
First Qualified:	1958 – London
Major Degrees:	DMRT, FRCP, FRCR
Academic:	Honorary Senior Lecturer, Heart and Lung Institute, London University
Specialist Training:	King George's Hospital, Ilford
Distinctions:	Honorary Consultant, King George's Hospital, Ilford, and Harold Wood Hospital, Romford

PHILLIPS, Dr Robert H.

Special interests:	**Breast cancer, prostate cancer; AIDS-associated Kaposis sarcoma**
NHS:	Consultant Radiotherapist and Physician in Medical Oncology
	Department of Clinical Oncology
	Charing Cross Hospital
	Fulham Palace Road
	London W6 8RF
Tel:	0181 846 1298 or 0181 746 8425
Fax:	0181 746 8429
Private:	Refer to address and number above
First Qualified:	1971 – Oxford
Major Degrees:	DMRT, FRCP, FRCR
Distinctions:	Honorary Consultant Radiotherapist to the Army

PLOWMAN, Dr P. Nicholas

Special interests:	**Neuro-oncology; breast cancer; urological cancer; paediatric cancers**
NHS:	Consultant Physician in Radiotherapy and Oncology
	St Bartholomew's Hospital
	West Smithfield
	London EC1A 7BE
Tel:	0171 601 8351
Fax:	0171 601 8364
and NHS:	Consultant Physician in Radiotherapy and Oncology
	Hospital for Sick Children
	34 Great Ormond Street
	London WC1N 3JH
Tel:	0171 405 9200
Fax:	0171 813 8588
Private:	14 Harmont House
	20 Harley Street
	London W1
Tel:	0171 631 1632
Fax:	0171 323 3487
First Qualified:	1974 – Cambridge (with Honours)
Major Degrees:	MD, FRCP, FRCR
Academic:	Honorary Senior Lecturer, Institute of Child Health, London
Specialist Training:	St Bartholomew's Hospital, London, and Cambridge

PRICE, Dr Patricia

Special interests:	**Gastric, pancreatic and colonic cancer**
NHS:	Consultant Clinical Oncologist and Reader in Clinical Oncology
	Hammersmith Hospital
	Du Cane Road
	London W12 0HS
Tel:	0181 740 3357
Fax:	0181 743 8766
Private:	Refer to address and number above
First Qualified:	1981 – Cambridge
Major Degrees:	FRCR
Academic:	Reader, Clinical Oncology, Royal Postgraduate Medical School, London
Specialist Training:	Royal Marsden Hospital, London
Distinctions:	Sterling Oncology Award 1989

SMEDLEY, Dr Howard Martin

Special interests:	**Breast cancer; testicular cancer; gastrointestinal cancer**
NHS:	Clinical Director
	Director of Oncology
	Kent and Canterbury Hospital
	Ethelbert Road
	Canterbury CT1 3NG
Tel:	01227 766877 Ext. 4567
Fax:	01227 783012
Private:	5 Dover Street
	Canterbury
	Kent CT1 3HD
Tel:	01227 764664
Fax:	01227 787767
First Qualified:	1977 – London
Major Degrees:	FRCR
Academic:	Previously Clinical Tutor, Kent and Canterbury Hospital
	Senior Clinical Scientist, Ludwig Institute for Cancer Research, Cambridge
Specialist Training:	Addenbrooke's Hospital, Cambridge

SPITTLE, Dr Margaret F.

Special interests:	**Breast cancer, head and neck cancer, skin cancers; AIDS-related malignancies**
NHS:	Consultant Clinical Oncologist
	Meyerstein Institute of Oncology
	The Middlesex Hospital
	Mortimer Street
	London W1N 8AA
Tel:	0171 636 8333
Fax:	0171 436 0160
and:	Guy's Hospital
	St Thomas Street
	London SE1 9RT
Tel:	0171 955 5000
and:	St Thomas' Hospital
	Lambeth Palace Road
	London SE1 7EH
Tel:	0171 928 9292
Private:	Refer to first address and number above
First Qualified:	1963 – London
Major Degrees:	MSc. FRCP, FRCR
Academic:	Dean, Royal College of Radiologists
Specialist Training:	Westminster Hospital and Royal Postgraduate Medical School, London
Distinctions:	Vice-President, Royal Society of Medicine
	Honorary Consultant Radiotherapist, Royal Postgraduate Medical School, London
USA:	Previously Instructor, Stanford University Medical Centre, California

TIMOTHY, Dr Adrian

Special interests:	**Hodgkin's disease; breast cancer**
NHS:	Consultant Clinical Oncologist
	Department of Radiotherapy and Oncology
	St Thomas' Hospital
	Lambeth Palace Road
	London SE1 7EH
Tel:	0171 928 9292 Ext. 2416
Fax:	0171 928 9968
Private:	53 Harley Street
	London W1N 1DD
Tel:	0171 323 4332
Fax:	0171 636 4596
First Qualified:	1969 – London
Major Degrees:	FRCP, FRCR
Specialist Training:	St Bartholomew's Hospital, London
Distinctions:	Previously Hamilton–Fairley Fellow, St Bartholomew's Hospital, London
USA:	Previously Fellow in Radiation Therapy Harvard Medical School, Boston

TOBIAS, Dr Jeffrey S.

Special interests:	**Breast cancer, gynaecological cancer, head and neck cancer and myeloma**
NHS:	Clinical Director, Cancer Services
	Meyerstein Institute of Oncology
	The Middlesex Hospital
	Mortimer Street
	London W1N 8AA
Tel:	0171 380 9214
Fax:	0171 637 1201
Private:	Refer to address and number above
First Qualified:	1972 – Cambridge
Major Degrees:	MD, FRCP, FRCR
Academic:	Lecturer, Royal Marsden Hospitals, London
Specialist Training:	Royal Marsden and St Bartholomew's Hospitals, London
USA:	Previously Fellow in Medical Oncology, Harvard Medical School, Boston

ANGLIA AND OXFORD REGION

CAMBRIDGE

WATSON, Dr James

Special interests:	**Gynaecology; brain tumours**
NHS:	Consultant Clinical Oncology
	Addenbrooke's Hospital
	Hills Road
	Cambridge CB2 2QQ
Tel:	01223 245151 Ext. 2555
Fax:	01223 274409
Private:	No private work

WILSON, Dr Charles B. J. H.

Special interests:	**Breast and gastrointestinal malignancy**
NHS:	Consultant in Clinical Oncology
	Addenbrooke's Hospital
	Hills Road
	Cambridge CB2 2QQ
Tel:	01223 217110
Fax:	01223 274409
Private:	Evelyn Hospital
	4 Trumpington Road
	Cambridge CB2 2AF
Tel:	01223 370922
Fax:	01223 316068
First Qualified:	1980 – London
Major Degrees:	MD, MRCP, FRCR
Academic:	IRCF Fellow, Hammersmith MRC Cyctron Unit
Specialist Training:	Royal Marsden and Hammersmith Hospitals, London

NORTH WEST REGION

LIVERPOOL

COTTIER, Dr Brian

Special interests:	**Lung cancer**
NHS:	Consultant Clinical Oncologist
	Clatterbridge Centre for Oncology
	Clatterbridge Hospital
	Clatterbridge Road
	Bebington, Wirral, Merseyside L63 4JY
Tel:	0151 334 4092
Fax:	0151 604 7458
Private:	Refer to address and number above
First Qualified:	1974 – Liverpool
Major Degrees:	FRCP, FRCR
Academic:	Previously Senior Lecturer in Radiotherapy and
	Oncology, Liverpool University

MANCHESTER

JAMES, Dr Roger David

Special interests:	**Gastrointestinal cancers**
NHS:	Consultant Radiotherapist
	Christie Hospital
	Wilmslow Road
	Withington
	Manchester M20 9BX
Tel:	0161 446 3419
Fax:	0161 446 3352
Private:	Refer to address and number above
First Qualified:	1971 – Cambridge
Major Degrees:	FRCR
Academic:	Previously Honorary Lecturer, Meyerstein Institute, The Middlesex Hospital, London
Specialist Training:	Meyerstein Institute, The Middlesex Hospital, London
USA:	Berkeley Fellow, Massachusetts General Hospital, Boston

NORTHERN AND YORKSHIRE REGION

LEEDS

ASH, Dr Daniel

NHS:	Consultant Radiotherapist and Oncologist
	Cookridge Hospital
	Hospital Lane
	Cookridge
	Leeds LS16 6QB
Tel:	0113 267 3411 Ext. 4426
Fax:	0113 292 4214
Private:	Refer to address and number above
First Qualified:	1968 – London
Major Degrees:	FRCP, FRCR

SOUTH AND WEST REGION

BRISTOL

BARLEY, Dr Victor L.

Special interests:	**Head and neck cancers; gynaecological malignancy; skin cancer**
NHS:	Consultant Clinical Oncologist
	British Oncology Centre
	Horfield Road
	Bristol, Avon BS2 8ED
Tel:	0117 9282415
Fax:	0117 9282488
Private:	Refer to address and number above
First Qualified:	1966 – Cambridge
Major Degrees:	FRCS Ed, FRCR
Academic:	Clinical Teacher, Bristol
	Previously Demonstrator, Department of Anatomy, Oxford University
Specialist Training:	Churchill Hospital, Oxford

CHELTENHAM

OWEN, Dr John Roger

Special interests:	**Management of breast cancer, testicular cancer, head and neck tumours and the use of brachytherapy in treating cancer**
NHS:	Consultant Clinical Oncologist
	Gloucestershire Oncology Centre
	Cheltenham General Hospital
	Cheltenham, Gloucestershire GL53 7AN
Tel:	01242 222222 Ext. 4021
Fax:	01242 273506
Private:	Cotswold Nuffield Hospital
	Talbot Road, Cheltenham
	Gloucestershire
Tel:	Refer to number above
First Qualified:	1971 – London
Major Degrees:	MRCP, FRCR
Academic:	Previously Honorary Lecturer, Royal Postgraduate Medical School, London
Specialist Training:	Hôpital Henri Mondor, Cretere, Paris

PLYMOUTH

KELLY, Dr Steve A.

NHS:	Consultant Clinical Oncologist
	Director of Clinical Oncology
	Freedom Fields Hospital
	Plymouth PL4 7JJ
Tel:	01752 834243
Fax:	01752 601033
Private:	Refer to address and number above
First Qualified:	1980 – Leeds
Major Degrees:	PhD, FRCR
Academic:	Clinical Research Fellow, Imperial Cancer Research Fund
Specialist Training:	Hammersmith Hospital, London

TRENT REGION

NOTTINGHAM

BESSELL, Dr Eric

Special interests:	**Lymphomas**
NHS:	Consultant Oncologist
	Nottingham City Hospital
	Hucknall Road
	Nottingham NG5 1PB
Tel:	0115 969 1169 Ext. 46986
Fax:	0115 962 7994
Private:	Park Hospital
	Sherwood Lodge Drive
	Arnold
	Nottingham NG5 8RX
Tel:	0115 9670670 Ext. 326
Fax:	0115 9260905
First Qualified:	1978 – London
Major Degrees:	PhD, FRCP, FRCR
Specialist Training:	Royal Marsden Hospitals, London and Sutton, Surrey

WEST MIDLANDS

BIRMINGHAM

GLAHOLM, Dr John

Special interests:	**Head and neck cancers; thyroid cancer; urological cancer**
NHS:	Consultant Clinical Oncologist
	Birmingham Oncology Centre
	Queen Elizabeth Hospital
	Edgbaston
	Birmingham B15 2TH
Tel:	0121 472 1311 Ext. 2443
Fax:	0121 627 2496
Private:	Birmingham Nuffield Hospital
	22 Somerset Road
	Edgbaston
	Birmingham B15 2QQ
Tel:	0121 456 2000
Fax:	0121 454 5293
First Qualified:	1980 – London
Major Degrees:	FRCR

JAMES, Dr Nicholas David

Special interests:	**Urological oncology, lymphoma**
NHS:	Senior Lecturer and Honorary Consultant in Clinical Oncology
	CRC Institute for Cancer Studies
	Queen Elizabeth Hospital
	Edgebaston, Birmingham, B15 2TH
Tel:	0121 414 3803
Fax:	0121 414 3263
Private:	Birmingham Nuffield Hospital
	Somerset Road
	Edgbaston
	Birmingham B15 2QQ
Tel:	0121 456 2000 Ext. 217
Fax:	0121 455 8886
First Qualified:	1983 – London
Major Degrees:	BSc (1st Class Honours), PhD, MRCP, FRCR
Academic:	Lecturer in Oncology, Hammersmith and St Mary's Hospitals, London
Specialist Training:	St Bartholomew's, Hammersmith and Royal Marsden Hospitals, London
Distinctions:	Brackenbury and Bourne Scholarship, St Bartholomew's Hospital
	Frank Ellis Medal, Royal College of Radiologists
Japan:	Royal Society Fellowship, Cancer Institute, Tokyo

SCOTLAND

EDINBURGH

MacDOUGALL, Dr R. Hugh

Special interests:	**Head and neck cancers; colorectal cancer**
NHS:	Clinical Director
	Department of Clinical Oncology
	Western General Hospital
	Crewe Road
	Edinburgh EH4 2XU
Tel:	0131 537 1000 Ext. 2208
Fax:	0131 537 1029
Private:	Refer to address and number above
First Qualified:	1972 – St Andrews
Major Degrees:	DMRT, FRCS Ed, FRCR
Academic:	Honorary Senior Lecturer, Clinical Oncology, Edinburgh University

GLASGOW

BARRETT, Professor Ann

Special interests:	**Sarcomas; lymphomas**
NHS:	Professor of Radiotherapy Oncology
	Beatson Oncology Centre
	Western Infirmary
	Dumbarton Road
	Glasgow G11 6NT
Tel:	0141 211 1738
Fax:	0141 337 1712
Private:	No private work
First Qualified:	1968 – London
Major Degrees:	MD, FRCP, FRCR
Academic:	Previously Senior Lecturer, Royal Marsden Hospital, Sutton
Specialist Training:	Middlesex and Royal Marsden Hospitals, London, and Villejuif, Paris
Distinctions:	President of Scottish Radiological Society
	President European Society for Therapeutic Radiology and Oncology

WALES

CARDIFF

MASON, Dr Malcolm D.

Special interests:	**Prostate cancer**
NHS:	Consultant Clinical Oncologist
	Velindre Hospital
	Velindre Road
	Cardiff CF4 7XL
Tel:	01222 615888 Ext. 6202
Fax:	01222 522694
Private:	Refer to address and number above
First Qualified:	1979 – London
Major Degrees:	MD, FRCR
Academic:	Previously Lecturer, Institute of Cancer, and Royal Marsden Hospital, London

COLORECTAL SURGEONS

These surgeons treat ailments of the lower gastrointestinal tract. These include polyps, cancer, haemorrhoids and inflammatory diseases such as ulcerative colitis, which affects 80,000 people in the UK and Crohn's disease which affects roughly 40,000 people in the UK. Diagnosis is usually done by a gastroenterologist.

LONDON AND THE SOUTH EAST

HAWLEY, Mr Peter

Special interests:	**Colorectal cancer; recurrent colorectal cancer; irritable bowel disease; Crohn's disease**
NHS:	Consultant Surgeon
	St Mark's Hospital
	Northwick Park
	Watford Road
	Harrow, Middlesex HA1 3JU
Tel:	0181 235 4019
Fax:	0181 235 4001
Private:	149 Harley Street
	London W1N 2DE
Tel:	0171 935 2825
Fax:	0171 486 1406
and:	Consultant Surgeon
	King Edward VII Hospital
	10 Beaumont Street,
	London W1N 2AA
Tel:	0171 486 4411
Fax:	0171 935 6770
First Qualified:	1956 – London
Major Degrees:	MS, FRCS
Academic:	Previously Senior Lecturer, University College Hospital, London
	Fellow, University College London
Specialist Training:	St Mark's Hospital, London
Distinctions:	Consultant Colon and Rectal Surgeon to the Army
USA:	Previously Research Fellow in Surgery
	University of California, San Francisco

LEWIS, Mr A. Anthony M.

Special interests:	**Gastric and colorectal surgery**
NHS:	Consultant Surgeon
	Royal Free Hospital
	Pond Street
	London NW3 2QG
Tel:	0171 794 0500 Ext. 4832 or 0171 830 2069
Fax:	0171 431 4528
Private:	8 Upper Wimpole Street
	London W1M 7TD
Tel:	0171 935 1956
Fax:	0171 487 2894
First Qualified:	1963 – London
Major Degrees:	FRCS
Specialist Training:	Royal Free Hospital, London
Distinctions:	Surgeon to the Royal Household
USA:	Post-Doctoral Fellow, Stanford University Medical School, California

NICHOLLS, Mr R. John

Special interests:	**Inflammatory bowel disease; ulcerative colitis and Crohn's disease; large bowel cancer; functional bowel diseases including incontinence**
NHS:	Consultant Colorectal Surgeon
	St Mark's Hospital
	Northwick Park
	Watford Road
	Harrow, Middlesex HA1 3JU
Tel:	0181 235 4046
Fax:	0181 235 4039
Private:	149 Harley Street
	London W1N 2DE
Tel:	0171 935 4444
Fax:	0171 486 0665
First Qualified:	1968 – Cambridge
Major Degrees:	FRCS, MChir
Academic:	Dean, St Mark's Academic Institute
	Previously Senior Lecturer, St Bartholomew's Hospital, London
Specialist Training:	St Mark's and London Hospitals, London, and in Heidelberg, Germany
Distinctions:	Previously Hallet Prize, Royal College of Surgeons
	Editor, International Journal Colorectal Disease

NORTHOVER, Mr John M. A.

Special interests:	**Bowel cancer; Crohn's disease; ulcerative colitis; the surgery of incontinence; complex fistulae**
NHS:	Consultant Surgeon
	St Mark's Hospital
	Northwick Park
	Watford Road
	Harrow, Middlesex HA1 3JU
Tel:	0181 235 4250
Fax:	0181 235 4277
Private:	149 Harley Street
	London W1N 2DE
Tel:	0171 486 1008
Fax:	0171 486 0665
First Qualified:	1970 – London
Major Degrees:	FRCS
Academic:	Director, Imperial Cancer Research Fund, Colorectal Cancer Unit
Specialist Training:	St Mark's Hospital, Middlesex

SHAND, Mr William S.

Special interests:	**Colorectal surgery; endocrinology**
NHS:	Consultant Surgeon
	St Bartholomew's Hospital
	West Smithfield
	London ECIA 7BE
Tel:	0171 601 8888 Ext. 7032
Fax:	0171 601 7034
Private:	149 Harley Street
	London WIN 2DE
Tel:	0171 935 4444
Fax:	0171 486 3782
First Qualified:	1961 – Cambridge
Major Degrees:	MD, FRCS, FRCS Ed
Specialist Training:	St Mark's and St Bartholomew's Hospitals, London
Distinctions:	Honorary Consultant Surgeon, St Mark's Hospital, Middlesex
	Panel of Examiners, Edinburgh College
	Previously Court of Examiners, Royal College of Surgeons, England

SPRINGALL, Mr Roger G.

NHS:	Consultant Surgeon
	Charing Cross Hospital
	Fulham Palace Road
	London W6 8RF
Tel:	0181 846 1077
Fax:	0181 846 1111
Private:	149 Harley Street
	London W1N 1HG
Tel:	0171 486 7927
Fax:	0171 486 7927
First Qualified:	1973 – Liverpool
Major Degrees:	ChM, FRCS
Specialist Training:	St Bartholomew's and St Mark's Hospitals, London

---

THOMSON, Mr James P. S.

NHS:	Clinical Director and Consultant Surgeon
	St Mark's Hospital
	Northwick Park
	Watford Road
	Harrow, Middlesex HA1 3JU
Tel:	0181 235 4003/2
Fax:	0181 235 4001
Private:	The Robert and Lisa Sainsbury Wing
	St Mark's Hospital (see address above)
Tel:	01223 413500
Fax:	01223 413500
First Qualified:	1962 – London
Major Degrees:	DM, FRCS, MS
Academic:	Honorary Senior Clinical Lecturer, St Mary's Medical School, London
Specialist Training:	St Mark's and The Middlesex Hospitals, London
Distinctions:	President, Coloprotology Section, Royal Society of Medicine
	Civil Consultant Surgeon to the Royal Navy and the Royal Air Force
	Surgical Examiner, Universities of Cambridge and London and previously to The Royal College of Surgeons and Liverpool University

---

ANGLIA AND OXFORD REGION

OXFORD

MORTENSEN, Mr Neil

Special interests:	**Ulcerative colitis; Crohn's disease; anal sphincter injuries; cancer of the rectum; transanal endoscopic microsurgery**
NHS:	Consultant Colorectal Surgeon John Radcliffe Hospital Headley Way, Headington Oxford OX3 9DU
Tel:	01865 220926
Fax:	01865 60390
Private:	23 Banbury Road Oxford OX2 6NX
Tel:	01865 220926
Fax:	01865 60390
First Qualified:	1973 – Birmingham
Major Degrees:	MD, FRCS
Academic:	Reader in Colorectal Surgery, Oxford University Previously Senior Lecturer, Bristol University
Specialist Training:	St Mark's Hospital, London
Distinctions:	Arris and Gale Lecture, Royal College of Surgeons
USA:	Previously Paul Hawley International Scholar American College of Surgeons

NORTH WEST REGION

MANCHESTER

MacLENNAN, Mr Ian

NHS:	Consultant Surgeon Manchester Royal Infirmary Oxford Road Manchester M13 9WL
Tel:	0161 276 4170
Fax:	0161 276 4530
Private:	Refer to address and number above
First Qualified:	1967 – Manchester
Major Degrees:	FRCS, FRCS Ed
Academic:	Dean, Clinical Studies, Manchester University
Distinctions:	Councillor, Coloproctology section, Royal Society of Medicine
USA:	Research Fellow and Instructor, Harvard Medical School, Boston

NORTHERN AND YORKSHIRE REGION

LEEDS

FINAN, Mr Paul J.

NHS:	Consultant Surgeon
	Leeds General Infirmary
	Great George Street
	Leeds LS1 3EX
Tel:	0113 2432799
Fax:	0113 2923598
Private:	Refer to address and number above
First Qualified:	1974 – Bristol
Major Degrees:	MD, FRCS
Academic:	Previously Lecturer in Surgery, St James's University Hospital, Leeds
	Cancer Research Campaign
	Research Fellow, Medical Research Council Clinical Oncology and Radiotherapy Unit, Cambridge
Specialist Training:	St Mark's Hospital, London

NORTHALLERTON

WARD, Mr David C.

Special interests:	**Gastrointestinal surgery; colorectal surgery**
NHS:	Consultant Surgeon
	Friarage Hospital
	Northallerton
	North Yorkshire DL6 1JG
Tel:	01609 779911
Fax:	01609 777144
Private:	Culpepper House
	243 High Street
	Northallerton DL7 8DJ
Tel:	01609 780556
First Qualified:	1973 – Bangalore, India
Major Degrees:	ChM, FRCS
Academic:	Previously Lecturer in Surgery, Leeds University
Specialist Training:	Leeds University
Distinctions:	Callistas Francis Nazareth Prize in Medicine

WEST MIDLANDS

BIRMINGHAM

KEIGHLEY, Professor Michael Robert B.

Special interests:	**Inflammatory bowel disease; colorectal cancer; anorectal incontinence**
NHS:	Barling Professor of Surgery
	Honorary Consultant General Surgeon (Coloproctology)
	Queen Elizabeth Hospital
	Edgbaston
	Birmingham B15 2TH
Tel:	0121 472 1311
Fax:	0121 472 1230
Private:	Consulting Suites
	Priory Hospital
	Priory Road
	Edgbaston, Birmingham B5 7UG
Tel:	0121 440 2323 Ext. 2123
Fax:	0121 446 5686
First Qualified:	1967 – London
Major Degrees:	MS, FRCS, FRCS Ed
Academic:	Barling Professor of Surgery and Head, University Department of Surgery, Birmingham University
Distinctions:	President, Coloproctology Section, Royal Society of Medicine
	Previously Hunterian Professor, Royal College of Surgeons
	Prize, Royal College
	Penman Memorial Professor of Surgery, Cape Town University
	The Sir Alan Parks Professor, St Mark's Hospital, London
USA:	Harvard Professor of Surgery 1991

SCOTLAND

EDINBURGH

BARTOLO, Mr David C. C.

Special interests:	**Coloproctology: inflammatory bowel disease, rectal cancer, rectal prolapse**
NHS:	Consultant Colorectal Surgeon
	Edinburgh Royal Infirmary
	Lauriston Place
	Edinburgh EH3 9YW
Tel:	0131 536 1610
Fax:	0131 536 1510
Private:	BUPA Murrayfield Hospital
	122 Corstorphine Road
	Edinburgh EH12 6UD
Tel:	0131 334 0363
Fax:	0131 334 7338
First Qualified:	1973 – London
Major Degrees:	MS, FRCS, FRCS Ed
Academic:	Part-time Senior Lecturer, Royal Infirmary of Edinburgh
Specialist Training:	St Mark's Hospital, London
Distinctions:	Previously Hunterian Professor, Royal College of Surgeons
	Moynihan Fellowship
	Patey Prize, Surgical Research Society

GLASGOW

FINLAY, Mr Ian G.

Special interests:	**Colorectal cancer; inflammatory bowel disease; rectal prolapse; faecal incontinence**
NHS:	Consultant Colorectal Surgeon
	Royal Infirmary
	Glasgow G31 2ER
Tel:	0141 211 4084
Fax:	0141 211 4991
Private:	Ross Hall Hospital
	221 Crookston Road
	Glasgow G51
Tel:	0141 810 3151
First Qualified:	1976 – Manchester
Major Degrees:	FRCS (Glas), FRCS Ed, FRCPSP (Hon)
Academic:	Honorary Clinical Senior Lecturer, Department of Surgery, Glasgow University
	Previously Demonstrator in Anatomy, Manchester University
Specialist Training:	St Mark's Hospital, London, and Minnesota University, USA
Distinctions:	Patey Prize, Surgical Research Society
	Research Award, American Society of Colon and Rectal Surgeons
	Joint Winner, Moynihan Prize
	Smart Award (jointly with Biosil Ltd)
	Executive Officer, Royal College of Physicians and Surgeons, Glasgow
USA:	See under 'Specialist Training'

DERMATOLOGISTS

This area of medicine covers all conditions of the skin, hair, nails and external genitals and frequently the mouth. Many dermatologists now perform minor surgery for skin diseases. New technology has enabled dermatologists to use procedures such as laser surgery to remove portwine stains, warts and non-malignant lesions; and phototherapy using ultraviolet light therapy for the treatment of psoriasis, vitilgo and cutaneous T-cell lymphoma and the treatment of skin tumours. Skin cancer is the commonest cancer in the United Kingdom. If, once the treatment has been completed, aesthetic surgery needs to be done, the patient will then be sent to a plastic surgeon.

LONDON AND THE SOUTH EAST

ATHERTON, Dr David

Special interests:	**Paediatric dermatology; eczema; genetic skin disorders**
NHS:	Consultant Dermatologist
	Great Ormond Street Hospital for Children
	Great Ormond Street
	London WC1N 3JH
Tel:	0171 405 9200 Ext. 5601
Fax:	0171 813 8274
and:	Consultant Dermatologist
	St John's Institute of Dermatology
	St Thomas' Hospital
	Lambeth Palace Road
	London SE1 7EH
Tel:	0171 928 9292
Fax:	0171 922 8346
Private:	Private Consulting Rooms
	Great Ormond Street Hospital for Children
	Great Ormond Street
	London WC1N 3JH
Tel:	0171 829 8632
First Qualified:	1974 – Cambridge
Major Degrees:	FRCP
Academic:	Senior Lecturer, Institute of Child Health, London
Specialist Training:	Guy's Hospital and Institute of Child Health, London

BLACK, Dr Martin M.

NHS:	Consultant, St John's Institute of Dermatology
	St Thomas' Hospital
	Lambeth Palace Road
	London SE1 7EH
Tel:	0171 928 9292
Fax:	0171 922 8079
Private:	The Consulting Rooms
	York House
	199 Westminster Bridge Road
	London SE1 7UT
Tel:	0171 928 5485
Fax:	0171 928 3748
First Qualified:	1963 – Durham
Major Degrees:	MD, FRCP, FRCPath
Academic:	Senior Lecturer, Institute of Dermatology
	Chairman, Department of Dermatopathology
Specialist Training:	Institute of Dermatology, London, and
	Royal Victoria Infirmary, Newcastle
Distinctions:	Consultant Dermatologist to the Army
	Previously President, International Committee
	Dermatological Pathology
USA:	Gold Award, American Academy of Dermatology

BUNKER, Dr Christopher B.

Special interests:	**General dermatology; penile dermatological abnormalities**
NHS:	Consultant Dermatologist
	Chelsea and Westminster Hospital
	369 Fulham Road
	London SW10 9NH
Tel:	0181 746 8170
Fax:	0181 746 8578
Private:	152 Harley Street
	London W1N 1HH
Tel:	0171 935 0444
Fax:	0171 224 2574
First Qualified:	1981 – London
Major Degrees:	MD, MRCP
Specialist Training:	University College and Middlesex School of Medicine, London

du VIVIER, Dr Anthony W.

Special interests:	**Pigmented moles**
NHS:	Consultant Dermatologist
	King's College Hospital
	Denmark Hill
	London SE5 9RS
Tel:	0171 346 3258
Fax:	0171 346 3616
Private:	115a Harley Street
	London W1N 1DG
Tel:	0171 935 6465
Fax:	0171 935 5014
First Qualified:	1968 – London
Major Degrees:	MD, FRCP
Specialist Training:	St Mary's and St Bartholomew's Hospitals, London
USA:	Research Fellow, Scripps Clinic, La Jolla, California

GILKES, Dr Jeremy J. H.

Special interests:	**Especially skin diseases of the mouth**
NHS:	No NHS work
Private:	115a Harley Street
	London W1N 1DG
Tel:	0171 935 6465
Fax:	0171 935 5014
and:	Lister Hospital
	Chelsea Bridge Road
	London SW1W 8RH
Tel:	0171 730 3417
Fax:	0171 824 8867
First Qualified:	1964 – London
Major Degrees:	MD, FRCP
Academic:	Previously Senior Lecturer in Dermatology
	University College London
Specialist Training:	Guy's and St Bartholomew's Hospitals, London

GRIFFITHS, Dr William A. D.

Special interests:	**Industrial skin diseases**
NHS:	Consultant Dermatologist
	St John's Institute of Dermatology
	St Thomas' Hospital
	Lambeth Palace Road, London SE1 7EH
Tel:	0171 928 9292 Ext. 1309
Fax:	0171 922 8079
Private:	6 Harley Street
	London W1N 1AA
Tel:	0171 631 3459
Fax:	0171 631 3459
First Qualified:	1965 – Cambridge and London
Major Degrees:	MD, FRCP
Specialist Training:	St Thomas' Hospital and St John's Institute, London

HARPER, Dr John I.

Special interests:	**Children**
NHS:	Consultant Paediatric Dermatologist
	Great Ormond Street Hospital for Children
	Great Ormond Street
	London WC1N 3JH
Tel:	0171 405 9200 Ext. 5231
Fax:	0171 813 8274
Private:	Refer to address and number above
First Qualified:	1973 – London
Major Degrees:	MD, MRCP
Distinctions:	Author, Handbook of Paediatric Dermatology

LEIGH, Professor Irene M.

Special interests:	**Cultivation of patient's own skin for grafting; melanoma oncology/vulva diseases**
NHS:	Professor of Dermatology
	Department of Dermatology
	Royal London Hospital
	Whitechapel
	London E1 1BB
Tel:	0171 377 7724/49
Fax:	0171 247 6509
Private:	Department of Experimental Dermatology
	56 Ashfield Street
	London E1 2BL
First Qualified:	1971 – London
Major Degrees:	MD, FRCP
Specialist Training:	St John's Institute and Middlesex Hospital, London
Distinctions:	Director, Imperial Cancer Research Fund, Skin Tumour and Experimental Dermatology Research Laboratory

LEONARD, Dr Jonathan

Special interests:	**General dermatology**
NHS:	Consultant Dermatologist
	St Mary's Hospital
	Praed Street
	London W2 1NY
Tel:	0171 725 1194
Fax:	0171 725 1134
Private:	152 Harley Street
	London W1N 1HH
Tel:	0171 580 7914
Fax:	0171 580 9814
First Qualified:	1975 – London
Major Degrees:	MD, FRCP
Specialist Training:	Oxford, and St Mary's Hospital, London

MAYOU, Dr Susan C.

Special interests:	**Children's skin problems**
NHS:	Queen Mary's University Hospital
	Roehampton Lane
	London SW15 5PN
Tel:	0181 789 6611 Ext. 2774
Fax:	0181 789 0704
Private:	Lister Hospital
	Chelsea Bridge Road
	London SW1W 8RH
Tel:	0171 259 9892
Fax:	0171 259 9887
First Qualified:	1977 – London
Major Degrees:	MRCP
Specialist Training:	St Thomas' and St Bartholomew's Hospitals, London

PEMBROKE, Dr Andrew C.

NHS:	Consultant Dermatologist
	Bromley Hospitals NHS Trust
	Orpington Hospital
	Sevenoaks Road
	Orpington, Kent BR6 9JU
Tel:	01689 815070
Fax:	01689 896232
Private:	152 Harley Street
	London W1N 1HH
Tel:	0171 935 2477
Fax:	0171 224 2574
First Qualified:	1971 – Cambridge
Major Degrees:	FRCP
Specialist Training:	King's College and Royal London Hospitals, London

ROBINSON, Dr Trevor W.

NHS:	Consultant Dermatologist
	Edgware General Hospital
	Edgware, Middlesex HA3 OAD
Tel:	0181 732 6362
Fax:	0181 952 8696
Private:	Flat 3, 51 Harley Street
	London W1N 1DD
Tel:	0171 387 2160 or 0171 637 7325
Fax:	0171 637 5383
First Qualified:	1959 – Cambridge
Major Degrees:	MD, FRCP
Specialist Training:	St Bartholomew's and St John's Hospitals, London
Distinctions:	Emeritus Consultant, University College Hospital, London

RUSTIN, Dr Malcolm H. A.

Special interests:	**General dermatology; atopic eczema; connective tissue diseases**
NHS:	Consultant Dermatologist
	Department of Dermatology
	Royal Free Hospital
	Pond Street, London NW3 2QG
Tel:	0171 794 0500 Ext. 3508
Fax:	0171 830 2247
Private:	53 Wimpole Street
	London W1M 7DF
Tel:	0171 935 9266
Fax:	0171 935 9266
First Qualified:	1976 – London
Major Degrees:	MD, FRCP
Specialist Training:	University College and The Middlesex Hospitals, London

STAUGHTON, Dr Richard C.

Special interests:	**General dermatology; dermatological surgery; vulval problems**
NHS:	Consultant Dermatologist
	Chelsea and Westminster Hospital
	369 Fulham Road
	London SW10 9NH
Tel:	0181 746 8000 Ext. 8169
Fax:	0181 746 8111 or 8578
Private:	Lister Hospital
	Chelsea Bridge Road
	London SW1W 8RH
Tel:	0171 730 8308
Fax:	0171 823 5541
First Qualified:	1969 – Cambridge
Major Degrees:	FRCP
Specialist Training:	Cambridge and St Thomas' Hospital, London
Distinctions:	Honorary Consultant, King Edward VII Hospital for Officers and Royal Brompton Hospital, London

NORTHERN AND YORKSHIRE REGION

LEEDS

CUNLIFFE, Professor William J.

Special interests:	**Acne; psoriasis; baldness in women**
NHS:	Professor of Dermatology
	Leeds General Infirmary
	Great George Street
	Leeds LS1 3EN
Tel:	0113 2316446
Fax:	0113 2341154
Private:	Refer to address and number above
First Qualified:	1962 – Manchester
Major Degrees:	MD, FRCP
Academic:	Professor of Dermatology, Leeds
Specialist Training:	Royal Victoria Infirmary, Newcastle
USA:	Member, American Academy of Dermatology

WALES

ROBERTS, Dr Dafydd Lloyd

Special interests:	**Treatment of skin cancer especially malignant melanoma; acne in adolescents**
NHS:	Consultant Dermatologist
	Singleton Hospital
	Sketty
	Swansea SA2 8QA
Tel:	01792 285324
Fax:	01792 208647
Private:	38 Walter Road
	Swansea SA1 5NW
Tel:	01792 643945
Fax:	01792 648284
First Qualified:	1972 – London
Major Degrees:	FRCP
USA:	Fellow, American Academy of Dermatology

FINLAY, Dr Andrew Y.

NHS:	Consultant Dermatologist
	University Hospital of Wales
	Heath Park
	Cardiff CF4 4XW
Tel:	01222 747747
Fax:	01222 762314
Private:	Refer to address and number above
First Qualified:	1972 – London
Major Degrees:	FRCP
Academic:	Honorary Senior Lecturer, University Hospital, Cardiff
Specialist Training:	University Hospital, Cardiff
Distinctions:	Treasurer, British Association of Dermatologists
USA:	Research Fellow, Mount Sinai Medical Center, Miami Beach, Florida

DIABETOLOGISTS

(see also Endocrinologists)

Diabetologists specialise in the management of diabetes; many also treat endocrine problems as well as metabolic diseases. Around 3% of the UK's adult population have diabetes. Of the 1,400,000 people diagnosed, 20,000 are under the age of 20.

There are two types of diabetes:
a) Insulin-dependent diabetes, which is usually treated by insulin injections and a controlled diet;
b) Non-insulin-dependent diabetes, treated by diet alone or a combination of diet and pills.

Between 10–25% of people with diabetes are insulin-dependent. This type of diabetes usually develops in people under 30. It develops due to the failure of the pancreas beta cells to produce insulin. The cause is unknown although viruses may play a part.

It is estimated that 75-90% of diabetes sufferers are non-insulin-dependent. It usually develops in people over the age of 40. It is common among the elderly and overweight. The tendency to develop diabetes is passed from one generation to another although the development of the condition is not automatic.

LONDON AND THE SOUTH EAST

AMIEL, Professor Stephanie A.

Special interests:	**Diabetes mellitus**
NHS:	Professor of Diabetic Medicine
	King's College School of Medicine and Dentistry
	Bessemer Road
	London SE5 9PG
Tel:	0171 346 3241
Fax:	0171 346 3445
Private:	Refer to address and number above
First Qualified:	1978 – London
Major Degrees:	MD, FRCP
Academic:	RD Lawrence Professor of Diabetic Medicine
Distinctions:	RD Lawrence Lecturer 1994, British Diabetic Association
USA:	Previously Research Fellow, Yale University

BARNES, Dr Adrian J.

Special interests:	**Glandular aspects**
NHS:	Consultant Physician
	Barnet General Hospital
	Wellhouse Lane
	Barnet
	Herts EN5 3DJ
Tel:	0181 440 5111
Fax:	0181 732 4681
Private:	Refer to address above
Tel:	0181 732 4623
First Qualified:	1971 – London
Major Degrees:	MD, FRCP
Specialist Training:	Royal Postgraduate Medical School, London

BETTERIDGE, Dr D. John

Special interests:	**Diabetes mellitus; lipid disorders**
NHS:	Consultant Physician
	The Middlesex Hospital
	Mortimer Street
	London W1N 8AA
Tel:	0171 380 9336
Fax:	0171 380 9201
Private:	Woolavington Wing
	The Middlesex Hospital
Tel:	0171 380 9443
Fax:	0171 380 9440
First Qualified:	1972 – London
Major Degrees:	PhD, MD, FRCP
Academic:	Reader in Medicine, University College London
Specialist Training:	Hammersmith, Brompton and St Bartholomew's
	Hospitals, London
Distinctions:	Chairman, British Hyperlipidaemia Association
	Committee member, Royal Society of Medicine Lipid
	Forum
USA:	Member, American Diabetic Association and American
	Heart Association

CASSAR, Dr Joseph

Special interests:	**Endocrinology; diabetes mellitus**
NHS:	Consultant Physician and Endocrinologist
	West Middlesex University Hospital
	Twickenham Road
	Isleworth TW7 6AF
Tel:	0181 565 5390
Fax:	0181 565 2535
Private:	22 Harley Street
	London W1N 1AA
Tel:	0171 637 0491
First Qualified:	1964 – Royal University of Malta
Major Degrees:	PhD, FRCP
Academic:	Honorary Senior Lecturer, West Middlesex University Hospital, London
Specialist Training:	King's College Hospital, London
Distinctions:	Commonwealth Scholar
USA:	Rotating Intern, Middlesex Memorial Hospital Middletown, Connecticut

ELKELES, Dr Robert S.

NHS:	Consultant Physician
	St Mary's Hospital
	Praed Street
	London W2 1NY
Tel:	0171 725 6666 Ext. 6037
Fax:	0171 725 6200
Private:	The Consulting Rooms
	Wellington Hospital
	Wellington Place
	London NW8 9LE
Tel:	0171 586 3213 or 0171 586 5959
Fax:	0171 483 0297
First Qualified:	1965 – London
Major Degrees:	MD, FRCP
Specialist Training:	University Hospital, Cardiff
	Medical Research Council and Royal Postgraduate Medical School, London

GALE, Professor Edwin

Special interests:	**Diabetes**
NHS:	Consultant Physician
	St Bartholomew's Hospital
	West Smithfield
	London EC1A 7BE
Tel:	0171 601 7447
Fax:	0171 601 7449
Private:	Refer to address and number above
First Qualified:	1973 – Cambridge
Major Degrees:	FRCP
Academic:	Professor of Diabetes and Metabolism, St Bartholomew's Medical College, London
Specialist Training:	Oxford Diabetes Unit and St Bartholomew's Hospital, London

KURTZ, Dr Anthony B.

Special interests:	**Thyroid disorders**
NHS:	Consultant Physician
	The Middlesex Hospital
	Mortimer Street
	London W1N 8AA
Tel:	0171 380 9029
Fax:	0171 380 9201
Private:	Refer to address above
Tel:	0171 436 1536
Fax:	0171 631 0178
First Qualified:	1965 – Cambridge
Major Degrees:	FRCP
Academic:	Previously Reader, Diabetic Medicine, The Middlesex and University College Medical Schools, London
Specialist Training:	The Middlesex Hospital, London

LESLIE, Dr R. David G.

Special interests:	**Endocrinology; diabetes**
NHS:	Reader and Consultant Physician
	St Bartholomew's Hospital
	West Smithfield
	London EC1A 7BE
Tel:	0171 601 7450
Fax:	0171 601 7449
Private:	Lister Hospital
	Chelsea Bridge Road
	London SW1W 8RH
Tel:	0171 730 3417
Fax:	0171 824 8867
First Qualified:	1972 – London
Major Degrees:	MD, FRCP
Academic:	Wellcome Trust Senior Fellow and Consultant,
	King's College Hospital and Charing Cross and
	Westminster Medical School, London
Specialist Training:	King's College Hospital, London
	Chicago University, USA
Distinctions:	Erasmus Professor of Medicine, University of Rome,
	Italy
USA:	Medical Research Council Travelling Fellow
	Chicago University

LOWY, Dr Clara

Special interests:	**Diabetes and pregnancy**
NHS:	Honorary Consultant Physician
	Endocrine and Diabetic Day Centre
	St Thomas' Hospital
	London SE1 7EH
Tel:	0171 928 9292 Ext. 3791
Fax:	0171 922 8079
Private:	Refer to adddress and number above
First Qualified:	1958 – London
Major Degrees:	FRCP
Academic:	Reader, Guy's and St Thomas' United Medical Schools,
	London
Specialist Training:	Hammersmith Hospital, London

McHARDY-YOUNG, Dr Stuart

Special interests:	**Thyroid disorders within endocrinology**
NHS:	Consultant Physician
	Geoffrey Kelson Diabetic Centre
	Central Middlesex Hospital
	Acton Lane
	Park Royal
	London NW10 7NS
Tel:	0181 453 2401
Fax:	0181 453 2415
Private:	106 Harley Street
	London W1N 1AF
Tel:	0171 935 2797
Fax:	0181 453 2415
First Qualified:	1960 – London
Major Degrees:	MD, FRCP
Specialist Training:	Guy's Hospital, London
Distinctions:	Consultant, Royal Postgraduate Medical School, London
USA:	Previously Fellow, Stanford University School of Medicine, California

SIMPSON, Dr Robert David

NHS:	Consultant Physician
	St Richard's Hospital
	Chichester
	West Sussex PO19 4SE
Tel:	01243 788122 Ext. 2725
Fax:	01243 538417
Private:	The Sherbourne Hospital
	Broyle Road
	Chichester, West Sussex PO19 4BE
Tel:	01243 537117
Fax:	01243 532244
First Qualified:	1965 – Cambridge and London
Major Degrees:	MB, FRCP
Academic:	Previously Lecturer, Metabolic Unit, St Mary's Hospital, London
Specialist Training:	St Mary's Hospital, London, and Radcliffe Infirmary, Oxford
Distinctions:	Honorary Clinical Teacher, St Mary's Hospital, London

SONKSEN, Professor Peter H.

Special interests:	**Pituitary disorders**
NHS:	Honorary Consultant Physician
	St Thomas' Hospital
	Lambeth Palace Road
	London SE1 7EH
Tel:	0171 928 9292 Ext. 2265
Fax:	0171 922 8079
Private:	Refer to address and number above
First Qualified:	1960 – London
Major Degrees:	MD, FRCP
Academic:	Professor of Endocrinology, Guy's and St Thomas' United Medical Schools, London
Specialist Training:	The Middlesex Hospital, London
Distinctions:	Previously Editor, Clinical Endocrinology
USA:	Previously Harkness Fellow, Harvard University, Boston

VAUGHAN, Dr Nicholas J. A.

Special interests:	**Clinical Diabetes – treatment of pregnancy; information management; Clinical Endocrinology – pituitary disease**
NHS:	Clinical Director of Medicine
	Royal Sussex County Hospital
	Eastern Road
	Brighton BN2 5BE
Tel:	01273 696955 Ext. 4311
Fax:	01273 676345
Private:	Hove Nuffield Hospital
	55 New Church Road
	Hove BN3 4BG
Tel:	01273 627054
Fax:	01273 495489
First Qualified:	1974 – Cambridge and Middlesex (with Honours)
Major Degrees:	MA, MD, FRCP
Specialist Training:	The Middlesex and St George's Hospitals, London
Distinctions:	Chairman, Joint Colleges Information Management and Audit Committee
	Clinical Working Group Leader for Diabetes, NHS Executive

WATKINS, Dr Peter J.

Special interests:	**Neuropathy**
NHS:	Consultant Physician
	King's College Hospital
	Denmark Hill
	London SE5 9RS
Tel:	0171 737 4000 or 0171 346 3241
Fax:	0171 346 3407
Private:	Refer to address and number above
First Qualified:	1961 – Cambridge
Major Degrees:	MD, FRCP
Academic:	Senior Lecturer, General Medicine and Diabetes, Kings College Hospital, London
Specialist Training:	Birmingham and St Bartholomew's Hospital, London
Distinctions:	Chairman, Medical and Scientific Section, British Diabetic Association
	Honorary Treasurer, Association of Physicians of Great Britain and Ireland

YUDKIN, Professor John S.

Special interests:	**Takes no new cases, respected second opinion**
NHS and Academic:	Professor of Medicine
	Whittington Hospital
	Archway Road
	London N19 3UA
Tel:	0171 288 5218
Fax:	0171 288 5302
Private:	Refer to address and number above
First Qualified:	1967 – Cambridge
Major Degrees:	MD, FRCP
Specialist Training:	Royal London Hospital

NORTH WEST REGION

LIVERPOOL

GILL, Dr Geoffrey Victor

Special interests:	**Endocrinology**
NHS:	Consultant Physician
	Walton Hospital
	Rice Lane
	Liverpool L9 1AE
Tel:	0151 525 3611 Ext. 1749
Fax:	0151 529 4688
Private:	Refer to address and number above
First Qualified:	1972 – Newcastle (with Honours)
Major Degrees:	MD, FRCP
Academic:	Clinical Medical Lecturer, Liverpool University
	Honorary Lecturer, Liverpool School of Tropical Medicine

NORTHERN AND YORKSHIRE REGION

NEWCASTLE

ALBERTI, Professor K. George M. M.

Special interests:	**Metabolic defects in non-insulin-dependent diabetes; diabetes care in Africa**
NHS:	Honorary Consultant Physician
	Royal Victoria Infirmary
	Queen Victoria Road
	Newcastle upon Tyne NE1 4LP
Tel:	0191 222 7003
Fax:	0191 222 0723
Private:	Refer to address and number above
First Qualified:	1965 – Oxford
Major Degrees:	FRCPath, FRCP, FRCP Ed
Academic:	Dean of Medicine and Professor of Medicine, Medical School, Framlington Place, Newcastle upon Tyne
	Previously Professor of Clinical Biochemistry and Metabolic Medicine, Newcastle University
Distinctions:	Previously Vice-President, International Diabetic Federation
	Previously President, European Association for the study of Diabetes
	Director, WHO Collaborating Centre in Diabetes, Newcastle
USA:	Previously Research Fellow, Harvard University, Boston

TRENT REGION

NOTTINGHAM

TATTERSALL, Professor Robert B.

Special interests:	**Diabetes mellitus**
NHS:	Consultant Physician
	Queen's Medical Centre
	University Hospital
	Nottingham NG7 2UH
Tel:	01159 709100
Fax:	01159 701080
Private:	Refer to address and number above
First Qualified:	1967 – Cambridge
Major Degrees:	MD, FRCP
Academic:	Professor of Clinical Diabetes, Nottingham University
Specialist Training:	King's College Hospital, London
Distinctions:	Editor, Diabetes Mellitus Clinics in Endocrinology and Metabolism

SHEFFIELD

WARD, Professor John D.

Special interests:	**Diabetic neuropathy**
NHS:	Consultant Physician
	Royal Hallamshire Hospital
	Glossop Road
	Sheffield S10 2JF
Tel:	0114 2711900 Ext. 2938
Fax:	01142 766381
Private:	Refer to address and number above
First Qualified:	MD, FRCP
Major Degrees:	1961 – London
Academic:	Professor of Diabetic Medicine, Sheffield University
Specialist Training:	London Hospital
Distinctions:	Treasurer, European Association for the Study of Diabetes

DIAGNOSTIC RADIOLOGISTS

These doctors specialise in utilising imaging for diagnosis by utilising X-ray, CT (Computed Tomography) Scan and MRI (Magnetic Resonance Imaging) scanning. Their work includes mammograms and ultrasound angiography. Interventional treatments of a wide range of conditions are also done.

LONDON AND THE SOUTH EAST

BARTRAM, Dr Clive I.

Special interests:	**Gastrointestinal ultrasound and barium studies**
NHS:	Consultant Radiologist
	St Mark's Hospital
	Northwick Park, Watford Road
	Harrow, Middlesex HA1 3JU
Tel:	0181 235 4081
Fax:	0181 235 4001
Private:	Princess Grace Hospital
	Nottingham Place
	London W1AA 3FD
Tel:	0171 486 7401/1234
Fax:	0171 486 1084
First Qualified:	1966 – London
Major Degrees:	FRCP, FRCR
Specialist Training:	St Mark's and St Bartholomew's Hospitals, London

GISHEN, Dr Philip

Special interests:	**Interventional, keyhole radiology, including lungs and bones; diagnostic radiology and scanning**
NHS:	Consultant Radiologist
	King's Health Care Trust
	Denmark Hill
	London SE5 9RS
Tel:	0171 346 3413/2
Fax:	0171 346 3589
Private:	126 Harley Street
	London W1N 1AA
Tel:	0171 935 4072
Fax:	0171 224 2520
First Qualified:	1968 – Witwatersrand, South Africa
Major Degrees:	FRCR
Specialist Training:	Johannesburg General, South Africa, and King's College Hospital, London

LEES, Professor William R.

Special interests:	**Gastrointestinal ultrasound**
NHS:	Consultant Radiologist
	Department of Imaging
	The Middlesex Hospital
	Mortimer Street
	London W1N 8AA
Tel:	0171 636 8333 or 0171 436 2447
Fax:	0171 436 2447
Private:	Refer to address and number above
First Qualified:	1972 – London
Major Degrees:	FRCR
Academic:	Professor of Medical Imaging, The Middlesex Hospital, London
Specialist Training:	The Middlesex Hospital, London

LONGMORE, Professor Donald B.

Special interests:	**Noninvasive investigations of the heart**
NHS:	Director, Brompton M R Enterprises
	Chairman, M R 3000
	92 Fulham Road
	London SW3 6HR
Tel:	0171 581 9482/86
Fax:	0171 581 9475
Private:	Refer to address and number above
First Qualified:	1953 – London
Major Degrees:	FRCS, FRCR
Academic:	Professor Emeritus, Royal Brompton Hospital, London

MAISEY, Professor Michael

Special interests:	**Nuclear medicine; positron emission tomography**
NHS:	Consultant in Nuclear Medicine
	Guy's Hospital
	St Thomas Street
	London SE1 9RT
Tel:	0171 955 4531
Fax:	0171 955 4532
Private:	No private work
First Qualified:	1964 – London
Major Degrees:	FRCP, FRCR
Academic:	Professor of Radiological Science, Guy's Hospital, London
Specialist Training:	Guy's Hospital, London
Distinctions:	Consultant to the Army
USA:	Previously Research Fellow in Nuclear Medicine, Johns Hopkins, Baltimore, Maryland

McLEAN, Dr Alison

Special interests:	**Gastrointestinal disease, barium, ultrasound; CT Scanning; biopsy; breast ultrasound**
NHS:	Consultant Radiologist
	St Bartholomew's Hospital
	West Smithfield
	London EC1A 7BE
Tel:	0171 601 8329
Fax:	0171 601 8323
Private:	X-Ray Department
	Princess Grace Hospital
	42–52 Nottingham Place
	London W1M 3FD
Tel:	0171 486 1234
Fax:	0171 935 2198
First Qualified:	1975 – Cambridge
Major Degrees:	MRCP, FRCR
Specialist Training:	St Bartholomew's Hospital, London
USA:	Clinical Fellow, New England Hospital, Boston

PERRY, Dr Nicholas M.

Special interests:	**Breast disease particularly imaging and assessment of both benign and malignant breast conditions**
NHS:	Director of Breast Screening
	Breast Assessment Centre
	St Bartholomew's Hospital
	West Smithfield, London EC1 7BE
Tel:	0171 601 8840
Fax:	0171 601 7892
Private:	Consultant Radiologist
	Breast Clinic
	108 Harley Street
	London W1N 2ET
Tel:	0171 637 8820
Fax:	0171 436 2945
First Qualified:	1975 – London
Major Degrees:	FRCS, FRCR
Distinctions:	Director, Central and East London Breast Screening Service
	Consultant to the European Commission – Europe against Cancer Breast Screening Programme
	Chairman, National Co-ordinating Quality Assurance Group for National Breast Screening Programme

REZNEK, Dr Rodney H.

Special interests:	**Oncology; endocrinology; CT and MRI scanning**
NHS:	Consultant Radiologist
	St Bartholomew's Hospital
	West Smithfield
	London EC1A 7BE
Tel:	0171 601 8329
Fax:	0171 601 8323
Private:	X-Ray Department
	Princess Grace Hospital
	42–52 Nottingham Place
	London W1M 3FD
Tel:	0171 486 1234
Fax:	0171 486 1084
Major Degrees:	FRCP, FRCR
Distinctions:	Editor, British Journal of Radiology

RICKARDS, Dr David

Special interests:	**Ultrasound and CT Scans of male genital and urinary organs**
NHS:	Consultant Uroradiologist
	The Middlesex Hospital
	Mortimer Street
	London W1N 8AA
Tel:	0171 380 9070
Fax:	0171 380 9068
Private:	136 Harley Street
	London W1N 1AH
Tel:	0171 637 8207
Fax:	0171 436 7059
First Qualified:	1972 – South Africa
Major Degrees:	FRCR, FFR
Academic:	Senior Lecturer, Institute of Urology, London
Specialist Training:	Manchester University and The Middlesex Hospital, London
Distinctions:	Honorary Editor, British Journal of Radiology Bulletin

WESTABY, Dr David

Special interests:	**Endoscopic investigation**
NHS:	Consultant Physician and Gastroenterologist
	Chelsea and Westminster Hospital
	369 Fulham Road
	London SW10 9NH
Tel:	0181 746 8000 Ext. 1076
Fax:	0181 746 8100
Private:	Cromwell Hospital
	Cromwell Road
	London SW5 OTU
Tel:	0171 370 4233 Ext. 5081
Fax:	0171 835 1573
First Qualified:	1976 – Cambridge
Major Degrees:	FRCP
Specialist Training:	King's College Hospital, London

ANGLIA AND OXFORD REGION

CAMBRIDGE

DIXON, Professor Adrian K.

NHS and Academic:	Honorary Consultant Radiologist
	Department of Radiology
	Addenbrooke's Hospital
	Hills Road
	Cambridge CB2 2QQ
Tel:	01223 336893
Fax:	01223 330915
Private:	Refer to address and number above
First Qualified:	1972 – Cambridge
Major Degrees:	MD, FRCR, FRCP
Academic:	Professor of Radiology, Cambridge University
	Visiting Professor, Otago University, New Zealand
Specialist Training:	St Bartholomew's Hospital, London
Distinctions:	Fellow, Peterhouse, Cambridge University

FLOWER, Dr Christopher D. R.

Special interests:	**Thoracic radiology**
NHS:	Consultant Radiologist
	Department of Radiology
	Addenbrooke's Hospital
	Hills Road
	Cambridge CB2 2QQ
Tel:	01223 216203
Fax:	01223 217847
Private:	The Evelyn Hospital
	Cambridge CN2 2AF
Tel:	01223 370906
First Qualified:	1963 – Cambridge and London
Major Degrees:	FRCP (C), FRCR
Academic:	Toronto and Cambridge
Specialist Training:	Toronto and Cambridge

OXFORD

ANSLOW, Dr Philip L.

Special interests:	**Neuroradiology; ENT**
NHS:	Consultant Neuroradiologist
	Radcliffe Infirmary
	Woodstock Road
	Oxford OX2 6HE
Tel:	01865 311188
Fax:	01865 224315
Private:	Refer to address and number above
First Qualified:	1976 – Cambridge
Major Degrees:	FRCR
Specialist Training:	Radcliffe Infirmary, Oxford, and King's College, Cambridge

117

NORTHERN AND YORKSHIRE REGION

LEEDS

CHAPMAN, Dr Anthony H.

Special interests:	**Gastrointestinal radiology**
NHS:	Consultant Radiologist
	St James's University Hospital
	Beckett Street
	Leeds LS9 7TF
Tel:	0113 243 3144
Fax:	0113 283 6951
Private:	Wingfield House
	22 Street Lane
	Leeds LS8 2ET
Tel:	0113 237 0327
Fax:	0113 237 0336
First Qualified:	1969 – London
Major Degrees:	MRCP, FRCR
Academic:	Honorary Senior Lecturer, Leeds University

NORTH WEST REGION

LIVERPOOL

CARTY, Dr Helen M. L.

Special interests:	**Paediatric radiology especially orthopaedic**
NHS:	Consultant Radiologist
	Alder Hey Children's Hospital
	Eaton Road
	West Derby
	Liverpool L12 2AP
Tel:	0151 228 4811
Fax:	0151 252 5533
Private:	Refer to address and number above
First Qualified:	1967 – Ireland
Major Degrees:	FFR, FRCR
Specialist Training:	Broadgreen Hospital, Liverpool, and St Thomas' Hospital, London

SOUTH AND WEST REGION

BRISTOL

VIRJEE, Dr James

Special interests:	**Gastrointestinal radiology**
NHS:	Clinical Director
	Directorate of Clinical Radiology
	Bristol Royal Infirmary
	Marlborough Street
	Bristol BS2 8HW
Tel:	0117 9282729
Fax:	0117 9283267
Private:	Litfield House Medical Centre
	Litfield Place
	Clifton, Bristol
Tel:	0117 9736275
First Qualified:	1970 – Bristol
Major Degrees:	FRCR
Academic:	Fellow in Gastrointestinal Radiology
	McMaster Medical Centre, Hamilton, Ontario, Canada
USA and Canada:	See 'Academic' above

TRENT REGION

SHEFFIELD

CUMBERLAND, Professor David C.

Special interests:	**Interventional cardiology**
NHS:	Professor of Interventional Cardiology
	Northern General Hospital
	Herries Road
	Sheffield S5 7AU
Tel:	0114 243 4343
Fax:	0114 256 2366
Private:	Refer to address and number above
First Qualified:	1967 – Edinburgh
Major Degrees:	FRCP Ed, FRCS, FRCR
Academic:	Professor of Interventional Cardiology
	Sheffield University
Specialist Training:	Chalmers and City Hospitals, Edinburgh
USA:	Fellow, American College of Cardiology

EAR, NOSE AND THROAT SPECIALISTS

ENT surgeons specialise in the diagnosis, treatment and surgery for conditions related to the ear, nose and throat as well as related structures of the face, head and neck. ENT surgeons also do reconstructive head and neck surgery in conjunction with a plastic surgeon. Other operations include removal and management of skull base tumours and treatment for speech and hearing disorders as well as the treatment of allergies.

Continual advancement in this field of surgery plays an important role in restoring hearing and treating infections of the ear and mastoid. With microsurgery many patients can now be treated on a day case basis.

LONDON AND THE SOUTH EAST

BAILEY, Mr C. Martin

Special interests:	**Paediatric surgeon**
NHS:	Consultant ENT Surgeon
	Great Ormond Street Hospital for Children
	Great Ormond Street
	London WC1N 3JH
Tel:	0171 405 9200 Ext. 5362
Fax:	0171 829 8644
Private:	55 Harley Street
	London WC1N 1DD
Tel:	0171 580 2426
Fax:	0171 436 1645
First Qualified:	1973 – London
Major Degrees:	FRCS
Academic:	Senior Lecturer, Institute of Child Health and
	Institute of Laryngology and Otology, London
Specialist Training:	Sussex Throat and Ear Hospital and
	The Royal National Throat, Nose and Ear Hospital,
	London
Distinctions:	TWJ Foundation Clinical and Research Fellow Michigan
	University
USA:	See 'Distinctions' above

BELLMAN, Ms Susan C.

Special interests:	**Paediatric audiology**
NHS:	Consultant Physician in Audiological Medicine
	Great Ormond Street Hospital for Children
	Great Ormond Street
	London WC1N 3JH
Tel:	0171 405 9200 Ext. 5381
Fax:	0171 829 8643
Private:	Refer to address and number above
First Qualified:	1971 – Cambridge
Major Degrees:	FRCS
Specialist Training:	The Royal National Throat, Nose and Ear Hospital, London

BOOTH, Mr John B.

Special interests:	**The voice; otology; neuro-otology**
NHS:	Consultant ENT Surgeon
	Royal London Hospital
	Whitechapel
	London E1 1BB
Tel:	0171 377 7430
Fax:	0171 377 7361
and:	St Bartholomew's Hospital
	West Smithfield
	London EC1A 7BE
Tel:	0171 601 7173
Private:	18 Upper Wimpole Street
	London W1M 7TB
Tel:	0171 935 1304 / 5631
Fax:	0171 224 1645
First Qualified:	1963 – London
Major Degrees:	FRCS
Academic:	Lecturer, Institute of Laryngology and Otology, London
Specialist Training:	The Royal Free, The Royal National Throat, Nose and Ear and National Hospitals, London
Distinctions:	Civil Consultant to the Royal Air Force
	Laryngologist to the Royal Opera House and the Royal College of Music

BULL, Mr Tony R.

Special interests:	**Rhinoplasty and otosclerosis**
NHS:	Consultant ENT Surgeon
	Charing Cross Hospital
	Fulham Palace Road
	London W6 8RF
Tel:	0181 846 1234
Fax:	0181 846 1111
Private:	107 Harley Street
	London W1N 1DG
Tel:	0171 935 3171
First Qualified:	1958 – London
Major Degrees:	FRCS
Specialist Training:	The London and The Royal National Throat, Nose and Ear Hospitals, London
Distinctions:	Previously Yearsley Lecturer, Royal Society of Medicine
USA:	Previously Senior Fellow in Otology Memphis Foundation

CHEESMAN, Mr Anthony D.

Special interests:	**Head and neck surgery**
NHS:	Consultant Otolaryngologist
	Charing Cross Hospital
	Fulham Palace Road
	London W6 8RF
Tel:	0181 846 1234
Fax:	0181 846 1111
Private:	Cromwell Hospital
	Cromwell Road
	London SW5 OTU
Tel:	0171 370 4233
Fax:	0171 244 8891
First Qualified:	1965 – London
Major Degrees:	FRCS
Academic:	Honorary Senior Lecturer Gough Cooper, Department of Neurosurgery, National Hospital, London Previously Lecturer in Otolaryngology, West Indies University, Jamaica
Specialist Training:	The Royal National Throat, Nose and Ear Hospital, London
Distinctions:	Vice-President, Laryngology section, Royal Society of Medicine

CROFT, Mr Charles B.

Special interests:	**Sleep apnoea; snoring; surgical management of head and neck tumours**
NHS:	Consultant ENT Surgeon
	The Royal National Throat, Nose and Ear Hospital
	Gray's Inn Road
	London WC1X 8DA
Tel:	0171 837 8855
Fax:	0171 833 5518
Private:	55 Harley Street
	London W1N 1DD
Tel:	0171 580 2426
Fax:	0171 436 1645
First Qualified:	1965 – Leeds (with Honours)
Major Degrees:	FRCS
Specialist Training:	Leeds General Infirmary
Distinctions:	Civil Consultant in Laryngology to the Royal Air Force
	Examiner, Royal College of Surgeons, Edinburgh
	Consultant ENT Surgeon, National Heart and Chest
	Hospitals, London
USA:	Attending Head and Neck Surgeon
	Montefiore Hospital, New York
	Previously Associate Professor, Albert Einstein Medical
	School, New York

DOUEK, Mr Ellis E.

Special interests:	**Nose; sense of smell; otology**
NHS:	Consultant Otologist
	Guy's Hospital
	St Thomas Street
	London SE1 9RT
Tel:	0171 955 5000
Fax:	0171 955 8878
Private:	97 Harley Street
	London W1N 1DF
Tel:	0171 935 7828
Fax:	0171 224 6911
First Qualified:	1958 – London
Major Degrees:	FRCS
Specialist Training:	Royal Free and King's College Hospitals, London

FITZGERALD O'CONNOR, Mr Alexander Francis

Special interests:	**Otolaryngology**
NHS:	Clinical Director Otolaryngology and Plastic Surgery
	Churchill Clinic
	St Thomas' Hospital
	80 Lambeth Palace Road
	London SE1 7PW
Tel:	0171 261 9848
Fax:	0171 620 2795
Private:	38 Devonshire Street
	London W1N 1LD
Tel:	0171 261 9848
First Qualified:	1971 – Birmingham
Major Degrees:	FRCS
Specialist Training:	London Hospital

GARFIELD DAVIES, Mr David

Special interests:	**Vocal cords; sinus disease and snoring disorders**
NHS:	Senior Consultant
	Voice Clinic
	Royal National Throat, Nose and Ear Hospital
	Gray's Inn Road
	London WC1X 8DA
Tel:	0171 837 8855
Fax:	0171 833 5518
Private:	149 Harley Street
	London W1N 2DE
Tel:	0171 935 4444
Fax:	0171 333 0340
First Qualified:	1959 – London
Major Degrees:	FRCS
Academic:	Otolaryngologist Emeritus Middlesex and
	University Hospitals, London
Specialist Training:	The Royal National Throat, Nose and Ear and
	St Bartholomew's Hospitals, London
USA:	Lately Fellow in Otology, Massachusetts Eye and Ear
	Infirmary, Harvard Medical School, Boston

HAZELL, Mr Jonathan W. P.

Special interests:	**Tinnitus**
NHS:	Consultant Neuro-Otologist
	Royal Ear Hospital
	Cleveland Street
	London W1P 5FD
Tel:	0171 636 8333
Fax:	0171 580 6726
Private:	32 Devonshire Place
	London W1N 1PE
Tel:	0171 935 0382
Fax:	0171 486 2218
First Qualified:	1966 – Cambridge
Major Degrees:	FRCS
Academic:	Senior Lecturer in Neuro-Otology, University College London
Specialist Training:	University College and The Royal National Throat, Nose and Ear Hospitals, London
Distinctions:	Consultant in Neuro-Otology, Royal National Institute for the Deaf
USA:	Visiting Professor, Maryland University School of Medicine

HOWARD, Mr David J.

Special interests:	**Laryngology; head and neck oncology**
NHS:	Honorary Consultant ENT and Head and Neck Surgeon
	Royal National Throat, Nose and Ear Hospital
	330 Gray's Inn Road
	London WC1X 8DA
Tel:	0171 915 1305
Fax:	0171 833 9480
Private:	Refer to address and number above
First Qualified:	1972 – London
Major Degrees:	FRCS, FRCS Ed
Academic:	Senior Lecturer, Professorial Unit, Institute of Laryngology and Otology and The Royal National Throat, Nose and Ear Hospital, London
Specialist Training:	Sussex Throat, Nose and Ear Hospital, Brighton The Royal National Throat, Nose and Ear Hospital, London

KEENE, Mr Malcolm Howard

Special interests:	**Head and neck surgery**
NHS:	Consultant ENT Surgeon St Bartholomew's Hospital West Smithfield London EC1A 7BE
Tel:	0171 601 8888 or 0171 601 7173
Fax:	0171 601 7899
Private:	35 Wimpole Street London W1M 7AE
Tel:	0171 224 6249
Fax:	0171 224 4162
First Qualified:	1970 – London
Major Degrees:	FRCS
Specialist Training:	Middlesex and The Royal National Throat, Nose and Ear Hospitals, London, and University of Toronto, Canada

LAVELLE, Mr Richard J.

Special interests:	**Surgery of salivary glands**
NHS:	Consultant ENT Surgeon St Bartholomew's Hospital West Smithfield London EC1A 7BE
Tel:	0171 601 8888 or 0171 601 7172
Fax:	0171 601 8385
Private:	86 Harley Street London W1N 1AE
Tel:	0171 580 3625
Fax:	0171 637 7202
First Qualified:	1962 – London
Major Degrees:	FRCS
Specialist Training:	The Royal National Throat, Nose and Ear and Royal Marsden Hospitals, London

LUDMAN, Mr Harold

Special interests:	**Otology and neuro-otology**
NHS:	Consultant Otolaryngologist
	National Hospital for Neurology and Neurosurgery
	Queen Square
	London WC1N 3BG
Tel:	0171 837 3611
Fax:	0171 829 8720
Private:	149 Harley Street
	London W1N 2DE
Tel:	0171 935 4444
Fax:	0171 486 3782
First Qualified:	1957 – Cambridge (with first class Honours in natural science)
Major Degrees:	FRCS
Specialist Training:	King's College Hospital, London
Distinctions:	Previously President, British Association of Otolaryngologists and President, Otology Section, Royal Society of Medicine

LUND, Professor Valerie J.

Special interests:	**Rhinosinusitis; nose and sinus tumour, including endoscopic sinus surgery**
NHS and Academic:	Professor in Rhinology
	Professorial Unit
	The Royal National Throat, Nose and Ear Hospital
	Gray's Inn Road
	London WC1X 8DA
Tel:	0171 915 1495
Fax:	0171 833 9480
Private:	Refer to address and number above
First Qualified:	1977 – London
Major Degrees:	MS, FRCS, FRCS Ed
Specialist Training:	The Royal National Throat, Nose and Ear Hospital, London

LUXON, Professor Linda Maitland

Special interests:	**Neuro-otology**
NHS:	Consultant Physician in Neuro-otology
	National Hospital for Neurology and Neurosurgery
	Queen Square
	London WC1N 3BJ
Tel:	0171 837 3611
Fax:	0171 829 8775
Private:	15 Upper Wimpole Street
	London W1M 7TB
Tel:	0171 486 5787
Fax:	0171 486 5470
First Qualified:	1972 – London
Major Degrees:	FRCP
Academic:	Professor in Audiology, Institute of Laryngology and Otology, University College London
Specialist Training:	National Hospital for Nervous Diseases, London
Distinctions:	Vice-Chairman, British Association of Audiology Physicians

MACKAY, Mr Ian S.

Special interests:	**Rhinoplasty; rhinosinusitis; endoscopic sinus surgery; nasal polyps**
NHS:	Consultant ENT Surgeon
	Chelsea and Westminster Hospital
	369 Fulham Road
	London SW10 9NH
Tel:	0181 746 8000
Fax:	0181 746 8111
and:	Royal Brompton Hospital
	Sydney Street
	London SW3 6NB
Tel:	0171 352 8121
and:	Charing Cross Hospital
	Fulham Palace Road
	London W6 8RF
Private:	55 Harley Street
	London W1N 1DD
Tel:	0171 580 5070
Fax:	0171 323 5401
First Qualified:	1968 – London
Major Degrees:	FRCS
Academic:	Senior Lecturer, The Royal National Throat, Nose and Ear Hospital, London
Specialist Training:	The Royal National Throat, Nose and Ear Hospital, London

RHYS EVANS, Mr Peter H.

Special interests:	**Head and neck surgery and reconstruction; oncology; laryngology; salivary and thyroid tumours**
NHS:	Consultant ENT/Head and Neck Surgeon
	The Royal Marsden Hospital
	Fulham Road
	London SW3 6JJ
Tel:	0171 352 8171 Ext. 2731
Fax:	0171 351 3785
and:	King Edward VII Hospital for Officers
	Beaumont Street
	London W1N 2AA
Tel:	0171 486 4411
Private:	106 Harley Street
	London W1N 1AF
Tel:	0171 935 3525
Fax:	0171 935 7701
First Qualified:	1971 – London
Major Degrees:	DCC, FRCS
Academic:	Honorary Senior Lecturer and Tutor, Institute of Cancer Research, University of London; Previously Senior Lecturer in Otolaryngology, Birmingham University
Specialist Training:	The Royal National Throat, Nose and Ear Hospital, London and Gustave–Roussy Institute, Paris University
Distinctions:	Honorary ENT Surgeon, St Mary's Hospital, London; Honorary Civilian Consultant ENT Surgeon to the Royal Navy; Vice-President, European Academy of Facial Surgery Council RSM (Laryngology); Previously Leon Goldan Visiting Professor of Otolaryngology, Cape Town University
USA:	American Society for Head and Neck Surgeons

SCADDING, Dr Glenys K.

Special interests:	**Medical management of otitis media with effusion; chronic rhinosinusitis and the combination of asthma and rhinitis (especially with aspirin-sensitive patients)**
NHS:	Consultant Rhinologist
	The Royal National Throat, Nose and Ear Hospital
	Gray's Inn Road
	London WC1X 8DA
Tel:	0171 915 1310
Fax:	0171 833 9480
Private:	Refer to address and number above
First Qualified:	1973 – Cambridge
Major Degrees:	MD, FRCP
Specialist Training:	The Middlesex and Royal Brompton Hospitals, London

SHAH, Mr Navit

Special interests:	**Deafness; glue ear; middle-ear surgery**
NHS:	Consultant Otologist
	Nuffield Hearing and Speech Centre
	The Royal National Throat, Nose and Ear Hospital
	Gray's Inn Road
	London WC1X 8DA
Tel:	0171 915 1300
Fax:	0171 833 5518
Private:	80 Harley Street
	London W1N 1AE
Tel:	0171 580 3664
Fax:	0171 959 3711
First Qualified:	1958 – Bombay
Major Degrees:	FRCS, DLO
Academic:	Lately Vice-Dean, Institute of Laryngology and Otology, London
Specialist Training:	The Royal National Throat, Nose and Ear Hospital, London
Distinctions:	President, Otology Section, Royal Society of Medicine
	Honorary Professor, Portman Foundation, Bordeaux, France

WALSH-WARING, Mr Gerald P.

Special interests:	**Head and neck surgery**
NHS:	Consultant in Charge, Head and Neck Oncology
	St Mary's Hospital
	Praed Street
	London W2 1NY
Tel:	0171 725 6666
Fax:	0171 725 6200
Private:	2 Upper Wimpole Street
	London W1M 7TD
Tel:	0171 935 6172
Fax:	0171 224 6874
First Qualified:	1958 – London
Major Degrees:	FRCS
Specialist Training:	St Mary's and the Royal Marsden Hospitals, London
Distinctions:	Honorary Consultant ENT Surgeon
	Hammersmith Hospital, London

WRIGHT, Professor Anthony

Special interests:	**Ear disease in adults and children, complex middle-ear and mastoid work; stapedectomy for otosclerosis; surgery for acoustic neuromas; balance disorders: vertigo and dizziness**
NHS and Academic:	Professor of Otorhinolaryngology Institute of Laryngology and Otology The Royal National Throat, Nose and Ear Hospital Gray's Inn Road London WC1X 8DA
Tel:	0171 915 1308
Fax:	0171 833 9480
e-mail:	anthony.wright@ucl.ac.uk
Private:	Refer to address and number above
First Qualified:	1974 – Oxford
Major Degrees:	DM, FRCS

ANGLIA AND OXFORD REGION

CAMBRIDGE

MOFFAT, Mr David

Special interests:	**Otological; otoneurological and skull base surgery**
NHS:	Consultant in Otoneurological and Skull Base Surgery Department of Otolaryngology Addenbrooke's Hospital Hills Road Cambridge CB2 2QQ
Tel:	01223 217578
Fax:	01223 217559
Private:	Private Consulting Rooms Evelyn Hospital 4 Trumpington Road Cambridge CB2 1AF
Tel:	01223 303336, appointments: 01223 356201
First Qualified:	1971 – London
Major Degrees:	FRCS
Academic:	TWJ Travelling Scholar, Stanford University, California
Specialist Training:	Royal London Hospital and Stanford University Medical School, USA
Distinctions:	Dame Edith Forbes Memorial Scholarship; LeGrand Lecturer 1994; Vice-president, Otology Section, Royal Society of Medicine
USA:	Member, American Otological Society (by invitation); Editorial Board, American Journal of Otology and Ear, Nose and Throat Journal

NORTH WEST REGION

LIVERPOOL

SWIFT, Mr Andrew C.

Special interests:	**Paediatric ENT; infections after head and neck surgery**
NHS:	Consultant ENT Surgeon
	Walton Hospital
	Rice Lane
	Liverpool L9 1AE
Tel:	0151 529 4720
Fax:	0151 529 4033
Private:	Refer to address and number above
First Qualified:	1977 – Sheffield
Major Degrees:	ChM, FRCS, FRCS Ed
Academic:	Clinical Lecturer, Liverpool University

MANCHESTER

RAMSDEN, Professor Richard Thomas

Special interests:	**Neuro-otology; cochlear implantation; skull base surgery**
NHS:	Professor of Otolaryngology
	Manchester Royal Infirmary
	Oxford Road
	Manchester M13 9WL
Tel:	0161 276 4639
Fax:	0161 276 8511
email:	rramsden@fsl.mci.man.ac.uk
Private:	11 Lorne Street
	Manchester M13 OEZ
Tel:	0161 273 4231
Fax:	0161 273 8124
First Qualified:	1968 – St Andrews
Major Degrees:	FRCS
Academic:	Currently Professor of Otolaryngology, Manchester Royal Infirmary, Victoria University of Manchester
Specialist Training:	The London and Royal National Throat, Nose and Ear Hospitals, London
Distinctions:	President, Otology Section, Royal Society of Medicine; TWJ Travelling Fellow in Neuro-otology and Otolaryngology to North America; Dolby Prize and Medal, Royal Society of Medicine; McBride Lecturer, Edinburgh University; Sir William Wilde Discourse, Irish Otolaryngological Society and Gold Medal; Inaugural Graham Fraser Lecturer; V.S. Subramaniam Memorial Oration, The Indian Society of Otology; Member, Collegioum Oto-Rhino-Laryngologicum Amicitiae Sacrum
USA:	See 'Distinctions' above

SOUTH AND WEST REGION

BRISTOL

MAW, Mr A. Richard

Special interests:	**Otolaryngology, particularly related to chronic otitis media in children**
NHS:	Consultant Otolaryngologist
	Department of Otolaryngology
	St Michael's Hospital
	Southwell Street
	Bristol BS2 8EG
Tel:	0117 928 5870
Fax:	0117 928 5117
and:	Head and Neck Surgery
	Royal Hospital for Sick Children
	St Michael's Hill
	Bristol BS2 8BJ
Tel:	0117 921 5411
Fax:	0117 928 5820
and:	Bristol Royal Infirmary
	Maudlin Street
	Bristol BS2 8HW
Tel:	0117 923 0000
Fax:	0117 928 2000
Private:	Consulting Rooms
	Litfield House
	Litfield Place
	Clifton, Bristol BS8 3LS
Tel:	01179 731323
Fax:	01179 733303
First Qualified:	1963 – London
Major Degrees:	MS, FRCS
Academic:	Senior Clinical Lecturer, Otolaryngology, Bristol University
Specialist Training:	St Bartholomew's Hospital, London
Distinctions:	Wellcome Trust Travelling Research Fellow Uppsala University, Sweden

GLOUCESTER

ROBINSON, Mr James

Special interests:	**Otology; middle ear**
NHS:	Consultant ENT Surgeon
	Department of Otolaryngology
	Gloucester Royal Hospital
	Great Western Road
	Gloucester GL1 3NN
Tel:	01452 394207
Fax:	01452 394432
Private:	Refer to address and number above
First Qualified:	1966 – London
Major Degrees:	FRCS
Specialist Training:	United Bristol Hospitals, and The Royal National Throat, Nose and Ear Hospital, London
Distinctions:	President, Otology Section, Royal Society of Medicine

PLYMOUTH

BRIDGER, Mr Michael

Special interests:	**Head and neck cancer; medico-legal work**
NHS:	Consultant ENT Surgeon and Clinical Director for Head and Neck Services
	Derriford Hospital
	Derriford Road
	Plymouth PL6 8DH
Tel:	01752 763183
Fax:	01752 763185
Private:	Plymouth Nuffield Hospital
	Derriford Road
	Plymouth PL6 8BG
Tel:	01752 778892
Fax:	01752 778421
First Qualified:	1968 – London
Major Degrees:	FRCS, FRCS Ed
Academic:	Honorary Lecturer, Plymouth University
Specialist Training:	The Middlesex Hospital, London
	Department of ENT, Toronto General Hospital, Canada
Distinctions:	Wellcome Award 1977
USA:	Department of Otolaryngology, Tulane University, New Orleans

SOUTHAMPTON

HAACKE, Mr Norman P.

Special interests:	**Endoscopic sinus surgery; middle-ear disease; implants for profoundly deaf children**
NHS:	Consultant ENT Surgeon Southampton University Hospital Southampton SO9 4XY
Tel:	01703 825526
Fax:	01703 825688
Private:	Chalybeate Hospital Chalybeate Close Southampton SO16 6UQ
Tel:	01703 764308
Fax:	01703 785621
First Qualified:	1976 – Cambridge
Major Degrees:	FRCS, FRCSI
Academic:	Senior Lecturer, Otolaryngology, Southampton University
Specialist Training:	Royal Infirmary, Edinburgh, and The Royal National Throat, Nose and Ear Hospital, London
Distinctions:	Medical Director, South England Cochlear Implant Centre, Southampton Examiner, Royal College of Surgeons in Ireland
USA:	Lionel College Travelling Fellowship

WINCHESTER

GUERRIER, Mr Timothy H.

NHS:	Consultant ENT Royal Hampshire County Hospital Romsey Road Winchester Hampshire SO22 5DG
Tel:	01962 863535
Fax:	01962 824826
Private:	Refer to address and number above
First Qualified:	1966 – London
Major Degrees:	FRCS

TRENT REGION

NOTTINGHAM

GIBBIN, Mr Kevin P.

NHS:	Consultant ENT Surgeon
	Queen's Medical Centre
	University Hospital
	Nottingham NG7 2UH
Tel:	0115 9249924 Ext. 41275
Fax:	0115 9709748
Private:	Refer to address and number above
First Qualified:	1968 – Cambridge
Major Degrees:	FRCS
Specialist Training:	University Hospital, Wales

SHEFFIELD

BULL, Mr Peter D.

NHS:	Consultant Otolaryngologist
	Royal Hallamshire Hospital
	Glossop Road
	Sheffield S10 2JF
Tel:	0114 2711900
Fax:	0114 2712280
Private:	Consulting Rooms
	Thornbury Hospital
	312 Fulwood Road
	Sheffield S10 3BR
Tel:	0114 266 1133
Fax:	0114 268 6913
First Qualified:	1967 – Wales
Major Degrees:	FRCS
Distinctions:	Editorial Represenative, Laryngology Section,
	Royal Society of Medicine
	President, British Association, Paediatric Otolaryngology

WEST MIDLANDS REGION

BIRMINGHAM

JOHNSON, Mr Alan P.

NHS:	Consultant ENT Surgeon
	Queen Elizabeth Hospital
	Edgbaston
	Birmingham B15 2TH
Tel:	0121 627 2294
Fax:	0121 627 2291
Private:	Refer to address and number above
First Qualified:	1974 – Edinburgh
Major Degrees:	FRCS, FRCS Ed
Specialist Training:	St Bartholomew's Hospital, London

PROOPS, Mr David W.

Special interests:	**Paediatric ENT**
NHS:	Consultant ENT Surgeon
	Queen Elizabeth Hospital
	Edgbaston
	Birmingham B15 2TH
Tel:	0121 472 1311
Fax:	0121 627 2291
Private:	Refer to address and number above
First Qualified:	1975 – Birmingham
Major Degrees:	FRCS

SCOTLAND

DUNDEE

BLAIR, Mr Robert L.

Special interests:	**General Otolaryngology**
NHS:	Consultant Otolaryngologist
	Dundee Royal
	Barrack Road
	Dundee DD1 9ND
Tel:	01382 660111 Ext. 2162
Fax:	01382 632 816
Private:	Refer to address and number above
First Qualified:	1968 – Edinburgh
Major Degrees:	FRCS Ed
Academic:	Assistant Professor in Otolaryngology
	Toronto University, Canada
Distinctions:	Honour Award Canadian Society of Otolaryngology
USA and Canada:	See 'Academic' above

EDINBURGH

DALE, Mr Bryan A. B.

NHS:	ENT Department
	Royal Infirmary
	Edinburgh EH3 9YW
Tel:	0131 536 1000
Fax:	0131 536 3417
Private:	BUPA Murrayfield Hospital
	122 Corstorphine Road
	Edinburgh EH12 6UD
Tel:	0131 334 0363
Fax:	0131 334 7338
First Qualified:	1962 – Edinburgh
Major Degrees:	FRCS Ed
Specialist Training:	St Mary's Hospital, London

GLASGOW

BROWNING, Professor George G.

Special interests:	**The ear**
NHS:	ENT Department
	Royal Infirmary
	Glasgow G31 2ER
Tel:	0141 211 4367
Fax:	0141 211 4896
Private:	Refer to address and number above
First Qualified:	1958 – Glasgow
Major Degrees:	MD, FRCS Ed, FRCPS (Glas)
Academic:	Professor of Otolaryngology, ENT Department, Glasgow Royal Infirmary
Specialist Training:	Glasgow Royal Infirmary
Distinctions:	Consultant in Charge, Scottish School of Audiology
USA:	Medical Research Council Wernher–Piggot Travelling Fellow, Harvard University, Boston

ENDOCRINE SURGEONS

(see also General Surgeons)

LYNN, Mr John A.

Special interests:	**Thyroid, parathyroid and adrenal surgery**
NHS:	Consultant Endocrine and Breast Surgeon
	Hammersmith Hospital
	Du Cane Road
	London W12 OHS
Tel:	0181 743 2030 Ext. 4823
Fax:	0181 740 3360
Private:	Refer to address and number above
First Qualified:	1964 – London
Major Degrees:	MS, FRCS
Academic:	Honorary Senior Lecturer, Royal Postgraduate Medical School, London
Specialist Training:	Westminster Hospital and Royal Postgraduate Medical School, London
Distinctions:	Recognised teacher in Surgery, London University
	Arris and Gale Lecturer, Royal College of Surgeons
USA:	Surgical Research Fellow, Boston University Medical Centre, Boston

MAYNARD, Mr John D.

Special interests:	**Salivary glands; thyroid surgery**
NHS:	Retired from the NHS
Private:	97 Harley Street
	London WIN 1DF
Tel:	0171 935 4988
Fax:	0171 935 6617
First Qualified:	1954 – London
Major Degrees:	FRCS, MS
Specialist Training:	Royal London and Guy's Hospitals, London
Distinctions:	Previously Hunterian Professor, Royal College of Surgeons

ROSSWICK, Mr Robert P.

Special interests:	**Thyroids**
NHS:	No NHS work
Private:	79 Harley Street
	London W1N 1DE
Tel:	0171 935 3046
Fax:	0171 486 3927
First Qualified:	1955 – London
Major Degrees:	MS, FRCS
Academic:	Previously Honorary Senior Lecturer
	St George's Hospital, London
Specialist Training:	St George's Hospital, London
Distinctions:	Emeritus Surgeon
USA:	Previously Fellow in Surgery
	Presbyterian St Luke's Hospital, Chicago
	Master of Surgery, Illinois University

SHAHEEN, Mr Omar H.

Special interests:	**Thyroids**
NHS:	No NHS work
Private:	Emblem House
	London Bridge Hospital
	27 Tooley Street
	London SE1 2PR
Tel:	0171 403 4501
Fax:	0171 407 6172
First Qualified:	1954 – London
Major Degrees:	MS, FRCS
Specialist Training:	Guy's and The Royal National Throat, Nose and Ear
	Hospitals, London
Distinctions:	Previously President, Laryngology Section
	Royal Society of Medicine

YOUNG, Mr Anthony E.

Special interests:	**General breast and endocrine surgery**
NHS:	Consultant Surgeon
	Joint Medical Director Guy's and St Thomas' Hospital Trust
	St Thomas' Hospital
	Lambeth Palace Road
	London SE1 7EH
Tel:	0171 928 9292 Ext. 2688
Fax:	0171 922 8388
Private:	38 Devonshire Place
	London W1N 1PE
Tel:	0171 580 3612
Fax:	0171 224 0034
First Qualified:	1968 – Cambridge
Major Degrees:	FRCS, MChir
Specialist Training:	St Thomas' Hospital, London
Distinctions:	Joint Medical Director, Guy's and St Thomas' Hospital Trust
USA:	Fellow, Harvard Medical School, Boston

ANGLIA AND OXFORD REGION

OXFORD

ADAMS, Mr Christopher B. T.

Special interests:	**Pituitary tumour surgery; epilepsy; intracranial aneurysms**
NHS:	Head of Department and Consultant Neurosurgeon
	Department of Neurological Surgery
	Radcliffe Infirmary
	Oxford OX2 6HE
Tel:	01865 245389
Fax:	01865 245389
Private:	Refer to address and number above
First Qualified:	1963 – Cambridge
Major Degrees:	FRCS, FRCS Ed, MChir
Specialist Training:	Radcliffe Infirmary, Oxford

NORTHERN AND YORKSHIRE REGION

NEWCASTLE

LENNARD, Mr Thomas W. J.

Special interests:	**Breast and endocrine surgery; laparoscopic surgery**
NHS:	Consultant Surgeon
	Royal Victoria Infirmary
	Newcastle upon Tyne NE1 4LP
Tel:	0191 232 5131
Fax:	0191 232 5278
Private:	Refer to address and number above
First Qualified:	1977 – Newcastle
Major Degrees:	MD (Commendation) FRCS, FRCS Ed
Academic:	Senior Lecturer, Department of Surgery, Newcastle upon Tyne
Distinctions:	James IV Traveller
	Hunterian Professor, Royal College of Surgeons
	Moynihan Prize, Association of Surgeons
	Patey Prize, Surgical Research Society

SOUTH AND WEST REGION

BRISTOL

FARNDON, Professor John Richard

Special interests:	**Surgical endocrinology; breast disease**
NHS:	Professor of Surgery
	Department of Surgery
	Bristol Royal Infirmary
	Maudlin Street
	Bristol BS2 8HW
Tel:	01179 260601
Fax:	01179 252736
Private:	Refer to address and number above
First Qualified:	1970 – Newcastle
Major Degrees:	MD, FRCS
Academic:	Professor of Surgery, Bristol University
Distinctions:	Associate Editor, British Journal of Surgery; Previously Hunterian Professor, Royal College of Surgeons; Travelling Fellow, Royal Australasian College of Surgeons; James IV Travelling Fellow
USA:	Senior Resident Associate, Department of Surgery, Duke University Medical Centre, Durham, North Carolina

ENDOCRINOLOGISTS

(see also Diabetologists)

These are doctors who specialise in the management of all aspects of endocrine disorders. These include thyroid, pituitary, adrenocortila and adrenomedully disorders. They also treat diabetes, metabolic disorders, reproductive gynaecology, menstrual problems, sexual development and sexual problems linked to hormones as well as andrology, bone densitrometry, disorders of calcium and bone metabolism. Endocrinologists and gynaecologists work together on infertility problems resulting from a hormonal disorder.

LONDON AND THE SOUTH EAST

BESSER, Professor G. Michael

Special interests:	**Neuroendocrinology; pituitary disease; growth disorders; Cushing's syndrome; thryoid disease**
NHS:	Consultant Physician
	St Bartholomew's Hospital
	West Smithfield
	London EC1A 7BE
Tel:	0171 601 8344
Fax:	0171 601 8306
Private:	Refer to address above
Tel:	0171 601 8342
Fax:	0171 601 8505
First Qualified:	1960 – London (with distinctions in Medicine and Surgery)
Major Degrees:	DSc, MD, FRCP
Academic:	Professor of Endocrinology, St Bartholomew's Hospital, London
Specialist Training:	Royal Brompton and National Heart Hospitals, Royal Postgraduate Medical School and St Bartholomew's Hospital, London
Distinctions:	Consultant Endocrinologist to the Royal Navy
	President, Endocrine Section, Royal Society of Medicine
	Censor, Royal College of Physicians
USA:	Honorary Member, American Association of Physicians

BETTERIDGE, Dr D. John

Special interests:	**Diabetes mellitus; lipid disorders**
NHS:	Consultant Physician
	The Middlesex Hospital
	Mortimer Street
	London W1N 8AA
Tel:	0171 380 9336
Fax:	0171 380 9201
Private:	Woolavington Wing
	The Middlesex Hospital
Tel:	0171 380 9443
Fax:	0171 380 9440
First Qualified:	1972 – London
Major Degrees:	PhD, MD, FRCP
Academic:	Reader in Medicine, University College London
Specialist Training:	Hammersmith, Brompton and St Bartholomew's Hospitals, London
Distinctions:	Chairman, British Hyperlipidaemia Association Committee Member, Royal Society of Medicine Lipid Forum
USA:	Member, American Diabetic Association and American Heart Association

BLOOM, Professor Stephen R.

Special interests:	**Management of gastrointestinal endocrine tumours**
NHS:	Deputy Medical Director
	Department of Medicine
	Hammersmith Hospital
	Du Cane Road
	London W12 ONN
Tel:	0181 743 3242
Fax:	0181 740 3142
Private:	Refer to address and number above
First Qualified:	1967 – Cambridge
Major Degrees:	DSc, MD, FRCP, FRCPath
Academic:	Professor of Endocrinology, Royal Postgraduate Medical School, London
Specialist Training:	The Middlesex Hospital, London

FRANKS, Professor Stephen

Special interests:	**Hormonal aspects of gynaecology and fertility**
NHS:	The Samaritan and Western Eye Hospital
	171 Marylebone Road
	London NW1 5YE
Tel:	0171 402 4211 Ext. 455
Fax:	0171 258 3417
Private:	Consultant Physician
	St Mary's Hospital
	Praed Street
	London W2 1NY
Tel:	0171 725 1050
Fax:	0171 725 6054
First Qualified:	1970 – London
Major Degrees:	MD, FRCP, Hon MD Uppsala
Academic:	Professor of Reproductive Endocrinology
	St Mary's Hospital Medical School, London
Specialist Training:	Queen Elizabeth Hospital, Birmingham
	McGill University, Canada and
	The Middlesex Hospital, London
USA and Canada:	see 'Specialist Training' above

GROSSMAN, Professor Ashley B.

Special interests:	**Pituitary and thyroid disorders; pituitary and hypothalamic tumours; hirsutism**
NHS:	Consultant Physician
	St Bartholomew's Hospital
	West Smithfield
	London EC1A 7BE
Tel:	0171 601 8343
Fax:	0171 601 8505
Private:	Refer to address and number above
First Qualified:	1975 – London (with Honours)
Major Degrees:	MD, FRCP
Academic:	Professor of Neuroendocrinology, Medical College of St Bartholomew's, London
Specialist Training:	St Thomas' and National Hospitals, London

JACOBS, Professor Howard S.

Special interests:	**Hormonal aspects of gynaecology and fertility**
NHS:	Honorary Consultant Endocrinologist
	The Middlesex Hospital
	Mortimer Street
	London W1N 8AA
Tel:	0171 636 8333
Fax:	0171 636 9941
Private:	Refer to address and number above
First Qualified:	1962 – Cambridge
Major Degrees:	MD, FRCP
Academic:	Professor of Reproductive Endocrinology
	University College London Medical School, London
Specialist Training:	The Middlesex Hospital, London
Distinctions:	Civil Consultant to the Royal Air Force
	President Endocrine Section, Royal Society of Medicine
	Chairman, British Fertility Society
USA:	Previously Assistant Professor, University of California
	Medical School, Los Angeles

JOHNSTON, Professor Desmond G.

Special interests:	**Endocrinology; diabetes**
NHS:	Professor of Clinical Endocrinology
	St Mary's Hospital
	Praed Street
	London W2 1NY
Tel:	0171 725 1253
Fax:	0171 725 1790
Private:	Refer to address above
Tel:	0171 725 1209 (academic secretary)
Fax:	0171 725 1790
First Qualified:	1971 – Edinburgh
Major Degrees:	FRCP, PhD, FRCPath
Academic:	Professor of Clinical Endocrinology
	Unit of Metabolic Medicine, St Mary's Hospital, London
Specialist Training:	St Mary's Hospital, London

KURTZ, Dr Anthony B.

Special interests:	**Thyroid disorders**
NHS:	Consultant Physician
	The Middlesex Hospital
	Mortimer Street
	London W1N 8AA
Tel:	0171 380 9029
Fax:	0171 380 9201
Private:	Refer to address above
Tel:	0171 631 0178
Fax:	0171 436 1536
First Qualified:	1965 – Cambridge
Major Degrees:	FRCP
Academic:	Previously Reader, Diabetic Medicine, The Middlesex and University College Medical Schools, London
Specialist Training:	The Middlesex Hospital, London

MONSON, Dr John P.

Special interests:	**Pituitary, thyroid and adrenal disorders; gynaecological and general endocrinology**
NHS:	Consultant Physician
	Department of Endocrinology
	St Bartholomew's Hospital
	West Smithfield
	London EC1A 7BE
Tel:	0171 601 8345
Fax:	0171 601 8505
Private:	Refer to address and number above
First Qualified:	1973 – London
Major Degrees:	MD, FRCP
Academic:	Reader in Medicine, St Bartholomew's Hospital Medical College, London
Specialist Training:	London Hospital

SAVAGE, Dr Martin O.

Special interests:	**Paediatric and adolescent endocrinology; growth and development disorders; thyroid disease; paediatric neuroendocrinology**
NHS:	Honorary Consultant Paediatrician St Bartholomew's Hospital West Smithfield London EC1A 7BE
Tel:	0171 601 8888 Ext. 8953 or 0171 601 8468
Fax:	0171 601 8468
Private:	Refer to address and number above
First Qualified:	1968 – Cambridge
Major Degrees:	MD, FRCP
Academic:	Reader in Paediatric Endocrinology, St Bartholomew's Hospital, London Clinical Lecturer in Growth and Development, Institute of Child Health, London
Specialist Training:	Great Ormond Street Hospital for Children, London and Research Fellow in Paediatric Endocrinology, Hôpital St Vincent de Paul, Paris

SONKSEN, Professor Peter H.

Special interests:	**Pituitary disorders**
NHS:	Honorary Consultant Physician St Thomas' Hospital Lambeth Palace Road London SE1 7EH
Tel:	0171 928 9292 Ext. 2265
Fax:	0171 922 8079
Private:	Refer to address and number above
First Qualified:	1960 – London
Major Degrees:	MD, FRCP
Academic:	Professor of Endocrinology, Guy's and St Thomas' United Medical Schools, London
Specialist Training:	The Middlesex Hospital, London
Distinctions:	Previously Editor, Clinical Endocrinology
USA:	Previously Harkness Fellow, Harvard University, Boston

VAUGHAN, Dr Nicholas J. A.

Special interests: **Clinical Diabetes – treatment of pregnancy; information management; Clinical Endocrinology – pituitary disease**
NHS: Clinical Director of Medicine
Royal Sussex County Hospital
Eastern Road
Brighton BN2 5BE
Tel: 01273 696955
Fax: 01273 676345
Private: Hove Nuffield Hospital
55 New Church Road
Hove BN3 4BG
Tel: 01273 720217
Fax: 01273 495489
First Qualified: 1974 – Cambridge and Middlesex (with Honours)
Major Degrees: MA, MD, FRCP
Specialist Training: Middlesex and St George's Hospitals, London
Distinctions: Chairman, Joint Colleges Information Management and Audit Committee
Clinical Working Group Leader for Diabetes, NHS Executive

ANGLIA AND OXFORD REGION

OXFORD

WASS, Professor John A. H.

Special interests: **Pituitary, adrenal and thyroid disorders; impotence; hirsutism**
NHS: Consultant Endocrinologist
Radcliffe Infirmary
Woodstock Road
Oxford OX2 6HE
Tel: 01865 224 765
Fax: 01865 224 617
and: Nuffield Orthopaedic Centre
Windmill Road
Oxford OX3 7LD
Tel: 01865 227 621
Fax: 01865 742 348
Private: Refer to address and numbers above
First Qualified: 1971 – London
Major Degrees: MD, FRCP, MA
Academic: Professor of Endocrinology
Specialist Training: St Bartholomew's Hospital, London

NORTHERN AND YORKSHIRE REGION

NEWCASTLE

BAYLIS, Professor Peter Howard

Special interests:	**Pituitary**
NHS:	Consultant Physician
	Endocrine Unit
	Royal Victoria Infirmary
	Queen Victoria Road
	Newcastle upon Tyne NE1 4LP
Tel:	0191 232 5131
Fax:	0191 261 8505
Private:	Refer to address and number above
First Qualified:	1970 – Bristol
Major Degrees:	MD, FRCP
Academic:	Professor of Experimental Medicine, Newcastle University
Specialist Training:	Birmingham University
USA:	Clinical Fellow, Endocrinology, Indiana University

WEST MIDLANDS

BIRMINGHAM

FRANKLYN, Dr Jayne A.

Special interests:	**Pituitary and thyroid disorders**
NHS:	Honorary Consultant Physician
	Department of Medicine
	Queen Elizabeth Hospital
	Edgbaston
	Birmingham B15 2TH
Tel:	0121 472 1311
Fax:	0121 627 2384
Private:	Refer to address and number above
First Qualified:	1979 – Birmingham
Major Degrees:	MD, PhD, FRCP
Academic:	Reader in Medicine, Birmingham University
Distinctions:	Council Member, Endocrine Section, Royal Society of Medicine

SHEPPARD, Professor Michael Charles

Special interests:	**Thyroid disease**
NHS:	Honorary Consultant Physician
	Department of Medicine
	Queen Elizabeth Hospital
	Edgbaston
	Birmingham B15 2TH
Tel:	0121 472 1311
Fax:	0121 627 2384
Private:	Refer to address and number above
First Qualified:	1971 – Cape Town, South Africa
Major Degrees:	PhD, FRCP
Academic:	Professor of Medicine, Birmingham University
Specialist Training:	Queen Elizabeth Hospital, Birmingham
Distinctions:	President, Endocrine Section, Royal Society of Medicine

ENDOSCOPISTS

Endoscopists perform internal examination by direct vision through an illuminated tube, generally with a system of lenses. Advances in technology has produced new fibroscopic tubes allowing the examiner to look round curves and increase the usefulness of this method. The major areas where the endoscope is used include examination of the upper and lower gastrointestinal tract, the respiratory and urinary tracts and in performing laparoscopy, culdoscopy and colposcopy. Endoscopy is not strictly a speciality in its own right, practitioners in various specialities use this technique. They are mainly gastroenterologists and gynaecologists.

LONDON AND THE SOUTH EAST

FAIRCLOUGH, Dr Peter D.

Special interests:	**Biliary and pancreatic disorders; colonoscopy; ERCP; endoscopic ultrasound**
NHS:	Consultant Physician
	Department of Gastroenterology
	St Bartholomew's Hospital
	London EC1A 7BE
Tel:	0171 601 8516/7
Fax:	0171 982 6121/3
Private:	Endoscopy Unit, London Clinic
	20 Devonshire Place
	London W1N 2DH
Tel:	0171 935 4444
Fax:	0171 486 1755
First Qualified:	1969 – London
Major Degrees:	MD, FRCP
Academic:	Senior Lecturer, St Bartholomew's Medical College, London
Specialist Training:	St Mark's and St Bartholomew's Hospitals, London
Distinctions:	Previously Wellcome Senior Clinical Research Fellow, USA
USA:	See 'Distinctions' above

HATFIELD, Dr Adrian R. W.

Special interests:	**ERCP and non-surgical treatments of the liver and pancreas; insertion of bile duct stents**
NHS:	Consultant Physician and Gastroenterologist
	The Middlesex Hospital
	Mortimer Street
	London W1N 1HG
Tel:	0171 636 8333
Fax:	0171 380 9162
Private:	149 Harley Street
	London W1N 1HG
Tel:	0171 935 4444
Fax:	0171 486 1755
First Qualified:	1969 – London
Major Degrees:	MD, FRCP
Specialist Training:	Middlesex and Royal London Hospitals, London

KIRKHAM, Mr John Squire

Special interests:	**Gastrointestinal endoscopy, diagnostic and therapeutic, upper and lower; inguinal hernia repairs**
NHS:	Consultant Surgeon
	Queen Mary's Hospital
	Roehampton
	London SW15 5PN
Tel:	0181 789 6611
Fax:	0181 789 0704
Private:	149 Harley Street
	London W1N 2DE
Tel:	0171 935 4444
Fax:	0171 935 3690
and:	Parkside Hospital
	53 Parkside
	Wimbledon SW19 5NX
Tel:	0181 946 4202
Fax:	0181 946 7775
First Qualified:	1960 – Cambridge
Major Degrees:	MChir, FRCS
Academic:	Honorary Senior Lecturer, St George's Hospital Medical School, London
Distinctions:	Examiner, Royal College of Surgeons, Edinburgh Visiting Professor, University of Monache, Australia, University of Cairo, University of Alexandria, Mardi Hospital, Egypt and Medical School of Caracas, Venezuela

SILK, Dr David B.

Special interests: **Upper endoscopy and liver complaints**
NHS: Consultant Physician
Central Middlesex Hospital
Acton Lane
Park Royal
London NW10 7NS
Tel: 0181 965 5733 Ext. 2205
Fax: 0181 961 1317
Private: 55 Harley Street
London W1N 1DD
Tel: 0171 631 1595
Fax: 0171 323 5218
First Qualified: 1968 – London
Major Degrees: MD, FRCP
Specialist Training: King's College Hospital, London
USA: Previously Associate Professor, California University

SWAIN, Dr C. Paul

Special interests: **Therapeutic endoscopy; laser treatments**
NHS: Consultant Gastroenterologist
Royal London Hospital
Whitechapel Road
London E1 1BB
Tel: 0171 377 7000
Fax: 0171 377 7441
Private: Refer to address and number above
First Qualified: 1972 – London
Major Degrees: MD, FRCP
Academic: Senior Lecturer in Gastroenterology, Royal London
Hospital
Specialist Training: St George's Hospital, London

WESTABY, Dr David

Special interests: **Endoscopic investigation**
NHS: Consultant Physician and Gastroenterologist
Chelsea and Westminster Hospital
369 Fulham Road
London SW10 9NH
Tel: 0181 746 8000 Ext 1076
Fax: 0181 746 8100
Private: Cromwell Hospital
Cromwell Road
London SW5 0TU
Tel: 0171 370 4233 Ext. 5081
Fax: 0171 835 1573
First Qualified: 1976 – Cambridge
Major Degrees: FRCP
Specialist Training: King's College Hospital, London

WILLIAMS, Dr Christopher B.

Special interests:	**Gastrointestinal endoscopy; colonoscopy and colonic medicine**
NHS:	Consultant Physician
	Endoscopy Unit
	St Mark's Hospital
	Northwich Park
	Watford Road, Harrow HA1 3UJ
Tel:	0181 235 4000
Fax:	0181 235 4001
Private:	Endoscopy Unit
	London Clinic
	20 Devonshire Place
	London W1N 2DH
Tel:	0171 935 4444
Fax:	0171 486 1755
First Qualified:	1964 – Oxford
Major Degrees:	FRCP
Specialist Training:	St Mark's and St Bartholomew's Hospitals, London

ANGLIA AND OXFORD REGION

CAMBRIDGE

HUNTER, Dr John Oakley

Special interests:	**Intestinal disorders; inflammatory bowel disease; functional disorders of the gut**
NHS:	Consultant Physician
	Addenbrooke's Hospital
	Hills Road
	Cambridge CB2 2QQ
Tel:	01223 217469
Fax:	01223 211443
Private:	Bridge House
	Hildersham
	Cambridge CB1 6BU
Tel:	01223 890376
Fax:	01223 890377
First Qualified:	1964 – Cambridge
Major Degrees:	MA, MD, FRCP
Academic:	Associate Lecturer in Medicine, Cambridge University
Specialist Training:	St Mary's, Hammersmith and King's College Hospitals, London and Hôpital Beaujon Clichy, Paris
USA:	Fellow, American College of Gastroenterologists American Gastroenterological Association

IPSWICH

BELL, Dr Geoffrey Duncan

Special interests:	**Endoscopic treatment of helicobacter pylori infections**
NHS:	Consultant Physician and Gastroenterologist
	Department of Medicine
	The Ipswich Hospital
	Heath Road Wing
	Ipswich IP4 5PD
Tel:	01473 712233
Fax:	01473 702123
Private:	Refer to address and number above
First Qualified:	1968 – London (with Honours)
Major Degrees:	MD, FRCP
Specialist Training:	St Bartholomew's Hospital, London
	Research Fellow, Hammersmith Hospital, London
Distinctions:	Hunterian Professor, Royal College of Surgeons

NORTH WEST REGION

LIVERPOOL

MORRIS, Dr Anthony Isaac

NHS:	Consultant Physician and Gastroenterologist
	Royal Liverpool Hospital
	Prescot Street
	Liverpool L7 8XP
Tel:	0151 706 2000
Fax:	0151 706 5832
Private:	Lourdes Hospital
	57 Greenbank Road
	Liverpool L18 1HQ
Tel:	0151 722 5530
First Qualified:	1969 – Manchester
Major Degrees:	MD, FRCP
Academic:	Previously Senior Lecturer, Walton Hospital, Liverpool
Specialist Training:	University College and Whittington Hospitals, London

NORTHERN AND YORKSHIRE REGION

LEEDS

AXON, Professor Anthony T. R.

Special interests:	**Helicobacter pylori, gastric cancer and inflammatory bowel disease; endoscopic investigation**
NHS:	Professor of Gastroenterology
	Centre for Digestive Diseases
	Leeds General Infirmary
	Great George Street
	Leeds LS1 3EX
Tel:	0113 2922125
Fax:	0113 2926968
Private:	BUPA Hospital
	Jackson Avenue
	Leeds LS8 1NT
Tel:	0113 2693939
Fax:	0113 2681340
First Qualified:	1965 – London (with Honours)
Major Degrees:	MD, FRCP
Academic:	Professor of Gastroenterology, Leeds General Infirmary, University of Leeds Medical School
Specialist Training:	St Thomas' Hospital, London
Distinctions:	Previously Vice-President, Endoscopy section, British Society of Gastroenterology
	Previously Councillor, Royal College of Physicians
	Councillor, European Society of Gastrointestinal Endoscopy
USA:	Member, American Gastroenterology Association

NORTH WEST REGION

MANCHESTER

MARTIN, Dr Derrick F.

NHS:	Consultant Radiologist
	Withington Hospital
	West Didsbury
	Manchester M20 2LR
Tel:	0161 445 8111
Fax:	0161 448 1688
Private:	Refer to address and number above
First Qualified:	1972 – Birmingham
Major Degrees:	FRCP, FRCR
Academic:	Previously Lecturer in Radiology,
	Manchester University

ROTHERHAM

BARDHAN, Dr Karna Dev

Special interests:	**Gastrointestinal endoscopy**
NHS:	Consultant Physician and Gastroentcrologist
	Rotherham General Hospitals
	Moorgate Road
	Rotherham, South Yorkshire S60 2UD
Tel:	01709 820000
Fax:	01709 824168
Private:	Refer to address and number above
First Qualified:	1964 – Madras
Major Degrees:	FRCP, FRCP Ed
Academic:	Honorary Lecturer in Gastroenterology, Sheffield
	University
USA:	Member, American Gastroenterology Association

SOUTH AND WEST REGION

SWINDON

HELIER, Dr Michael D.

Special interests:	**Gastrointestinal endoscopy**
NHS:	Consultant Physician and Gastroenterologist
	Princess Margaret Hospital
	Okus Road
	Swindon SN1 4UJ
Tel:	01793 536231
Fax:	01793 426035
Private:	Ridgeway Hospital
	Moormead Road, Wroughton
	Swindon, Wiltshire SN4 9DD
Tel:	01793 814848
Fax:	01793 814852
First Qualified:	1966 – Cambridge
Major Degrees:	MD, FRCP
Specialist Training:	St Thomas' Hospital, London

TRENT

STOKE

GREEN, Dr Jonathan Rupert B.

NHS:	Consultant Physician and Gastroenterologist
	North Staffordshire Hospital
	City General
	Newcastle Road
	Stoke-on-Trent ST4 6QG
Tel:	01782 715444
Fax:	01782 712052
Private:	Refer to address and number above
First Qualified:	1970 – Oxford
Major Degrees:	DM, FRCP
Academic:	Previously Honorary Lecturer, St Bartholomew's Hospital, London
Specialist Training:	St Mary's Hospital, London

WEST MIDLANDS

WOLVERHAMPTON

SWARBRICK, Dr Edwin T.

Special interests:	**General gastroenterological endoscopy**
NHS:	Consultant Physician and Gastroenterologist
	Royal Wolverhampton Hospitals NHS Trust
	Wolverhampton Road
	Wolverhampton WV10 0QP
Tel:	01902 307999 Ext. 3027
Fax:	01902 643192
Private:	Refer to address and number above
First Qualified:	1968 – London (with Honours)
Major Degrees:	MD, FRCP
Specialist Training:	St Mark's Hospital, London

WALES

SWANSEA

KINGHAM, Dr Jeremy G. C.

Special interests:	**Gastrointestinal and liver disease**
NHS:	Consultant Physician
	Singleton Hospital
	Sketty
	Swansea SA2 0FB
Tel:	01792 205666
Fax:	01792 285506
Private:	Refer to address and number above
First Qualified:	1970 – London
Major Degrees:	MD, FRCP
Specialist Training:	St Bartholomew's Hospital, London

GASTROENTEROLOGISTS

These physicians specialise in the medicine of the digestive tract (oesophagus, stomach, small and large intestines) and the liver, biliary system and pancreas. State-of-the-art equipment has revolutionised this medical sector and the use of endoscopes to examine many parts of the tract is widely used for diagnosis and treatment of gastrointestinal diseases. When an operation is needed patients are sent to a surgeon listed in the section General Surgeons. See Endoscopists section for gastrointestinal endoscopy. The most common digestive disease in later years is cancer, which can affect any part of the digestive tract, accounting for more than 41,000 deaths each year.

LONDON AND THE SOUTH EAST

BOWN, Professor Stephen G.

Special interests:	**Laser treatment of gastroenterological disorders**
NHS:	Director, National Medical Laser Centre
	Department of Surgery
	Rayne Institute
	5 University Street
	London WC1E 6JJ
Tel:	0171 380 9802
Fax:	0171 383 3780
Private:	Refer to address and number above
First Qualified:	1971 – Cambridge
Major Degrees:	MD, FRCP
Academic:	Imperial Cancer Relief Fund, Professor of Laser Medicine and Surgery, University College Hospital, London
Specialist Training:	University College Hospital, London
Distinctions:	Previously Editor, Lasers in Medical Science
	Previously President, British Medical Laser Association
USA:	AM (Harvard)

CICLITIRA, Professor Paul J.

Special interests:	**General gastroenterology; general internal medicine; peptic ulcers; inflammatory bowel disease; coeliac disease**
NHS and Academic:	Professor of Gastroenterology
	Gastroenterology Unit, UMDS
	St Thomas' Hospital,
	Lambeth Palace Road
	London SE1 7EH
Tel:	0171 928 9292 Ext. 2354
Fax:	0171 620 2597
Private:	Refer to number below
Tel:	0171 928 5485
First Qualified:	1971 – London
Major Degrees:	MD, PhD, FRCP
Specialist Training:	Medical Research Council, Cambridge
	St Bartholomew's, Guy's and St Thomas' Hospitals, London
Distinctions:	British Gastroenterology Research Medal 1986
	UK and European Gastroenterology Award 1988
	Editor, standard work on molecular biology in gastroenterology

DAWSON, Sir Anthony

NHS:	No NHS work
Private:	149 Harley Street
	London W1N 2DE
Tel:	0171 935 4444 Ext. 4001
Fax:	0171 935 2539
First Qualified:	1951 – London
Major Degrees:	MD, FRCP
Specialist Training:	Massachusetts General Hospital, Boston and Royal Free Hospital, London
Distinctions:	KCVO; Previously Physician to HM The Queen and Head of HM's Medical Household
	Treasurer, Royal College of Physicians
	Chairman of Council, British Heart Foundation
USA:	See 'Specialist Training' above

DOWLING, Professor R. Hermon

Special interests:	**Gallstones**
NHS and Academic:	Professor of Gastroenterology and Consulting Physician
	Guy's Hospital
	St Thomas Street
	London SE1 9RT
Tel:	0171 955 5000 Ext. 2123
Fax:	0171 955 4230 or 0171 407 6689
Private:	Refer to address and number above
First Qualified:	1968 – Belfast
Major Degrees:	MD, FRCP
Academic:	Professor of Gastroenterology, United Medical and Dental Schools, Guy's and St Thomas' Hospitals, London
Distinctions:	Ex-President, European Society for Clinical Investigation President, British Gastroenterology Association
USA:	Previously Senior Research Fellow, Boston University

FARTHING, Professor Michael J. G.

Special interests:	**Infections; coelic disease; inflammatory bowel disease; endocrine abnormals in gastrointestinal disease**
NHS:	Professor of Gastroenterology and Honorary Consultant Physician
	Department of Gastroenterology
	St Bartholomew's Hospital
	West Smithfield
	London EC1A 7BE
Tel:	0171 601 8888 Ext. 8517
Fax:	0171 982 6121
Private:	Refer to address and number above
First Qualified:	1972 – London
Major Degrees:	MD, FRCP
Academic:	Professor of Gastroenterology, St Bartholomew's Hospital, London
Specialist Training:	Cambridge; and St Mark's Hospital, London
USA:	Previously Assistant Professor in Medicine Tufts University, Boston

FORBES, Dr Alastair

Special interests:	**Management of colorectal disorders including inflammatory bowel disease and functional bowel disease**
NHS:	Consultant Physician and Gastroenterologist
St Mark's Hospital
Northwick Park
Watford Road
Harrow, Middlesex HA1 3JU
Tel:	0181 235 4000
Fax:	0181 235 4001
Private:	Refer to address and number above
First Qualified:	1979 – London
Major Degrees:	MD, MRCP
Academic:	Honorary Senior Lecturer, St Bartholomew's Hospital Medical College, London
Research Fellow, Liver Unit, King's College Hospital, London
Specialist Training:	Middlesex, Charing Cross and Westminster Hospitals, London
Distinctions:	Author and Co-editor, *Atlas of Clinical Gastroenterology*

FORGACS, Dr Ian C.

Special interests:	**Gallbladders and bile ducts**
NHS:	Consultant Physician and Gastroenterologist
King's College Hospital
Denmark Hill
London SE5 9RS
Tel:	0171 737 4000 Ext. 2728
Fax:	0171 346 6474
Private:	Refer to address and number above
First Qualified:	1975 – London
Major Degrees:	MD, MRCP
Academic:	Postgraduate Dean, King's College Hospital Medical School, London
Specialist Training:	St Thomas' Hospital, London, and Addenbrooke's Hospital, Cambridge
Distinctions:	Associate Editor, British Medical Journal

HATFIELD, Dr Adrian R. W.

Special interests:	**ERCP and non-surgical treatments of the liver and pancreas; insertion of bile duct stents**
NHS:	Consultant Physician and Gastroenterologist
	Middlesex Hospital
	Mortimer Street
	London W1N 1HG
Tel:	0171 636 8333
Fax:	0171 380 9162
Private:	149 Harley Street
	London W1N 1HG
Tel:	0171 935 4444
Fax:	0171 486 1755
First Qualified:	1969 – London
Major Degrees:	MD, FRCP
Specialist Training:	The Middlesex and Royal London Hospitals, London

MAXWELL, Dr J. Douglas

Special interests:	**General gastroenterology; liver disease**
NHS:	Consultant Physician
	St George's Hospital
	Blackshaw Road
	London SW17 0QT
Tel:	0181 672 1255 Ext. 1541
Fax:	0181 725 3520
Private:	Refer to address and number above
First Qualified:	1964 – Glasgow
Major Degrees:	MD, FRCP
Academic:	Clinical Dean and Reader in Medicine, St George's Hospital Medical School, London
Specialist Training:	King's College and St George's Hospitals, London
USA:	Previously Research Fellow, University of California Medical School, San Francisco

MISIEWICZ, Dr Jerzy J. (George)

Special interests:	**Peptic ulcer; helicobacter pylori; irritable bowel syndrome; colitis; Crohn's disease**
NHS:	Consultant Gastroenterologist
	Central Middlesex Hospital
	Acton Lane
	Park Royal, London NW10 7NS
Tel:	0181 453 2202
Fax:	0181 961 1317
Private:	The Consulting Rooms
	Princess Grace Hospital
	42–52 Nottingham Place
	London W1M 3FD
Tel:	0171 486 1234
Fax:	0171 487 4476
First Qualified:	1956 – London
Major Degrees:	FRCP
Specialist Training:	Royal Postgraduate Medical School, Royal Brompton and St Bartholomew's Hospitals, London
Distinctions:	Consultant Gastroenterologist to the Royal Navy and British Airways
	Editor, European Journal of Gastroenterology and Hepatology
	Ex-President, British Society of Gastroenterology

MURRAY-LYON, Dr Iain M.

Special interests:	**All aspects of liver disease particularly chronic viral liver disease, alcohol and liver damage, and liver tumours**
NHS:	Consultant Physician and Gastroenterologist
	Department of Gastroenterology
	Chelsea and Westminster Hospital
	369 Fulham Road
	London SW10 9NH
Tel:	0181 746 8000
Fax:	0171 746 8111
Private:	149 Harley Street
	London W1N 2DH
Tel:	0171 935 6747 or 0171 935 4444
Fax:	0171 935 7017
First Qualified:	1964 – Edinburgh (with Honours)
Major Degrees:	MD, FRCP
Specialist Training:	Royal Infirmary Edinburgh, Liver Unit, King's College Hospital, London

POUNDER, Professor R. E. Roy

Special interests:	**Peptic ulceration; inflammatory bowel disease**
NHS:	Honorary Consulting Physician and Gastroenterologist
	Royal Free Hospital
	Pond Street
	London NW3 2QG
Tel:	0171 794 0500 Ext. 3990 or 0171 830 2243
Fax:	0171 435 5803
Private:	See address and number above
First Qualified:	1969 – Cambridge
Major Degrees:	MD, D.Sc., FRCP
Academic:	Professor of Medicine, Royal Free Hospital and School of Medicine, London
Specialist Training:	St Thomas', Hammersmith and Central Middlesex Hospitals, London
Distinctions:	Co-editor, *Alimentary Pharmacology and Therapy*
USA:	Member, American Gastroenterology Association

SILK, Dr David B.

Special interests:	**Including upper endoscopy and liver complaints**
NHS:	Consultant Physician
	Central Middlesex Hospital
	Acton Lane
	Park Royal
	London NW10 7NS
Tel:	0181 965 5733 Ext. 2205
Fax:	0181 961 1317
Private:	55 Harley Street
	London W1N 1DD
Tel:	0171 631 1595
Fax:	0171 323 5218
First Qualified:	1968 – London
Major Degrees:	MD, FRCP
Specialist Training:	King's College Hospital, London
USA:	Previously Associate Professor, California University

SWAIN, Dr C. Paul

Special interests:	**Therapeutic endoscopy; laser treatments**
NHS:	Consultant Gastroenterologist
	Royal London Hospital
	Whitechapel Road
	London E1 1BB
Tel:	0171 377 7000 or 0171 377 7443
Fax:	0171 377 7441
Private:	Refer to address and number above
First Qualified:	1972 – London
Major Degrees:	MD, FRCP
Academic:	Senior Lecturer in Gastroenterology, Royal London Hospital
Specialist Training:	St George's Hospital, London

THOMPSON, Dr Richard P. H.

Special interests:	**Liver disease**
NHS:	Consultant Physician
	The Rayne Institute
	St Thomas' Hospital
	London SE1 7EH
Tel:	0171 928 9292 Ext. 2650
Fax:	0171 922 8079
Private:	Consulting Rooms
	York House
	199 Westminster Bridge Road
	London SE1 7UT
Tel:	0171 928 5485
Fax:	0171 928 3748
First Qualified:	1964 – Oxford
Major Degrees:	DM, FRCP
Academic:	Senior Lecturer, Liver Unit, King's College Hospital
Distinctions:	Physician to HM the Queen
	Previously Physician to the Royal Household
	MRC Clinical Research Fellow
USA:	Research Assistant, Gastroenterology Unit, Mayo Clinic, Rochester, Minnesota

ZEEGEN, Dr Ronald, OBE

Special interests:	**Gall bladder, pancreas, and gut; liver problems**
NHS:	Consultant Physician and Gastroenterologist
	Chelsea and Westminster Hospital
	369 Fulham Road
	London SW10 9NH
Tel:	0181 746 8106
Fax:	0181 746 8100
Private:	Lister Hospital
	Chelsea Bridge Road
	London SW1W 8RH
Tel:	0171 730 3417
Fax:	0171 824 8867
and:	Chelsea and Westminster Hospital
	369 Fulham Road
	London SW10 9NH
Tel:	0181 746 8000
Fax:	0181 746 8111
First Qualified:	1962 – London
Major Degrees:	FRCP
Specialist Training:	Westminster and St Bartholomew's Hospitals, London

ANGLIA AND OXFORD

CAMBRIDGE

HUNTER, Dr John Oakley

Special interests:	**Intestinal disorders; inflammatory bowel disease; functional disorders of the gut**
NHS:	Consultant Physician
	Addenbrooke's Hospital
	Hills Road
	Cambridge CB2 2QQ
Tel:	01223 217469
Fax:	01223 211443
Private:	Bridge House
	Hildersham
	Cambridge CB1 6BU
Tel:	01223 890376
Fax:	01223 890377
First Qualified:	1964 – Cambridge
Major Degrees:	MA, MD, FRCP
Academic:	Associate Lecturer in Medicine, Cambridge University
Specialist Training:	St Mary's, Hammersmith and King's College Hospitals, London, and Hôpital Beaujon Clichy, Paris
USA:	Fellow, American College of Gastroenterologists
	American Gastroenterological Association

OXFORD

CHAPMAN, Dr Roger W.

Special interests:	**Cholestatic liver disease**
NHS:	Consultant Gastroenterologist
	John Radcliffe Hospital
	Headley Way, Headington
	Oxford OX3 9DU
Tel:	01865 220618
Fax:	01865 751100
Private:	23 Banbury Road
	Oxford
Tel:	01865 515036
First Qualified:	1973 – London
Major Degrees:	MD, FRCP
Academic:	Honorary Senior Lecturer in Medicine
	Oxford University Medical School
	Previously Lecturer in Medicine, Royal Free Hospital, London
Specialist Training:	Southampton General Hospital and Royal Free Hospital, London
Distinctions:	Previously Secretary/Treasurer, British Association for the Study of the Liver
	Associate Editor, Gut
	Frewin Award, Clinical Research 1984
USA:	Previously Visiting Scientist, Washington University, Seattle

JEWELL, Dr Derek P.

Special interests:	**Inflammatory bowel disease; coeliac disease**
NHS:	Consultant Gastroenterologist
	John Radcliffe Hospital
	Headley Way, Headington
	Oxford OX2 6HE
Tel:	01865 741166 or 01865 220960
Fax:	01865 790792
Private:	Refer to address and number above
First Qualified:	1966 – Oxford
Major Degrees:	FRCP
Academic:	Previously Clinical Senior Lecturer, Oxford University
	Senior Lecturer in Medicine, London University
Specialist Training:	Oxford
USA:	Previously Assistant Professor, Stanford University, California

NORTH WEST REGION

STOCKPORT

DYMOCK, Dr Iain William

Special interests:	**Liver disease**
NHS:	Consultant Physician
	Stepping Hill Hospital
	Poplar Grove
	Stockport SK2 7JE
Tel:	0161 483 1010
Fax:	0161 419 5930
Private:	Consulting Rooms
	87 Palatine Road
	Manchester M20 8JQ
Tel:	0161 434 3399
Fax:	0161 445 7468
First Qualified:	1962 – Glasgow
Major Degrees:	FRCP Ed, FRCP
Academic:	Previously Senior Lecturer in Medicine
	Manchester University
	MRC Research Fellow, Liver Group, King's College
	Hospital, London

NORTHERN AND YORKSHIRE

LEEDS

AXON, Professor Anthony T. R.

Special interests:	**Helicobacter pylori, gastric cancer and inflammatory bowel disease; endoscopic investigation**
NHS:	Professor of Gastroenterology
	Centre for Digestive Diseases
	Leeds General Infirmary
	Great George Street
	Leeds LS1 3EX
Tel:	0113 2922125
Fax:	0113 2926968
Private:	BUPA Hospital
	Jackson Avenue
	Leeds LS8 1NT
Tel:	0113 2693939
Fax:	0113 2681340
First Qualified:	1965 – London (with Honours)
Major Degrees:	MD, FRCP
Academic:	Professor of Gastroenterology, Leeds General Infirmary, University of Leeds Medical School
Specialist Training:	St Thomas' Hospital, London
Distinctions:	Previously Vice-President, Endoscopy Section, British Society of Gastroenterology
	Previously Councillor, Royal College of Physicians
	Councillor, European Society of Gastrointestinal Endoscopy
USA:	Member, American Gastroenterology Association

WEST MIDLANDS

BIRMINGHAM

ALLAN, Dr Robert N.

Special interests:	**Colitis; Crohn's disease**
NHS:	Consultant Physician
	Queen Elizabeth Hospital
	Edgbaston
	Birmingham B12 2TH
Tel:	0121 472 1311 Ext. 3377
Fax:	0121 472 8135
Private:	No private work
First Qualified:	1964 – Birmingham
Major Degrees:	MD, PhD, FRCP
Specialist Training:	United Birmingham Hospitals
USA:	Previously, N.I.H.Research Fellow, Mayo Graduate Medical School, Rochester, Minnesota

COVENTRY

LOFT, Dr Duncan Edward

Special interests:	**Coeliac disease; oesophageal carcinoma; endoscopy**
NHS:	Consultant Gastroenterologist
	Walsgrave Hospital
	Clifford Bridge Road
	Coventry CV2 2DX
Tel:	01203 602020
Fax:	01203 538793
Private:	Refer to address and number above
First Qualified:	1978 – Birmingham
Major Degrees:	MD, MRCP
Academic:	MRC Research Fellow, Hope Hospital, Salford
Specialist Training:	Central Middlesex Hospital, London
	Hope Hospital, Salford

SCOTLAND

ABERDEEN

BRUNT, Dr Peter William, OBE

Special interests:	**Liver and biliary system**
NHS:	Consultant Physician and Gastroenterologist
	Aberdeen Royal Infirmary
	Foresterhill
	Aberdeen AB9 2ZB
Tel:	01224 681818
Fax:	01224 840711
Private:	Refer to address and number above
First Qualified:	1959 – Liverpool
Major Degrees:	MD, FRCP Ed, FRCP
Academic:	Clinical Senior Lecturer in Medicine, Aberdeen University
	Previously Honorary Senior Lecturer in Medicine, Royal Free Hospital, London
Specialist Training:	Edinburgh University
Distinctions:	Physician to HM the Queen in Scotland
USA:	Previously Fellow, Johns Hopkins Hospital, Baltimore

EDINBURGH

FERGUSON, Professor Anne

Special interests:	**Gastrointestinal immunology**
NHS:	Consultant Physician
	Gastrointestinal Unit
	Western General Hospital
	Crewe Road
	Edinburgh EH4 2XU
Tel:	0131 537 1000
Fax:	0131 537 1007
Private:	Refer to address and number above
First Qualified:	1964 – Glasgow
Major Degrees:	PhD, FRCP Ed, FRCPath
Academic:	Professor of Gastroenterology, Edinburgh University
Specialist Training:	Royal Infirmary, Glasgow

FINLAYSON, Dr Niall D. C.

Special interests:	**Liver disease**
NHS:	Clinical Director and Consultant Physician
	Centre for Liver and Digestive Disorders
	Edinburgh Royal Infirmary
	1 Lauriston Place
	Edinburgh EH3 9YW
Tel:	0131 536 2178
Fax:	0131 536 2197
Private:	No private work
First Qualified:	1964 – Edinburgh
Major Degrees:	PhD, FRCP, FRCP Ed
Academic:	Honorary Senior Lecturer in Medicine, Edinburgh University
Specialist Training:	Previously New York Hospital, Cornell Medical Centre, New York
USA:	See 'Specialist Training' above

HEADING, Dr Robert Campbell

NHS:	Consultant Physician
	Royal Infirmary
	Edinburgh Royal Infirmary
	1 Lauriston Place
	Edinburgh EH3 9YW
Tel:	0131 536 1000 Ext. 62241
Fax:	0131 536 2197
Private:	Refer to address and number above
First Qualified:	1966 – Edinburgh
Major Degrees:	MD, FRCP Ed
Academic:	Reader in Medicine, Edinburgh University
USA:	Fellow, University of Iowa Medical College
	International Member, American Gastroenterology Association

WALES

RHODES, Professor John

Special interests:	**Crohn's disease; ulcerative colitis**
NHS:	Consultant Gastroenterologist
	University Hospital of Wales
	Heath Park
	Cardiff CF4 4XW
Tel:	01222 743292
Fax:	01222 743821
Private:	Refer to address and number above
First Qualified:	1960 – Manchester
Major Degrees:	MD, FRCP
Academic:	Honorary Professor, University Hospital of Wales, Cardiff
Specialist Training:	Manchester Royal Infirmary
USA:	Previously Research Assistant, Gastroenterology Unit, Mayo Clinic, Rochester, Minnesota

GENERAL SURGEONS

To find the doctor for your condition look under the special interest headings to check what area of surgery is the doctor's main area of expertise. The following are the main categories covered under this section.

Breast and Endocrine Surgery: *also included under Endocrine Surgeons*

Gastrointestinal surgery: *includes surgery of the gall bladder, stomach and intestines.*

Surgical Oncology: *Roughly 30% of general surgeons' work is concerned with the management of cancer. Many surgeons are now channelling their surgical speciality to cancer patients and devoting much of their time to the surgery of certain types of cancer or particular problems in oncology. Increasingly surgeons are working in conjunction with clinical and medical oncologists. See sections on Medical Oncologists and Clinical Oncologists.*

Minimally invasive surgery: *This is one of the great innovations of health care in the twentieth century. With minimal disruption to the patient's body or way of life, outcomes are at least as effective as, and procedures are safer than, conventional surgery. The widespread use of minimally invasive techniques has important implications for hospital and health workers. As more patients are treated on an outpatient basis, fewer hospital beds will be needed and traditional operating rooms will have to adapt to a greater turnover of patients. At present the areas of surgery that have benefited from such techniques are gastrointestinal, gynaecological, colorectal and hernia operations. Surgeons are having to acquire new operating skills, possibly requiring formal training and accreditation.*

LONDON AND THE SOUTH EAST

ALLUM, Mr William H.

NHS:	Consultant Surgeon
	Epsom General Hospital
	Dorking Road, Epsom KT18 7EG
Tel:	01372 735735 Ext. 5107
Fax:	01372 743421
Private:	Refer to address and number above
First Qualified:	1977 – Birmingham
Major Degrees:	MD, FRCS
Specialist Training:	Birmingham and Leicester
Distinctions:	Secretary, British Stomach Cancer Group
USA:	Oncology Unit, University of Houston, Texas

BAUM, Professor Michael

Special interests:	**Breast cancer**
NHS:	Consultant Surgeon
	Royal Marsden Hospital
	Fulham Road
	London SW3 6JJ
Tel:	0171 352 9162
Fax:	0171 351 5410
Private:	Refer to address and number above
First Qualified:	1960 – Birmingham
Major Degrees:	MD (HC), ChM, FRCS
Academic:	Emeritus Professor of Surgery, Institute of Cancer Research; Visiting Professor, Department of Surgery, University College, London; Previously Professor of Surgery, King's College, London
Specialist Training:	University of Wales
Distinctions:	Emeritus Professor of Surgery of the Institute of Cancer Research; President, British Oncological Association; Vice–President, European Society of Mastology; Chairman, Cancer Research Campaign Breast Cancer Trials Group; Chairman, UK Co-ordinating Committee of Breast Cancer Research
USA:	Previously Instructor in Surgery, Pittsburgh University, Pennsylvania

BISHOP, Mr Christopher C. R.

Special interests:	**Laparoscopic cholecystectomy**
NHS:	Consultant Surgeon
	The Middlesex Hospital
	Mortimer Street
	London W1N 8AA
Tel:	0171 636 8333
Fax:	0171 637 5541
Private:	149 Harley Street
	London W1 2DE
Tel:	0171 235 6086
Fax:	0171 235 6052
First Qualified:	1978 – Cambridge
Major Degrees:	MChir, FRCS
Specialist Training:	St Thomas' Hospital, London, and Scripps Clinic, La Jolla, California
USA:	See 'Specialist Training' above

COCHRANE, Mr John P. S.

NHS:	Consultant Surgeon
	Whittington Hospital
	Highgate Hill
	Archway
	London N19 5NF
Tel:	0171 288 5411
Fax:	0171 288 5417
Private:	19 Wimpole Street
	London W1M 7AD
Tel:	0171 637 9755
Fax:	0171 637 2789
First Qualified:	1967 – London
Major Degrees:	MS, FRCS
Specialist Training:	The Middlesex Hospital, London, and at Leicester

EARLAM, Mr Richard J.

NHS:	Consultant Surgeon
	Royal London Hospital
	Whitechapel
	London E1 1BB
Tel:	0171 377 7439
Fax:	0171 377 7439
Private:	Cromwell Hospital
	Cromwell Road
	London SW5 0TU
Tel:	0171 370 4233
Fax:	0171 370 4063
First Qualified:	1958 – Cambridge
Major Degrees:	MChir, FRCS
Specialist Training:	Liverpool Royal Infirmary and Munich, Germany
Distinctions:	Examiner, Royal College of Surgeons
	Chairman, International Society of Gastric Society
USA:	Previously Research Assistant, Mayo Clinic, Rochester, Minnesota

FERNANDO, Mr Oswald N.

Special interests:	**Kidney transplants**
NHS:	Consultant Surgeon, Department of Nephrology and Renal Transplantation Royal Free Hospital Pond Street London NW3 2QG
Tel:	0171 794 0500
Fax:	0171 435 5342
Private:	Refer to address and number above
First Qualified:	1960 – Sri Lanka
Major Degrees:	FRCS
Academic:	Previously Research Fellow, Royal Free Hospital, London
Specialist Training:	Royal Free Hospital, London
Distinctions:	Honorary Consultant Surgeon, Great Ormond Street Hospital for Children, London

GILMORE, Mr O. Jeremy

Special interests:	**Diagnosis and management of early breast cancer and benign breast disease**
NHS:	No NHS work
Private:	108 Harley Street London WIN 2ET
Tel:	0171 637 8820
Fax:	0171 436 2945
First Qualified:	1966 – London (with special award)
Major Degrees:	MS, FRCS, FRCS Ed
Academic:	Previously Senior Lecturer, London University
Specialist Training:	St Bartholomew's Hospital, London
Distinctions:	Lately Hunterian Professor, Royal College of Surgeons Moynihan Medal, Association of Surgeons of Great Britain and Ireland Hamilton Bailey Prize, International College of Surgeons Previously Hunterian Professor, Royal College of Surgeons Previously Director, Breast Clinic, St Bartholomew's Hospital, London

GLAZER, Mr Geoffrey

Special interests:	**Gastroenterology; pancreatitis; thyroid disease**
NHS:	Consultant Surgeon
	St Mary's Hospital
	Praed Street
	London W1N 1AA
Tel:	0171 725 6041
Fax:	0171 725 1571
Private:	22 Harley Street
	London W1N 1AA
Tel:	0171 483 3020
Fax:	0171 483 3087
and:	Wellington Hospital
	Wellington Place
	London NW8 9LE
Tel:	0171 586 5959
Fax:	0171 258 1960
First Qualified:	1964 – London
Major Degrees:	MS, FRCS, FACS
Specialist Training:	St Mary's Hospital, London

HABIB, Mr Nagy

NHS:	Consultant Surgeon
	Hammersmith Hospital
	Du Cane Road
	London W12 0HS
Tel:	0181 743 2030
Fax:	0181 740 3212
Private:	Refer to address and number above
First Qualified:	1978 – London
Major Degrees:	MS, FRCS
Specialist Training:	Royal Postgraduate Medical School, London

JACKSON, Mr Barry T.

Special interests: **Gastrointestinal surgeon**
NHS: Consultant Surgeon
St Thomas' Hospital
Lambeth Palace Road
London SE1 7EH
Tel: 0171 928 9292 Ext. 2997
Fax: 0171 922 8086
Private: The Consulting Rooms
York House
199 Westminster Bridge Road
London S12 7UT
Tel: 0171 928 5485
Fax: 0171 928 3748
First Qualified: 1963 – London
Major Degrees: MS, FRCS
Specialist Training: St Thomas' Hospital, London
Distinctions: President, Association of Surgeons of Great Britain and
Ireland; Previously Surgeon to the Royal Household;
Honorary Consultant Surgeon to the Army; Previously
Thomas Vicary Lecturer, Royal College of Surgeons;
Ex-President, Coloproctology Section, Royal Society of
Medicine

KIRKHAM, Mr John Squire

Special interests: **Upper and lower gastrointestinal cancer**
NHS: Consultant Surgeon
Queen Mary's Hospital
Roehampton
London SW15 5PN
Tel: 0181 789 6611
Fax: 0181 789 0704
Private: 149 Harley Street
London W1N 2DE
Tel: 0171 935 4444
Fax: 0171 935 3690
and: Parkside Hospital
53 Parkside
Wimbledon SW19 5NX
Tel: 0181 946 4202
Fax: 0181 946 7775
First Qualified: 1960 – Cambridge
Major Degrees: MChir, FRCS
Academic: Honorary Senior Lecturer, St George's Hospital Medical
School, London
Distinctions: Examiner, Royal College of Surgeons, Edinburgh
Visiting Professor, University of Monache, Australia,
University of Cairo, University of Alexandria, Mardi
Hospital, Egypt and Medical School of Caracas,
Venezuela

MAYNARD, Mr John D.

Special interests:	**Salivary glands; thyroid surgery**
NHS:	Retired from the NHS
Private:	97 Harley Street
	London WIN 1DF
Tel:	0171 935 4988
Fax:	0171 935 6617
First Qualified:	1954 – London
Major Degrees:	FRCS, MS
Specialist Training:	Royal London and Guy's Hospitals, London
Distinctions:	Previously Hunterian Professor, Royal College of Surgeons

McCOLL, Professor Rt. Hon. Lord

Special interests:	**Laparoscopic cholecystectomy**
NHS:	Professor of Surgery
	Guy's Hospital
	St Thomas Street
	London SE1 9RT
Tel:	0171 955 4466
Fax:	0171 403 0212
Private:	Refer to address and number above
First Qualified:	1957 – London
Major Degrees:	FRCS, FACS
Academic:	Professor of Surgery, Guy's and St Thomas' United Medical Schools
Distinctions:	Honorary Consultant Surgeon to the Army
	Honorary Surgeon, King's College
	Adviser on Medical Features, BBC TV
	Councillor, Royal College of Surgeons and the Imperial Cancer Research Fund
USA:	Research Fellow, Harvard Medical School, Boston

MENZIES-GOW, Mr Neil

Special interests:	**Laparoscopic surgery of the abdomen, appendix, gall bladder**
NHS:	Senior Consultant Surgeon and Director of the Surgical Directorate Central Middlesex Hospital Medical School Acton Lane Park Royal, London NW10 7NS
Tel:	0181 965 5733
Fax:	0181 453 2733
Private:	Princess Grace Hospital 42–52 Nottingham Place London WIM 3FD
Tel:	0171 486 1234
Fax:	0171 487 4476
First Qualified:	1969 – London
Major Degrees:	FRCS

ROSIN, Mr R. David

Special interests:	**Minimal access surgery; surgery for skin cancer, carcinoma and pancreatic endocrine tumours**
NHS:	Consultant Surgeon St Mary's Hospital Praed Street London W2 1NY
Tel:	0171 725 1242
Fax:	0171 725 1571
Private:	6 Harley Street London W1N 1AA
Tel:	0171 631 3447
Fax:	0171 631 3447
First Qualified:	1966 – London
Major Degrees:	MS, FRCS
Specialist Training:	Westminster Hospital, London
Distinctions:	Previously Hunterian Professor, Royal College of Surgeons Previously Arris and Gale Lecturer, Arnott Lecturer and Penrose May Tutor, Royal College of Surgeons; Examiner, Royal College of Surgeons, Edinburgh Ex-President, Melanoma Study Group

SCURR, Mr John H.

NHS:	Consultant Surgeon
	Middlesex Hospital
	Mortimer Street
	London W1N 8AA
Tel:	0171 380 9414
Fax:	0171 380 9413
Private:	Lister Hospital
	Chelsea Bridge Road
	London SW1W 8RH
Tel:	0171 730 9563
Fax:	0171 259 9938
First Qualified:	1972 – London (with Honours)
Major Degrees:	FRCS
Academic:	Senior Lecturer, The Middlesex Hospital, London
Specialist Training:	Westminster Hospital, London

SINNETT, Mr Hugh Dudley

Special interests:	**Breast diseases and soft tissue tumours**
NHS:	Consultant in Breast Surgery
	Department of Surgery
	Charing Cross Hospital
	Fulham Palace Road
	London W6 8RF
Tel:	0181 846 7303
Fax:	0181 846 1617
Private:	Refer to address and number above
First Qualified:	1972 – London
Major Degrees:	FRCS
Academic:	Senior Lecturer, Royal Marsden Hospital, London
Specialist Training:	St Bartholomew's Hospital, London
Distinctions:	Member, Court of Examiners, Royal College of Surgeons
	Honorary Consultant Surgeon, Royal Marsden Hospital, London

THOMAS, Mr J. Merion

Special interests:	**Breast cancer, soft tissue sarcoma, malignant melanoma and head/neck surgery. 'Leading authority on soft tissue sarcomas and melanomas'**
NHS:	Consultant Surgical Oncologist
	Chelsea and Westminster Hospital
	369 Fulham Road
	London SW10 9NH
Tel:	0181 746 8549
Fax:	0181 746 8544
and:	Consultant Surgical Oncologist
	Royal Marsden Hospital
	Fulham Road
	London SW3 6JJ
Tel:	0171 352 2269
Fax:	0171 351 5410
Private:	Lister Hospital
	Chelsea Bridge Road
	London SW1W 8RH
Tel:	0171 631 4498
Fax:	0171 259 9552
First Qualified:	1969 – London
Major Degrees:	MS, MRCP, FRCS
Specialist Training:	Royal Marsden and St Mark's Hospitals, London

WASTELL, Professor Christopher

Special interests:	**Laparoscopic surgery; surgery of gastrointestinal disease and surgery in relation to HIV infection**
NHS and Academic:	Honorary Consultant Surgeon and Professor of Surgery
	Chelsea and Westminster Hospital
	369 Fulham Road
	London SW10 9NH
Tel:	0181 746 8000 Ext. 8466
Fax:	0181 746 8282
Private:	Refer to address and number above
First Qualified:	1957 – London
Major Degrees:	MS, FRCS
Specialist Training:	Westminster Hospital, London
Distinctions:	Previously President, Hunterian Society
	Hunterian Professor, Royal College of Surgeons
	Hunterian Society Orator
	Professor Examiner, Royal College of Surgeons
USA:	Previously Research Fellow in Surgery, Mount Sinai Medical Center, New York
	Thomas Bombeck Lecturer, Chicago, Illinois

WELLWOOD, Mr James M.

Special interests:	**Breast Cancer; laparoscopic surgery of the abdomen, appendix, gall bladder, abdominal wall, inguinal and hiatus hernia repairs**
NHS:	Clinical Director
	Breast Cancer Screening Unit
	Whipps Cross Hospital
	Whipps Cross Road
	Leytonstone, London E10
Tel:	0181 539 5522
Fax:	0181 558 8115
Private:	134 Harley Street
	London W1N 1AH
Tel:	0171 487 4212
Fax:	0171 486 1042
First Qualified:	1966 – Cambridge
Major Degrees:	Mchir, FRCS
Academic:	Honorary Senior Lecturer, St Bartholomew's Medical College, London
Distinctions:	Previously Honorary Secretary, British Association of Surgical Oncology; Member, United Kingdom Council of the Association of Endoscopic Surgeons of Great Britain and Ireland; Trainer, Minimal Access Training Unit, Royal College of Surgeons, London
USA:	Specialist training and research, Lahey Clinic, Boston

WILLIAMS, Professor Norman S.

Special interests:	**Gastrointestinal surgery; inflammatory bowel disease surgery**
NHS:	Honorary Consultant
	Royal London Hospital
	Whitechapel Road
	London E1 1BB
Tel:	0171 377 7098
Fax:	0171 377 7283
Private:	Refer to address and number above
First Qualified:	1970 – London
Major Degrees:	MS, FRCS
Academic:	Professor of Surgery, London Hospital Medical College
Specialist Training:	London Hospital
Distinctions:	Vice-President; British Journal of Surgery; President, Ileostomy Association of Great Britain and Ireland; Previously Moynihan Fellowship; Patey Prize Surgical Research Society
USA:	Research Fellow, University of California, Los Angeles

YOUNG, Mr Anthony E.

Special interests:	**General breast and endocrine surgery**
NHS:	Consultant Surgeon
	Joint Medical Director Guy's and St Thomas' Hospital Trust
	St Thomas' Hospital
	Lambeth Palace Road
	London SE1 7EH
Tel:	0171 928 9292 Ext. 2688
Fax:	0171 922 8388
Private:	38 Devonshire Place
	London W1N 1PE
Tel:	0171 580 3612
Fax:	0171 224 0034
First Qualified:	1968 – Cambridge
Major Degrees:	FRCS, MChir
Specialist Training:	St Thomas' Hospital, London
Distinctions:	Joint Medical Director Guy's and St Thomas' Hospital Trust
USA:	Fellow, Harvard Medical School, Boston

ANGLIA AND OXFORD REGION

CAMBRIDGE

DUNN, Mr David Christy

Special interests:	**Minimally invasive surgery of the abdomen (hiatus hernia, stomach, gall bladder, appendix, colon) and sympathectomy for hyperhidrosis**
NHS:	Consultant Surgeon
	Addenbrooke's Hospital
	Hills Road
	Cambridge CB3 2QQ
Tel:	01223 216992
Fax:	01223 216015
Private:	Evelyn Hospital
	4 Trumpington Road
	Cambridge CB2 2AF
Tel:	01223 303336
Fax:	01223 354438
First Qualified:	1963 – Cambridge
Major Degrees:	MChir, FRCS
Academic:	Lecturer in Surgery, University of Cambridge Clinical School
Distinctions:	National Secretary, Association of Endoscopic Surgeons of Great Britain and Ireland; Director, Comparative Audit Service, Royal College of Surgeons; Penrose May Tutor, Royal College of Surgeons
USA:	Faculty Member, International Minimal Access Surgery Symposium, Kansas City

NORTHERN AND YORKSHIRE REGION

HULL

ROYSTON, Mr Christopher M. S.

Special interests:	**Upper gastroenterology; minimally invasive surgery**
NHS:	Consultant Surgeon
	Hull Royal Infirmary
	Anlaby Road
	Hull HU3 2JZ
Tel:	01482 674 708
Fax:	01482 586 560
Private:	43 Newland Park
	Hull HU5 2DN
Tel:	01482 342314
First Qualified:	1965 – London
Major Degrees:	FRCS
Specialist Training:	Hammersmith Hospital, London

LEEDS

JOHNSTON, Professor David

Special interests:	**Gastric Cancer – bringing survival rates for gastric cancer up from British 10 per cent to Japan's 50 per cent. Surgery for obesity – pioneered new operation 'Magenstrasse and Mill' procedure; Preservation of the anal sphincter, both for ulcerative cancer and ulcerative colitis**
NHS:	Honorary Consultant Surgeon
	General Infirmary at Leeds
	Great George Street
	Leeds LS1 3EX
Tel:	0113 292 3467
Fax:	0113 292 3635
Private:	Refer to address and number above
First Qualified:	1960 – Glasgow (with Honours and Brunton Prize)
Major Degrees:	MD, ChM, FRCS Ed, FRCS
Academic:	Professor of Surgery, Leeds University
Distinctions:	Previously Macewan Medal, Royal College Society, Glasgow

McMAHON, Professor Michael J.

Special interests:	**Gastrointestinal surgery**
NHS:	Director, Institute for Miminally Invasive Surgery
	General Infirmary at Leeds
	Great George Street
	Leeds LS1 3EX
Tel:	0113 2432799
Fax:	0113 2926305
Private:	Refer to address and number above
First Qualified:	1966 – Sheffield
Major Degrees:	PhD, ChM, FRCS
Academic:	Reader in Medicine, Leeds University

NEWCASTLE

LENNARD, Mr Thomas W. J.

Special interests:	**Breast cancer; surgical endocrinology and laparoscopic surgery**
NHS:	Consultant Surgeon
	Royal Victoria Infirmary
	Newcastle upon Tyne NE1 4LP
Tel:	0191 232 5131
Fax:	0191 232 5278
Private:	Refer to address and number above
First Qualified:	1977 – Newcastle
Major Degrees:	MD (Commendation), FRCS, FRCS Ed
Academic:	Senior Lecturer, Department of Surgery, Newcastle upon Tyne
Distinctions:	James IV Traveller
	Hunterian Professor, Royal College of Surgeons
	Moynihan Prize, Association of Surgeons
	Patey Prize, Surgical Research Society

NORTH WEST REGION

MANCHESTER

MacLENNAN, Mr Ian

NHS:	Consultant Surgeon
	Manchester Royal Infirmary
	Manchester M13 9WL
Tel:	0161 276 4170
Fax:	0161 276 4530
Private:	Refer to address and number above
First Qualified:	1967 – Manchester
Major Degrees:	FRCS, FRCS Ed
Academic:	Dean, Clinical Studies, Manchester University
Distinctions:	Councillor, Coloproctology Section, Royal Society of Medicine
USA:	Research Fellow and Instructor
	Harvard Medical School, Boston

LIVERPOOL

SUTTON, Mr Robert

Special interests:	**Minimally invasive anti-reflux surgery**
NHS:	Senior Lecturer in Surgery
	Department of Surgery
	University of Liverpool
	Liverpool L69 3BX
Tel:	0151 706 4187
Fax:	0151 706 5826
Private:	Refer to address and number above
First Qualified:	1980 – London
Major Degrees:	DPhil, FRCS
Academic:	Senior Lecturer, Liverpool University
Distinctions:	Jacksonian Prize and Hunterian Professor
	Royal College of Surgeons

SOUTH AND WEST REGION

BRISTOL

ESPINER, Mr Harry

Special interests:	**Development of minimal access surgery**
NHS:	Consultant Surgeon
	Bristol Royal Infirmary
	Maudlin Street
	Bristol BS2 8HW
Tel:	0117 928 2808
Fax:	0117 928 2000
Private:	2 Clifton Park
	Bristol BS8 3BS
Tel:	0117 973 3290
Fax:	0117 973 0887
First Qualified:	1955 – Otago, New Zealand
Major Degrees:	FRCS
Academic:	Previously Research Associate and Honorary Consultant Senior Lecturer, Bristol University;
Distinctions:	Moynihan Prize, Association of Surgeons of Great Britain and Ireland

PLYMOUTH

KINGSNORTH, Professor Andrew

Special interests:	**Pancreatitis; Barrett's oesophagus; hernia surgeon – introduced 'safer more durable technique from America which can be performed under local anaesthetic'**
NHS:	Professor of Surgery
	University of Plymouth
	Derriford Hospital
	Derriford Road
	Plymouth PL6 8DH
Tel:	01752 777111
Fax:	01752 768976
Private:	No private work
First Qualified:	1973 – London
Major Degrees:	MS, FRCS
Academic:	Previously Reader in Surgery, Liverpool University
Specialist Training:	Cape Town University, South Africa
Distinctions:	Committee member, Surgical Research Society; Member, Court of Examiners, Royal College of Surgeons of England; Secretary, Oesophaegeal Section, British Society of Gastroenterology
USA:	Harvard Medical School, Boston

WEST MIDLANDS

BIRMINGHAM

FIELDING, Mr John W. L.

Special interests:	**Surgical oncology: particularly gastric and breast cancer; gastrointestinal cancer**
NHS:	Consultant Surgeon
	Queen Elizabeth Hospital
	University Hospital Trust
	Edgbaston, Birmingham B15 2TH
Tel:	0121 627 2272
Fax:	0121 627 2273
Private:	Priory Hospital
	Priory Road
	Edgbaston B5 7UG
Tel:	0121 440 2323
First Qualified:	1971 – Birmingham
Major Degrees:	MD, FRCS
Academic:	Previously Senior Lecturer in Surgery
	Birmingham University
Specialist Training:	Queen Elizabeth Hospital, Birmingham
Distinctions:	Chairman, British Stomach Cancer Group
	British Representative on WHO for Gastric Cancer, Japan
	Council member, International Gastric Cancer Association

KEIGHLEY, Professor Michael Robert B.

Special interests:	**Inflammatory bowel disease; colorectal cancer; anorectal incontinence**
NHS:	Honorary Consultant General Surgeon and Barling Professor of Surgery Queen Elizabeth Hospital Queen Elizabeth Medical Centre Edgbaston Birmingham B15 2TH
Tel:	0121 472 1311 or 0121 627 2275
Fax:	0121 472 1230
Private:	Consulting Suites Priory Hospital Priory Road Edgbaston, Birmingham B5 7UG
Tel:	0121 440 2323 Ext. 2123
Fax:	0121 446 5686
First Qualified:	1967 – London
Major Degrees:	FRCS, FRCS Ed
Academic:	Barling Professor of Surgery and Head, University Department of Surgery Birmingham University
Distinctions:	President, Coloproctology Section, Royal Society of Medicine Previously Hunterian Professor, Royal College of Surgeons; Prize, Royal College, Penman Memorial Professor of Surgery, Cape Town University, The Sir Alan Parks Professor, St Mark's Hospital, London
USA:	Harvard Professor of Surgery 1991

SCOTLAND

DUNDEE

CUSCHIERI, Professor Alfred

Special interests:	**Minimally invasive gastroenterology; cancer; pancreatic and hepatobiliary surgery**
NHS:	Professor of Surgery Department of Surgery Ninewells Hospital and Medical School Dundee DD1 9SY
Tel:	01382 660111 Ext. 2174
Fax:	01382 641795
Private:	Refer to address and number above
First Qualified:	1961 – Malta
Major Degrees:	ChM, FRCS Ed, FRCS
Academic:	Professor of Surgery, Dundee University
Distinctions:	Moynihan Prize

GENITO-URINARY PHYSICIANS

These doctors diagnose and treat all aspects of genito-urinary medicine including chronic genital infections and sexually transmitted diseases. Surgery is performed by a urologist.

LONDON AND THE SOUTH EAST

ADLER, Professor Michael W.

Special interests:	**Sexually transmitted diseases**
NHS:	Professor of Genito-Urinary Medicine
	University College London Medical School
	The Mortimer Market Centre
	off Capper Street
	London WC1E 6AU
Tel:	0171 380 9660
Fax:	0171 380 9669
Private:	Refer to address and number above
First Qualified:	1965 – London
Major Degrees:	MD, FFCM, FRCP
Academic:	Professor of Genito-Urinary Medicine
	University College London Medical School
Specialist Training:	The Middlesex Hospital, London

BARLOW, Dr David

Special interests:	**Gonorrhoea**
NHS:	Consultant Physician, Genito-Urinary Medicine
	St Thomas' Hospital
	Lambeth Palace Road
	London SE1 7EH
Tel:	0171 928 9292 Ext. 2849
Fax:	0171 620 0903
Private:	Refer to address and number above
First Qualified:	1969 – Oxford
Major Degrees:	MPPF, FRCP
Specialist Training:	St Thomas' Hospital, London
Distinctions:	Councillor, Medical Society for Venereal Disease

BARTON, Dr Simon E.

Special interests:	**Sexual health problems especially chronic vulvo vaginal problems in women**
NHS:	Consultant in Genito-Urinary and HIV Medicine
	Chelsea and Westminster Hospital
	369 Fulham Road
	London SW10 9TH
Tel:	0181 846 6184
Fax:	0181 846 6198
Private:	Lister Hospital
	Chelsea Bridge Road
	London SW1W 8RH
Tel:	0171 730 3417
Fax:	0171 259 9218
First Qualified:	1987 – London
Major Degrees:	MD, MRCOG
Specialist Training:	St Mary's, Westminster and St Stephen's Hospitals, London

---

BINGHAM, Dr James S.

Special interests:	**Herpes; genital warts and HIV infection**
NHS:	Consultant, Genito-Urinary Medicine
	St Thomas' Hospital
	Lambeth Palace Road
	London SE1 7EH
Tel:	0171 928 9292 Ext. 1696
Fax:	0171 922 8291
Private:	Consulting Rooms
	York House
	199 Westminster Bridge Road
	London SE1 7UT
Tel:	0171 928 5485
Fax:	See fax number above
First Qualified:	1969 – Belfast
Major Degrees:	FRCOG, FRCP Ed
Specialist Training:	The Middlesex Hospital, London, and Vancouver, Canada

---

BOAG, Dr Fiona C.

Special interests:	**Including psychosocial aspects of sexually transmitted disease**
NHS:	Consultant Physician
	Department Genito-Urinary Medicine
	Chelsea and Westminster Hospital
	369 Fulham Road
	London SW10 9TH
Tel:	0181 746 5625
Fax:	0181 846 6198
Private:	Refer to address and number above
First Qualified:	1980 – London
Major Degrees:	MRCP
Specialist Training:	Royal Free and University College Hospitals, London

BRADBEER, Dr Caroline S.

Special interests:	**Women's genital problems, including irritation and abnormalities of the cervix**
NHS:	Consultant Physician
	Department of Genito-Urinary Medicine
	St Thomas' Hospital
	Lambeth Palace Road
	London SE1 7EH
Tel:	0171 928 9292 Ext. 1696
Fax:	0171 922 8291
Private:	Refer to address and number above
First Qualified:	1979 – London
Major Degrees:	FRCP
Specialist Training:	St Thomas' Hospital, London

EVANS, Dr Brian A.

Special interests:	**Sexually transmitted diseases; HIV**
NHS:	Director, Genito-Urinary Medicine Clinic
	Charing Cross Hospital
	Fulham Palace Road
	London W6 8RF
Tel:	0181 846 1577
Fax:	0181 846 7582
Private:	Refer to address and number above
First Qualified:	1959 – London
Major Degrees:	FRCP
Specialist Training:	The Middlesex Hospital, London
Distinctions:	Previously President, Medical Society for Venereal Disease

HARRIS, Dr John W.

Special interests:	**Sexually transmitted diseases; prostatitis and sexual dysfunction**
NHS:	Consultant in Venerology and Genito-Urinary Medicine St Mary's Hospital Praed Street London W2 1NY
Tel:	0171 725 6754/6630
Fax:	0171 725 6617
Private:	77 Harley Street London W1N 1DE
Tel:	0171 486 4166
Fax:	0171 725 6617
First Qualified:	1967 – Belfast
Major Degrees:	FRCP
Specialist Training:	King's College Hospital, London
USA:	Visiting Consultant, VD Control Center, Atlanta, Georgia

HAWKINS, Dr David A.

Special interests:	**HIV testing; management of HIV disease; diagnosis and treatment of all types of genital infections including chlamydial (nongonococcal) infections**
NHS:	Consultant, Genito-Urinary Medicine Chelsea and Westminster Hospital 369 Fulham Road London SW10 9TH
Tel:	0181 846 6158
Fax:	0181 846 6198
Private:	Cromwell Hospital Cromwell Road London SW5 OTU
Tel:	0171 370 4223
Fax:	0171 370 4063
First Qualified:	1977 – London
Major Degrees:	FRCP
Specialist Training:	Northwick Park, The Middlesex, and St Mary's Hospitals, London

KITCHEN, Dr Valerie S.

Special interests:	**Cervical and vaginal infections**
NHS:	Senior Lecturer and Consultant
	Genito-Urinary Medicine and Communicable Diseases
	St Mary's Hospital
	London W2 1NY
Tel:	0171 725 6604
Fax:	0171 725 6604
Private:	Lister Hospital
	Chelsea Bridge Road
	London SW1W 8RH
Tel:	0181 846 7886
Fax:	0181 846 7886
First Qualified:	1981 – Leicester
Major Degrees:	MRCP
Academic:	Senior Lecturer, Genito-Urinary Medicine and
	Communicable Diseases, St Mary's Hospital, London
Specialist Training:	St Mary's Hospital, London
USA:	Visiting Associate Professor, Department of Obstetrics
	and Gynaecology, New York University Medical Centre
	(January 1996 – April 1996)

LIM, Dr Frederick T. K. S.

Special interests:	**Sexually transmitted hepatitis, viral infections**
	and non-surgical gynaecological and urological
	problems
NHS:	No NHS work
Private:	Flat 6, 26 Devonshire Place
	London W1N 1PD
Tel:	0171 487 3529
Fax:	0171 224 1784
First Qualified:	1971 – London
Major Degrees:	MRCP
Specialist Training:	The Middlesex and Charing Cross Hospitals, London
Distinctions:	Previously Consultant in Genito-Urinary Medicine,
	King's College Hospital, London

McMANUS, Dr Thomas J.

Special interests:	**HIV infection**
NHS:	Consultant Genito-Urinary Physician
	King's College Hospital
	Denmark Hill
	London SE5 9RS
Tel:	0171 346 3470
Fax:	0171 346 3486
Private:	Refer to address and number above
First Qualified:	1972 – Glasgow
Major Degrees:	FRCOG, FRCP
Distinctions:	Secretary, Medical Society for Venereal Disease

SIMMONS, Dr Paul D.

Special interests:	**Hepatitis B in homosexuals; chlamydial infection; genital warts; prostatitis**
NHS:	Consultant Physician in Charge
	Department of Genito-Urinary Medicine
	St Bartholomew's Hospital
	West Smithfield
	London EC1 7BE
Tel:	0171 601 8092
Fax:	0171 601 8601
Private:	Refer to address and number above
First Qualified:	1971 – Leeds
Major Degrees:	MB, FRCP
Specialist Training:	St Bartholomew's and St Thomas' Hospitals, London
Distinctions:	Honorary Medical Consultant, Society of Health Advisors in Sexually Transmitted Diseases

SYMONDS, Dr Michael A. E.

NHS:	Consultant Physician in Genito-Urinary Medicine
	Herts and Essex Hospital
	Haymeads Lane
	Bishop's Stortford
	Herts CM23 5JH
Tel:	01279 444455 Ext. 4158
Fax:	01279 651399
Private:	Refer to address and number above
First Qualified:	1958 – London
Major Degrees:	FRCP
Specialist Training:	St Thomas' Hospital, London
Distinctions:	Previously, Honorary Consultant in Genito-Urinary Medicine, St Thomas' Hospital, London

THIN, Dr R. Nicol

Special interests:	**Sexually transmitted diseases**
NHS:	Consultant, Genito-Urinary Medicine
	St Thomas' Hospital
	Lambeth Palace Road
	London SE1 7EH
Tel:	0171 928 9292 Ext. 1696
Fax:	0171 922 8291
Private:	Refer to address and number above
First Qualified:	1959 – Edinburgh
Major Degrees:	MD, FRCP Ed, FRCP
Distinctions:	Ex-President, Medical Society for Venereal Disease

WELCH, Dr Jan M.

Special interests:	**Women's sexual health including the management of women who have been sexually assaulted, and HIV disease in women**
NHS:	Consultant Genito-Urinary Physician King's College Hospital Denmark Hill London SE5 9RS
Tel:	0171 346 3478
Fax:	0171 346 3486
Private:	Refer to address and number above
First Qualified:	1980 – London
Major Degrees:	FRCP
Specialist Training:	St Thomas' Hospital, London

NORTH WEST REGION

CHESTER

O'MAHONEY, Dr Colm

NHS:	Department of Genito-Urinary Medicine Chester Royal Infirmary St Martin's Way Chester CH1 2AZ
Tel:	01244 363091
Fax:	01244 636095
Private:	Refer to address and number above
First Qualified:	1981 – Dublin
Major Degrees:	MD, MRCP
Academic:	Postgraduate Clinical Tutor, Liverpool University Honorary Clinical Teacher, Wales University
Distinctions:	Councillor, Welsh Section, Medical Society for Venereal Disease

LIVERPOOL

CAREY, Dr Peter

Special interests:	**Sexually transmitted disease**
NHS:	Consultant in Genito-Urinary Medicine
	Royal Liverpool University Hospital
	Prescot Street
	Liverpool L7 8XP
Tel:	0151 706 2000 Ext. 2647
Fax:	0151 706 5806
Private:	Refer to address and number above
First Qualified:	1970 – Liverpool
Major Degrees:	FRCP

TRENT REGION

SHEFFIELD

KINGHORN, Dr George

Special interests:	**HIV**
NHS:	Consultant in Genito-Urinary Medicine
	Royal Hallamshire Hospital
	Glossop Road
	Sheffield S10 2JF
Tel:	0114 276 6928
Fax:	0114 275 9081
Private:	Refer to address and number above
First Qualified:	1972 – Sheffield
Major Degrees:	MD, FRCP
Distinctions:	Clinical Director, Communicable Disease Centre, Sheffield University Hospital
	Chairman Royal College of Physicians, Genito-Urinary Medicine Committee
	Chairman Trent Regional ASC in Genito-Urinary Medicine

WEST MIDLANDS

BIRMINGHAM

SHAHMANESH, Dr Mohsen

NHS:	Consultant in Genito-Urinary Medicine
	Department of Genito-Urinary Medicine
	Whittal Street
	Birmingham B4 6D
Tel:	0121 236 8611
Fax:	0121 233 9810
Private:	Refer to address and number above
First Qualified:	1965 – London
Major Degrees:	MD, FRCP

REDDITCH

GODLEY, Dr Margaret Joan

NHS:	Consultant in Genito-Urinary Medicine
	The Alexandra Hospital
	Redditch
	Worcestershire B98 7UB
Tel:	01527 503030 Ext. 4095
Fax:	01527 517432
Private:	Refer to address and number above
First Qualified:	1976 – Liverpool
Major Degrees:	MRCOG
Distinctions:	Honorary Secretary, Association of Genito-Urinary Medicine

GERIATRICIANS

Geriatricians specialise in the diagnosis and management of problems of the elderly. They have special training in preventive and rehabilitative care. Many afflictions of the elderly are caused by mental conditions, which are treated by Old Age Psychiatrists, who are listed under the Psychiatrists section.

LONDON AND THE SOUTH EAST

BEYNON, Dr Gareth

NHS:	No NHS work
Private:	King Edward VII Hospital for Officers
	Beaumont Street
	London W1N 2AA
Tel:	01923 852329
Fax:	01923 852329
and:	St John and St Elizabeth Hospital
	Grove End Road
	London NW8 9NH
First Qualified:	1964 – Cambridge
Major Degrees:	FRCP
Specialist Training:	The Middlesex Hospital, London

CROKER, Dr John

NHS:	Consultant Physician and Geriatrician
	University College Hospital
	25 Grafton Way
	London WC1E 6DB
Tel:	0171 380 9910
Fax:	0171 380 9652
Private:	152 Harley Street
	London W1N 1HH
Tel:	0171 935 8868
Fax:	0171 224 2574
First Qualified:	1970 – Oxford
Major Degrees:	FRCP
Academic:	Senior Lecturer, University College and Middlesex School of Medicine, London
Specialist Training:	St Thomas' and The Middlesex Hospitals, London

YOUNG, Professor Archie

Special interests:	**Exercise and rehabilitation especially concerning muscle structure and function**
NHS:	Professor of Geriatric Medicine
	Royal Free Hospital
	Pond Street
	London NW3 2QG
Tel:	0171 794 0500 Ext. 5240
Fax:	0171 830 2202
Private:	Refer to address and number above
First Qualified:	1971 – Glasgow (with Honours)
Major Degrees:	FRCP, FRCP Glas
Academic:	Visiting Professor, Zimbabwe University
Specialist Training:	Hammersmith Hospital, London
Distinctions:	Eli Lilley Prize Lecturer

ANGLIA AND OXFORD REGION

CAMBRIDGE

WEBSTER, Dr Stephen G. P.

Special interests:	**Techniques for avoiding disability in old age; management of acute and chronic illness in later life**
NHS:	Consultant Physician, Geriatric Medicine
	Addenbrooke's Hospital
	Hills Road
	Cambridge CB2 2QQ
Tel:	01223 245151 Ext. 3599
Fax:	01223 217783
Private:	Refer to address and number above
First Qualified:	1964 – London
Major Degrees:	MD FRCP
Academic:	Associate Lecturer in Faculty of Medicine
	Cambridge University

NORTHERN AND YORKSHIRE REGION

KEIGHLEY

HARRINGTON, Dr Mary G.

NHS:	Consultant Physician in Medicine for the Elderly
	Airedale General Hospital
	Skipton Road
	Steeton
	Keighley, West Yorkshire BD20 8TT
Tel:	01535 652511
Fax:	01535 655207
Private:	Refer to address and number above
First Qualified:	1976 – London
Major Degrees:	FRCP
Academic:	Previously Honorary Senior Lecturer, King's College School of Medicine and Dentistry, London
Specialist Training:	The Middlesex and University College Hospitals, London

HAEMATOLOGISTS

These physicians treat diseases of the blood, spleen and lymph glands such as anaemia. Other areas covered include clotting disorders, sickle cell disease, haemophilia, leukaemia and lymphoma. In some leukaemia units the clinical haematologist carries the major responsibility for the management of patients with leukaemia.

LONDON AND THE SOUTH EAST

CATOVSKY, Professor Daniel

Special interests:	**Leukaemia**
NHS:	Honorary Consultant Physician
	Royal Marsden Hospital
	Fulham Road
	London SW3 6JJ
Tel:	0171 352 8171 Ext. 2875
Fax:	0171 351 6420
Private:	Refer to address and number above
First Qualified:	1961 – Buenos Aires
Major Degrees:	FRCP, FRCPath
Academic:	Professor of Haematology, Institute of Cancer Research, Royal Marsden Hospital, London

GOLDMAN, Professor John M.

Special interests:	**Leukaemia**
NHS:	Chairman, Department of Haematology
	Director, Centre for Adult Leukaemia
	Hammersmith Hospital
	Du Cane Road
	London W12 ONN
Tel:	0181 740 3238
Fax:	0181 740 9679
Private:	Refer to address and number above
First Qualified:	1963 – London
Major Degrees:	DM, FRCP, FRCPath
Academic:	Professor of Leukaemia Biology, Royal Postgraduate Medical School, London
Specialist Training:	Royal Postgraduate Medical School and St Bartholomew's Hospitals, London
USA:	Lately, Fellow in Medicine, Miami University, Florida, and Massachusetts General Hospital, Boston

GOLDSTONE, Dr Anthony H.

Special interests: **Leukaemia; bone marrow transplants; paediatric cancer**
NHS: Consultant Haematologist
University College London
Gower Street
London WC1E 6AU
Tel: 0171 387 9300
Fax: 0171 387 9977
Private: Private Patients Wing
University College Hospital
Grafton Way
London WC1
Tel: 0171 387 9709
Fax: 0171 380 9816
First Qualified: 1968 – Oxford
Major Degrees: FRCP
Academic: Previously Postgraduate Dean, University College Hospital Medical School
Specialist Training: Addenbrooke's Hospital, Cambridge
Cancer Research Institute

HOFFBRAND, Professor A. Victor

Special interests: **General haematology; leukaemia and lymphoma**
NHS: Consultant Physician
Royal Free Hospital
Pond Street
London NW3 2QG
Tel: 0171 794 0500 Ext. 3258
Fax: 0171 431 4537
Private: Refer to address and number above
First Qualified: 1959 – Oxford
Major Degrees: DSc, DM, FRCP, FRCPath
Academic: Professor of Haematology, Royal Free Hospital Medical School
Previously, Senior Lecturer, Royal Postgraduate Medical School, London
Specialist Training: Royal Postgraduate Medical School and Hammersmith Hospitals, London

LEE, Dr Christine A.

Special interests:	**Investigation and treatment of bleeding and thrombotic disorders; haemophilia**
NHS:	Consultant Haematologist Haemophilia Centre Royal Free Hospital Pond Street London NW3 2QG
Tel:	0171 794 0500 Ext. 3808 or 0171 830 2238
Fax:	0171 830 2178
Private:	Refer to address and number above
First Qualified:	1969 – Oxford
Major Degrees:	MA, MD, FRCPath
Specialist Training:	Royal Free, Westminster and Charing Cross Hospitals, London

MURPHY, Dr Michael F.

Special interests:	**General haematology; blood transfusion; immune thrombocytopenias including the antenatal management of alloimmune neonatal thrombocytopenia**
NHS:	Senior Lecturer and Consultant Haematologist St Bartholomew's Hospital West Smithfield London EC1A 7BE
Tel:	0171 601 8888 Ext. 8216
Fax:	0171 601 8200
Private:	Refer to address and number above
First Qualified:	1973 – London
Major Degrees:	MD, FRCP, FRCPath
Distinctions:	Previously Secretary, British Committee for Standards in Haematology Currently Member of Blood Transfusion Task Force of the British Society for Haematology

ANGLIA AND OXFORD REGION

CAMBRIDGE

MARCUS, Dr Robert

Special interests:	**Leukaemia; lymphoma; myeloma; Hodgkin's disease; bone marrow and peripheral transplantation**
NHS:	Consultant Haematologist and Director East Anglia Bone Marrow Transplant Unit Department of Haematology Addenbrooke's Hospital Hills Road Cambridge CB2 2QQ
Tel:	01223 217071
Fax:	01223 217017
Private:	Evelyn Hospital 4 Trumpington Road Cambridge CB2 2AF
Tel:	01223 303336
Fax:	Use above fax number
First Qualified:	1977 – London
Major Degrees:	FRCP, FRCPath
Academic:	Honorary Senior Lecturer, Cambridge University
Specialist Training:	Royal Postgraduate Medical School, Royal Free and University College Hospitals, London
Distinctions:	Director, East Anglian Bone Marrow Transplant Unit

HEPATOLOGISTS

(Liver Physicians)

These physicians cover all diseases related to the liver.

LONDON AND THE SOUTH EAST

BURROUGHS, Dr Andrew K.

Special interests:	**Liver and biliary disease; liver transplantation**
NHS:	Consultant Physician
	Hepato-Biliary and Liver Transplantation Unit
	Royal Free Hospital
	Pond Street
	London NW3 3QG
Tel:	0171 794 0500 Ext. 3978
Fax:	0171 794 4688
Private:	Refer to address and number above
First Qualified:	1976 – Liverpool
Major Degrees:	MD, FRCS
Academic:	Senior Lecturer, Royal Free Hospital, London
Distinctions:	Councillor, British Association for the Study of the Liver, British Society of Gastroenterology
USA:	Member, American Association of the Study of the Liver

MAXWELL, Dr J. Douglas

Special interests:	**Gastroenterology; liver disease**
NHS:	Consultant Physician
	St George's Hospital
	Blackshaw Road
	London SW17 0QT
Tel:	0181 672 1255 Ext. 1541
Fax:	0181 725 3520
Private:	Refer to address and number above
First Qualified:	1964 – Glasgow
Major Degrees:	MD, FRCP
Academic:	Clinical Dean and Reader in Medicine St George's Hospital Medical School, London
Specialist Training:	King's College and St George's Hospitals, London
USA:	Previously Research Fellow, University of California Medical School, San Francisco

MURRAY-LYON, Dr Iain M.

Special interests:	**All aspects of liver disease particularly chronic viral liver disease, alcohol and liver damage, and liver tumours**
NHS:	Consultant Physician and Gastroenterologist
	Department of Gastroenterology
	Chelsea and Westminster Hospital
	369 Fulham Road
	London SW10 9NH
Tel:	0181 746 8000
Fax:	0171 746 8111
Private:	149 Harley Street
	London W1N 2DH
Tel:	0171 935 6747 or 0171 935 4444
Fax:	0171 935 7017
First Qualified:	1964 – Edinburgh (with Honours)
Major Degrees:	MD, FRCP
Specialist Training:	Royal Infirmary Edinburgh, Liver Unit, King's College Hospital, London

THOMAS, Professor Howard C.

Special interests:	**Hepatitis B and C; primary liver cancer**
NHS:	Consultant Physician and Director, Hepatology Unit
	St Mary's Hospital
	Praed Street
	London W2 1PG
Tel:	0171 725 6454
Fax:	0171 724 9369
Private:	Refer to address and number above
First Qualified:	1969 – Newcastle
Major Degrees:	PhD, FRCP, FRCPS, FRCPath
Academic:	Professor of Medicine, St Mary's Hospital, London
Specialist Training:	Glasgow, and Royal Free, London
Distinctions:	President-Elect, British and European Associations for the Study of the Liver

THOMPSON, Dr Richard P. H.

Special interests:	**Liver disease**
NHS:	Consultant Physician
	The Rayne Institute
	St Thomas' Hospital
	London SE1 7EH
Tel:	0171 928 9292 Ext. 2650
Fax:	0171 922 8079
Private:	Consulting Rooms
	York House
	199 Westminster Bridge Road
	London SE1 7UT
Tel:	0171 928 5485
Fax:	0171 928 3748
First Qualified:	1964 – Oxford
Major Degrees:	DM, FRCP
Academic:	Senior Lecturer, Liver Unit, King's College Hospital
Distinctions:	Physician to HM the Queen
	Previously Physician to the Royal Household
	MRC Clinical Research Fellow
USA:	Research Assistant, Gastroenterology Unit, Mayo Clinic, Rochester, Minnesota

WESTABY, Dr David

Special interests:	**Endoscopic investigation**
NHS:	Consultant Physician and Gastroenterologist
	Chelsea and Westminster Hospital
	369 Fulham Road
	London SW10 9NH
Tel:	0181 746 8000
Fax:	0181 746 8100
Private:	Cromwell Hospital
	Cromwell Road
	London SW5 OTU
Tel:	0171 370 4233 Ext. 5081
Fax:	0171 835 1573
First Qualified:	1976 – Cambridge
Major Degrees:	FRCP
Specialist Training:	King's College Hospital, London

WILLIAMS, Professor Roger, CBE

NHS:	Director of the Institute of Liver Studies
	King's College Hospital
	Bessemer Road
	London SE5 9PJ
Tel:	0171 346 3254
Fax:	0171 346 3167
Private:	Cromwell Hospital
	Cromwell Road
	London SW5 0TU
Tel:	0171 370 4233
Fax:	0171 244 8176
and:	Private Wing
	King's College Hospital
First Qualified:	1953 – London
Major Degrees:	MD, FRCP, FRCS
Specialist Training:	Royal Postgraduate Medical School and Royal Free Hospitals, London
Distinctions:	Consultant in Medicine to the Army and the Liver Research Trust
USA:	Lately Fellow, Columbia Presbyterian Hospital, New York

ZEEGEN, Dr Ronald, OBE

Special interests:	**Gall bladder, pancreas and gut; liver problems**
NHS:	Consultant Physician and Gastroenterologist
	Chelsea and Westminster Hospital
	369 Fulham Road
	London SW10 9NH
Tel:	0181 746 8106
Fax:	0181 746 8100
Private:	Lister Hospital
	Chelsea Bridge Road
	London SW1W 8RH
Tel:	0171 730 3417
Fax:	0171 824 8867
and:	Chelsea and Westminster Hospital
	369 Fulham Road
	London SW10 9NH
First Qualified:	1962 – London
Major Degrees:	FRCP
Specialist Training:	Westminster and St Bartholomew's Hospitals, London

ANGLIA AND OXFORD REGION

OXFORD

CHAPMAN, Dr Roger W.

Special interests:	**Cholestatic liver disease**
NHS:	Consultant Gastroenterologist
	John Radcliffe Hospital
	Headley Way, Headington
	Oxford OX3 9DU
Tel:	01865 220618
Fax:	01865 751100
Private:	23 Banbury Road
	Oxford
Tel:	01865 515036
First Qualified:	1973 – London
Major Degrees:	MD, FRCP
Academic:	Honorary Senior Lecturer in Medicine
	Oxford University Medical School
	Previously Lecturer in Medicine, Royal Free Hospital, London
Specialist Training:	Southampton General Hospital and Royal Free Hospital, London
Distinctions:	Previously Secretary/Treasurer, British Association for the Study of the Liver
	Associate Editor, Gut
	Frewin Award, Clinical Research 1984
USA:	Previously Visiting Scientist, Washington University, Seattle

SCOTLAND

EDINBURGH

FINLAYSON, Dr Niall D. C.

Special interests:	**Liver Disease**
NHS:	Clinical Director and Consultant Physician
	Centre for Liver and Digestive Disorders
	Edinburgh Royal Infirmary
	1 Lauriston Place
	Edinburgh EH3 9YW
Tel:	0131 536 2178
Fax:	0131 536 2197
Private:	No private work
First Qualified:	1964 – Edinburgh
Major Degrees:	PhD, FRCP, FRCP Ed
Academic:	Honorary Senior Lecturer in Medicine
	Edinburgh University
Specialist Training:	Previously New York Hospital, Cornell Medical Center, New York

HEPATO-PANCREATO-BILIARY SURGEONS

These surgeons operate on the liver, gall bladder, bile duct and pancreas.

LONDON AND SOUTH EAST

BENJAMIN, Professor Irving S.

Special interests:	**Liver cancer**
NHS:	Professor of Surgery
	King's College Hospital
	Denmark Hill
	London SE5 9RS
Tel:	0171 346 3017
Fax:	0171 346 3438
Private:	Refer to address and number above
First Qualified:	1971 – Glasgow
Major Degrees:	MD, FRCS
Academic:	Professor of Surgery, King's College School of Medicine, London
Specialist Training:	Groote Schuur Hospital, Cape Town, South Africa
	Royal Postgraduate Medical School, London
Distinctions:	Honorary Consultant in Surgery, Royal Postgraduate Medical School and Hammersmith Hospital, London

HOBBS, Professor Kenneth E. F.

Special interests:	**Hepatobiliary pancreatic surgery**
NHS:	Professor of Surgery and Consultant Surgeon
	Royal Free Hospital
	Pond Street
	London NW3 2QG
Tel:	0171 435 6121
Fax:	0171 431 4528
Private:	Refer to address and number above
First Qualified:	1960 – London
Major Degrees:	ChM, FRCS
Academic:	Professor of Surgery, Royal Free Hospital School of Medicine, London University, since 1974
	Previously Consultant Senior Lecturer in Surgery Bristol University
Distinctions:	Previously Honorary Fellow, Sri Lanka College of Surgeons; International Master Surgeon, International College of Surgeons; Honorary Member, Hellenic Surgical Surgical Society
USA:	Previously Research Fellow, Harvard Medical School, Boston

KNIGHT, Mr Michael J.

Special interests:	**Pancreatic and biliary surgery**
NHS:	Consultant Surgeon
	St George's Hospital
	Blackshaw Road
	London SW17 OQT
Tel:	0181 672 1255
Fax:	0181 672 8114
Private:	135 Harley Street
	London W1N 1DJ
Tel:	0171 487 3501
Fax:	0171 935 3148
First Qualified:	1963 – London
Major Degrees:	MS, FRCS
Academic:	Previously Hunterian Professor, Royal College of Surgeons
	Honorary Senior Lecturer, St George's Hospital Medical School, London
Specialist Training:	St George's Hospital, London
Distinctions:	Previously President, Pancreatic Society
	Member, Court of Examiners, Royal College of Surgeons
	Examiner in Surgery, London University
USA:	Research Fellow in Surgery, Washington University, St Louis, Missouri

RUSSELL, Mr R. Christopher G.

Special interests:	**Pancreatic and biliary surgery**
NHS:	Consultant Surgeon
	The Middlesex Hospital
	Mortimer Street
	London W1N 8AA
Tel:	0171 636 8333 Ext. 9202
Fax:	0171 380 9162
Private:	149 Harley Street
	London W1N 2DE
Tel:	0171 486 1164
Fax:	0171 487 5997
First Qualified:	1963 – London
Major Degrees:	MS, FRCS
Specialist Training:	St Mary's and Central Middlesex Hospitals, London

WILLIAMSON, Professor Robin C. N.

Special interests:	**Pancreatic and biliary surgery**
NHS:	Director of Surgery
	Hammersmith Hospital
	Du Cane Road
	London W12 OHS
Tel:	0181 740 3210
Fax:	0181 740 3023
Private:	Refer to address and number above
First Qualified:	1968 – Cambridge (1st class honours)
Major Degrees:	MD, MChir, FRCS
Academic:	Professor of Surgery, Royal Postgraduate Medical School, London
	Previously Professor of Surgery, Bristol University
Specialist Training:	United Hospitals, Bristol, and Harvard Medical School and Massachusetts General Hospital, Boston, USA
Distinctions:	Editor, *British Journal of Surgery*
	Research Medal, British Society of Gastroenterology; Hallett Prize, Hunterian Professor and Arris and Gale Lecturer, Royal College of Surgeons
USA:	Previously Fulbright Fellow, Harvard, and Massachusetts General Hospital, Boston

---

WEST MIDLANDS

BIRMINGHAM

BUCKELS, Mr John Anthony Charles

Special interests:	**Pancreatic and hepatobiliary surgery; liver transplantation**
NHS:	Consultant Surgeon
	Liver Unit
	Queen Elizabeth Hospital
	Birmingham B15 2TH
Tel:	0121 627 2418
Fax:	0121 414 1833
Private:	Prior Hospital
	Priory Road
	Edgbaston, Birmingham B5 7UG
Tel:	0121 440 2323
First Qualified:	1972 – Birmingham
Major Degrees:	MD, FRCS
Academic:	Senior Clinical Lecturer, Birmingham University
Specialist Training:	Birmingham and West Midlands
USA:	Previously Research Fellow, UCLA Medical Centre, Los Angeles

---

SCOTLAND

EDINBURGH

CARTER, Professor David C.

Special interests:	**Hepatobiliary and pancreatic surgery**
NHS:	Honorary Consultant Surgeon
	Royal Infirmary
	Lauriston Place
	Edinburgh EH3 9YW
Tel:	0131 536 3812
Fax:	0131 228 2661
Private:	No private work
First Qualified:	1964 – St Andrews
Major Degrees:	MD, FRCS, FRCP, FRS Ed
Academic:	Regius Professor of Clinical Surgery
Specialist Training:	Royal Infirmary of Edinburgh
USA:	Previously Senior Research Fellow, Center for Ulcer Research and Education, University of California at Los Angeles

GARDEN, Mr Oliver James

Special interests:	**Hepatobiliary surgery**
NHS:	Honorary Consultant Surgeon
	Scottish Liver Transplant Unit
	Clinical Director of Organ Transplantation
	University Department of Surgery
	Royal Infirmary
	Lauriston Place
	Edinburgh EH3 9YW
Tel:	0131 536 1000
Fax:	0131 228 2661
Private:	Refer to address and number above
First Qualified:	1977 – Edinburgh
Major Degrees:	MD, FRCS Ed
Academic:	Senior Lecturer, Edinburgh University

HIV/AIDS Physicians

Many physicians who treat HIV/AIDS are often specialists in allergy and immunology, as well as infectious disease and respiratory/chest physicians. See appendix 1(v) for a list of specialist units focusing on HIV/AIDS.

LONDON AND THE SOUTH EAST

BARTON, Dr Simon E.

Special interests:	**Sexual health problems especially chronic vulvo vaginal problems in women**
NHS:	Consultant in Genito-Urinary and HIV Medicine Chelsea and Westminster Hospital 369 Fulham Road London SW10 9TH
Tel:	0181 846 6184
Fax:	0181 846 6198
Private:	Lister Hospital Chelsea Bridge Road London SW1W 8RH
Tel:	0171 730 3417
Fax:	0171 259 9218
First Qualified:	1982 – London
Major Degrees:	MD, MRCOG
Specialist Training:	St Mary's, Westminster and St Stephen's Hospitals, London
Distinctions:	Co-author, *HIV and AIDS – Your Questions Answered*

GAZZARD, Dr Brian G.

Special interests:	**HIV/AIDS; gastroenterology**
NHS:	Consultant Physician Chelsea and Westminster Hospital 369 Fulham Road London SW10 9NH
Tel:	0181 746 8000
Fax:	0181 746 5611
Private:	Cromwell Hospital Cromwell Road London SW5
Tel:	0171 370 4233
Fax:	0171 244 6678
First Qualified:	1970 – Cambridge (with Honours)
Major Degrees:	MD, FRCP
Academic:	Lecturer, Liver Unit, King's College Hospital, London
Specialist Training:	St Bartholomew's and King's College Hospitals, London

GRIFFIN, Professor George E.

Special interests:	**HIV and the intestine**
NHS:	Honorary Consultant Physician and Professor of Infectious Diseases Division of Communicable Diseases St George's Hospital Blackshaw Road London SW17 0QT
Tel:	0181 672 9944
Fax:	0181 725 3487
Private:	Refer to address and number above
First Qualified:	1974 – London
Major Degrees:	PhD, FRCP, FRCP Ed
Academic:	Professor of Infectious Diseases, St George's Hospital Medical School
Specialist Training:	Hammersmith Hospital, London
USA:	Honorary Professor of Medicine, Michigan University Harkness Fellow, Harvard University, Boston

JOHNSON, Dr Margaret

Special interests:	**HIV disease; HIV testing; HIV in women**
NHS:	Clinical Director and Consultant Physician in Charge HIV/AIDS Clinic Royal Free Hospital Pond Street London NW3 2QG
Tel:	0171 794 0500 Ext. 3082 or 0171 830 2775
Fax:	0171 830 2201
Private:	Refer to address and number above
First Qualified:	1975 – London
Major Degrees:	MD, FRCP
Academic:	Honorary Senior Lecturer, Royal Free Hospital, London
Specialist Training:	Brompton Hospital, London
Distinctions:	Member, Expert Advisory Group on Aids

MAIN, Dr Janice

Special interests:	**Infectious diseases; HIV**
NHS:	Senior Lecturer and Consultant Physician
	Department of Medicine and Infectious Diseases
	St Mary's Hospital
	Praed Street
	London W2 INY
Tel:	0171 725 1926
Fax:	0171 724 9369
Private:	Lindo Wing – as above and refer to number above
First Qualified:	1980 – Dundee
Major Degrees:	FRCP Ed, FRCP
Academic:	Senior Lecturer in Infectious Diseases
	St Mary's Hospital Medical School, London
Specialist Training:	St Mary's Hospital, London
Distinctions:	Jean Tulloch Award (Top Female Graduate), Alexander Prize in Surgery
	Tulloch Prize for contributions to infectious diseases

PINCHING, Professor Anthony J.

Special interests:	**HIV/AIDS**
NHS:	Professor of Immunology
	St Bartholomew's Hospital
	West Smithfield
	London EC1A 7BE
Tel:	0171 601 8428
Fax:	0171 600 3839
Private:	Refer to address and number above
First Qualified:	1973 – Oxford
Major Degrees:	FRCP
Academic:	Professor of Immunology, St Bartholomew's Medical School, London;
Specialist Training:	Royal Postgraduate Medical School and St Mary's Hospitals, London

POZNIAC, Dr Anton

NHS:	Consultant Physician, HIV/AIDS Clinic
	King's College Hospital
	Denmark Hill
	London SE5 9RS
Tel:	0171 346 3687
Fax:	0171 346 3723
Private:	Refer to address and telephone number above
First Qualified:	London
Major Degrees:	MD, FRCP
Specialist Training:	Middlesex and King's College Hospitals, London

ANGLIA AND OXFORD REGION

CONLON, Dr Christopher Peter

Special interests:	**HIV; tropical medicine; infections associated with prosthetic material; home intravenous antibiotic administration; general infectious diseases**
NHS:	Consultant Physician in Infectious Diseases Nuffield Department of Medicine John Radcliffe Hospital Headley Way Oxford OX3 9DU
Tel:	01865 220154
Fax:	01865 222901
e-mail:	chris.conlon@ndm.ox.ac.uk
Private:	No private work
First Qualified:	1980 – London
Major Degrees:	MD, MRCP
Academic:	Previously Research Fellow, Department of Immunology, St Marys Hospital, London Previously Visiting Lecturer, Zimbabwe University Previously Lecturer, University of Zambia
Specialist Training:	East Birmingham Hospital, St Mary's Hospital, London, and John Radcliffe Hospital, Oxford

NORTH WEST REGION

LIVERPOOL

BEECHING, Mr Nicholas John

Special interests:	**HIV including tropical disease aspects; infections related to drug abuse**
NHS:	Honorary Consultant Physician Infectious Diseases Unit Fazakerley Hospital Liverpool L9 7AL
Tel:	0151 529 3833
Fax:	0151 529 3762
and:	Liverpool School of Tropical Medicine Pembroke Place Liverpool L3 5QA
Tel:	0151 708 9393
Fax:	0151 708 8733
First Qualified:	1977 – Oxford
Major Degrees:	FRCP, FRACP, DCH, DTM
Academic:	Senior Clinical Lecturer in Infectious Diseases, Liverpool School of Tropical Medicine
Specialist Training:	Liverpool, Birmingham, and Auckland, New Zealand

SQUIRE, Dr S. Bertel

Special Interests:	**Tuberculosis; clinical management of HIV/AIDS**
NHS:	Tropical Physician
	Liverpool School of Tropical Medicine
	Pembroke Place
	Liverpool L36 5QA
Tel:	0151 708 9393
Fax:	0151 708 8733
Private:	Refer to address and number above
First Qualified:	1984 – Cambridge
Major Degrees:	MD, MRCP
Distinctions:	Wellcome Trust Fellow, Royal Free Hospital, London

MANCHESTER

BIBHAT, Dr Mandal K.

NHS:	Consultant Physician in Infectious Diseases and Tropical medicine
	North Manchester General Hospital;
	Delaunays Road
	Crumpsall, Manchester M8 5RB
Tel:	0161 720 2792
Fax:	0161 720 2732
Private:	Refer to address and number above
First Qualified:	1959 – Calcutta
Major Degrees:	FRCP Ed
Academic:	Lecturer in Infectious Diseases, Manchester University
Specialist Training:	Seacroft Hospital, Leeds, Leeds General Infirmary

TRENT REGION

SHEFFIELD

KINGHORN, Dr George

Special Interests	**HIV**
NHS:	Consultant in Genito-Urinary Medicine
	Royal Hallamshire Hospital
	Glossop Road
	Sheffield S10 2JP
Tel:	0114 276 6928
Fax:	0114 275 9081
Private:	Refer to address and number above
First Qualified:	1972 – Sheffield
Major Degrees:	MD, FRCP
Distinctions:	Clinical Director, Communicable Disease Centre, Sheffield University Hospital; Chairman Royal College of Physicians, Genito-Urinary Medicine Committee; Chairman Trent Regional ASC in Genito-Urinary Medicine

SCOTLAND

EDINBURGH

BRETTLE, Dr Raymond P.

Special Interests;	**HIV infection and drug abuse**
NHS:	Consultant Physician Infectious Diseases Unit
	Infectious Diseases Unit
	City Hospital
	51 Greenbank Drive
	Edinburgh EH10 5SB
Tel:	0131 536 6484
Fax:	0131 452 9720
Private:	Refer to address and number above
First Qualified:	1974 – Edinburgh
Major Degrees:	FRCP Ed
Academic:	Part-time Senior Lecturer, Edinburgh University
Specialist Training:	Edinburgh, and Hammersmith Hospital, London
Distinctions:	Alastair Ironside Memorial Lecturer
	Wilfred Card Lecturer
	Croom Lecturer, Royal College of Physicians, Edinburgh
USA:	Fellowship, Medical School North Carolina

LEEN, Dr Clifford

Special Interests:	**HIV**
NHS:	Edinburgh Royal Infirmary
	City Hospital
	51 Greenbank Drive
	Edinburgh EH10 5SB
Tel:	0131 536 6484
Fax:	0131 536 6749
Private:	Refer to address and number above

MEDICAL ONCOLOGISTS

These doctors specialise in the diagnosis, medical treatment, symptom control and prevention of cancer and benign tumours. Their work is integrated with that of clinical oncologists, haematologists and palliative consultants. When a patient needs surgery they are sent to a Surgical Oncologist (see General Surgeons section). (See appendix 1(i) for a list of specialist cancer units.)

LONDON AND THE SOUTH EAST

COOMBES, Dr R. Charles

Special interests:	**Breast cancer**
NHS:	Professor of Medical Oncology
	Department of Medical Oncology
	Charing Cross Hospital
	Fulham Palace Road
	London W6 8RF
Tel:	0181 846 1418
Fax:	0181 846 1111
Private:	Refer to address and number above
First Qualified:	London – 1971
Major Degrees:	MD, PhD, FRCP
Academic:	Senior Lecturer, Institute of Cancer Research; Senior Clinical Scientist, Ludwig Institute of Cancer Research
Specialist Training:	Royal Marsden and Royal Postgraduate Medical School, London
Distinctions:	Honorary Consultant Physician, Royal Marsden Hospital; Honorary Consultant Physician, Hammersmith Hospitals Trust

CUNNINGHAM, Dr David

Special interests:	**Gastrointestinal cancer and lymphoma, including bone marrow transplantation**
NHS:	Consultant Physician
	Head Gastrointestinal and Lymphoma Units
	Royal Marsden Hospital
	Downs Road
	Sutton
	Surrey SM2 5PT
Tel:	0181 642 6011 Ext. 3157
Fax:	0181 643 9414
Private:	Refer to address and number above
First Qualified:	1978 – Glasgow
Major Degrees:	MD, FRCP
Specialist Training:	St Mary's Hospital, London

GOLDMAN, Professor John M.

Special interests:	**Leukaemia**
NHS:	Chairman, Department of Haematology
	Director, Centre for Adult Leukaemia
	Hammersmith Hospital
	Du Cane Road
	London W12 ONN
Tel:	0181 740 3238
Fax:	0181 740 9679
Private:	Refer to address and number above
First Qualified:	1963 – London
Major Degrees:	DM, FRCP, FRCPath
Academic:	Professor of Leukaemia Biology, Royal Postgraduate Medical School, London
Specialist Training:	Royal Postgraduate Medical School and St Bartholomew's Hospital, London
USA:	Previously, Fellow in Medicine, Miami University, Florida, and Massachusetts General Hospital, Boston

GOLDSTONE, Dr Anthony H.

Special interests:	**Leukaemia and bone marrow transplants; paediatric cancer**
NHS:	Consultant Haematologist
	University College London
	Gower Street
	London WC1E 6AU
Tel:	0171 387 9300
Fax:	0171 387 9816
Private:	Private Patients Wing
	University College London
	Grafton Way
	London WC1E 6AU
Tel:	0171 387 9709
Fax:	0171 387 9816
First Qualified:	1968 – Oxford
Major Degrees:	FRCP, FRCPath
Academic:	Previously Postgraduate Dean, University College Hospital Medical School, London
Specialist Training:	Addenbrooke's Hospital, Cambridge, and Cancer Research Institute, London

GORE, Dr Martin E.

Special interests:	**Gynaecology cancer; melanoma**
NHS:	Consultant Medical Oncologist
	Royal Marsden Hospital
	Fulham Road
	London SW3 6JJ
Tel:	0171 352 8171 Ext. 2198
Fax:	0171 352 5441
Private:	Refer to address and number above
First Qualified:	1974 – London
Major Degrees:	PhD, FRCP
Academic:	Honorary Senior Lecturer, Institute of Cancer Research, London and Sutton
Specialist Training:	University College Hospital, London
	Senior Lecturer, Institute Cancer Research, Sutton

HARPER, Dr Peter G.

Special interests:	**Breast cancer**
NHS:	Consultant Physician and Medical Oncologist
	Guy's Hospital
	St Thomas Street
	London SE1 9RT
Tel:	0171 955 4623
Fax:	0171 955 2714
Private:	97 Harley Street
	London W1N 1DE
Tel:	0171 935 6698
Fax:	0171 224 6504
First Qualified:	1970 – London
Major Degrees:	FRCP
Academic:	Honorary Senior Lecturer, UMDS Guy's and St Thomas' Hospitals, London
Specialist Training:	University College, Whittington and St Mary's Hospitals, London

HOFFBRAND, Professor A. Victor

Special interests: **General haematology; leukaemia and lymphoma**
NHS: Consultant Physician
Royal Free Hospital
Pond Street
London NW3 2QG
Tel: 0171 794 0500 Ext. 3258
Fax: 0171 431 4537
First Qualified: 1959 – Oxford
Major Degrees: DSc, DM, FRCP, FRCPath
Academic: Professor of Haematology, Royal Free Hospital Medical School, London
Previously, Senior Lecturer, Royal Postgraduate Medical School, London
Specialist Training: Royal Postgraduate Medical School and Hammersmith Hospital, London

LISTER, Professor T. Andrew

Special interests: **Leukaemia; lymphoma; myeloma**
NHS: Professor of Clinical Oncology
Department of Medical Oncology
St Bartholomew's Hospital
West Smithfield
London EC1A 7BE
Tel: 0171 601 7462
Fax: 0171 796 3979
Private: Refer to address and number above
First Qualified: 1969 – Cambridge
Major Degrees: MD, FRCP, FRCPath
Academic: Professor of Medical Oncology, St Bartholomew's Hospital, London
Previously Reader in Medical Oncology
Specialist Training: St Bartholomew's Hospital, London
Dane Farber Cancer Centre,
Harvard Medical School, Boston
Distinctions: Director, Imperial Cancer Research Fund Medical Oncology Unit; Director of Cancer Services and Clinical Haematology at Royal Hospital NHS Trust, London
USA: Member, American Society for Cancer Research, American Society of Clinical Oncology, American Society of Haematology

MALPAS, Professor James S.

Special interests:	**Paediatric cancer; haematological lymphomas**
NHS:	Honorary Consultant Physician
	Department of Medical Oncology
	St Bartholomew's Hospital
	West Smithfield
	London EC1A 7BE
Tel:	0171 601 7456
Fax:	0171 796 3979
Private:	Refer to address and number above
First Qualified:	MD, FRCP, FRCR
Major Degrees:	1955 – London
Academic:	Emeritus Professor in Medical Oncology
	St Bartholomew's Hospital, London
Specialist Training:	Radcliffe Infirmary, Oxford
	Royal Postgraduate Medical School and
	St Bartholomew's Hospital, London
Distinctions:	Examiner to Universities of London and Oxford
	Director, Imperial Cancer Research Fund
	President, Association of Cancer Physicians
	Lockyer Lecturer, Royal College of Physicians
	President, Association Cancer Physicians
	Ex-President St Bartholomews Hospital Medical College

NEWLANDS, Professor Edward S.

Special interests:	**Gestational choriocarcinoma; testicular cancer; brain tumours**
NHS:	Professor of Cancer Medicine
	Charing Cross Hospital
	Fulham Palace Road
	London W6 8RF
Tel:	0181 846 1419
Fax:	0181 846 1443
Private:	Refer to address and numbers above
First Qualified:	1966 – Oxford
Major Degrees:	PhD, FRCP
Academic:	Professor of Medical Oncology, Charing Cross and
	Westminster Medical Schools, London
Specialist Training:	Westminster and Charing Cross Hospitals, London

OLIVER, Professor R. Timothy

Special interests:	**Bladder, kidney and testicular cancer**
NHS:	Professor of Medical Oncology
	Department of Medical Oncology
	St Bartholomew's Hospital
	West Smithfield
	London EC1A 7BE
Tel:	0171 601 8522
Fax:	0171 601 7577
Private:	Refer to address and number above
First Qualified:	1966 – London
Major Degrees:	MD, FRCP
Academic:	Professor of Medical Oncology, Honorary Senior Lecturer, St Bartholomew's Hospital, London
Specialist Training:	London and St Bartholomew's Hospitals, London

POWLES, Dr Ray L.

Special interests:	**Leukaemia; lymphoma; bone marrow transplantation**
NHS:	Head and Physician in Charge
	Leukaemia and Myeloma Units
	Royal Marsden Hospital
	Downs Road
	Sutton, Surrey SN2 5PT
Tel:	0181 770 1027
Fax:	0181 770 7313
e-mail:	leukaemia@delphi.com
e-mail:	myeloma@delphi.com
Private:	Refer to address and number above
First Qualified:	1964 – London
Major Degrees:	MD, BSc, FRCP, FRCPath
Academic:	Clinical Tutor, Royal College of Physicians
Specialist Training:	St Bartholomew's Hospital
Distinctions:	Member, British Society Haematology
	British Transplantation Society
	Board Member, European Society for Medical Oncology
	Member, European Bone Marrow Transplantation Society
	UK Cancer Co-ordinating Sub-Committee on Leukaemia and Bone Marrow Transplantation
	Published over 450 papers on malignant disease and bone marrow transplantation

POWLES, Dr Trevor J.

Special interests:	**Breast cancer**
NHS:	Consultant Medical Oncologist
	Medical Breast Unit
	Royal Marsden Hospital
	Downs Road
	Sutton, Surrey SN2 5PT
Tel:	0181 642 6011 Ext. 3361
Fax:	0181 770 7313
Private:	Refer to address and number above
First Qualified:	1964 – London
Major Degrees:	PhD, FRCP
Academic:	Senior Lecturer, Institute of Cancer Research, London
	Teacher and Head Breast Unit, London University
Specialist Training:	Royal Postgraduate Medical School and Royal Marsden Hospital, London
Distinctions:	Previously Chairman, Medical Division, Royal Marsden Hospital, London

PRENTICE, Professor H. Grant

Special interests:	**Leukaemia; lymphoma; bone marrow transplantation**
NHS:	Director, Bone Marrow Transplantation Programme
	Royal Free Hospital
	Pond Street
	London NW3 2QG
Tel:	0171 794 0500 or 0171 830 2301
Fax:	0171 794 0645
Private:	Refer to address and number above
First Qualified:	1968 – London
Major Degrees:	MD, FRCP, FRCPath
Academic:	Professor of Haematological Oncology, Royal Free School of Medicine, London
Specialist Training:	St George's and Royal Marsden Hospitals, London

RUSTIN, Dr Gordon J. S.

Special interests:	**Germ cell and gynaecological cancers; drug development**
NHS:	Consultant Medical Oncologist and Director of Medical Oncology Mount Vernon Hospital Rickmansworth Road Northwood, Middlesex HA6 2RN
Tel:	01923 844389
Fax:	01923 844138
Private:	Refer to address and number above
First Qualified:	1971 – London
Major Degrees:	MD, FRCP
Specialist Training:	Royal Postgraduate Medical School and Charing Cross Hospital, London

SIKORA, Professor Karol

Special interests:	**Investigational therapies, gene therapy**
NHS:	Director, Department of Clinical Oncology Hammersmith Hospital Du Cane Road London W12 OHS
Tel:	0181 740 3057
Fax:	0181 743 8766
Private:	Refer to address and number above
First Qualified:	1973 – Cambridge
Major Degrees:	PhD, FRCP, FRCR
Academic:	Professor of Clinical Oncology, Royal Postgraduate Medical School, London
Specialist Training:	Cambridge, and St Bartholomew's Hospital, London
Distinctions:	Twining Medal, Royal College of Radiology
USA:	Previously Fellow in Medical Oncology Stanford University, Palo Alto, California

SLEVIN, Dr Maurice L.

Special interests:	**Gastrointestinal tumours; gynaecological cancer; breast cancer; lung cancer**
NHS:	Consultant Physician
	St Bartholomew's Hospital
	West Smithfield
	London EC1A 7BE
Tel:	0171 606 6662
Fax:	0171 796 3979
Private:	149 Harley Street
	London W1N 1HG
Tel:	0171 224 0685
Fax:	0171 224 1722
First Qualified:	1973 – Cape Town, South Africa
Major Degrees:	MD, FRCP
Specialist Training:	Groote Schuur, Cape Town, South Africa, and St Bartholomew's Hospital, London

SMITH, Dr Ian E.

Special interests:	**Breast cancer; lung cancer**
NHS:	Head, Section of Medicine
	Consultant Medical Oncologist
	Royal Marsden Hospital
	Fulham Road
	London SW3 6JJ
Tel:	0171 352 8171
Fax:	0171 352 5441
Private:	Refer to address and number above
First Qualified:	1971 – Edinburgh
Major Degrees:	MD, FRCP, FRCP Ed
Specialist Training:	Edinburgh Royal Infirmary and Royal Marsden Hospitals
USA:	Member, American Society of Medical Oncologists

SOUHAMI, Professor Robert L.

Special interests:	**Sarcoma; lung cancer**
NHS:	Consultant Physician and Professor of Clinical Oncology
	Meyerstein Institute of Oncology
	The Middlesex Hospital
	Mortimer Street
	London W1N 8AA
Tel:	0171 380 9092
Fax:	0171 436 2956
Private:	Refer to address and number above
First Qualified:	1962 – London
Major Degrees:	MD, FRCP, FRCR
Academic:	Professor of Clinical Oncology, University College and The Middlesex Hospitals, London
Specialist Training:	University College and St Mary's Hospitals, London
Distinctions:	Chairman, Association of Cancer Physicians
	Chairman, Cancer Therapy Committee of the Medical Research Council

WAXMAN, Dr Jonathan

Special interests:	**Prostate cancer**
NHS:	Consultant Physician and Reader in Oncology
	Hammersmith Hospital
	Du Cane Road
	London W12 OHS
Tel:	0181 743 6112
Fax:	0181 743 8766
Private:	Refer to address and number above
First Qualified:	1975 – London
Major Degrees:	MD, FRCP
Academic:	Reader, Royal Postgraduate Medical School, London
Specialist Training:	University College Hospital, London and Addenbrooke's Hospital, Cambridge
Distinctions:	Honorary Consultant Physician, West Middlesex Hospital, London
	Directs research programme at the Hammersmith Hospital on behalf of National Prostate Cancer Research Commission. The laboratory contains numerically the most important group for prostate cancer research in the UK

ANGLIA AND OXFORD REGION

OXFORD

HARRIS, Professor Adrian L.

Special interests:	**Breast cancer; melanoma and renal cancer; interests include new drugs agains novel targets: anti-angiogenesis, gene therapy, blockade of signalling systems in cancer cells; mechanisms to overcome drug resistance**
NHS:	Honorary Consultant Medical Oncologist Imperial Cancer Research Fund Clinical Oncology Unit Churchill Hospital Headington, Oxon OX3 7LJ
Tel:	01865 226184
Fax:	01865 226179
Private:	Refer to address and number above
First Qualified:	1972 – Liverpool
Major Degrees:	DPhil, MA, FRCP
Academic:	ICRF Professor of Clinical Oncology, Oxford University Head of Growth Factor Group, Institute of Molecular Medicine

NORTH WEST REGION

LANCASTER

McILLMURRAY, Dr Malcolm B.

Special interests:	**Psycho-oncology; relaxation therapy and supportive care**
NHS:	Macmillan Consultant in Medical Oncology and Palliative Care Director of St John's Hospice, Lancaster Royal Lancaster Infirmary Ashton Road Lancaster LA1 4RP
Tel:	01524 583510
Fax:	01524 846346
Private:	Beech House Over Kellet, Carnforth Lancs LA6 1DL
Tel:	01524 732921
First Qualified:	1968 – London
Major Degrees:	DM, FRCP

MANCHESTER

CROWTHER, Professor Derek

Special interests:	**Haematological lymphomas; gynaecological cancer; sarcomas**
NHS:	Professor of Medical Oncology
	Christie Hospital
	Wilmslow Road
	Withington, Manchester M20 9BX
Tel:	0161 446 3000 Ext. 3208
Fax:	0161 446 3109
Private:	Refer to address and number above
First Qualified:	1963 – Cambridge
Major Degrees:	PhD, FRCP
Academic:	Professor of Medical Oncology, Christie Hospital, and Holt Radium Institute, Manchester, and Manchester University
Specialist Training:	Royal Marsden Hospital and Chester Beatty Research Institute, London
USA:	Member, American Society of Clinical Oncology and Cancer Research

HUNTER, Dr Robert D.

Special interests:	**Gynaecology**
NHS:	Director of Clinical Oncology
	Christie Hospital
	Department of Clinical Oncology
	Wilmslow Road
	Withington, Manchester
Tel:	0161 446 3000 Ext. 3406
Fax:	0161 446 3084
Private:	Refer to address and number above
Major Degrees:	FRCP, FRCR

NORTHERN AND YORKSHIRE REGION

LEEDS

SELBY, Professor Peter

Special interests:	**Medical management of cancer: lymphoma, myeloma, lung cancer, urological cancer and melanoma**
NHS:	Consultant Physician
	St James University Hospital
	Beckett Street
	Leeds, West Yorkshire LS9 7TF
Tel:	0113 244 2007
Fax:	0113 342 9886
Private:	Refer to address and number above
First Qualified:	1974 – Cambridge and London
Major Degrees:	FRCP, FRCR
Academic:	Professor of Cancer Medicine, Leeds University
Specialist Training:	Royal Marsden Hospital, London
USA and Canada:	Training in Toronto, Canada

SOUTH AND WEST REGION

SOUTHAMPTON

MEAD, Dr Graham

Special interests:	**Testicular cancer; lymphoma; bladder cancer**
NHS:	Consultant in Medical Oncology
	Royal South Hampshire Hospital
	Brintons Terrace
	off St Mary's Road
	Southampton SO14 0YG
Tel:	01703 634288 Ext. 2973
Fax:	01703 825441
Private:	Refer to address above
Tel:	01703 825973
Fax:	01703 825441
First Qualified:	1972 – London
Major Degrees:	DM, FRCP
Specialist Training:	Stanford University Medical Centre, California
USA:	See 'Specialist Training' above

WHITEHOUSE, Professor Michael

NHS:	Consultant Physician
	Director, CRC Western Medical Oncology Unit
	Southampton General Hosptial
	Tremona Road
	Southampton SO16 6YD
Tel:	01703 796185
Fax:	01703 783839
Private:	Refer to address and number above
First Qualified:	1966 – Cambridge
Major Degrees:	FRCP, FRCR
Academic:	Professor of Medical Oncology, Southampton University
Distinctions:	Joint Chairman, Council for Clinical Oncology, Royal College of Physicians and Royal College of Radiology
	Chairman, Association of Cancer Physicians
	Previously Acting Director, ICRF Medical Oncology Unit, St Bartholomew's Hospital, London

TRENT REGION

NOTTINGHAM

CARMICHAEL, Professor James

Special interests:	**Breast cancer; lung cancer; colorectal cancer**
NHS:	Professor of Clinical Oncology
	Department of Clinical Oncology
	City Hospital
	Hucknall Road
	Nottingham NG5 1PB
Tel:	0115 969 1169
Fax:	0115 962 7923
Private:	Refer to address and number above
First Qualified:	1975 – Edinburgh
Major Degrees:	MD, FRCP
Academic:	ICRF, Senior Lecturer, Churchill Hospital, Oxford
	Lecturer, Newcastle General Hospital and Western General Hospital, Edinburgh
USA:	Research Fellow, National Cancer Institute, Bethesda, Maryland

SHEFFIELD

COLEMAN, Dr Robert Edward

Special interests:	**Breast cancer; bone metastases; ovarian cancer; germ cell tumours**
NHS:	Consultant Medical Oncologist
	YCRC Department of Clinical Oncology
	Weston Park Hospital
	Whitham Road
	Sheffield S10 2SJ
Tel:	0114 267 0222
Fax:	0114 267 8140
Private:	No private work
First Qualified:	1978 – London
Major Degrees:	MD, FRCP
Academic:	Senior Lecturer, Sheffield University
Specialist Training:	Edinburgh, and Guy's Hospital, London

HANCOCK, Professor Barry W.

Special interests:	**Lymphoma**
NHS:	Head of Department of Clinical Oncology
	Weston Park Hospital
	Whitham Road
	Sheffield S10 2SJ
Tel:	0114 268 4389
Fax:	0114 267 8140
Private:	Refer to address and number above
First Qualified:	1969 – Sheffield (with Honours)
Major Degrees:	MD, FRCP, FRCR
Academic:	YCRC Professor of Clinical Oncology, Sheffield University
Distinctions:	Director, Supraregional Gestational Trophoblastic Tumour Centre
	Honorary Director, Trent Palliative Care Centre
	Trial Co-ordinator British National Lymphoma Investigation
	Council Member, British Oncology Association

WEST MIDLANDS

BIRMINGHAM

KERR, Professor David James

Special interests:	**Colorectal cancer; early clinical trials**
NHS:	Professor of Clinical Oncology
	CRC Institute for Cancer Studies
	University of Birmingham
	Birmingham
	B15 2TT
Tel:	0121 414 3802
Fax:	0121 414 3263
Private:	No private work
First Qualified:	1980 – Glasgow
Major Degrees:	MD, PhD, FRCP Glas
Academic:	Professor of Clincal Oncology and Clinical Director,
	CRC Institute for Cancer Studies
	Honorary Professor, Department of Pharmacy and
	Pharmacology, Strathclyde University
	Visiting Professor, Athens University, Greece
Distinctions:	European School of Oncology Award for Outstanding
	Research in Molecular Biology and Cytoxic Therapy

SCOTLAND

EDINBURGH

SMYTH, Professor John F.

Special interests:	**Ovarian and lung cancer; the evaluation of new anti-cancer medicines including supportive care**
NHS:	Professor of Medical Oncology
	Directorate of Clinical Oncology
	Western General Hospital NHS Trust
	Crewe Road
	Edinburgh
	EH4 2XU
Tel:	0131 467 8449
Fax:	0131 332 8494
Private:	No private work
First Qualified:	1970 – Cambridge and London
Major Degrees:	MD, MSc, FRCP Ed, FRCS Ed
Academic:	Previouly Senior Lecturer, Royal Marsden Hospital, London
Specialist Training:	St Bartholomew's and Royal Marsden Hospitals, London
USA:	Fogerty International Travelling Fellowship
	National Cancer Institute

GLASGOW

KAYE, Professor Stanley B.

Special interests:	**Cancer of urological testis (germ cell or teratoma), breast and gynaecological ovarian**
NHS:	Professor of Medical Oncology
	Beatson Oncology Centre
	Western Infirmary
	Dumbarton Road
	Glasgow G11 6NT
Tel:	0141 211 2318
Fax:	0141 211 1869
Private:	Refer to address and number above
First Qualified:	1972 – London
Major Degrees:	MD, FRCP, FRCR
Academic:	Professor of Medical Oncology, Glasgow University
Specialist Training:	Ludwig Institute of Cancer Research, Sydney, Australia, and Charing Cross Hospital, London

---

SOUKOP, Dr Michael

Special interests:	**Management of lymphomas, breast, gastrointestinal and ovarian cancers; high dose chemotherapy**
NHS:	Consultant Physician and Medical Oncologist
	Glasgow Royal Infirmary
	Glasgow G4 0SF
Tel:	0141 211 4270
Fax:	0141 211 4855
Private:	Ross Hall Hospital
	221 Crookston Road
	Glasgow G52 3MQ
Tel:	0141 810 3151
Fax:	0141 882 7439
and:	Glasgow Nuffield Hospital
	Beaconsfield Road
	Glasgow G12 0PJ
Tel:	0141 334 9441
First Qualified:	1971 – St Andrews
Major Degrees:	FRCP Ed, FRCP
Academic:	Honorary Senior Lecturer, Glasgow University
Specialist Training:	Department of Medical Oncology, Glasgow University
USA:	Visiting Research Lecturer, Department Human Oncology, Winconsin University, Madison

NEPHROLOGISTS

(Kidney Physicians)

Nephrologists deal with kidney disorders, hypertension and fluid and mineral balance. They direct dialysis treatment for patients in kidney failure. They work closely with urological surgeons.

LONDON AND THE SOUTH EAST

BAKER, Dr Laurence R. I.

Special interests:	**Stone diseases; chronic renal failure; dialysis**
NHS:	Consultant Physician and Nephrologist
	Director of Renal Medicine and Transplantation
	St Bartholomew's Hospital
	West Smithfield
	London EC1A 7BE
Tel:	0171 601 8787
Fax:	0171 601 8529
Private:	149 Harley Street
	London W1N 2DE
Tel:	0171 935 4444
Fax:	0171 486 3782
First Qualified:	1964 – Cambridge
Major Degrees:	MD, FRCP, FRCP Ed
Academic:	Previously Research Fellow, St Mary's Hospital, London
Specialist Training:	Royal Postgraduate Medical School and St Mary's Hospital, London
Distinctions:	Examiner, Royal College of Physicians
	Previously Postgraduate Dean, St Bartholomew's, London

CUNNINGHAM, Dr John

Special interests:	**Dialysis and transplantation; metabolic bone disease; runs osteoporosis diagnostic service at Royal London Hospital**
NHS:	Consultant Physician and Nephrologist
	Royal London Hospital
	Whitechapel
	London E1 1BB
Tel:	0171 377 7366
Fax:	0171 377 7003
and:	King Edward VII Hospital For Officers
	Beaumont Street
	London W1N 2AA
Tel:	0171 486 4411
Fax:	0171 935 6770
Private:	London Independent Hospital
	1 Beaumont Square
	London E1 4NL
Tel:	0171 791 2200
Fax:	0171 377 7003
First Qualified:	1973 – Oxford
Major Degrees:	DM, FRCP
Academic:	Sub-Dean for Medical Student Admissions, London Hospital Medical College
Specialist Training:	Oxford, London and United States
Distinctions:	Physician to the Royal Household
USA:	Previously Fellow in Metabolism, Washington University, St Louis, Missouri

EISINGER, Dr Anthony John

Special interests:	**Dialysis**
NHS:	Consultant Physician and Nephrologist
	St Helier Hospital
	Carshalton
	Surrey SM5 1AA
Tel:	0181 644 4343
Fax:	0181 641 8560
Private:	54 Wimpole Street
	London W1M 7DF
Tel:	0181 644 1168
First Qualified:	1965 – Cambridge (with Honours)
Major Degrees:	FRCP
Specialist Training:	The Middlesex, Royal Brompton and St Thomas' Hospitals, London
Distinctions:	Director, South West Thames Regional Renal Unit

GOWER, Dr Peter Edward

Special interests:	**General renal problems**
NHS:	Consultant Physician
	Charing Cross Hospital
	Fulham Palace Road
	London W6 8RF
Tel:	0181 846 1753
Fax:	0181 846 7589
Private:	Refer to address and number above
First Qualified:	1962 – London
Major Degrees:	MD, FRCP
Academic:	Honorary Senior Lecturer, Charing Cross Hospital
	Previously Lecturer in Medicine, Charing Cross and Westminster Medical School, London
Specialist Training:	Charing Cross Hospital, London

HILTON, Dr Philip J.

Special interests:	**Hypertension**
NHS:	Consultant Physician
	St Thomas' Hospital
	Lambeth Palace Road
	London SE1 7EH
Tel:	0171 928 9292 Ext. 3059
Fax:	0171 922 8329
Private:	134 Harley Street
	London W1N 1AH
Tel:	0171 486 1042
Fax:	0171 486 1042
and:	The Consulting Rooms
	York House
	199 Westminster Bridge Road
	London SE1 7UT
Tel:	0171 928 5485
First Qualified:	1963 – Cambridge
Major Degrees:	MD, FRCP
Specialist Training:	St Thomas' Hospital, London

JONES, Dr Norman F.

NHS:	Retired from NHS
Private:	Private Consulting Rooms
	St Thomas' Hospital
	Lambeth Palace Road
	London SE1 7EH
Tel:	0171 928 5485
Fax:	0171 928 3748
First Qualified:	1956 – Cambridge
Major Degrees:	MD, FRCP
Specialist Training:	St Thomas' Hospital, London
Distinctions:	Honorary Consultant to the Army
	Treasurer, Royal College of Physicians
	Previously MRC Travelling Fellow

MARSH, Dr Francis (Frank) P.

Special interests:	**General nephrology; renal failure; urinary infection; hypertension**
NHS:	Consultant Nephrologist
	Royal London Hospital
	Whitechapel
	London E1 1BB
Tel:	0171 377 7367
Fax:	0171 377 7003
Private:	London Independent Hospital
	1 Beaumont Square
	London E1 4NL
Tel:	0171 790 0990
Fax:	0171 265 9032
First Qualified:	1960 – Cambridge
Major Degrees:	FRCP
Academic:	Dean of Medical Studies, London Hospital Medical College
Specialist Training:	London Hospital

MOORHEAD, Professor John F.

Special interests:	**Nephrotic syndrome; cholesterol metabolism in kidney disease; lipids in progressive glomerular disease**
NHS:	Consultant Physician
	Director, Department of Nephrology and Transplantation
	Royal Free Hospital
	Pond Street
	London NW3 2QG
Tel:	0171 794 0500 Ext. 4132 or 0171 830 2930
Fax:	0171 830 2125
Private:	Honorary Consultant Nephrologist
	St John and St Elizabeth Hospital
	60 Grove End Road
	Swiss Cottage
	London NW8 9NH
Tel:	0171 286 5126
Fax:	0171 266 2316
First Qualified:	1957 – Liverpool
Major Degrees:	FRCP
Academic:	Professor of Renal Medicine, Royal Free Hospital, London
Distinctions:	Examiner, University of London

NEILD, Professor Guy H.

Special interests:	**Diabetic nephrology**
NHS:	Professor of Nephrology
	The Middlesex Hospital
	Mortimer Road
	London W1N 8AA
Tel:	0171 380 9302
Fax:	0171 637 7006
Private:	Refer to address and number above
First Qualified:	1971 – London
Major Degrees:	MD, FRCP
Academic:	Professor of Nephrology, University College and Middlesex Medical Schools, London
	Previously Senior Lecturer, Institute of Urology, London

OGG, Dr C. Stuart

Special interests:	**Kidney stones**
NHS:	Renal Physician and Director of Renal Services
	Guy's Hospital
	St Thomas Street
	London SE1 9RT
Tel:	0171 955 5000 Ext. 3844
Fax:	0171 955 4909
Private:	Emblem House
	London Bridge Hospital
	27 Tooley Street
	London SE1 2PR
Tel:	0171 403 4884 Ext. 2106
Fax:	0171 407 3162
First Qualified:	1961 – London (with Distinction)
Major Degrees:	MD, FRCP
Specialist Training:	Guy's, St Philip's, St Peter's and St Paul's Hospitals, London
Distinctions:	Consultant, Renal Disease, to the Royal Navy

PALMER, Dr Andrew

Special interests:	**Glomerular disease; acute and chronic renal failure; renal transplantation**
NHS:	Consultant Nephrologist
	St Mary's Hospital
	Praed Street
	London W2 1NY
Tel:	0171 725 1615/6599
Fax:	0171 725 1707
Private:	The Clementine Churchill Hospital
	Sudbury Hill
	Harrow, Middlesex HA1 3RX
Tel:	0181 422 3464
Fax:	0181 864 1747
First Qualified:	1980 – London
Major Degrees:	MRCP
Specialist Training:	St Mary's, Dulwich and King's College Hospitals, London

PHILLIPS, Dr Malcolm E.

Special interests:	**Renal bone disease**
NHS:	Chief of Service, Renal Medicine and Transplantation
	Consultant Physician and Nephrologist
	Charing Cross Hospital
	Fulham Palace Road
	London W6 8RF
Tel:	0181 846 7592
Fax:	0181 846 7592
and:	West Middlesex University Hospital
	Twickenham Road
	Isleworth
	Middlesex TW7 6AF
Tel:	0181 560 2121
Fax:	0181 560 5425
Private:	Refer to address and number above
First Qualified:	1964 – London
Major Degrees:	MD, FRCP
Specialist Training:	Charing Cross Hospital, London and the University of Naples, Italy

PUSEY, Professor Charles Dickson

Special interests:	**Immunological aspects of renal disease; acute renal failure**
NHS:	Consultant Physician
	Royal Postgraduate Medical School
	Hammersmith Hospital
	Du Cane Road
	London W12 0HS
Tel:	0181 743 2030
Fax:	0181 740 3169
Private:	Refer to address and number above
First Qualified:	1972 – Cambridge
Major Degrees:	MSc, FRCP
Academic:	Professor of Renal Medicine, Royal Postgraduate Medical School, London
	Previously Reader in Renal Medicine and Senior Lecturer in Medicine, Royal Postgraduate Medical School, London
Distinctions:	Editor, Immunological Renal Disease

REES, Professor Andrew J.

Special interests:	**Autoimmune disease**
NHS:	Professor of Nephrology
	Royal Postgraduate Medical School
	Hammersmith Hospital
	Du Cane Road
	London W12 0HS
Tel:	0181 743 2030
Fax:	0181 740 3169
Private:	Refer to address and number above
First Qualified:	1969 – Liverpool
Major Degrees:	FRCP
Academic:	Professor of Nephrology, Royal Postgraduate Medical School, London
Specialist Training:	Royal Postgraduate Medical School, London
Distinctions:	Previously Goulstonian Lecturer, Royal School of Physicians

---

TAUBE, Dr H. David

Special interests:	**Management of transplants**
NHS:	Consultant Nephrologist
	Renal and Transplant Unit
	St Mary's Hospital
	London W2 1NY
Tel:	0171 725 6726
Fax:	0171 724 0678
and:	Northwick Park and St Mark's Hospital
	Watford Road
	Harrow, Middlesex HA1 3UJ
Tel:	0181 869 2604/3247
Fax:	0181 869 2009
Private:	66 Harley Street
	London W1N 1AE
Tel:	0171 636 6628
Fax:	0171 631 5341
First Qualified:	1973 – Oxford
Major Degrees:	FRCP
Specialist Training:	Guy's Hospital, London

WING, Dr Anthony J.

NHS:	Consultant Physician
	St Thomas' Hospital
	Lambeth Palace Road
	London SE1 7EH
Tel:	0171 928 9292 Ext. 3059
Fax:	0171 922 8079
Private:	Refer to address and number below
First Qualified:	1958 – Oxford
Major Degrees:	DM, FRCP
Specialist Training:	Charing Cross Hospital, London
Distinctions:	Chairman, European Dialysis and Transplant Association

---

ANGLIA AND OXFORD REGION

CAMBRIDGE

EVANS, Mr David Bernard

Special interests:	**Glomerulonephritis; renal transplantation**
NHS:	Consultant Physician
	Renal Unit
	Addenbrooke's Hospital
	Hills Road
	Cambridge CB2 2QQ
Tel:	01223 217828
Fax:	01223 217825
Private:	Evelyn Hospital
	Trumpington Road
	Cambridge CB22
Tel:	01223 303336
Fax:	01223 316068
First Qualified:	1957 – Cardiff
Major Degrees:	FRCP
Academic:	Associated Lecturer, Clinical Medicine, Cambridge University
Specialist Training:	Charing Cross Hospital, London
USA:	Dialysis training, Seattle, Washington

NORTH WEST REGION

MANCHESTER

MALLICK, Professor Netar

Special interests:	**Transplantation; 'appointed by the government to sort out kidney medicine in London'**
NHS:	Honorary Consultant Physician
	Department of Renal Medicine
	Manchester Royal Infirmary
	Oxford Road
	Manchester M13 9WL
Tel:	0161 276 4411
Fax:	0161 273 4834
Private:	No private work
First Qualified:	1959 – Manchester
Major Degrees:	FRCP, FRCP Ed
Academic:	Professor in Renal Medicine, Manchester University
Distinctions:	Previously President, Renal Association

SOUTH AND WEST REGION

PORTSMOUTH

MASON, Dr Juan Corlett

NHS:	Consultant Physician
	Renal Unit
	St Mary's Hospital
	Milton Road
	Portsmouth PO3 6AD
Tel:	01705 822331
Fax:	01705 866413
Private:	Refer to address and number above
First Qualified:	1976 – Oxford
Major Degrees:	MRCP
Specialist Training:	St Thomas' Hospital, London

TRENT REGION

LEICESTER

WALLS, Professor John

Special interests:	**Urinary tract infections; stones; tubular disorders**
NHS:	Consultant Nephrologist
	Department of Nephrology
	Leicester General Hospital
	Leicester LE5 4PW
Tel:	01162 490490
Fax:	01162 734989
Private:	Refer to address and number above
First Qualified:	1963 – Leeds
Major Degrees:	FRCP
Academic:	Professor of Nephrology, Leicester University
	Clinical Sub-Dean, Leicester University
USA:	Previously Assistant Professor in Medicine
	Washington University, St Louis, Missouri

SHEFFIELD

BROWN, Dr Colin B.

Special interests:	**Renal bone disease; dialysis**
NHS:	Consultant Renal Physician
	Sheffield Kidney Institute
	Northern General Hospital
	Herries Road
	Sheffield
Tel:	01142 434343
Fax:	01142 562514
Private:	Refer to address and number above
First Qualified:	1968 – London
Major Degrees:	FRCP
Specialist Training:	Guy's Hospital, London
Distinctions:	Chairman Public Committee, International Society of Peritoneal Dialysis

WEST MIDLANDS REGION

BIRMINGHAM

MICHAEL, Dr Jonathan

Special interests:	**Cation transport and renal disease; renal failure; renal disease in pregnancy**
NHS:	Consultant Physician and Nephrologist
	Queen Elizabeth Hospital
	Edgbaston
	Birmingham B15 2TH
Tel:	0121 472 1311
Fax:	0121 627 2547
Private:	Refer to address and number above
First Qualified:	1970 – London
Major Degrees:	FRCP
Academic:	Honorary Senior Clinical Lecturer
	Birmingham University
Specialist Training:	St Thomas' Hospital, London

NEUROLOGISTS

Neurologists diagnose and treat disorders affecting nerves, the brain and spinal cord. Ailments they typically see include stroke, chronic pain or headaches, movement disorders and epilepsy. If surgery is required they refer the patient to a neurosurgeon.

NOTE: The National Hospital refers to the National Hospital for Neurology and Neurosurgery based at Queen Square, London

LONDON AND THE SOUTH EAST

BLAU, Dr Nathan

Special interests:	**Migraines; headaches and facial pain**
NHS:	Consultant Neurologist
	National Hospital
	Queen Square
	London WC13BG
Tel:	0171 837 3611 Ext. 8732
Fax:	0171 833 8658
Private:	Refer to address above
Tel:	0171 829 8732
Fax:	0171 833 8658
First Qualified:	1952 – London
Major Degrees:	MD, FRCP, FRCPath
Specialist Training:	London Hospital
Distinctions:	Honorary Director, City London Migraine Clinic, London
	Honorary Medical Advisor British Migraine Association
	Author, *Understanding Headaches and Migraines*
USA:	Nuffield Medical Research Fellow
	Massachusetts General Hospital, Boston

BRONSTEIN, Dr Adolfo

Special interests:	**Balance and eye movement problems**
NHS:	Honorary Consultant Physician
	National Hospital
	Queen Square
	London WC1N 3BG
Tel:	0171 837 3611 Ext. 4112
Fax:	0171 837 7281
Private:	Refer to address and number above
First Qualified:	1975 – Buenos Aires, Argentina
Major Degrees:	PhD
Academic:	Honorary Senior Lecturer, Institute of Neurology, London
Specialist Training:	National Hospital, London, and Buenos Aires, Argentina

BROWN, Dr Martin Meredith

Special interests:	**Cerebrovascular disease**
NHS:	Consultant Neurologist
	St George's Hospital
	Blackshaw Road
	London SW17 0QT
Tel:	0181 725 4683
Fax:	0181 725 4700
and:	Atkinson Morley's Hospital
	31 Copse Hill
	London SW20 0NE
Tel:	0181 946 7711
Fax:	0181 947 8389
Private:	Refer to address and number above
First Qualified:	1975 – Cambridge and London
Major Degrees:	MA, MD, FRCP
Academic:	Reader in Neurology, St George's Hospital Medical School, London
Specialist Training:	Royal London and National Hospitals, London
USA and Canada:	Research Fellow, University of Western Ontario, Canada

DICK, Dr Jeremy P. R.

NHS:	Consultant Neurologist
	Royal London Hospital
	Whitechapel Road
	London E1 1BB
Tel:	0171 377 7421
Fax:	0171 377 7008
Private:	Refer to address and number above
First Qualified:	1977 – Cambridge
Major Degrees:	PhD, MRCP
Academic:	Reader in Neurology, Institute of Neurology, London
Specialist Training:	Charing Cross Hospital, London, and Manchester

DUNCAN, Dr John S.

Special interests:	**Epilepsy**
NHS:	Honorary Consultant Neurologist
	National Hospital
	Queen Square
	London WC1N 3BG
Tel:	0171 837 3611 Ext. 4259
Fax:	0171 837 3941
Private:	Refer to address and number above
First Qualified:	1979 – Oxford
Major Degrees:	MA, MD, FRCP
Academic:	Reader in Neurology, Institute of Neurology, London
Specialist Training:	Radcliffe Infirmary, Oxford, and National Hospital for Nervous Diseases, London

EARL, Dr Christopher

Special interests:	**Creutzfeldt-Jakob disease; multiple sclerosis**
NHS:	Retired from the NHS
Private:	149 Harley Street
	London W1N 1HG
Tel:	0171 935 4444
Fax:	0171 935 5742
First Qualified:	1948 – London
Major Degrees:	MD, FRCP
Specialist Training:	Councillor, Medical Defence Union
Distinctions:	Ex-President, British Association of Neurologists
USA:	Member, American Association of Neurologists

GAWLER, Dr Jeffrey G.

Special interests:	**Neurological aspects of systemic diseases**
NHS:	Consultant Neurologist
	St Bartholomew's Hospital
	West Smithfield
	London EC1A 7BE
Tel:	0171 601 8888 Ext. 7668
Fax:	0171 601 7899
and:	Royal London Hospital
	Whitechapel Road
	London E1 1BB
Tel:	0171 377 7000
Private:	149 Harley Street
	London W1N 2DE
Tel:	0171 224 0640
Fax:	0171 935 7245
First Qualified:	1968 – London (with Honours)
Major Degrees:	FRCP
Specialist Training:	National Hospital for Nervous Diseases

GIBBERD, Dr Frederick B.

Special interests:	**Refsum's disease; Parkinson's disease; epilepsy**
NHS:	Consultant Neurologist
	Chelsea and Westminster Hospital
	369 Fulham Road
	London SW10 9NH
Tel:	0181 746 8320
Fax:	0181 846 7872
Private:	Refer to address and number above
First Qualified:	1957 – Cambridge
Major Degrees:	MD, FRCP
Specialist Training:	Royal London and National Hospitals, London
Distinctions:	Examiner, Royal College of Physicians, London

GIBBS, Dr Jeremy

Special interests:	**General neurology**
NHS:	Consultant Neurologist
	Department of Neuroscience
	Royal Free Hospital
	Pond Street NW3 2QG
Tel:	0171 794 0500 Ext. 4965
Fax:	0171 431 1577
Private:	Refer to address and number above
First Qualified:	1975 – Cambridge
Major Degrees:	MD, MRCP
Academic:	Honorary Senior Lecturer, Royal Free School of Medicine, London
Specialist Training:	National Hospital and King's College, London

GUILOFF, Dr Roberto J.

Special interests:	**Peripheral nerve disease**
NHS:	Consultant Neurologist
	Chelsea and Westminster Hospital
	369 Fulham Road
	London SW10 9NH
Tel:	0181 746 8322
Fax:	0181 846 7872
and:	Charing Cross Hospital
	Fulham Palace Road
	London W6 8RF
Tel:	0181 846 1196
Fax:	0181 846 1195
Private:	Refer to the Charing Cross Hospital address and number above
First Qualified:	1967 – Santiago, Chile
Major Degrees:	MD, FRCP
Specialist Training:	National Hospital, London

HARVEY, Dr Peter K. P.

Special interests:	**General neurology; epilepsy**
NHS:	Consultant Neurologist
	Royal Free Hospital
	Pond Street
	London NW3 2QG
Tel:	0171 794 0500 Ext. 4365
Fax:	0171 435 5342
and:	Chase Farm Hospital
	The Ridgeway
	Enfield
	Middlesex EN2 8JL
Tel:	0181 366 6600
Fax:	0181 367 5982
Private:	134 Harley Street
	London W1N 1AH
Tel:	0171 486 8005
Fax:	0171 224 3905
First Qualified:	1966 – Cambridge
Major Degrees:	FRCP
Academic:	Honorary Senior Lecturer, Royal Free Hospital School of Medicine, London
Specialist Training:	National Hospital for Nervous Diseases, London

HOPKINS, Dr Anthony P.

Special interests:	**Epilepsy, seizures and headaches**
NHS:	No NHS work at present
Private:	149 Harley Street
	London W1N 2DE
Tel:	0171 935 4444
Fax:	0171 486 3782
First Qualified:	1960 – London
Major Degrees:	MD, FRCP
Specialist Training:	National Hospital for Neurology and Neurosurgery, London
	L'Hôpital Salpêtrière, Paris, and Mayo Clinic, Rochester, USA
Distinctions:	Director, Research Unit, Royal College of Physicians
USA:	Corresponding Fellow, American Academy of Neurologists

HUGHES, Professor Richard A. C.

Special interests:	**Peripheral neuropathies; multiple sclerosis; Guillain Barre Syndrome**
NHS:	Honorary Consultant Neurologist
	Department of Neurology
	Guy's Hospital
	London Bridge
	London SE1 9RT
Tel:	0171 955 4398
Fax:	0171 378 1221
Private:	Refer to address and number above
First Qualified:	1967 – Cambridge
Major Degrees:	MD, FRCP
Academic:	Professor and Chairman of Neurology, United Medical and Dental Schools, Guy's and St Thomas' Hospitals, London
Specialist Training:	Hammersmith, University College London and National Hospital for Nervous Diseases, London
Distinctions:	Previously Goulstonian Lecturer, Royal College of Physicians
	Erasmus Wilson Lecturer, Royal College of Surgeons
	Editor, Journal of Neurology, Neurosurgery and Psychiatry
USA:	Visiting Professor, Department of Pathology, UCSD San Diego

KENNARD, Professor Christopher

Special interests:	**Neurological ophthalmology**
NHS:	Professor of Clinical Neurology
	Charing Cross Hospital
	Fulham Palace Road
	London W6 8RF
Tel:	0181 846 1195
Fax:	0181 846 1195
Private:	Refer to address and number above
Tel:	0181 846 7598
Fax:	0181 846 7715
First Qualified:	1970 – London
Major Degrees:	PhD, FRCP
Academic:	Professor, Academic Unit of Neuroscience, Charing Cross and Westminster Medical School, London
Specialist Training:	Royal London Hospital
USA:	Research Neurologist, University of California Medical Center, San Francisco

KOCEN, Dr Roman S.

Special interests:	**Diagnosis of complex neurological conditions; peripheral nerve disorders**
NHS:	Consultant Neurologist
	National Hospital
	Queen Square
	London WC1N 3BG
Tel:	0171 837 3611 Ext. 3419
Fax:	0171 829 8720
and:	Edgware General Hospital
	Edgware
	Middlesex HA8 0AD
Tel:	0181 952 2381
Fax:	0181 951 3078
Private:	Refer to address and number above
First Qualified:	1956 – Leeds (with Honours)
Major Degrees:	FRCP
Academic:	Previously Sub-Dean, Institute of Neurology, London University
Specialist Training:	National Hospital for Nervous Diseases and The Middlesex Hospitals, London
Distinctions:	Honorary Consultant, Royal Free Hospital and St Luke's Hospital for Clergy, London
	Consultant Neurologist to the Royal Air Force and British Airways

LEES, Dr Andrew John

Special interests:	**Parkinson's disease and syndrome movement disorders**
NHS:	Consultant Neurologist
	National Hospital
	Queen Square
	London WC1N 3BG
Tel:	0171 837 3611 Ext. 3414
Fax:	0171 829 8748
Private:	Private Wing
	University College Hospital
	25 Grafton Way
	London WC1
Tel:	0171 388 3894
Fax:	0171 380 9816
First Qualified:	1970 – London
Major Degrees:	MD, FRCP
Specialist Training:	National Hospital for Neurology and Neurosurgery, London
	L'Hôpital Salpêtrière, Paris
Distinctions:	Neurological Advisor, British Boxing Board of Control Council Member, Medical Advisory Panel, Parkinson's Disease Society

LEGG, Dr Nigel J.

Special interests:	**Migraines; headaches**
NHS:	Consultant Neurologist
	Hammersmith Hospital
	Du Cane Road
	London W12 0HS
Tel:	0181 740 3986
Fax:	0181 259 8999
Private:	152 Harley Street
	London W1N 1HH
Tel:	0171 935 8868
Fax:	0171 224 2574
First Qualified:	1959 – London (with Honours)
Major Degrees:	FRCP
Academic:	Senior Lecturer in Neurology, Royal Postgraduate Medical School, London
Specialist Training:	National Hospital for Nervous Diseases

LUXON, Professor Linda Maitland

Special interests:	**Neuro-otology**
NHS:	Consultant Physician in Neuro-otology
	National Hospital for Neurology and Neurosurgery
	Queen Square
	London WC1N 3BJ
Tel:	0171 837 3611
Fax:	0171 829 8775
Private:	15 Upper Wimpole Street
	London W1M 7TB
Tel:	0171 486 5787
Fax:	0171 486 5470
First Qualified:	1972 – London
Major Degrees:	FRCP
Academic:	Professor in Audiology, Institute of Laryngology and Otology, University College London
Specialist Training:	National Hospital for Nervous Diseases, London
Distinctions:	Vice-Chairman, British Association of Audiology Physicians

MARSDEN, Professor C. David

Special interests:	**Movement disorders including Parkinson's disease**
NHS:	Professor of Neurology
	National Hospital
	Queen Square
	London WC1N 3BG
Tel:	0171 837 3611 Ext. 4252
Fax:	0171 278 5616
Private:	Refer to address and number above
Tel:	0171 837 3611 Ext. 8742
Fax:	0171 713 1407
First Qualified:	1963 – London
Major Degrees:	DSc, FRCP, MRCPsych
Academic:	Previously Professor of Neurology, Institute of Psychiatry and King's College Hospital, London
Specialist Training:	King's College and Maudsley Hospitals, London

McDONALD, Professor W. Ian

Special interests: **Multiple sclerosis**
NHS: Professor of Clinical Neurology
National Hospital
Queen Square
London WC1N 3BG
Tel: 0171 837 3611 Ext. 3416
Fax: 0171 278 5616
Private: Refer to address and number above
First Qualified: 1957 – New Zealand
Major Degrees: PhD, FRCP, FRCOphth
Academic: Professor of Clinical Neurology, Institute of Neurology, London
Distinctions: Editor of *Brain*
Honorary Consultant, Moorfields and National Hospitals, London
President, Association of British and Europan Neurologists
USA: Research Fellow, Harvard Medical School

MEADOWS, Dr John C.

NHS: Retired from the NHS
Private: 143 Harley Street
London W1N 1DJ
Tel: 0171 935 1802
Fax: 0171 935 1479
First Qualified: 1965 – Cambridge
Major Degrees: MD, FRCP
Academic: Honorary Senior Lecturer, St George's Hospital, London
Specialist Training: St Thomas' Hospital and National Hospital for Nervous Diseases, London

MORGAN-HUGHES, Dr John A.

Special interests: **Muscular disorders; metabolic myopathies**
NHS: Consultant Physician
National Hospital
Queen Square
London WC1N 3BG
Tel: 0171 837 3611 Ext. 8719
Fax: 0171 813 2123
Private: Refer to address and number above
First Qualified: 1957 – Cambridge
Major Degrees: MD, FRCP
Academic: Senior Lecturer, Institute of Neurology, London
Previously Lecturer, Department of Clinical Neurology, National Hospital, London
Specialist Training: National Hospital, London
USA: Postdoctoral Research Fellow, National Institute of Health, Bethesda, Maryland

PARKES, Professor J. David

Special interests:	**Myasthenia; Parkinson's disease; narcolepsy**
NHS:	Professor of Clinical Neurology
	Neurology Institute and King's College Hospital
	Denmark Hill
	London SE5 9RS
Tel:	0171 737 4000 Ext. 3874
Fax:	0171 708 0159
Private:	Refer to address and number above
First Qualified:	1964 – Cambridge
Major Degrees:	MD, FRCP
Academic:	Previously, Reader in Neurology, Neurology Institute and King's College Hospital, London
Specialist Training:	Maudsley and National Hospitals, London
Distinctions:	Honorary Consultant Neurologist, Maudsley Hospital and King's College Hospital, London

PERKIN, Dr George

NHS:	Consultant Neurologist
	Regional Neurosciences Unit
	Charing Cross Hospital
	Fulham Palace Road
	London W6 8RF
Tel:	0181 846 1153
Fax:	0181 846 7487
Private:	Refer to address and number above
First Qualified:	1966 – Cambridge
Major Degrees:	FRCP
Specialist Training:	University College Hospital, London

REYNOLDS, Dr Edward H.

Special interests:	**Epilepsy**
NHS:	Consultant Neurologist
	King's College Hospital
	Denmark Hill
	London SE5 9RS
Tel:	0171 703 6333
Fax:	0171 919 2171
and:	Chairman, Centre for Epilepsy
	Maudsley Hospital
	Denmark Hill
	London SE5 8AZ
Tel:	0171 919 2505
Fax:	0171 703 6396
Private:	Refer to address and number above
Tel:	01737 360867
Fax:	01737 363415
First Qualified:	1959 – Cardiff
Major Degrees:	MD, FRCP, FRCPsych
Academic:	Director, Institute of Epileptology, King's College, London
	Senior Lecturer, Department of Neurology, Institute of Psychiatry, London
Specialist Training:	National Hospital and Medical Research Council Neuropsychiatric Research Unit
Distinctions:	President, International League against Epilepsy
	President British Chapter, International League against Epilepsy
USA:	Previously, Assistant Professor Yale University Medical School

ROSSOR, Dr Martin N.

Special interests:	**Alzheimer's disease and related neurodegenerative conditions**
NHS:	Consultant Neurologist
	St Mary's Hospital
	Praed Street
	London W2 1NY
Tel:	0171 725 6666 or 0171 725 1264
Fax:	0171 725 6200
and:	National Hospital
	Queen Square
	London WC1N 3BG
Tel:	0171 837 3611
Fax:	0171 829 8720
Private:	Refer to address and number above
First Qualified:	1975 – Cambridge
Major Degrees:	MD, FRCP
Academic:	Senior Lecturer, Institute of Neurology, London
Specialist Training:	Cambridge, and at King's College and National Hospitals, London
Distinctions:	Associate Member, Royal College of Psychiatrists

SCADDING, Dr John W.

Special interests:	**Neurogenic pain; peripheral neuropathy**
NHS:	Consultant Neurologist
	National Hospital
	Queen Square
	London WC1N 3BG
Tel:	0171 837 3611 Ext. 3426
Fax:	0171 813 2126
Private:	Refer to address above
Tel:	0171 829 8741
Fax:	0171 833 8658
First Qualified:	1972 – London
Major Degrees:	MD, FRCP
Academic:	Honorary Senior Lecturer, Institute of Neurology, London

SCHOTT, Dr Geoffrey Denis

Special interests:	**Neurology and pain**
NHS:	Consultant Neurologist
	National Hospital
	Queen Square
	London WC1N 3BG
Tel:	0171 837 3611 Ext. 3066
Fax:	0171 829 8720
Private:	Refer to address above
Tel:	0171 837 3611 or 0171 829 8743
Fax:	0171 833 8659
First Qualified:	1968 – Cambridge
Major Degrees:	MD, FRCP
Specialist Training:	King's College Hospital and University Department of Clincal Neurology, National Hospital for Nervous Diseases, London

SHORVON, Professor Simon

Special interests:	**Epilepsy**
NHS:	Consultant Neurologist
	National Hospital
	Queen Square
	London WC1N 3BG
Tel:	0171 837 3611 Ext. 3422
Fax:	0171 837 3941
Private:	No private work
First Qualified:	1973 – Cambridge and London
Major Degrees:	MD, FRCP
Academic:	Professor in Clinical Neurology, Institute of Neurology, London
	Medical Director, National Society for Epilepsy
Distinctions:	Vice-President, International League against Epilepsy
USA:	Visiting Scientist, Virginia University

THOMAS, Dr David J.

Special interests:	**Strokes and stroke prevention**
NHS:	Consultant Neurologist
	St Mary's Hospital
	Praed Street
	London W2 1NY
Tel:	0171 725 1216
Fax:	0171 725 1422
and:	National Hospital
	Queen Square
	London WC1N 3BG
Tel:	0171 837 3611
Fax:	0171 829 8720
Private:	Refer to address and number above
First Qualified:	1969 – Cambridge
Major Degrees:	MD, FRCP
Specialist Training:	Queen Elizabeth Hospital, Birmingham, St Thomas' and National Hospitals, London
Distinctions:	Chairman, Charitable Association Supplying Hospitals

WADE, Dr John Philip Huddart

Special interests:	**Cerebrovascular disease**
NHS:	Consultant Neurologist
	Charing Cross Hospital
	Fulham Palace Road
	London W6 8RF
Tel:	0181 846 1303
Fax:	0181 846 7487
Private:	Thames Valley Nuffield Hospital
	Wexham
	Slough SL3 6NH
Tel:	01753 662241 Ext. 236
Fax:	01753 662129
First Qualified:	1974 – Cambridge
Major Degrees:	MA, MD, FRCP
Specialist Training:	National Hospital for Neurology and Neurosurgery, London
USA and Canada:	Reseach Fellow, University of Western Ontario, Canada

ZILKHA, Dr Kevin J.

Special interests:	**Dietary and hormonal factors in migraine and multiple sclerosis**
NHS:	Retired from the NHS
Private:	Cromwell Hospital
	Cromwell Road
	London SW5
Tel:	0171 370 4233 Ext. 5668
Fax:	0171 460 5669
and:	National Hospital
	Queen Square
	London WC1N 3BG
Tel:	0171 837 3611
Fax:	0171 713 1407
First Qualified:	1953 – London
Major Degrees:	MD, FRCP
Academic:	Previously Sub-Dean, Institute of Neurology, London
Specialist Training:	National, Hospital for Sick Children and Guy's Hospitals, London
Distinctions:	Honorary Consultant, Maudsley Hospital, London, the Army and Royal Hospital, Chelsea

ANGLIA AND OXFORD REGION

CAMBRIDGE

COMPSTON, Professor David Alastair Standish

Special interests:	**Multiple sclerosis**
NHS:	Professor of Neurology
	University of Cambridge Clinical School
	Addenbrooke's Hospital
	Hills Road, Cambridge CB2 2QQ
Tel:	01223 217091
Fax:	01223 336941
Private:	Refer to address and number above
First Qualified:	1971 – London
Major Degrees:	PhD, FRCP
Academic:	Formerly Professor of Neurology, University of Wales
Specialist Training:	National Hospital, London

HODGES, Dr John Russell

Special interests:	**Behavioral neurology: memory disorders and dementia**
NHS:	Consultant Neurologist
	Department of Neurology
	Addenbrooke's Hospital
	Hills Rd, Cambridge CB2 2QQ
Tel:	01223 217697
Fax:	01223 336941
Private:	No private work
First Qualified:	1975 – London (Distinction in Medicine)
Major Degrees:	MD, FRCP
Academic:	Lecturer, Cambridge University Clinical School
Specialist Training:	Radcliffe Infirmary, Oxford and UCSD, California USA
Distinctions:	Visiting Professor, Pennsylvania University and MacQuaire University, Sydney; Founding Co-Editor, Neurocare; Editorial Board, Journal of Neurology, Neurosurgery and Psychiatry and Journal of Neurology
USA:	See' Specialist Training' and 'Distinctions' above

OXFORD

DONAGHY, Dr Michael John

Special interests:	**Peripheral neuropathies**
NHS:	Consultant Neurologist
	Department of Clinical Neurology
	University of Oxford
	Radcliffe Infirmary
	Woodstock Road
	Oxford OX2 6HE
Tel:	01865 224 698
Fax:	01865 790 493
Private:	Refer to address and number above
First Qualified:	1978 – London (with Honours)
Major Degrees:	DPhil, FRCP
Academic:	Clinical Reader in Neurology, Oxford University
Specialist Training:	St Bartholomew's, National Hospital for Nervous Diseases and The Middlesex Hospitals, London
Distinctions:	Honorary Consultant Neurologist, Radcliffe Infirmary, Oxford, and Horton General Hospital, Banbury

---

NEWSOM-DAVIS, Professor John Michael

Special interests:	**Myasthenic disorders; neuroimmunological disorders; paraneoplastic syndromes**
NHS:	Professor of Neurology
	Department of Clinical Neurology
	Radcliffe Infirmary
	Woodstock Road
	Oxford OX2 6HE
Tel:	01865 224205
Fax:	01865 790493
Private:	Refer to address and number above
First Qualified:	1960 – Cambridge and London
Major Degrees:	MA, MD, FRCP
Academic:	MRC Clinical Research Professor of Neurology Royal Free Hospital Medical School, Institute of Neurology 1980–87
	Professor of Clinical Neurology, University of Oxford 1987 – present
Specialist Training:	National Hospital for Nervous Diseases and Institute of Neurology, London
Distinctions:	FRS 1991, CBE 1996
USA:	Research Fellow, Department of Neurology, New York Hospital, Cornell Medical Centre, New York 1969–70

OXBURY, Dr John Michael

Special interests:	**Epilepsy**
NHS:	Consultant Neurologist
	Department of Neurology
	Radcliffe Infirmary
	Oxford OX2 6HE
Tel:	01865 224487
Fax:	01865 224303
Private:	Refer to address and number above
First Qualified:	1963 – Cambridge
Major Degrees:	FRCP
Academic:	Clinical Lecturer in Neurology, Oxford University
Specialist Training:	Oxford

SLOUGH

See above: WADE, Dr John Philip Huddart

NORTH WEST REGION

LIVERPOOL

CHADWICK, Professor David W.

Special interests:	**Epilepsy; myoclonus**
NHS:	Professor of Neurology
	Department of Neuroscience
	Walton Hospital
	Rice Lane
	Liverpool L9 1AE
Tel:	0151 525 3611 Ext. 4819
Fax:	0151 525 3857
Private:	Refer to address and number above
First Qualified:	1971 – Oxford
Major Degrees:	DM, FRCP
Academic:	Professor of Neurology, Liverpool University

HUMPHREY, Dr Peter R. D.

Special interests:	**Strokes**
NHS:	Consultant Neurologist
	The Walton Centre for Neurology and Neurosurgery
	Rice Lane
	Liverpool L9 1AE
Tel:	0151 529 4596
Fax:	0151 529 4514
Private:	88 Rodney Street
	Liverpool L1 9AR
Tel:	0151 525 3611
Fax:	0151 529 4514
and:	The Grosvenor Nuffield Hospital
	Wrexham Road
	Chester CH4 7QP
Tel:	01224 680444
First Qualified:	1972 – Oxford
Major Degrees:	DM, FRCP
Academic:	Lecturer in Neurology, Liverpool University
Specialist Training:	National and St Bartholomew's Hospitals, London

NORTHERN AND YORKSHIRE REGION

LEEDS

JOHNSON, Dr Michael Harvey

Special interests:	**Neuroimmunology**
NHS:	Consultant Neurologist
	St James University Hospital
	Beckett Street
	Leeds LS9 7TF
Tel:	01132 433144 Ext. 4454
Fax:	01132 465231
Private:	Refer to address and number above
First Qualified:	1974 – Oxford
Major Degrees:	DM, FRCP
Academic:	Clinical Lecturer in Medicine, Leeds Univesity
Specialist Training:	National Hospital for Nervous Diseases and Middlesex Hospital, London

NEWCASTLE

BATES, Dr David

NHS:	Consultant Neurologist
	Royal Victoria Infirmary
	Newcastle upon Tyne NE1 4LP
Tel:	0191 232 5131 Ext. 24949
Fax.	0191 261 0881
Private:	Refer to address and number above
First Qualified:	1968 – Cambridge
Major Degrees:	FRCP
Academic:	Senior Lecturer in Neurology, Newcastle University

SHEFFIELD

VENABLES, Dr Graham Stuart

NHS:	Consultant Neurologist
	Royal Hallamshire Hospital
	Sheffield S10 2JF
Tel:	01142 766222 Ext. 2197
Fax:	01142 713684
Private:	Refer to address and number above
First Qualified:	1973 – Oxford
Major Degrees:	DM, FRCP
Academic:	Associate Post-Dean, Sheffield Medical School

EDINBURGH

WARLOW, Professor Charles Picton

Special interests:	**Strokes; cerebrovascular disease**
NHS:	Professor of Medical Neurology
	Department of Clinical Neurosciences
	Western General Hospital
	Crewe Road
	Edinburgh EH4 2XU
Tel:	0131 537 2081 or 0131 537 2082
Fax:	0131 332 7886
e-mail:	dcn@skull.dcn.ed.ac.uk
Private:	Refer to address and number above
First Qualified:	1968 – Cambridge
Major Degrees:	MD, FRCP Glas, FRCP Ed, FRCP
Academic:	Professor Medical Neurology, Edinburgh University
	Previously Clinical Reader in Neurology, Oxford University
Specialist Training:	National Hospital for Nervous Diseases, London

NEUROSURGEONS

Neurosurgeons operate or use non-operative procedures to treat problems affecting the nerves, the brain and the spinal cord, such as brain tumours and slipped discs. They also treat congenital neurological conditions such as spina bifida and hydrocephalus. Head injuries affecting the brain are operated on by a neurosurgeon.

LONDON AND THE SOUTH EAST

AFSHAR, Mr Farhad

Special interests:	**Stereotaxic surgery; vascular and pituitary lesions; brain and spinal tumours**
NHS:	Consultant Neurosurgeon
	Royal London Hospital
	Whitechapel Road
	London E1 1BB
Tel:	0171 377 7000 Ext. 7211
Fax:	0171 377 7002
and:	St Bartholomew's Hospital
	West Smithfield
	London EC1A 7BE
Tel:	0171 601 8888
Fax:	0171 601 7899
Private:	149 Harley Street
	London W1 2DE
Tel:	0171 935 7505
Fax:	0171 935 7245
First Qualified:	1967 – London
Major Degrees:	MD, FRCS
Academic:	Senior Lecturer and Honorary Consultant Neurosurgeon, London Hospital
	Honorary Lecturer, London University
Specialist Training:	St Bartholomew's and Royal London Hospitals, London
Distinctions:	Hallett Prize, Royal College of Surgeons; Sir Hugh Cairns Memorial Travelling Neurosurgical Scholarship, Society British Neurosurgeons
USA:	Previously Fellow in Neurosurgery, Ohio State University, Columbus
	Consultant Neurosurgeon, Hartford, Connecticut
	Member, American Congress of Neurosurgeons

BRADFORD, Mr Robert

Special interests:	**Surgery of glioma, stereotaxis; management of acute spinal injury**
NHS:	Consultant Neurosurgeon
	Royal Free Hospital
	Pond Street
	London NW3
Tel:	0171 794 0500 Ext. 3356
Fax:	0171 830 2866
Private:	Refer to address and number above
First Qualified:	1979 – London
Major Degrees:	MD, FRCS
Academic:	Senior Lecturer, Royal Free Hampstead Trust
Distinctions:	Councillor, Neurology Section, Royal Society of Medicine
	MRC Brain Tumour working party
	Advanced trauma life support instructor, Royal College of Surgeons

CROCKARD, Mr H. Alan

Special interests:	**Complex spinal problems**
NHS:	Consultant Neurosurgeon
	National Hospital
	Queen Square
	London WC1N 3BG
Tel:	0171 646 4191
Fax:	0171 722 3141
Private:	Refer to address and number above
First Qualified:	1966 – Belfast
Major Degrees:	FRCS, FRCS Ed
Specialist Training:	Institute of Neurology, London, and University of Chicago
Distinctions:	Co-founder and Secretary, British Cervical Spine Society
	Surgical Workshop Tutor, Royal College of Surgeons
	Hunterian Professor and Arnott Demonstration, Royal College of Surgeons
	Olivecrona Lecturer, Karolinska Institute Stockholm
USA:	Member, American Academy of Neurological Surgeons
	See 'Specialist Training' above

HAYWARD, Mr Richard D.

Special interests: **Paediatric neurosurgery; craniofacial surgery**
NHS: Consultant Surgeon
Great Ormond Street Hospital for Children
Great Ormond Street
London WC1N 3JH
Tel: 0171 405 9200
Fax: 0171 242 5800
Private: The Private Consulting Rooms
National Hospital
Queen Square
London WC1N 3BG
Tel: 0171 829 8792
Fax: 0171 833 8658
First Qualified: 1966 – London
Major Degrees: FRCS
Specialist Training: St Mary's and National Hospitals, London
Distinctions: Honorary Consultant Neurosurgeon, King Edward VII
Hospital, London

POWELL, Mr Michael P.

Special interests: **Pituitary surgery**
NHS: Director of Surgery
Consultant Neurosurgeon
National Hospital
Queen Square
London WC1N 3BG
Tel: 0171 837 3611 Ext. 3176
Fax: 0171 833 8658
Private: Refer to address above
Tel: 0171 829 8717
Fax: 0171 833 8658
First Qualified: 1975 – London
Major Degrees: FRCS
Specialist Training: National Hospital
Distinctions: Honorary Consultant Neurosurgeon, St Luke's Hospital
for Clergy, Whittington Hospital and King Edward VII
Hospital for Officers and St Thomas' Hospitals, London

THOMAS, Professor David G. T.

Special interests:	**Head injuries; malignant brain tumours**
NHS:	Professor of Neurological Surgery
	National Hospital
	Queen Square
	London WC1N 3BG
Tel:	0171 837 3611 Ext. 3410
Fax:	0171 278 7894
and:	Consultant Neurosurgeon
	Northwick Park and St Mark's Hospital
	Watford Road
	Harrow, Middlesex HA1 3UJ
Tel:	0181 864 3232
Fax:	0181 869 2009
Private:	Refer to address and number above
First Qualified:	1966 – Cambridge
Major Degrees:	FRCP, FRCS
Academic:	Senior Lecturer, Institute of Neurology
Specialist Training:	Institute of Neurological Science, Glasgow, and St Mary's Hospital, London
Distinctions:	Consultant Neurosurgeon, Medical Research Council
	Cheadle Medal and Prize, St Mary's
	Cairns Memorial Prize, Society Neurosurgeons
	Wellcome Surgical Fellowship

ANGLIA AND OXFORD REGION

CAMBRIDGE

HARDY, Mr David Gordon

Special interests:	**Surgery of meningioma; acoustic neuroma and tumours of the skull base**
NHS:	Consultant Neurosurgeon
	Addenbrooke's Hospital
	Hills Road
	Cambridge CB2 2QQ
Tel:	01223 216302
Fax:	01223 216302
Private:	BUPA Cambridge Lea Hospital
	30 New Road
	Impington, Cambridge CB4 4EL
Tel:	01223 216302
Fax:	01223 216302
First Qualified:	1965 – Edinburgh
Major Degrees:	FRCS Ed, FRCS
Academic:	Associate Lecturer, Cambridge University
	Previously Senior Lecturer, London Hospital Medical College
Specialist Training:	London Hospital
USA:	Previously Research Fellow, Department of Neurosurgery, Florida University

---

OXFORD

ADAMS, Mr Christopher B. T.

Special interests:	**Pituitary tumour surgery; epilepsy; intracranial aneurysms; cervical spondylosis**
NHS:	Consultant Neursurgeon
	Department of Neurological Surgery
	Radcliffe Infirmary
	Oxford OX2 6HE
Tel:	01865 512433
Fax:	01865 512433
Private:	Refer to address and number above
First Qualified:	1963 – Cambridge
Major Degrees:	FRCS, FRCS Ed, MChir
Specialist Training:	Radcliffe Infirmary, Oxford

NORTH WEST REGION

LIVERPOOL

FINDLAY, Mr Gordon

Special interests:	**Back surgery**
NHS:	Consultant Neurosurgeon
	Walton Hospital
	Rice Lane
	Liverpool L9 1AE
Tel:	0151 525 3611 Ext. 4694
Fax:	0151 529 4772
Private:	Refer to address and number above
First Qualified:	1974 – Edinburgh
Major Degrees:	FRCS

MANCHESTER AND SALFORD

COWIE, Mr Richard A.

Special interests:	**Spinal surgery**
NHS:	Consultant Neurosurgeon
	Neuroscience Unit
	Alexandra Hospital
	Mill Lane
	Cheadle, Cheshire SK8 2PX
Tel:	0161 491 1606
Fax:	0161 491 1645
and:	Royal Manchester Children's Hospital
	Hospital Road
	Pendlebury
	Manchester M27 1HA
Tel:	0161 794 4696
Fax:	0161 794 5929
and:	Consultant Neurosurgeon
	Hope Hospital
	Stott Lane
	Salford M6 8HD
Tel:	0161 789 7373
Fax:	0161 787 4606
Private:	Refer to address and number above
First Qualified:	1973 – Edinburgh
Major Degrees:	FRCS
Specialist Training:	Western General Hospital, Edinburgh

NORTHERN AND YORKSHIRE REGION

NEWCASTLE

MENDELOW, Professor Alexander David

Special interests:	**Vascular neurosurgery: aneurysms, arteriovenous malformation, carotid endarterectomy, carotid stenosis/occlusions; neurotrauma**
NHS:	Consultant Neurosurgeon
	Newcastle General Hospital
	Westgate Road
	Newcastle upon Tyne NE4 6BE
Tel:	0191 273 8811 Ext. 22269
Fax:	0191 226 0543
Private:	Refer to address and number above
First Qualified:	1969 – Witwatersrand, Johannesburg, South Africa
Major Degrees:	PhD FRCS Ed (Surgical Neurology)
Academic:	Professor of Neurosurgery, Newcastle University
Distinctions:	Honorary Consultant Neurosurgeon, Southern General Hospital, Glasgow
	Clinical Director, Regional Neurosciences Centre, Newcastle
	Govenor, British Neurosurgery Research Group

SOUTH AND WEST REGION

BRISTOL

SANDEMAN, Mr David R.

Special interests:	**Epilepsy surgery; neuro-oncology; interactive image-neurosurgery**
NHS:	Consultant Neurosurgeon
	Department of Neurosurgery
	Frenchay Hospital
	Bristol BS16 1LE
Tel:	0117 975 3833
Fax:	0117 970 1161
Private:	15 Fremantle Road
	Cotham
	Bristol BS6 5SY
Tel:	0117 924 7346
Fax:	0117 970 1161
First Qualified:	1979 – London
Major Degrees:	FRCS
Specialist Training:	Walton Hospital, Liverpool, Manchester Royal Infirmary and Hope Hospital, Salford

SCOTLAND

GLASGOW

HIDE, Mr Thomas A. H.

NHS:	Consultant Neurosurgeon
	Institute of Neurological Sciences
	Southern General Hospital
	1345 Govan Road
	Glasgow G51 4TF
Tel:	0141 445 2466 or 0141 201 1100 Ext. 2024
Fax:	0141 425 1442
Private:	Refer to address and number above
First Qualified:	1960 – Glasgow
Major Degrees:	FRCS
Specialist Training:	Atkinson Morley's Hospital and National Hospital for Nervous Diseases, London

JOHNSTON, Mr Robin A.

Special interests:	**Spinal surgery**
NHS:	Consultant Neurosurgeon
	Institute of Neurological Sciences
	Southern General Hospital
	1345 Govan Road
	Glasgow G51 4TF
Tel:	0141 201 1100
Fax:	0141 201 2999
Private:	Refer to address and number above
First Qualified:	1974 – Dublin
Major Degrees:	MD, FRCS Ed
USA:	Hagar Clinical Resident Fellow in Neurology, Texas University

OBSTETRICIANS AND GYNAECOLOGISTS

Obstetricians and Gynaecologists treat medical and surgical ailments affecting the female reproductive system. Obstetricians care for women during pregnancy and childbirth and many serve as a woman's primary care physician. Gynaecologists treat all conditions affecting the female reproductive system but not pregnant women; this includes treatment of gynaecological cancers and infertility. Endocrinologists may also be consulted if there is an infertility problem.

LONDON AND THE SOUTH EAST

ABDALLA, Mr Sam

Special interests:	**In vitro fertilisation**
NHS:	Consultant Gynaecologist
	Chelsea and Westminster Hospital
	369 Fulham Road, London SW10 9NH
Tel:	0181 746 8000 or 0181 746 8585
Fax:	0181 746 8921
Private:	Director of IVF Clinic
	Lister Hospital
	Chelsea Bridge Road
	London SW1W 8RH
Tel:	0171 730 3417
Fax:	0171 259 9039
First Qualified:	1977 – Bagdad, Iraq
Major Degrees:	MRCOG

ARMSTRONG, Mr N. Paul

Special interests:	**Pregnancy; recurrent miscarriage; minimal access surgery**
NHS:	Consultant Obstetrician and Gynaecologist
	Royal London Hospital
	Whitechapel Road, London E1 1BB
Tel:	0171 377 7055
Fax:	0171 377 7171
Private:	The Portland Hospital
	209 Great Portland Street
	London W1N 6AH
Tel:	0171 580 5754
Fax:	0171 631 1170 or 0171 580 8754
First Qualified:	1976 – Manchester
Major Degrees:	MD, MRCOG
Academic:	Senior Lecturer in Obstetrics and Gynaecology, London Hospital Medical College
Specialist Training:	University College and Royal London Hospital

BEARD, Mr Robert John

Special interests:	**Menopause**
NHS:	Consultant Obstetrician and Gynaecologist
	Brighton General Hospital
	Elm Grove
	Brighton BN2 3EW
Tel:	01273 696955
Fax:	01273 665023
Private:	75 Dyke Road
	Hove, East Sussex BN3 6DA
Tel:	01273 541642
Fax:	01273 552165
First Qualified:	1964 – London (with Honours)
Major Degrees:	FRCS Ed, FRCS, FRCOG

BEARD, Professor Richard W.

Special interests:	**Diabetic pregnancy; pelvic pain**
NHS:	Samaritan Hospital for Women
	171 Marylebone Rd
	London NW1 5YE
Tel:	0171 402 4211 Ext. 454
Private:	Refer to the number below
Tel:	0171 725 1461
Fax:	0171 725 6054
First Qualified:	1956 – London
Major Degrees:	MD, FRCOG
Academic:	Professor of Obstetrics and Gynaecology, St Mary's Hospital, London
Specialist Training:	King's College and Queen Charlotte's Hospitals, London
Distinctions:	President, European College of Obstetricians and Gynaecologists
	Civilian Consultant to the Royal Air Force

BRIDGES, Ms Jane

Special interests:	**Gynaecological cancer**
NHS:	Consultant Gynaecologist
	Chelsea and Westminster Hospital
	369 Fulham Road
	London SW10 9NH
Tel:	0181 746 8218
Fax:	0181 846 7998
Private:	Lister Hospital
	Chelsea Bridge Road
	London SW1W 8RH
Tel:	0171 730 3417 Ext. 252
Fax:	0171 259 0465
First Qualified:	1981 – Leicester
Major Degrees:	MRCOG

CAMPBELL, Professor Stuart

Special interests:	**Prenatal diagnosis**
NHS and academic:	Professor of Obstetrics and Gynaecology
	St George's Hospital
	Blackshaw Road
	London SW17 0QT
Tel:	0181 672 1255
Fax:	0181 725 5958
Private:	Refer to address above
Tel:	0171 935 2243 for private appointments
First Qualified:	1961 – Glasgow
Major Degrees:	FRCOG
Academic:	Professor of Obstetrics and Gynaecology, St George's Hospital, London
Specialist Training:	Queen Charlotte's Hospital, London
USA:	Fellow, American Institute of Ultrasound

CARDOZO, Professor Linda

Special interests:	**Management of female urinary incontinence; pelvic reconstructive surgery**
NHS and Academic:	Professor of Urogynaecology
	King's College Hospital
	Denmark Hill, London SE5 9RS
Tel:	0171 737 4000 Ext. 4561
Fax:	0171 346 3603
Private:	8 Devonshire Place
	London W1N 1PB
Tel:	0171 935 2357
Fax:	0171 224 2797
First Qualified:	1974 – Liverpool
Major Degrees:	MD, FRCOG
Specialist Training:	St George's Hospital, London

COLTART, Mr Timothy M.

NHS:	Consultant Gynaecologist and Obstetrician
	Queen Charlotte's Hospital
	Goldhawk Road, London W6 0XG
Tel:	0181 748 4666
Fax:	0181 740 3419
Private:	92 Harley Street
	London WIN IAF
Tel:	0171 935 6836
Fax:	0171 487 2550
First Qualified:	1963 – Cambridge
Major Degrees:	PhD, FRCS, FRCOG
Specialist Training:	Queen Charlotte's Hospital, London

FERGUSSON, Mr Ian L. C.

NHS:	Consultant Obstetrician and Gynaecologist
	St Thomas' Hospital
	Lambeth Palace Road
	London SEI 7EH
Tel:	0171 928 9292 Ext. 2320
Fax:	0171 922 8351
Private:	10 Upper Wimpole Street
	London W1M 7TD
Tel:	0171 935 8273
Fax:	0171 487 5715
First Qualified:	1967 – Cambridge
Major Degrees:	FRCS Ed, FRCOG
Distinctions:	Senior Civilian Gynaecologist to the Royal Navy

GILLARD, Mr Malcolm G.

Special interests:	**Pregnancy**
NHS:	No NHS work
Private:	1 Devonshire Place
	London WIN 1PA
Tel:	0171 486 2856
Fax:	0171 486 2858
First Qualified:	1972 – London (with Honours)
Major Degrees:	FRCS, FRCOG
Academic:	Lately Dean, Institute of Obstetrics and Gynaecology
Specialist Training:	Queen Charlotte's, London
Distinctions:	Hallet Prize, Royal College of Surgeons

KENNEY, Mr Anthony

Special interests:	**Obstetrics**
NHS:	Consultant Obstetrician and Gynaecologist
	St Thomas' Hospital
	Lambeth Palace Road
	London SEI 7EH
Tel:	0171 928 9292 Ext. 2320
Fax:	0171 922 8351
Private:	17 Wimpole Street, London W1M 7AD
Tel:	0181 942 0440
Fax:	0181 949 9100
First Qualified:	1966 – Cambridge
Major Degrees:	FRCS, FRCOG
Specialist Training:	The London and Westminster Hospitals, London
Distinctions:	Examiner, Royal College of Obstetrics and Gynaecology

LLOYD, Mrs Ursula E.

Special interests:	**General Obstetrics and Gynaecology**
NHS:	None
Private:	Portland Hospital
	209 Great Portland Street
	London W1N 6AH
Tel:	0171 935 3732
Fax:	0171 935 3732
First Qualified:	1967 – London
Major Degrees:	FRCOG
Specialist Training:	Queen Charlotte's Hospital, London

LOEFFLER, Mr Frank E.

Special interests:	**Detection of foetal abnormalities during pregnancy**
NHS:	Consultant Obstetrician and Gynaecologist
	St Mary's Hospital
	Praed Street
	London W2 1NY
Tel:	0171 725 6666 or 0171 725 1567
Fax:	0171 725 6200
and:	Queen Charlotte's Hospital
	Goldhawk Road
	London W6 OXG
Tel:	0181 748 4666
Fax:	0181 740 3588
Private:	86 Harley Street
	London W1N 1AE
Tel:	0171 486 2966
Fax:	0171 637 0994
First Qualified:	1956 – Cambridge
Major Degrees:	FRCS, FRCOG
Specialist Training:	Queen Charlotte's Hospital, London
Distinctions:	Previously Editor, British Journal of Obstetrics and Gynaecology

MAGOS, Mr Adam L.

Special interests:	**Minimally invasive surgery; gynaecological endoscopy**
NHS:	Consultant, University Department of Obstetrics and Gynaecology
	Royal Free Hospital
	Pond Street
	London NW3 2QG
Tel:	0171 794 0500 Ext. 3868 or 0171 431 1321
Fax:	0171 431 1321
Private:	10 Harley Street
	London W1N 1AA
Tel:	0171 636 6504
Fax:	0171 637 5227
First Qualified:	1978 – London
Major Degrees:	MD, MRCOG
Specialist Training:	King's College Hospital, London, and John Radcliffe Hospital, Oxford

MALVERN, Mr John

Special interests:	**Urogynaecological/obstetrics; general gynaecology**
NHS:	Consultant Obstetrician and Gynaecologist
	Queen Charlotte's Hospital
	Goldhawk Road
	London W6 0XG
Tel:	0181 748 4666
Fax:	0181 740 3419
Private:	84 Harley Street
	London WIN 1AE
Tel:	0171 636 2766
Fax:	0171 631 5371
First Qualified:	1960 – London
Major Degrees:	FRCS, FRCOG
Academic:	Senior Lecturer, Institute of Obstetrics and Gynaecology, London
Specialist Training:	Queen Charlotte's Hospital and Chelsea Hospital for Women, London
Distinctions:	Honorary Treasurer and Examiner, Royal College of Obstetrics and Gynaecologists

MARWOOD, Mr Roger P.

Special interests:	**Gynaecology; obstetric care**
NHS:	Consultant Obstetrician and Gynaecologist
	Chelsea and Westminster Hospital
	369 Fulham Road
	London SW10 9NH
Tel:	0181 746 8000
Fax:	0181 746 8111
Private:	96 Harley Street
	London W1N 1AF
Tel:	0171 637 7977
Fax:	0171 486 2022
First Qualified:	1969 – London
Major Degrees:	FRCOG
Specialist Training:	Guy's and St Mary's Hospitals, London

MASON, Mr Peter W.

Special interests:	**Cancer**
NHS:	Consultant Obstetrician and Gynaecologist
	Samaritans Hospital
	171 Marylebone Road
	London NW1 5YE
Tel:	0171 402 4211
Fax:	0171 259 3417
Private:	106 Harley Street
	London W1N 1AF
Tel:	0171 935 7952
Fax:	0171 935 7044
First Qualified:	1972 – Bristol
Major Degrees:	FRCS, FRCOG
Specialist Training:	St Mary's Hospital, London

McMILLAN, Mr Lindsay

Special interests:	**Minimally invasive surgery; oncology**
NHS:	Consultant Gynaecologist
	Whipp's Cross Hospital
	Whipp's Cross Road
	Leytonstone
	London E11 1NR
Tel:	0181 535 6536
Fax:	0181 558 8115
Private:	17 Wimpole Street
	London W1M 7AD
Tel:	0171 631 0914
Fax:	0171 323 9126
First Qualified:	1977 – London
Major Degrees:	MRCOG
Specialist Training:	Royal Free Hospital, London

NAYLOR, Mr Christopher Hardy

Special interests:	**Complicated pregnancy and delivery; therapeutic termination of pregnancy; endometriosis; menorrhagia; management of the menopause**
NHS:	Retired from the NHS
Private:	116 Harley Street
	London W1N 1AG
Tel:	0171 935 6911
Fax:	0171 935 5411
First Qualified:	1958 – Cardiff
Major Degrees:	FRCOG
Academic:	Honorary Senior Lecturer, University College Hospital, London
Specialist Training:	Queen Charlotte's Hospital, London

NICOLAIDES, Professor Kyprianos H.

Special interests:	**Pre-natal diagnosis and treatment of the foetus**
NHS:	Consultant, Harris Birthright Research Centre for Foetal Medicine
	King's College Hospital Medical School
	Denmark Hill
	London SE5 9RS
Tel:	0171 346 3040
Fax:	0171 738 3740
Private:	Refer to address and number above
First Qualified:	1978 – London
Major Degrees:	FRCOG
Academic:	Professor, Harris Birthright Research Centre for Foetal Medicine
Specialist Training:	King's College Hospital, London

ORAM, Mr David H.

Special interests:	**Gynaecological cancer; colposcopy; ovarian cancer screening**
NHS:	Consultant Obstetrician and Gynaecologist
	St Bartholomew's Hospital
	West Smithfield
	London EC1A 7BE
Tel:	0171 601 7186
Fax:	0171 601 7182
and:	Royal London
	Whitechapel Road
	London E1 1BB
Tel:	0171 377 7000 Ext. 7225
Fax:	0171 377 7396/7122
Private:	121 Harley Street
	London W1N 1DM
Tel:	0171 935 7111
Fax:	0171 935 7111
First Qualified:	1971 – London
Major Degrees:	FRCOG
Specialist Training:	Durban, South Africa, and Georgetown University, Washington D.C.
USA:	See 'Specialist Training' above

OSBORNE, Mr John L.

Special interests:	**Urogynaecology and female incontinence**
NHS:	Consultant Obstetrician and Gynaecologist
	Queen Charlotte's Hospital
	Goldhawk Road
	London W6 0XG
Tel:	0181 748 4666
Fax:	0181 740 3419
and:	Elizabeth Garrett Anderson Hospital
	University College Hospital
	Euston Road
	London NW1 2AP
Tel:	0171 387 2501
Fax:	0171 388 9632
Private:	77 Harley House
	Marleybone Road
	London NW1 5HN
Tel:	0171 935 1682
Fax:	0171 487 4650
First Qualified:	1966 – London
Major Degrees:	FRCOG
Academic:	Honorary Senior Lecturer, Institute of Obstetrics and Gynaecology; Honorary Senior Lecturer, Institute of Urology; Honorary Senior Lecturer, University College Hospital Medical School, London
Specialist Training:	The Middlesex and Queen Charlotte's Hospitals, London

PAWSON, Mr Michael E.

Special interests:	**Holistic gynaecology**
NHS and Academic:	Senior Lecturer and Consultant in Gynaecology
	Chelsea and Westminster Hospital
	369 Fulham Road
	London SW10 9NH
Tel:	0181 746 8000
Fax:	0181 846 7998
Private:	55 Wimpole Street
	London W1
Tel:	0171 935 1964
Fax:	0171 486 1212
First Qualified:	1962 – London
Major Degrees:	FRCOG
Specialist Training:	Queen Charlotte's Hospital, London
Distinctions:	Examiner, London University and Royal College of Obstetrics and Gynaecology

SAVVAS, Mr Michael

Special interests:	**PMT; menopause; infertility**
NHS:	Consultant Obstetrician and Gynaecologist
	Lewisham Hospital
	High Street
	Lewisham, London SW13 6LH
Tel:	0181 333 3000 Ext. 3065
Fax:	0181 690 1963
Private:	London Bridge Hospital
	Emblem House
	27 Tooley Street
	London SE1
Tel:	0171 403 3363
First Qualified:	1980 – London
Major Degrees:	MRCOG
Specialist Training:	King's College Hospital, London

SETCHELL, Mr Marcus E.

Special interests:	**Fertility; minimally invasive surgery**
NHS:	Consultant Gynaecological Surgeon
	St Bartholomew's and Homerton Hospital
	Homerton Row
	London E9 6SR
Tel:	0171 919 5555
Fax:	0171 919 7787
and:	Director, In-Vitro Fertilisation Clinic
	St Bartholomew's Hospital
	West Smithfield
	London EC1 7BE
Tel:	0171 601 8888 Ext. 7186
Fax:	0171 601 7182
Private:	137 Harley Street
	London W1N 1DJ
Tel:	0171 935 6122
Fax:	0171 935 6122
and:	Director, Fertility Clinic
	The Portland Hospital
	209 Great Portland Street
	London W1N 6AH
Tel:	0171 580 4400
Fax:	0171 390 8012
First Qualified:	1968 – Cambridge
Major Degrees:	FRCS, FRCOG
Distinctions:	Gynaecologist to HM the Queen; Examiner to the Universities of London and Cambridge and the Royal College of Obstetricians and Gynaecologists

SHEPHERD, Mr John

Special interests:	**Gynaecological cancer**
NHS:	Consultant Gynaecological Surgeon
	St Bartholomew's Hospital
	West Smithfield, London EC1A 7BE
Tel:	0171 601 8888 Ext. 7180
Fax:	0171 601 7182
and:	Royal Marsden Hospital
	Fulham Road
	London SW3 6JJ
Private:	149 Harley Street
	London W1N 2DE
Tel:	0171 935 4444
Fax:	0171 935 6224
First Qualified:	1971 – London
Major Degrees:	FRCS, MRCOG
Specialist Training:	Queen Charlotte's Hospital, London
Distinctions:	Previously Royal College of Obstetricians and Gynaecologists Gold Medallist
USA:	Visiting Professor, Universities of Virginia and South Florida

SILVERSTONE, Mr Anthony C.

Special interests:	**Gynaecological cancer**
NHS:	Consultant Obstetrician and Gynaecologist
	The Middlesex Hospital
	Mortimer Street
	London W1N 8AA
Tel:	0171 636 8333
Fax:	0171 323 0397
Private:	The Portland Hospital
	209 Great Portland Street
	London W1N 6AH
Tel:	0171 383 7884
Fax:	0171 580 4400
First Qualified:	1969 – Birmingham
Major Degrees:	FRCS, FRCOG
Specialist Training:	Queen Charlotte's Hospital for Women, London
	John Radcliffe Hospital, Oxford
	General and Princess Margaret Hospitals, Toronto, Canada
USA and Canada:	See 'Specialist Training' above

SINGER, Professor Albert

Special interests:	**Non-surgical treatment of gynaecological problems**
NHS and Academic:	Professor of Gynaecology
	The Whittington Hospital
	St Mary's Wing
	Highgate Hill
	London N19 5NF
Tel:	0171 272 3070
Fax:	0171 288 5066
Private:	148 Harley Street
	London W1N 1DJ
Tel:	0171 935 1900
Fax:	0181 458 0168
First Qualified:	1962 – Sydney, Australia
Major Degrees:	PhD, DPhil, FRCOG
Academic:	Professor of Gynaecology, University College London
Specialist Training:	Oxford and Sheffield

STANTON, Mr Stuart L. R.

Special interests:	**Urogynaecology including incontinence, prolapse and the elderly**
NHS:	Consultant Gynaecologist St George's Hospital Blackshaw Road London SW17 0QT
Tel:	0181 725 5949
Fax:	0181 725 2999
Private:	Flat 10, 43 Wimpole Street London WIM 7AF
Tel:	0171 486 0677
Fax:	0171 486 6792
First Qualified:	1961 – London
Major Degrees:	FRCS, FRCOG
Academic:	Senior Lecturer, St George's Hospital Medical School, London
Specialist Training:	Institute of Urology and The Middlesex Hospital, London
Distinctions:	Examiner, Royal College of Obstetricians and Gynaecologists
USA:	Visiting Professor to Emory and to Iowa

STEER, Professor Philip J.

Special interests:	**Foetal monitoring**
NHS:	Professor of Obstetrics Chelsea and Westminster Hospital 369 Fulham Road London SW10 9NH
Tel:	0181 746 8000 Ext. 7892
Fax:	0181 846 7880
Private:	Refer to address and number above
First Qualified:	1971 – London
Major Degrees:	MD, FRCOG
Academic:	Professor of Obstetrics
Specialist Training:	Queen Charlotte's Hospital and Chelsea Hospital for Women, London
Distinctions:	Councillor, British Association of Perinatal Medicine

STUDD, Mr John W. W.

Special interests:	**Premenstrual, menopause and infertility**
NHS:	Consultant Obstetrician and Gynaecologist
	Chelsea and Westminster Hospital
	369 Fulham Road
	London SW10 9NH
Tel:	0181 746 8000
Fax:	0181 746 8111
Private:	120 Harley Street
	London W1N 1AG
Tel:	0171 486 0497
Fax:	0171 224 4190
and:	Director, Infertility and Endocrine Centre
	Lister Hospital
	Chelsea Bridge Road
	London SW1N 8RH
Tel:	0171 730 5433
Fax:	0171 823 6108
First Qualified:	1962 – Birmingham
Major Degrees:	DSc, MD, FRCOG
Specialist Training:	Universities of Birmingham and Nottingham
Distinctions:	President, International Society of Reproductive Medicine
	Chairman, National Osteoporosis Society
	Examiner to the RCOG and the Universities of London, Birmingham, Cambridge and Nottingham
USA:	Visiting Professor, Yale and Duke University

SUTTON, Mr Christopher James Gabert

Special interests:	**Laparoscopic and hysteroscopic laser surgery; laser treatment of endometriosis**
NHS:	Consultant Gynaecologist and Minimal Access Surgeon Chelsea and Westminster Hospital 369 Fulham Road London SW10 9NH
Tel:	0181 846 1083
Fax:	0181 846 7998
and:	Royal Surrey County Hospital Egerton Road Guildford Surrey GU25 5XX
Tel:	01483 571122
Fax:	01483 451815
Private:	Waterdean Road Private Clinic 8 Waterdean Road Guildford
Tel:	01483 568286
Fax:	01483 440063
First Qualified:	1967 – Cambridge and London
Major Degrees:	FRCOG
Academic:	Honorary Lecturer, Royal London Hospital, London University
Specialist Training:	Addenbrooke's Hospital, Cambridge and St Mary's Hospital, London
Distinction:	Founder and Previously President, British Society for Gynaecological Endoscopy Vice President, European Socity of Gynaecological Endoscopy; Director, Minimal Access Therapy Training Unit, Royal Surrey, Guildford

THOM, Ms Margaret H.

Special interests:	**Including pregnancy**
NHS:	Consultant Obstetrician and Gynaecologist Guy's Hospital St Thomas Street London SE1 9RT
Tel:	0171 955 5000 Ext. 4520
Fax:	0171 955 4199
Private:	97 Harley Street, London W1 1DE
Tel:	0171 486 9272
Fax:	0171 224 5906
First Qualified:	1973 – London
Major Degrees:	FRCOG
Specialist Training:	Queen Charlotte's and King's College Hospitals, London

WEEKES, Mr Anthony R. L.

Special interests:	**Gynaecological endoscopy; oncology**
NHS:	Consultant Obstetrician and Gynaecologist
	Oldchurch Hospital
	Oldchurch Road
	Romford RM7 0BE
Tel:	01708 746090
Fax:	01708 708044
Private:	The BUPA Roding Hospital
	Roding Lane South
	Ilford
	Essex IG4 5PZ
Tel:	0181 550 3849
Fax:	0181 550 3849
First Qualified:	1966 – Calcutta
Major Degrees:	FRCS Ed, FRCOG
Specialist Training:	Liverpool Maternity Hospital

WINSTON, Professor Lord Robert M. L.

Special interests:	**Fertility**
NHS:	Consultant Gynaecologist
	Hammersmith Hospital
	Du Cane Road, London W12 0HS
Tel:	0181 743 2030 Ext. 3272 or 0181 740 3272
Fax:	0181 749 6973
Private:	Refer to address and number above
Major Degrees:	MD, FRCOG
Academic:	Professor of Fertility Studies, Royal Postgraduate Medical School, London
Specialist Training:	Royal Postgraduate Medical School

WRIGHT, Mr Charles Stewart Weatherley

Special interests:	**Normal and high risk pregnancy care**
NHS:	Consultant Obstetrician and Gynaecologist
	Hillingdon Hospital
	Pield Health Road
	Uxbridge
	Middlesex UB8 2NN
Tel:	01895 279446
Fax:	01895 279989
Private:	152 Harley Street
	London W1N 1HH
Tel:	0171 935 2477
Fax:	0171 224 2574
First Qualified:	1969 – Cambridge and London
Major Degrees:	FRCOG
Academic:	Previously Lecturer, St Mary's Hospital, London
Specialist Training:	Queen Charlotte's Maternity Hospital and Soho Hospital for Women, London
USA:	Research Fellow, Vanderbilt University Nashville, USA

ANGLIA AND OXFORD REGION

CAMBRIDGE

MILTON, Mr Peter J. D.

Special interests:	**Gynaecology, endocrinology and infertility**
NHS:	Consultant Gynaecologist
	Addenbrooke's Hospital
	Hills Road
	Cambridge CB2 2QQ
Tel:	01223 245151
Fax:	01223 216122
Private:	Refer to address and number above
First Qualified:	1964 – London
Major Degrees:	MD, FRCOG
Academic:	Associate Lecturer, Cambridge University Medical School

NORWICH

WARREN, Mr Richard Charles

Special interests:	**Hormone replacement therapy; menstrual disorders; foetal medicine**
NHS:	Consultant Obstetrician and Gynaecologist
	Norfolk and Norwich Hospital
	Brunswick Road
	Norwich, Norfolk NR1 2BB
Tel:	01603 286788
Fax:	01603 286781
Private:	14 Christchurch Road
	Norwich NR2 2AE
Tel:	01603 454173
First Qualified:	1977 – London
Major Degrees:	DCH, MRCOG
Academic:	Harris Birthright Centre for Foetal Medicine King's College Hospital, London
Specialist Training:	King's College Hospital, London

NORTH WEST REGION

LIVERPOOL

ATLAY, Mr Robert

Special interests:	**General gynaecology; colposcopy laser; HRT; respected second opinion director of the largest specialist obstetrics and gynaecology hospital in Europe**
NHS:	Medical Director
	Liverpool Women's Hospital
	Crown Street
	Liverpool L8 7SS
Tel:	0151 708 9988
Fax:	0151 702 4137
Private:	35 Rodney Street
	Liverpool L1 9EN
Tel:	0151 708 9528
First Qualified:	1960 – Liverpool
Major Degrees:	FRCOG
Academic:	Clinical Lecturer, Liverpool University; Chairman, Board of Faculty of Medicine; University Examiner, Cambridge, London, Liverpool, Glasgow, Manchester; Postgraduate Examiner, Royal College of Gynaecology
Specialist Training:	Nottingham Hospital for Women; Sheffield Jessop Hospital for Women
Distinctions:	Chairman, European Committee Royal College of Gynaecology; Member, Council Royal College for Gynaecology; Previously, Honorary Secretary Royal College of Gynaecologists

GARDEN, Miss Anne S.

Special interests:	**MRI in pregnancy; maternal serum alpha protein screening; chorionic villus sampling**
NHS:	Honorary Consultant Obstetrician and Gynaecologist
	Liverpool Women's Hospital
	Crown Street
	Liverpool L8 7SS
Tel:	0151 708 9988
Fax:	0151 702 4028 or 0151 702 7137
Private:	Refer to address and number above
First Qualified:	1973 – Aberdeen
Major Degrees:	FRCOG
Academic:	Senior Lecturer in Obstetrics and Gynaecology, Liverpool University
Specialist Training:	Royal Infirmary and Simpson Maternity Memorial Pavilion, Edinburgh, and Groote Schuur Hospital, Cape Town, South Africa

HEWITT, Mr Jonathan

Special interests: **Infertility: In vitro fertilisation therapy; pre-conceptional sex selection; laparoscopic gynaecological surgery**

NHS: Consultant Obstetrician and Gynaecologist
Medical Director of Reproductive Medicine Unit
Liverpool Women's Hospital
Crown Street
Liverpool L8 7SS

Tel: 0151 708 9988
Fax: 0151 702 4137

Private: Lourdes Hospital
57 Greenbank Road
Liverpool L18 1HQ

Tel: 0151 733 7123
Fax: 0151 735 0446
First Qualified: 1978 – Liverpool
Major Degrees: MRCOG
Academic: Honorary Clinical Lecturer, Liverpool University
Specialist Training: Bourn Hall IVF Clinic, Bourne, Cambridge
USA: FMG, EMS Passed 1990

KINGSLAND, Mr Charles

Special interests: **Infertility and Menopause**
NHS: Consultant Obstetrician and Gynaecologist
Liverpool Women's Hospital
Crown Street
Liverpool L8 7SS

Tel: 0151 702 4215 Ext. 4594
Fax: 0151 702 4137

Private: 27 Rodney Street
Liverpool L1 9EH

Tel: 0151 708 0532
First Qualified: 1982 – Liverpool
Major Degrees: MD, MRCOG

KINGSTON, Mr Robert E.

Special interests: **Gynaecological cancer**
NHS: Consultant Obstetrician and Gynaecologist
Liverpool Women's Hospital
Crown Street
Liverpool L8 7SS

Tel: 0151 708 9988
Private: Refer to address and number above
First Qualified: 1975 – Leeds
Major Degrees: FRCS, FRCOG
Academic: Previously Lecturer in Obstetrics and Gynaecology,
Leeds University
USA: Clinical Fellow, Gynaecology Oncology

MANCHESTER

SMITH, Dr Anthony R. B.

Special interests:	**Genital prolapse, urinary and faecal incontinence, menstrual dysfunction, minimal access/endoscopic surgery**
NHS:	Director, Department of Urological Gynaecology
	St Mary's Hospital
	Whitworth Park
	Manchester M13 0JH
Tel:	0161 276 6570
Fax:	0161 248 0696
Private:	23 Anson Road
	Victoria Park
	Manchester M14 5BZ
Tel:	0161 225 1616
Fax:	0161 225 6488
First Qualified:	1977 – Manchester
Major Degrees:	MD, FRCOG
Specialist Training:	Manchester
USA:	Visiting Professor, Texas

LIEBERMAN, Dr Brian

Special interests:	**Infertility and IVF**
NHS:	Consultant Gynaecologist and Obstetrician
	Director Regional IVF and DI Unit
	St Mary's Hospital
	Manchester
Tel:	0161 276 6216
Fax:	0161 224 0957
Private:	Russell House
	Russell Road
	Whalley Range, Manchester
Tel:	0161 226 0662
Fax:	0161 860 6120
First Qualified:	1965 – Witwatersrand, Johannesburg, South Africa
Major Degrees:	FRCOG
Academic:	Honorary Senior Lecturer, Manchester University
Specialist Training:	St Mary's Hospital, London

NORTHERN AND YORKSHIRE REGION

LEEDS

JARVIS, Mr Gerald Joseph

Special interests:	**Female urinary incontinence**
NHS:	Clinical Director of Women's Services
	Consultant Obstetrician and Gynaecologist
	St James's University Hospital
	Leeds LS7 7TF
Tel:	0113 243 3144
Fax:	0113 242 6496
Private:	BUPA Hospital
	Jackson Avenue, Leeds LS8 1NT
Tel:	0113 269 3939
Fax:	0113 268 1340
First Qualified:	1971 – Oxford
Major Degrees:	FRCS Ed, FRCOG
Academic:	Honorary Senior Clinical Lecturer, University of Leeds
Specialist Training:	Sheffield and Leeds
Distinctions:	Member, Royal College of Gynaecologists Subspecialist Training Committee; Representative, Gynaecology on National Enquiry into Post-Operative Deaths

NEWCASTLE

HILTON, Dr Paul

Special interests:	**Urogynaecology; reconstructive gynaecological surgery**
NHS:	Consultant Gynaecologist
	Royal Victoria Infirmary
	Queen Victoria Road
	Newcastle upon Tyne NE1 4LP
Tel:	0191 232 5131
Fax:	0191 227 5173
Private:	No private work
First Qualified:	1974 – Newcastle
Major Degrees:	MD, MRCOG
Academic:	Senior Lecturer in Urogynaecology, Newcastle University
Specialist Training:	St George's Hospital Medical School, London, and Newcastle
Distinctions:	Blair Bell Memorial Lecturer, Royal College of Gynaecologists; Green Armytage and Spackman Travelling Scholar, Royal College of Gynaecologists, Royal College of Gynaecologists Historical Lecturer; Visiting Professor, Auckland University

SOUTH AND WEST REGION

BRISTOL

HULL, Professor Michael G. R.

Special interests:	**Reproductive endocrinology and all aspects of male and female infertility**
NHS:	Honorary Consultant Obstetrician and Gynaecologist
	Department of Obstetrics and Gynaecology
	St Michael's Hospital
	Southwell Street
	Bristol BS2 8EG
Tel:	0117 921 5411
Fax:	0117 927 2792
Private:	University of Bristol
	Department of Obstetrics and Gynaecology
	St Michael's Hospital
	Southwell Street
	Bristol BS2 8EG
Tel:	0117 928 5763
Fax:	0117 927 2792
First Qualified:	1962 – London
Major Degrees:	MD, FRCOG
Academic:	Lecturer, St Mary's Hospital Medical School, London
Specialist Training:	Women's Hospital, Liverpool
	Queens Charlotte's Hospital, London
Distinctions:	Green Armytage Anglo-American
	Lecturer, Royal College of Gynaecologists
USA:	Visiting Professor, Royal Society of Medicine
	Foundation, New York

MURDOCH, Mr John B.

Special interests:	**Gynaecological oncologist**
NHS:	Consultant Gynaecologist and Gynaecological Oncologist
	Department of Gynaecology
	St Michael's Hospital
	Southwell Street
	Bristol BS2 8EG
Tel:	0117 928 5810
Fax:	0117 928 5775
Private:	2 Clifton Park
	Bristol BS8 3BS
Tel:	0117 923 8217
Fax:	0117 973 0887
First Qualified:	1978 – Glasgow
Major Degrees:	MRCOG, MD
Academic:	Previously Senior Lecturer, Obstetrics and Gynaecology, Sheffield University
Specialist Training:	Gateshead

WARDLE, Mr Peter G.

Special interests:	**Reproductive medicine and surgery, especially male and female infertility**
NHS:	Consultant and Senior Lecturer in Obstetrics and Gynaecology
	University of Bristol
	St Michael's Hospital
	Southwell Street, Bristol BS2 8EG
Tel:	0117 921 5411 or 0117 928 5805
Fax:	0117 927 2792
Private:	Consultant Senior Lecturer
	University of Bristol
	Department of Obstetrics and Gynaecology
	St Michael's Hospital
	Bristol BS2 8EG
Tel:	0117 928 5624
First Qualified:	1975 – Bristol
Major Degrees:	FRCS, MRCOG, MD
Academic:	Consultant Senior Lecturer, St Michael's Hospital, Bristol
Specialist Training:	Bristol Maternity Hospital
Distinctions:	Advisory Board, Royal College of Gynaecologists

SOUTHAMPTON

GILLIBRAND, Mr Pharic N.

Special interests:	**Gynaecological oncology; endometrial ablative surgery**
NHS:	Consultant Gynaecologist
	Southampton University Hospital
	Princess Anne Hospital
	Coxford Road
	Southampton SO9 4HA
Tel:	01703 796039
Fax:	01703 794243
Private:	Hamilton
	Chilworth Road
	Southampton SO16 7JT
Tel:	01703 768618
Fax:	01703 760757
First Qualified:	1958 – London
Major Degrees:	MD, FRCOG
Academic:	Examiner for Royal College of Obstetricians and Gynaecologists
Specialist Training:	St Mary's and St George's Hospitals, London

SAUNDERS, Mr Nigel

Special interests:	**General gynaecological surgery; high risk obstetrics**
NHS:	Consultant Obstetrician and Gynaecologist
	Princess Anne Hospital
	Coxford Road
	Southampton SO9 4HA
Tel:	01703 777222
Fax:	01703 794243
Private:	BUPA Chalybeate Hospital
	Chalybeate
	Southampton SO16 6UQ
Tel:	01703 775544
Fax:	01703 701160
First Qualified:	1977 – Manchester
Major Degrees:	MD, MRCOG, FRCS Ed
Academic:	Previously Senior Lecturer, St Mary's Medical School, London

WEST MIDLANDS

BIRMINGHAM

CHAN, Mr Kong Kiong

Special interests:	**Colposcopy; gynaecological cancer**
NHS:	Consultant Gynaecological Surgery and Gynaecological Oncologist
	Birmingham Women's Hospital
	Edgbaston
	Birmingham B15 2TG
Tel:	0121 472 1377
Fax:	0121 627 2602
Private:	81 Harborne Road
	Edgbaston
	Birmingham B15 3HG
Tel:	0121 455 9496
Fax:	0121 455 0288
First Qualified:	1970 – London
Major Degrees:	FRCS, FRCOG
Academic:	Previously Senior Lecturer, Birmingham University
Specialist Training:	Hong Kong University

EMENS, Mr Michael

Special interests:	**Gynaecological infections and pre-invasive disease of the lower genital tract; diethylstilbestrol exposure**
NHS:	Consultant Gynaecologist The Women's Hospital Edgbaston Birmingham B15 2TG
Tel:	0121 472 1377
Fax:	0121 627 2602
Private:	14 Church Road Edgbaston B12 3SR
Tel:	0121 454 7576
Fax:	0121 454 7576
First Qualified:	1964 – Newcastle upon Tyne
Major Degrees:	MD, FRCOG
Academic:	Honorary Senior Lecturer, Birmingham University
Specialist Training:	MD Anderson, Houston, Texas, and Birmingham, Alabama
USA:	See 'Specialist Training' above

JORDAN, Mr Joseph Allan

Special interests:	**Gynaecological oncology and management of premalignant disease; management of the menopause**
NHS:	Consultant Gynaecologist and Medical Director Birmingham Women's Hospital Edgbaston, Birmingham B15 2TG
Tel:	0121 607 4715
Fax:	0121 627 2667
Private:	20 Church Road Edgbaston Birmingham B15 2TA
Tel:	0121 454 2345
Fax:	0121 454 5129
First Qualified:	1960 – Durham
Major Degrees:	MD, FRCOG
Academic:	Senior Lecturer, Birmingham University
Specialist Training:	Birmingham University and Birmingham Women's Hospital
Distinctions:	President, Birmingham and Midlands Obstetrical and Gynaecological Society Previously President, Section of Obstetrics and Gynaecology, Royal Society of Medicine Previously Member of Council, Royal College of Obstetrics and Gynaecologists
USA:	Previously President, Pan-American Cancer Cytology Society

WALES

SWANSEA

BOWEN–SIMKINS, Mr Peter

Special interests:	**Menopause; fertility; gynaecological surgery**
NHS:	Consultant Gynaecological
	Singleton Hospital
	Sketty Lane
	Sketty, Swansea SA2 8QA
Tel:	01792 285314
Fax:	01792 285874
Private:	38 Walter Road
	Swansea SA1 5NW
Tel:	01792 655600
Fax:	01792 648284
First Qualified:	1966 – Cambridge and London
Major Degrees:	FRCOG, MFFP
Academic:	Lecturer in Obstetrics and Gynaecology, Middlesex Hospital, London
	Lecturer in Family Planning, Margaret Pyke Centre, London
Specialist Training:	Queen Charlotte's, Samaritan's Hospital for Women and Hospital for Women, Soho Square, London

OPHTHALMOLOGISTS

Ophthalmologists specialise in the diagnosis plus medical/surgical treatment of diseases and defects of the eye and related structures. Treatments cover eye injuries, glaucoma, cataracts and nerve and muscle problems. All Ophthalmologists are surgeons.

LONDON AND THE SOUTH EAST

ACHESON, Mr James F.

Special interests:	**Neuro-ophthalmology; ocular motor problems**
NHS:	Consultant Ophthalmologist
	The Western Eye Hospital
	171 Marylebone Road
	London NW1 5YE
Tel:	0171 402 4211
Fax:	0171 723 3621
Private:	Refer to address and number above
First Qualified:	1980 – Southampton
Major Degrees:	FRCS Glas, FRCOphth
Specialist Training:	Moorfields Eye Hospital, London

ARNOTT, Mr Eric J.

Special interests:	**Cataract surgery; largest private practice in London and leads a team of ophthalmologists at the Arnott Eye Centre**
NHS:	No NHS work
Private:	Arnott Eye Centre
	22a Harley Street
	London W1N 2BP
Tel:	0171 580 1074
Fax:	0171 255 1524
First Qualified:	1954 – Dublin
Major Degrees:	FRCS, FRCOphth
Specialist Training:	Moorfields Eye Hospital and University College Hospital, London
Distinctions:	Director, International Phacoemulsificat and Cataract Methodology Society

BLACH, Mr Rolf K.

Special interests:	**The retina and diabetic eyes**
NHS:	Retired from the NHS
Private:	Lister House
	11–12 Wimpole Street
	London W1M 7AB
Tel:	0171 636 3407
Fax:	0171 436 2870
First Qualified:	1955 – Cambridge
Major Degrees:	MD, FRCS, FRCOphth
Academic:	Previously Dean, Institute of Ophthalmology, London
Specialist Training:	Moorfields Eye Hospital, London
Distinctions:	Consultant Surgeon, Moorfields Eye Hospital
	Consultant Ophthalmologist, St Dunstan's

CHIGNELL, Mr Anthony H.

Special interests:	**Retinal detachment**
NHS:	Consultant Ophthalmologist
	St Thomas' Hospital
	Lambeth Palace Road
	London SE1 7EH
Tel:	0171 928 9292 Ext. 1535
Fax:	0171 922 8079
Private:	44 Wimpole Street
	London W1M 7DG
Tel:	0171 935 7022
Fax:	0171 224 3722
First Qualified:	1962 – London
Major Degrees:	FRCS, FRCOphth
Specialist Training:	St Thomas' and Moorfields Eye Hospitals, London
Distinctions:	Consultant Ophthalmologist to the Army

COLLIN, Mr Richard

Special interests:	**Plastic and reconstructive surgery of the eyelids, including children's**
NHS:	Consultant Ophthalmic Surgeon
	Moorfields Eye Hospital
	City Road
	London EC1V 2PD
Tel:	0171 253 3411
Fax:	0171 566 2019
Private:	67 Harley Street
	London W1N 1DE
Tel:	0171 486 2699
Fax:	0171 486 8626
First Qualified:	1968 – Cambridge
Major Degrees:	FRCS
Academic:	Previously, Senior Lecturer Moorfields Eye Hospital, London
Specialist Training:	Moorfields Eye Hospital, London
Distinctions:	Honorary Consultant Ophthalmic Surgeon, Hospital for Sick Children, London
	Secretary, European Society Ophthalmic Plastic and Reconstructive Surgery
USA:	Previously Fellow in Ophthalmic Plastic and Reconstructive Surgery, University of California Medical School, San Francisco

COOLING, Mr Robert J.

Special interests:	**Eye injuries**
NHS:	Consultant Ophthalmic Surgeon and Medical Director
	Moorfields Eye Hospital
	City Road
	London EC1V 2PD
Tel:	0171 253 3411
Fax:	0171 253 4696
Private:	'Burnhams', 25 Totteridge Common
	London N20 8LR
Tel:	0181 906 4640
Fax:	0181 906 4024
First Qualified:	1970 – Liverpool (with Honours)
Major Degrees:	FRCS, FRCOphth
Specialist Training:	Moorfields Eye Hospital, London
Distinctions:	Honorary Consultant to the Royal Navy

DANIEL, Mr Reginald

Special interests:	**General eye surgery**
NHS:	Retired from the NHS
Private:	Emblem House
	London Bridge Hospital
	27 Tooley Street
	London SE1 2PR
Tel:	0171 403 4884
Fax:	0171 407 3162
First Qualified:	1964 – London
Major Degrees:	FRCS, FRCOphth
Specialist Training:	Professorial Surgical Unit, Westminster and Moorfields Eye Hospitals, London

DART, Mr John K. G.

Special interests:	**Corneal and external eye disease; corneal surgery; small incision cataract surgery**
NHS:	Consultant Ophthalmic Surgeon
	Moorfields Eye Hospital
	City Road
	London EC1V 2PD
Tel:	0171 253 3411
Fax:	0171 253 4696
Private:	8 Upper Wimpole Street
	London W1M 7DT
Tel:	0171 486 2257
Fax:	0171 487 3764
First Qualified:	1976 – Oxford
Major Degrees:	DM, FRCOphth
Academic:	Clinical Teacher, Institute of Ophthalmology, University College London
Specialist Training:	Moorfields Eye Hospital, London

DAVIES, Mr Geoffrey E. W.

Special interests:	**Eye problems of diabetics and retinal detachment**
NHS:	No NHS work
Private:	148 Harley Street
	London W1N 1AH
Tel:	0171 580 1631
Fax:	0171 224 1528
First Qualified:	1955 – Cambridge
Major Degrees:	FRCS, FRCOphth
Specialist Training:	St Mary's and Moorfields Eye Hospitals, London

FALCON, Mr Michael G.

Special interests:	**The cornea**
NHS:	Consultant Surgeon in Ophthalmology
	St Thomas' Hospital
	Lambeth Palace Road
	London SE1 7EH
Tel:	0171 928 9292 Ext. 3242
Fax:	0171 922 8156
Private:	25 Wimpole Street
	London W1M 7AD
Tel:	0171 580 7199
Fax:	0171 580 6855
First Qualified:	1967 – Cambridge
Major Degrees:	FRCP, FRCS, FRCOphth
Specialist Training:	Moorfields Eye Hospitals, London

FELLS, Mr Peter

Special interests:	**Problems with ocular movements, squints and double vision; thyroid eye disease; orbital wall fractures**
NHS:	Retired from the NHS
Private:	Honorary Consultant Ophthalmic Surgeon
	Lower Corridor Suite
	Moorfields Eye Hospital
	City Road
	London EC1V 2PD
Tel:	0171 566 2605
Fax:	0171 566 2608
First Qualified:	1959 – Cambridge
Major Degrees:	FRCS, FRCOphth
Distinctions:	Member Court of Examiners, Royal College of Surgeons
	Fellow, British Orthoptic Society
	Past President, European Strasbismological Association
	Council Member, International Strasbismological Association
USA:	Previously Harkness Fellow in Ophthalmology

ffYTCHE, Mr Timothy

Special interests:	**The retina; tropical eye diseases**
NHS:	Consultant Surgeon in Ophthalmology
	St Thomas' Hospital
	Lambeth Palace Road
	London SE1 7EH
Tel:	0171 928 9292
Fax:	0171 922 8079
and:	Moorfields Eye Hospital
	City Road
	London EC1V 2PD
Tel:	0171 253 3411
Fax:	0171 253 4696
and:	Hospital for Tropical Diseases
	4 St Pancras Way
	London NW1
Tel:	0171 530 3500
Fax:	0171 388 7645
Private:	149 Harley Street
	London W1N 2DE
Tel:	0171 935 4444
Fax:	0171 486 3782
First Qualified:	1961 – London
Major Degrees:	FRCS, FRCOphth
Specialist Training:	The Middlesex and Moorfields Eye Hospitals, London
Distinctions:	Surgeon Oculist to the Royal Household

FRANKS, Miss Wendy A.

Special interests:	**Glaucoma; retinal surgery**
NHS:	Consultant Surgeon in Ophthalmology
	Moorfields Eye Hospital
	City Road
	London EC1V 2PD
Tel:	0171 253 3411
Fax:	0171 253 4696
Private:	Refer to address and number above
First Qualified:	1980 – Cambridge
Major Degrees:	FRCS, FRCOphth
Specialist Training:	Moorfields Eye Hospital and St Thomas' Hospital, London
Distinctions:	Retinal Fellow, Royal Victoria Eye and Ear Hospital, Melbourne, Australia

---

GRAHAM, Dr Elizabeth M.

Special interests:	**Medical ophthalmology; uveitis**
NHS:	Consultant Medical Ophthalmologist Medicine
	Medical Eye Unit
	St Thomas' Hospital
	London SE1 7EH
Tel:	0171 928 9292 Ext. 1535
Fax:	0171 922 8079
Private:	Refer to address and number above
First Qualified:	1972 – London
Major Degrees:	FRCP, FRCOphth
Distinctions:	Iris Research Fellow, St Thomas' Hospital, London

GREGOR, Mr Zdenek

Special interests:	**Retinal detachment including diabetic and surgical treatment of disciform degeneration of the macula**
NHS:	Consultant Ophthalmic Surgeon
	Moorfields Eye Hospital
	City Road
	London EC1V 2PD
Tel:	0171 253 3411 Ext. 2022
Fax:	0171 253 4696
Private:	Consultant Ophthalmologist
	94 Harley Street
	London W1N 1AF
Tel:	0171 935 0777
Fax:	0171 935 6860
First Qualified:	1971 – London
Major Degrees:	FRCS, FRCOphth
Specialist Training:	Moorfields Eye Hospital, London
USA:	Previously Assistant Professor, University of Southern California, Los Angeles

HAMILTON, Mr A. M. Peter

Special interests:	**Medical retina; diabetic retinopathy**
NHS:	Consultant Ophthalmic Surgeon
	Moorfields Eye Hospital
	City Road
	London EC1V 2PD
Tel:	0171 253 3411 Ext. 2011
Fax:	0171 253 4696
Private:	Consultant Ophthalmic Surgeon
	149 Harley Street
	London W1N 2DE
Tel:	0171 935 4444 Ext. 4029
Fax:	0171 935 3061
First Qualified:	1964 – London
Major Degrees:	FRCS, FRCOphth
Specialist Training:	The Middlesex and Moorfields Eye Hospitals, London

HITCHINGS, Mr Roger A.

Special interests:	**Glaucoma**
NHS:	Consultant Ophthalmologist
	Moorfields Eye Hospital
	City Road
	London EC1V 2PD
Tel:	0171 253 3411 Ext. 2625
Fax:	0171 253 4696
Private:	36 Devonshire Place
	London W1N 1PE
Tel:	0171 486 6987
Fax:	0171 487 5017
First Qualified:	1966 – London
Major Degrees:	FRCS, FRCOphth
Specialist Training:	Moorfields Eye Hospital, London
Distinctions:	Executive Member, European Glaucoma Society
USA:	Previously Clinical Fellow in Ophthalmology, Wills Eye Hospital, Philadelphia

HOLMES SELLORS, Mr Patrick J.

Special interests:	**Respected medico-legal opinion concerning eyes**
NHS:	Part-time Consultant
	Royal Marsden Hospital
	Downs Road
	Sutton, Surrey SN2 5PT
Private:	149 Harley Street
	London W1N 1DE
Tel:	0171 935 4444 Ext. 4051
Fax:	0171 486 4616
First Qualified:	1958 – Oxford
Major Degrees:	FRCS, FRCOphth
Specialist Training:	The Middlesex and Moorfields Eye Hospitals, London
Distinctions:	Ophthalmic Surgeon to HM the Queen

HUNGERFORD, Mr John L.

Special interests:	**Tumours of the eye**
NHS:	Consultant Ophthalmologist
	Moorfields Eye Hospital
	City Road
	London EC1V 2PD
Tel:	0171 253 3411 Ext. 2021
Fax:	0171 253 4696
Private:	114 Harley Street
	London W1N 1AJ
Tel:	0171 935 1565
Fax:	0171 224 1752
First Qualified:	1969 – Cambridge
Major Degrees:	FRCS, FRCOphth

HUNTER, Mr Paul A.

Special interests:	**Corneal surgery**
NHS:	Consultant Ophthalmic Surgeon
	King's College Hospital
	Denmark Hill
	London SE5 9RS
Tel:	0171 737 4000 Ext. 2854
Fax:	0171 346 3738
Private:	94 Harley Street
	London W1N 1AF
Tel:	0171 935 0777
Fax:	0171 935 6860
First Qualified:	1970 – Cambridge
Major Degrees:	FRCS, FRCOphth
Specialist Training:	The Middlesex and Moorfields Eye Hospitals, London

JAGGER, Mr Jonathan D.

Special interests:	**The retina**
NHS:	Consultant Ophthalmologist
	Royal Free Hospital
	Pond Street
	London NW3 2GQ
Tel:	0171 794 0500 Ext. 3772
Fax:	0171 435 5342
Private:	2 Harley Street
	London W1N 1AA
Tel:	0171 935 3934
Fax:	0171 935 3934
First Qualified:	1974 – London
Major Degrees:	FRCS, FRCOphth
Specialist Training:	Moorfields Eye Hospital, London

KERR MUIR, Mr Malcolm G.

Special interests:	**Small incision cataract surgery; corneal disease**
NHS:	Consultant Ophthalmic Surgeon
	Addenbrooke's Hospital
	Hills Road
	Cambridge CB2 2QQ
Tel:	01223 245151 Ext. 2432
Fax:	01223 217968
Private:	21 Upper Wimpole Street
	London W1M 7TA
Tel:	0171 935 2552
Fax:	0171 935 2432
First Qualified:	1970 – London
Major Degrees:	FRCS, FRCOphth
Specialist Training:	Moorfields Eye Hospitals, London and Liverpool

LEAVER, Mr Peter K.

Special interests:	**Retinal surgery**
NHS:	Consultant Ophthalmologist
	Moorfields Eye Hospital
	City Road
	London EC1V 2PD
Tel:	0171 253 3411 Ext. 2576
Fax:	0171 253 4696
Private:	114 Harley Street
	London W1N 1AG
Tel:	0171 935 1565
Fax:	0171 224 1752
First Qualified:	1963 – London
Major Degrees:	FRCS, FRCOphth
Specialist Training:	Royal Postgraduate Medical School
	St Bartholomew's and Moorfields Eye Hospitals, London

LEE, Mr John P.

Special interests:	**Squint and ocular motility**
NHS:	Consultant Ophthalmic Surgeon
	Moorfields Eye Hospital
	City Road
	London EC1V 2PD
Tel:	0171 253 3411
Fax:	0171 253 4696
Private:	62 Wimpole Street
	London W1M 7DE
Tel:	0171 935 5801
Fax:	0171 486 3589
First Qualified:	1971 – Oxford
Major Degrees:	FRCS, FRCP, FRCOphth
Academic:	Previously Clinical Sub-Dean, Institute of Ophthalmology, London
Specialist Training:	Moorfields Eye Hospital, London
USA:	Fellow in Paediatric Ophthalmology and Neurophthalmology, Bascom Palmer Eye Institute, Miami

LEVY, Mr Ivor S.

Special interests:	**Neuro-ophthalmology and laser surgery, including correction of short-sightedness**
NHS:	Senior Consultant Ophthalmic Surgeon
	Royal London Hospital
	Whitechapel Road
	London E1 1BB
Tel:	0171 377 7000 Ext. 7426
Fax:	0171 377 7396/7112
Private:	75 Harley Street
	London WIN 1DE
Tel:	0171 486 1138
Fax:	0171 224 6214
First Qualified:	1965 – London
Major Degrees:	FRCP, FRCS, FRCOphth
Specialist Training:	Moorfields Eye Hospital, London
USA:	Visiting Professor, Cleveland Clinic

MARSH, Mr Ronald J.

Special interests:	**Cataracts; corneal grafts; herpes zoster eye infections**
NHS:	Consultant Ophthalmic Surgeon
	Western Eye Hospital
	Marylebone Road
	London NW1 5YE
Tel:	0171 402 4211
Fax:	0171 723 3621
and:	Moorfields Eye Hospital
	City Road
	London EC1V 2PD
Tel:	0171 253 3411
Fax:	0171 253 4696
Private:	149 Harley Street
	London W1N 2DE
Tel:	0171 935 3934
Fax:	0171 935 3934
First Qualified:	1963 – London (with Honours)
Major Degrees:	FRCS, FRCOphth
Specialist Training:	Western Eye and Moorfields Eye Hospitals, London

MIGDAL, Mr Clive

Special interests:	**Glaucoma**
NHS:	Consultant Ophthalmologist
	Western Eye Hospital
	Marylebone Road
	London NW1 5YE
Tel:	0171 402 4211 Ext. 464
Fax:	0171 723 3621
Private:	149 Harley Street
	London W1
Tel:	0171 935 4444
Fax:	0171 486 3782
First Qualified:	1971 – Cape Town, South Africa
Major Degrees:	FRCS, FRCOphth
Academic:	Research Fellow, Glaucoma Unit, Institute of Ophthalmology, London
Specialist Training:	St Bartholomew's and Moorfields Eye Hospitals, London

MUSHIN, Mr Alan S.

Special interests:	**Paediatric ophthalmology**
NHS:	Consultant Ophthalmic Surgeon
	Royal London Hospital
	Whitechapel Road
	London E1 1BB
Tel:	0171 377 7426
Fax:	0171 377 8112
and:	Great Ormond Street Hospital for Children
	Great Ormond Street
	London WC1N 3JH
Tel:	0171 405 9200
Fax:	0171 829 8643
Private:	82 Harley Street
	London W1N 1AE
Tel:	0171 580 3116
Fax:	0171 580 6996
First Qualified:	1960 – London
Major Degrees:	FRCS, FRCOphth
Specialist Training:	Royal Postgraduate Medical School, University College and Moorfields Eye Hospitals, London

RICE, Mr Noel S. C.

Special interests:	**Cornea and glaucoma**
NHS:	Retired from the NHS
Private:	25 Wimpole Street
	London W1M 7AD
Tel:	0171 935 6305
Fax:	0171 436 7349
First Qualified:	1956 – London
Major Degrees:	MD, FRCS, FRCOphth
Specialist Training:	St Bartholomew's and Moorfields Eye Hospitals, London

RIORDAN EVA, Mr Paul

Special interests:	**Neuro-ophthalmology**
NHS:	Consultant Neuro-ophthalmologist
	National Hospital for Neurology and Neurosurgery
	Queen Square
	London WC1N 3BG
Tel:	0171 837 3611 Ext. 3388
Fax:	0171 209 0751
and:	Moorfields Eye Hospital
	City Road
	London EC1V 2PD
Tel:	0171 253 3411
Fax:	0171 253 4696
Private:	Refer to address and number above
First Qualified:	1983 – Cambridge
Major Degrees:	FRCS, FRCOphth
Specialist Training:	National and Moorfields Eye Hospitals, London
Distinctions:	Co-editor, General Ophthalmology

ROSE, Mr Geoffrey E.

Special interests:	**Adnexal**
NHS:	Consultant Ophthalmic Surgeon
	Moorfields Eye Hospital
	City Road
	London EC1V 2PD
Tel:	0171 253 3411
Fax:	0171 253 4696
and:	Honorary Consultant Surgeon
	Great Ormond Street Hospital for Children
	Great Ormond Street
	London WC1N 3JH
Tel:	0171 405 9200
Fax:	0171 829 8643
Private:	Refer to address and number above
First Qualified:	1979 – London
Major Degrees:	FRCS, FRCOphth, MS
Academic:	Lecturer, Institute of Ophthalmology, London
Specialist Training:	Moorfields Eye Hospital, London

SANDERS, Mr Michael D.

Special interests:	**Neuro-ophthalmology**
NHS:	Consultant Ophthalmologist
	National Hospital
	Queen Square
	London WC1N 3BG
Tel:	0171 837 3611
Fax:	0171 829 8720
Private:	8 Upper Wimpole Street
	London W1M 7TD
Tel:	0171 935 5038
Fax:	0171 487 2968
First Qualified:	1959 – London
Major Degrees:	FRCP, FRCS, FRCOphth
Specialist Training:	Moorfields Eye Hospitals, London
Distinctions:	President, International Neuro-Ophthalmologist Society
	Honorary Consultant, University of Sydney, Australia
	Civilian Consultant, Royal Air Force
USA:	Previously Fellow, University of California

SPALTON, Mr David J.

Special interests:	**Cataract surgery; uveitis; neuro-ophthalmology**
NHS:	Consultant Ophthalmologist
	St Thomas' Hospital
	Lambeth Palace Road
	London SE1 7EH
Tel:	0171 928 9292
Fax:	0171 922 8157
Private:	59 Harley Street
	London W1N 1DD
Tel:	0171 935 6174
Fax:	0181 789 8309
First Qualified:	1970 – London
Major Degrees:	FRCP, FRCS, FCOphth
Specialist Training:	Moorfields Eye and St Thomas' Hospitals, London

STEELE, Mr Arthur D. M.

Special interests:	**Cornea, cataract and laser correction of sight**
NHS:	Retired from the NHS
Private:	62 Wimpole Street
	London W1M 7DE
Tel:	0171 637 7400
Fax:	0171 224 6216
First Qualified:	1960 – Australia
Major Degrees:	FRCS, FRACO, FRCOphth
Specialist Training:	Croyden Eye Unit and Moorfields Eye Hospital, London
Distinctions:	Councillor, College of Ophthalmology
	Editor, Major recent work on cataract surgery

TAYLOR, Mr David S. I.

Special interests:	**Children's eye problems**
NHS:	Consultant Ophthalmologist
	Great Ormond Street Hospital for Children
	Great Ormond Street
	London WC1N 3JH
Tel:	0171 405 9200
Fax:	0171 829 8643
Private:	1 Harmont House
	20 Harley Street
	London W1N 1AL
Tel:	0171 935 7916
Fax:	0171 323 5430
First Qualified:	1967 – Liverpool
Major Degrees:	FRCP, FRCS, FRCOphth
Academic:	Senior Lecturer, Institute of Child Health, London
Specialist Training:	National Hospital for Nervous Diseases, London
USA:	Previously, Fellow, Neuro-Ophthalmology, University of California; Member, American Association of Paediatric Ophthalmology

TOWNSEND, Mr Calver

Special interests:	**Cataract, implant surgery and laser treatment for diabetic retinopathy; other forms of vascular eye diseases: retinal thrombosis**
NHS:	Retired from the NHS
Private:	114 Harley Street
	London W1N 1AG
Tel:	0171 935 1565
Fax:	0171 224 1752
First Qualified:	1967 – London
Major Degrees:	FRCS, FRCOphth
Specialist Training:	Middlesex, Western and Moorfields Eye Hospitals, London
Distinctions:	Honorary Consultant, Western Eye Hospital, London

WRIGHT, Mr John E.

Special interests:	**Orbital diseases of the eye**
NHS:	Consultant Surgeon
	Moorfields Eye Hospital
	City Road
	London EC1V 2PD
Tel:	0171 253 3411 Ext. 2010
Fax:	0171 253 4696
Private:	44 Wimpole Street
	London W1M 7DG
Tel:	0171 580 1251
Fax:	01628 533458
First Qualified:	1956 – Liverpool
Major Degrees:	FRCS, FRCOphth, MS
Specialist Training:	Western and Moorfields Eye Hospitals, London
	The Royal Army Medical Corps

ANGLIA AND OXFORD REGION

CAMBRIDGE

KERR MUIR, Mr Malcolm G.

Special interests:	**Small incision cataract surgery; corneal disease**
NHS:	Consultant Ophthalmic Surgeon
	Addenbrooke's Hospital
	Hills Road
	Cambridge CB2 2QQ
Tel:	01223 245151 Ext. 2432
Fax:	01223 217968
Private:	21 Upper Wimpole Street
	London W1M 7TA
Tel:	0171 935 2552
Fax:	0171 935 2432
First Qualified:	1970 – London
Major Degrees:	FRCS, FRCOphth
Specialist Training:	Moorfields Eye Hospitals, London and Liverpool

MOORE, Mr Anthony Thomas

Special interests:	**Paediatric ophthalmology and strabismus; inherited eye disease**
NHS:	Consultant Ophthalmic Surgeon
	Addenbrooke's Hospital
	Hills Road
	Cambridge CB2 2QQ
Tel:	01223 216700
Fax:	01223 217968
Private:	Refer to address and number above
First Qualified:	1974 – Oxford
Major Degrees:	FRCS, FRCOphth
Academic:	Previously Lecturer, Institute of Ophthalmology and Institute of Child Health, London
Specialist Training:	Moorfields Eye Hospital, London
Distinctions:	Fellow in Paediatric Ophthalmology, Hospital for Sick Children, Toronto, Canada

SCOTT, Mr James D.

Special interests:	**Retinal detachment**
NHS:	Consultant Ophthalmic Surgeon
	Addenbrooke's Hospital
	Hills Road
	Cambridge CB2 2QQ
Tel:	01223 245151
Fax:	01223 217968
Private:	Refer to address and number above

OXFORD

BRON, Professor Anthony John

Special interests:	**External diseases**
NHS:	Clinical Professor of Ophthalmology
	Nuffield Laboratory
	Walton Street
	Oxford OX2 6AW
Tel:	01865 248996
Fax:	01865 794508
Private:	Refer to address and number above
First Qualified:	1961 – London
Major Degrees:	FRCS, FRCOphth
Academic:	Clinical Professor in Ophthalmology, Oxford University
Distinctions:	Chairman, Association of Eye Research; Ex-President, Ophthalmology Section, Royal Society of Medicine; Councillor, Oxford Ophthalmologists
USA:	Member Society Fellowship, Johns Hopkins University

SALMON, Mr John Frank

Special interests:	**Glaucoma**
NHS:	Consultant Ophthalmic Surgeon
	Oxford Eye Hospital
	Radcliffe Infirmary
	Woodstock Road
	Oxford OX2 6HE
Tel:	01865 311188
Fax:	01865 224360
Private:	Refer to address and number above
First Qualified:	1976 – Pretoria
Major Degrees:	FRCS Ed

NORTH WEST REGION

MANCHESTER

McLEOD, Professor David

Special interests:	**Vitreoretinal and diabetic retinopathy**
NHS:	Honorary Consultant Ophthalmologist
	Department of Ophthalmology
	Royal Eye Hospital
	Oxford Road
	Manchester M13 9WH
Tel:	0161 276 5620
Fax:	0161 273 6354
Private:	Refer to address and number above
First Qualified:	1969 – Edinburgh (with Honours)
Major Degrees:	FRCS, FRCOphth
Academic:	Professor of Ophthalmology, Manchester University
Distinctions:	Civilian Consultant Ophthalmologist to the Royal Air Force
USA:	International Member American Academy of Ophthalmologists

---

TULLO, Mr Andrew B.

Special interests:	**Corneal and external eye disease problems**
NHS:	Consultant Ophthalmologist
	Department of Ophthalmology
	Royal Eye Hospital
	Oxford Road
	Manchester M13 9WH
Tel:	0161 276 5522
Fax:	0161 272 6618
Private:	Refer to address and number above
First Qualified:	1974 – Bristol
Major Degrees:	MD, FRCS Glas
Specialist Training:	Manchester Royal Eye Hospital
Distinctions:	Wellcome Trust Research Fellow, Bristol University

NORTHERN AND YORKSHIRE REGION

BRADFORD

ATKINSON, Mr Peter L.

Special interests:	**General ophthalmology**
NHS:	Consultant Ophthalmic Surgeon
	Bradford Royal Infirmary
	Duckworth Lane
	Bradford BD9 6RJ
Tel:	01274 542200
Fax:	01274 364895
Private:	Refer to address and number above
First Qualified:	1983 – Leicester
Major Degrees:	FRCS, FRCOphth
Specialist Training:	King's College Hospital, London

SOUTH AND WEST REGION

BRISTOL

EASTY, Professor David L.

Special interests:	**Corneal grafting, corneal and retinal eye disease; eye banking**
NHS:	Professor of Ophthalmology
	University of Bristol
	Department of Ophthalmology
	Bristol Eye Hospital
	Bristol BS1 2LX
Tel:	0117 923 0060
Fax:	0117 925 1421
Private:	Refer to address and number above
First Qualified:	1959 – Manchester
Major Degrees:	MD, FRCS, FRCOphth
Academic:	Professor of Ophthalmology, Bristol University

HARRAD, Mr Richard A.

Special interests:	**Strabismus**
NHS:	Consultant Ophthalmologist
	Bristol Eye Hospital
	Lower Maudlin Street
	Bristol BS1 2LX
Tel:	0117 923 0060
Fax:	0117 928 4686
Private:	Refer to address and number above
First Qualified:	1978 – London
Major Degrees:	FRCS, FRCOphth
Specialist Training:	Moorfields Eye Hospital, London

POTTS, Mr Michael J.

Special interests:	**Adnexal eye disease**
NHS:	Consultant Ophthalmologist
	Department of Ophthalmology
	Bristol Eye Hospital
	Bristol BS1 2LX
Tel:	0117 923 0060
Fax:	0117 928 4686
Private:	Refer to address and number above
First Qualified:	1981 – Bristol
Major Degrees:	PhD, FRCS, FRCOphth
Specialist Training:	Moorfields Eye Hospital, London
Distinctions:	Previously, Oculoplastic Fellow, Moorfields Eye Hospital, London

ORTHOPAEDIC SURGEONS

These doctors use medication or surgery to treat bone and muscle problems, including fractures, congenital malformations, degenerative joint ailments and sports injuries. Joint replacement surgery forms a major part of the surgeon's work as the technological advancement of artifical joints increases.

LONDON AND THE SOUTH EAST

ALLEN, Mr Paul Richard

Special interests:	**Knee**
NHS:	Consultant Orthopaedic Surgeon
	Bromley Hospital
	17 Cromwell Avenue
	Bromley Kent BR2 9AJ
Tel:	0181 289 7000 Ext. 7008
Fax:	0181 289 7127
Private:	Refer to address and number above
First Qualified:	1970 – London
Major Degrees:	FRCS
Specialist Training:	St Thomas' Hospital, London

BIRCH, Mr Rolfe

Special interests:	**Peripheral nerve surgery of the upper limbs, including repair of nerve damage caused in orthopaedic surgery**
NHS:	Consultant Orthopaedic Surgeon
	Royal National Orthopaedic Hospital
	Brockley Hill
	Stanmore
	Middlesex HA7 4LP
Tel:	0181 954 2300 Ext. 567
Fax:	0181 420 6582
Private:	62 Wimpole Street
	London W1M 7DE
Tel:	0171 935 8400
Fax:	0171 935 3910
First Qualified:	1970 – Cambridge
Major Degrees:	FRCS, MChir
Specialist Training:	Cambridge, St Bartholomew's and Royal National Orthopaedic Hospitals, London
Distinctions:	Honorary Civilian Consultant to the Royal Navy; Regional Advisor, Royal College of Surgeons, Edinburgh; Honorary Orthopaedic Surgeon, Postgraduate Medical School Hammersmith, Hospital for Sick Children and National Hospitals, London

BUCKNILL, Mr Thomas M.

Special interests:	**Knee injuries; complex hip replacements**
NHS:	Consultant Orthopaedic Surgeon
	Royal London Hospital
	Whitechapel Road
	London E1 1BB
Tel:	0171 377 7000 Ext. 2408
Fax:	0171 377 7198
Private:	134 Harley Street
	London W1N 1AH
Tel:	0171 486 2622
Fax:	0171 224 1481
First Qualified:	1964 – London
Major Degrees:	RD, FRCS
Specialist Training:	Royal National Orthopaedic Hospital, London
Distinctions:	Previously Surgeon Commander, Royal Navy
USA:	Previously Orthopaedic Clinical Research Fellow, Harvard Medical School, Boston

CALVERT, Mr Paul T.

Special interests:	**Shoulders**
NHS:	Consultant Orthorpaedic Surgeon
	St George's Hospital
	Blackshaw Road
	London SW17 0QT
Tel:	0181 672 1255
Fax:	0181 725 3610
Private:	Refer to address and number above
First Qualified:	1974 – Cambridge
Major Degrees:	FRCS
Specialist Training:	Royal National Orthopaedic Hospital
USA:	Clinical Fellow in Paediatric Orthopaedics Children's Hospital, Boston

CHAPMAN, Mr Robin H.

NHS:	Consultant Orthopaedic Surgeon
	Kingston Hospital
	Galsworthy Road
	Kingston upon Thames, Surrey
Tel:	0181 546 7711 Ext. 2400
Fax:	0181 549 6558
Private:	New Victoria Hospital
	184 Coombe Lane West
	Kingston
	Surrey KT2 7EG
Tel:	0181 949 9000 Ext. 220/221
Fax:	0181 949 9099
Secretary's Number:	Tel/Fax: 01737 813 095
First Qualified:	1967 – London
Major Degrees:	FRCS
Specialist Training:	Royal London Hospital, London
USA:	Previously Orthopaedic Resident, Vanderbilt University Hospital, New York

COBB, Mr Justin P.

Special interests:	**Hips**
NHS:	Consultant Orthopaedic Surgeon
	The Middlesex Hospital
	Mortimer Street
	London WIN 8AA
Tel:	0171 380 9216
Fax:	0171 380 9081
Private:	149 Harley Street
	London W1N 2DE
Tel:	0171 224 0326
Fax:	0171 487 5997
First Qualified:	1982 – Oxford
Major Degrees:	FRCS
Specialist Training:	The Middlesex Hospital, London

DOWD, Mr George S. E.

Special interests:	**The knee**
NHS:	Consultant Orthopaedic Surgeon
	The Royal London Hospital
	Whitechapel Road
	London E11BB
Tel:	0171 377 7000 Ext. 7198
Fax:	0171 377 7198
Private:	Refer to address and number above
First Qualified:	1971 – Liverpool
Major Degrees:	MD, FRCS
Academic:	Senior Lecturer, Institute of Orthopaedics, London University
Specialist Training:	Royal Liverpool Hospital
Distinctions:	Previously British Orthopaedics Research Society President Medal; Honorary Consultant, Royal National Orthopaedic Hospital, London; Hunterian Professor, Royal College of Surgeons
USA:	Travelling Fellow North America and Canada

EDGAR, Mr Michael A.

Special interests:	**General orthopaedics, including paediatric orthopaedics; spine**
NHS:	Consultant Orthopaedic Surgeon
	The Middlesex Hospital
	Mortimer Street
	London WIN 8AA
Tel:	0171 380 9037
Fax:	0171 323 0397
Private:	149 Harley Street
	London W1N 2DE
Tel:	0171 486 0027
Fax:	0171 487 5997
First Qualified:	1964 – Cambridge
Major Degrees:	FRCS, MChir
Specialist Training:	The Orthopaedic Hospital, Oswestry, and The Middlesex Hospital, London
Distinctions:	Civil Consultant to the Royal Air Force President British Scoliosis Society Secretary, British Orthopaedic Association

EMERY, Mr Roger J.

Special interests:	**Shoulder**
NHS:	Consultant Orthopaedic Surgeon
	St Mary's Hospital
	Praed Street
	London W2 1NY
Tel:	0171 725 1329 or 0171 725 1627
Fax:	0171 725 1766
Private:	Refer to address and number above
First Qualified:	1979 – London
Major Degrees:	FRCS Ed
Specialist Training:	Addenbrooke's Hospital, Cambridge
Distinctions:	Wellcome Surgical Fellowship
	Secretary, British Society

EVANS, Mr Michael J.

Special interests:	**Trauma hip and knee replant surgery; ankle arthroplasty and revision arthroplasty**
NHS:	Consultant Orthopaedic Surgeon
	Hammersmith Hospital
	Du Cane Road
	London WI2 0HS
Tel:	0181 743 2030 Ext. 3943
Fax:	0181 967 5630
e-mail:	mje@evanorth.demon.co.uk
Private:	144 Harley Street
	London WIN IAH
Tel:	0171 935 0023
Fax:	0171 935 5972
First Qualified:	1962 – Birmingham
Major Degrees:	FRCS
Academic:	Honorary Senior Lecturer, Royal Postgraduate Medical School, London
Specialist Training:	The Middlesex and Royal National Orthopaedic Hospitals, London

FIXSEN, Mr John A.

Special interests:	**Congenital disorders in children, of feet, hips and spine**
NHS:	Consultant Orthopaedic Surgeon
	Great Ormond Street Hospital for Children
	Great Ormond Street
	London WC1N 3JH
Tel:	0171 405 9200 Ext. 8830
Fax:	0171 813 8243
Private:	Refer to address and number above
First Qualified:	1962 – Cambridge
Major Degrees:	FRCS, MChir
Specialist Training:	Royal National Orthopaedic Hospital, London
Distinctions:	Civilian Consultant in Children's Orthopaedics to the Army, Navy and Royal Air Force

FREEMAN, Mr Michael A. R.

Special interests:	**The knee**
NHS:	Consultant Orthopaedic Surgeon
	Royal London Hospital
	Whitechapel Road
	London E1 1BB
Tel:	0171 377 7766
Fax:	0171 377 7763
Private:	149 Harley Street
	London W1N 2DE
Tel:	0171 935 4444
Fax:	0171 935 7780
First Qualified:	1956 – Cambridge
Major Degrees:	MD, FRCS
Specialist Training:	Middlesex and Westminster Hospitals, London
USA:	Member, American Academy of Orthopaedic Surgeons

HALL, Mr Anthony J.

Special interests:	**Knee injuries**
NHS:	Consultant Orthopaedic Surgeon
	Chelsea and Westminster Hospital
	369 Fulham Road
	London SW10 9NH
Tel:	0181 237 5415
Fax:	0181 746 8846
Private:	126 Harley Street
	London WIN IAH
Tel:	0171 486 1096
Fax:	0171 224 2520
First Qualified:	1962 – London
Major Degrees:	FRCS
Academic:	Previously Postgraduate Dean, Charing Cross Hospital
Specialist Training:	Royal National Orthopaedic Hospital, Middlesex
	Previously Clinical Fellow in Orthopaedics, Toronto General Hospital
Distinctions:	Honorary Consultant in Orthopaedics to the Royal Marsden and Queen Charlotte's Hospitals, London
	Member, Court of Examiners, Royal College of Surgeons

HUGHES, Professor Sean P. F.

Special interests:	**Lumbar and cervical spine surgery, and infections of the bones**
NHS:	Professor of Orthopaedic Surgery
	Hammersmith Hospital
	Du Cane Road
	London W12 0HS
Tel:	0181 740 3215
Fax:	0181 742 9202
Private:	The Stamford Rooms
	Hammersmith Hospital
	Du Cane Road
	London W12 0HS
Tel:	0181 740 3215
Fax:	0181 742 9202
First Qualified:	1966 – London
Major Degrees:	MS, FRCS, FRCS Ed Orth.
Academic:	Previously Professor of Orthopaedic Surgery, Edinburgh University
Specialist Training:	Royal Postgraduate Medical School, The Middlesex and Royal National Orthopaedic Hospitals, London
Distinctions:	Civilian Orthopaedic Surgeon to the Royal Navy
	Author of standard works on orthopaedics
USA:	Research Fellow, Mayo Clinic, Rochester, Minnesota

HUNT, Mr David M.

Special interests:	**Knee injuries; paediatric orthopaedic problems**
NHS:	Consultant Orthopaedic Surgeon
	St Mary's Hospital
	Praed Street
	London W2 1NY
Tel:	0171 725 1930
Fax:	0171 725 1766
Private:	106 Harley Street
	London WIN 1AF
Tel:	0171 935 6347
Fax:	0171 935 2788
First Qualified:	1971 – London
Major Degrees:	FRCS
Specialist Training:	St Mary's Hospital, London

IRELAND, Mr John

Special interests:	**Knee surgery**
NHS:	NO NHS work
Private:	Private Consulting Rooms
	Royal National Orthopaedic Hospital
	45 Bolsover Street
	London W1P 8AQ
Tel:	0181 505 3211
Fax:	0181 559 1161
and:	Knee Surgery Unit
	Holly House Hospital
	High Road
	Buckhurst Hill
	Essex IG9 5HX
Tel:	0181 505 3211
Fax:	0181 559 1161
First Qualified:	1966 – London
Major Degrees:	FRCS
Specialist Training:	Royal National Orthopaedic Hospital, London

JACKSON, Mr Andrew M.

Special interests:	**Knee surgery including knee replacement, arthroscopy and ligament reconstruction; paediatric orthopaedics excluding the spine**
NHS:	Consultant Orthopaedic Surgeon
	St George's Hospital
	Blackshaw Road
	London SW17 0QT
Tel:	0181 672 1255 or 0181 725 3242
Fax:	0181 725 3610
Private:	107 Harley Street
	London WIN 1DG
Tel:	0171 935 9521
Fax:	0171 935 5187
First Qualified:	1969 – London
Major Degrees:	FRCS
Specialist Training:	Royal National Orthopaedic Hospital, London
Distinctions:	Honorary Consultant Surgeon, Royal National Orthopaedic Hospital, London

JOHNSON, Mr Jonathan R.

Special interests:	**The back**
NHS:	Consultant Orthopaedic Surgeon
	St Mary's Hospital
	Praed Street
	London W2 INY
Tel:	0171 725 6666
Fax:	0171 725 1766
and:	Royal National Orthopaedic Hospital
	Stanmore
	Middlesex HA7 4LP
Tel:	0181 954 2300
Private:	The Consulting Rooms
	Princess Grace Hospital
	42–52 Nottingham Place
	London W1M 3FD
Tel:	0171 935 6485
Fax:	0171 487 4476
First Qualified:	1971 – London
Major Degrees:	FRCS
Specialist Training:	Royal National Orthopaedic Hospital, University College and Westminster Hospitals, London

JONES, Mr David

Special interests:	**Paediatric orthopaedics**
NHS:	Consultant Orthopaedic Surgeon
	Great Ormond Street Hospital for Children
	Great Ormond Street
	London WC1N 3JH
Tel:	0171 405 9200
Fax:	0171 813 8243
Private:	Refer to address and number above
Fax:	0171 829 8650

MORLEY, Mr Timothy R.

Special interests:	**Scoliosis; the spine**
NHS:	Royal National Orthopaedic Hospital
	Brockley Hill
	Stanmore
	Middlesex HA7 4LP
Tel:	0181 954 2300 Ext. 720
Fax:	0181 420 6582
Private:	148 Harley Street
	London W1N 1AH
Tel:	0171 487 5020
Fax:	0171 224 1528
First Qualified:	1965 – Cambridge
Major Degrees:	FRCS
Specialist Training:	King's College and Royal National Orthopaedic Hospitals, London

MUIRHEAD-ALLWOOD, Ms Sarah K.

Special interests:	**Complex hip replacement revisions**
NHS:	Consultant Orthopaedic Surgeon
	The Whittington Hospital
	Highgate Hill
	London N19 5NF
Tel:	0171 288 5667
Fax:	0171 288 3147
Private:	19 Wimpole Street
	London W1M 7AD
Tel:	0171 935 8488
Fax:	0171 636 5758
First Qualified:	1971 – London
Major Degrees:	FRCS
Academic:	Honorary Senior Clinical Lecturer, London University
Specialist Training:	Westminster, University College and Royal National Orthopaedic Hospitals, London.
Distinctions:	Honorary Orthopaedic Consultant, St Luke's Hospital for the Clergy, London

RANSFORD, Mr Andrew O.

Special interests: **Cervical spine problems; children's spinal deformities; low back pain and disc disease**

NHS: Consultant Orthopaedic Surgeon
Royal National Orthopaedic Hospital
Brockley Hill
Stanmore
Middlesex HA7 4LP

Tel: 0181 954 2300 Ext. 231
Fax: 0181 420 6582
Private: 107 Harley Street
London W1N 1DG

Tel: 0171 486 1088
Fax: 0171 935 5187
First Qualified: 1966 – Cambridge
Major Degrees: FRCS
Specialist Training: University College and Royal National Orthopaedic Hospitals, London
USA: Previously Orthopaedic Fellow, Rancho Los Amigos Hospital, Downey, California

REYNOLDS, Mr David A.

Special interests: **Developmental problems of the hip in young adults**

NHS: Director, Department of Orthopaedic Surgery
St Thomas' Hospital
Lambeth Palace Road
London SE1 7EH

Tel: 0171 928 9292 Ext. 2292
Fax: 0171 922 8079
Private: The Churchill Clinic
80 Lambeth Road
London SE1 7PW

Tel: 0171 620 1590
Fax: 0171 938 1702
First Qualified: 1960 – London
Major Degrees: FRCS
Specialist Training: King's College and St Thomas' Hopitals, London
Distinctions: Consultant Orthopaedic Surgeon to the Metropolitan Police
USA: Previously Associate Professor in Orthopaedics, Einstein College, New York

SCOTT, Mr Gareth

Special interests:	**Hip and knee replacement including primary and revision surgery**
NHS:	Consultant Orthopaedic Surgeon
	Royal London Hospital
	Whitechapel Road
	London E1 1BB
Tel:	0171 377 7766
Fax:	0171 377 7763
Private:	149 Harley Street
	London W1
Tel:	0171 935 4444
Fax:	0171 486 3782
First Qualified:	1979 – London
Major Degrees:	FRCS, FRCS Ed
Specialist Training:	Royal London and Royal National Orthopaedic Hospitals, London

SCOTT, Mr James E.

Special interests:	**Adult reconstructive surgery, particulary spinal surgery; hip surgery; knee surgery**
NHS:	Consultant Orthopaedic Surgeon
	Chelsea and Westminster Hospital
	369 Fulham Road
	London SW10 9NH
Tel:	0181 746 8164
Fax:	0181 746 8846
Private:	The Lister Hospital
	Chelsea Bridge Road
	London SW1W 8RH
Tel:	0171 730 9560
Fax:	0171 730 7726
First Qualified:	1968 – Oxford
Major Degrees:	FRCS
Specialist Training:	The Middlesex and Royal National Orthopaedic Hospitals, London

VICKERS, Mr Roger H.

Special interests:	**Hip replacement; medico-legal opinions**
NHS:	Consultant Orthopaedic Surgeon
	St George's Hospital
	Blackshaw Road
	London SW17 0QT
Tel:	0181 725 1331
Fax:	0181 725 3610
Private:	149 Harley Street
	London W1N 1HJ
Tel:	0171 935 4444
Fax:	0171 935 5742
First Qualified:	1970 – Oxford
Major Degrees:	FRCS
Specialist Training:	Watford General and Charing Cross Hospitals, London
Distinctions:	Consultant Orthopaedic Surgeon to the Army

WATSON, Mr Michael S.

Special interests:	**Shoulder and elbow**
NHS:	Consultant Orthopaedic Surgeon
	Guy's Hospital
	St Thomas Street
	London SE1 9RT
Tel:	0171 955 5000 Ext. 2757
Fax:	0171 955 2759
Private:	Suite 306, Emblem House
	London Bridge Hospital
	Tooley Street
	London SE1 2PN
Tel:	0171 403 5858
Fax:	0171 357 8192
First Qualified:	1967 – Cambridge
Major Degrees:	FRCS
Specialist Training:	Westminster and Royal National Orthopaedic Hospitals, London
Distinctions:	Executive, European Society for Surgery of the Shoulder and Elbow
	Previously President, European Society for Shoulder and Elbow Surgery
USA:	Member, American Shoulder and Elbow Surgeons

ANGLIA AND OXFORD REGION

CAMBRIDGE

DANDY, Mr David J.

Special interests:	**International reputation for knee surgery**
NHS:	Consultant Orthopaedic Surgeon
	Addenbrooke's Hospital
	Hills Road
	Cambridge CB2 2QQ
Tel:	01223 245151 or 01223 216103
Fax:	01223 217307
Private:	The Old Vicarage
	Great Wilbraham
	Cambridge CB1 5JF
Tel:	01223 880006
Fax:	01223 881779
First Qualified:	1965 – Cambridge
Major Degrees:	MD, FRCS
Specialist Training:	St Bartholomew's Hospital, London, and Toronto General Hospital, Canada
Distinctions:	Honorary Civilian Consultant Adviser in Orthopaedic Surgery to the Royal Air Force and Royal Navy; Frank N Windsor studentship Emmanuel College Cambridge; Robert Milne Prize for Surgery, London Hospital; James Berry Prize, Royal College of Surgeons; Robert Jones Prize; Munsif Memorial Lecturer, Bombay; Naughton Dunn Lecture; Hunterian Professor; Councillor, Royal College of Surgeons and Fellow, British Orthopaedics Association; Formerly President British Arthroscopy Association

NORWICH

GLASGOW, Mr Malcolm M. S.

Special interests:	**The knee**
NHS:	Consultant Orthopaedic Surgeon
	Norfolk and Norwich Hospital
	Brunswick Road
	Norwich NR1 3SR
Tel:	01603 286286
Fax:	01603 287498
Private:	Refer to address and number above
First Qualified:	1970 – London
Major Degrees:	FRCS
Specialist Training:	Westminster Hospital, London

PHILLIPS, Mr Hugh

Special interests:	**Hip revision surgery**
NHS:	Consultant Orthopaedic Surgeon
	Norfolk and Norwich Hospital
	Brunswick Road
	Norwich NR1 3SR
Tel:	01603 286286
Fax:	01603 287498
Private:	Refer to address and number above
First Qualified:	1964 – London
Major Degrees:	FRCS
Specialist Training:	St Bartholomew's Hospital
Distinctions:	Ex-President, Orthopaedic Section, Royal Society of Surgeons; Member Specialist Advisory Committee of Orthopaedic Surgeons; Secretary, British Hip Society

NORTH WEST REGION

MANCHESTER

ROSS, Mr Raymond

Special interests:	**Spinal disc implants**
NHS:	Consultant Orthopaedic Surgeon
	Hope Hospital
	Stott Lane
	Salford 6, M6 8HD
Tel:	0161 787 4879
Fax:	0161 787 5263
Private:	87 Palatine Rd
	Didsbury, Manchester M20 3JQ
Tel:	0161 445 4871
Fax:	0161 445 7468
Major Degrees:	FRCS

WIGAN

STANLEY, Mr John Knowles

Special interests:	**Hand and upper limb surgery; problems of the wrist and carpus**
NHS:	Consultant Hand and Upper Limb Surgeon
	Wrightington Hospital
	Hall Lane
	Wrightington
	Wigan WN6 9EP
Tel:	01257 256259
Fax:	01257 253809
Private:	20 Derby Street West
	Ormskirk
	Lancashire L39 2NH
Tel:	01695 575210
Fax:	01695 575210
First Qualified:	1968 – Liverpool
Major Degrees:	MCh Orth, FRCS
Academic:	Honorary Clinical Lecturer, Department of Orthopaedic Surgery, Manchester University
Distinctions:	Previously President, British Association of Hand Therapist
	Founder member, British Shoulder and Elbow Society
USA:	Trained in the US under H Kleinert, AB Swanson, E Nalebuff, R Curtis and J Hunter

SOUTH AND WEST REGION

TAUNTON

WEBB, Mr Peter J.

Special interests:	**Scoliosis, general spine problems; general paediatric orthopaedics**
NHS:	Musgrove Park Hospital
	Taunton TA1 5DA
Tel:	01823 333444
Fax:	01823 336877
Private:	Somerset Nuffield
	Staplegrove Elm
	Taunton, Somerset TA2 6AN
Tel:	01823 286991
Fax:	01823 338951
First Qualified:	1969 – London
Major Degrees:	FRCS
Specialist Training:	Royal National Orthopaedic Hospital and Hospital for Sick Children, London

TRENT REGION

NOTTINGHAM

COLTON, Professor Christopher L.

Special interests:	**Skeletal trauma, especially reconstruction; fractures in children; skeletal infection, nonunion and malunion**
NHS:	Nottingham University Hospital
	Nottingham NG7 2UH
Tel:	0115 924 9924
Fax:	0115 942 3656
Private:	34 Regent Street
	Nottingham NG1 5BT
Tel:	0115 956 1307
Fax:	0115 942 3606
First Qualified:	1960 – London
Major Degrees:	FRCS, FRCS Ed

SCOTLAND

GLASGOW

EDMOND, Mr Peter, CBE

NHS:	National Spinal Unit
	1345 Govan Road
	Southern General Hospital
	Glasgow G51 4TF
Tel:	0141 201 1100 Ext. 2555
Fax:	0141 201 2991
Private:	Refer to address and number above
First Qualified:	1958 – Edinburgh
Major Degrees:	FRCS
Academic:	Previously Part-time Senior Lecturer, Royal Infirmary Edinburgh
Distinctions:	Director, National Spinal Unit, Scotland
	Honorary Surgeon to HM the Queen

PAEDIATRICS

Paediatricians are doctors who treat children up to the age of 16. Subspecialities within this section include neonatal physicians (babies up to four weeks old). See appendix 1(i) for a list of specialist paediatric cancer units and appendix1(iii) for a list of children's hospitals

PAEDIATRIC CARDIOLOGISTS

LONDON AND THE SOUTH EAST

TYNAN, Professor Michael J.

Special interests:	**Interventional cardiology**
NHS:	Consultant Paediatric Cardiologist Guy's Hospital London SE1 9RT
Tel:	0171 955 5000 Ext. 4615
Fax:	0171 955 4614
Private:	Refer to address and number above
First Qualified:	1968 – London
Major Degrees:	MD, FRCP
Academic:	Professor of Paediatric Cardiology, Guy's Hospital Medical School, London

RIGBY, Dr Michael L.

Special interests:	**Congenital heart disease; echocardiography; interventional cardiology**
NHS:	Director and Consultant Paediatric Cardiologist Royal Brompton Hospital Sydney Street London SW3 6NP
Tel:	0171 351 8542
Fax:	0171 351 8547
Private:	Refer to address and number above
First Qualified:	1970 – Leeds
Major Degrees:	MD, FRCP
Specialist Training:	Royal Brompton Hospital, London, and Hospital for Sick Children, Toronto, Canada
Distinctions:	Fellow, Canadian Heart Foundation, Hospital for Sick Children, Toronto, Canada

SHARLAND, Dr Gurleen K.

Special interests:	**Fetal diagnosis of congenital heart disease**
NHS:	Consultant Paediatric and Foetal Cardiologist Guy's Hospital London SE1 9RT
Tel:	0171 955 5000 Ext. 4615
Fax:	0171 955 4614
Private:	Refer to address and number above
First Qualified:	1982 – London
Major Degrees:	MD, MRCP
Academic:	Senior Lecturer in Perinatal Cardiology, Guy's Hospital, London

SHINEBOURNE, Dr Elliot A.

Special interests:	**Heart disorders in children**
NHS:	Consultant Paediatric Cardiologist Royal Brompton Hospital Sydney Street London SW3 6NP
Tel:	0171 352 8541
Fax:	0171 351 8544
Private:	Private Consulting Rooms Royal Brompton Hospital Sydney Street London SW3 6NP
Tel:	0171 352 6468
Fax:	0171 351 8544
First Qualified:	1963 – London (with Honours)
Major Degrees:	MD, FRCP
Academic:	Senior Lecturer, National Heart and Lung Institute, London
Specialist Training:	St Bartholomew's and National Heart Hospitals, London
USA:	Previously American Heart Association Travelling Fellow in Cardiovascular Medicine, University College, San Francisco

TAYLOR, Dr James Francis N.

Special interests:	**Congenital heart disease; physiology of newborn circulation**
NHS:	Consultant Paediatric Cardiologist
	Great Ormond Street Hospital for Children
	Great Ormond Street
	London WC1N 3JH
Tel:	0171 405 9200
Fax:	0171 430 2995
Private:	Refer to address and number above
First Qualified:	1962 – Cambridge
Major Degrees:	MD, FRCP
Specialist Training:	Great Ormond Street Hospital for Children and St Thomas' Hospitals, London

PAEDIATRIC CARDIOTHORACIC SURGEONS

(Heart Surgeons)

LONDON AND THE SOUTH EAST

ANDERSON, Mr David Robert

Special interests:	**Congenital defects; neonatal correction**
NHS:	Consultant Cardiac Surgeon
	Department of Cardiac Surgery
	Guy's Hospital
	St Thomas Street
	London SE1 9RT
Tel:	0171 955 4065
Fax:	0171 955 4858
Private:	Guy's Nuffield House
	London SE1
Tel:	0171 955 4752
Fax:	0171 955 4858
First Qualified:	1979 – Cambridge
Major Degrees:	FRCS, FRCS Ed
Academic:	Senior Lecturer, Guy's Hospital, London
Specialist Training:	Guy's and St George's Hospitals, London, and Birmingham Children's Hospital
Distinctions:	Previously Hunterian Professor, Royal College of Surgeons
USA:	Research Fellow, Pennsylvania University
	Research Fellow, Wayne State University, Michigan

de LEVAL, Mr Marc R.

Special interests:	**Doyen of children's heart surgery**
NHS:	Consultant Cardiothoracic Surgeon
	Great Ormond Street Hospital for Children
	Great Ormond Street
	London WC1N 3JH
Tel:	0171 404 4383
Fax:	0171 831 4931
Private:	Refer to address and number above
First Qualified:	1966 – Liège, Belgium
Major Degrees:	MD, FRCS

DEVERALL, Mr Philip B.

Special interests:	**Patients of all ages from newborn to elderly, congenital heart disease, valve heart disease and all types of degenerative disease of the structures of the heart with particular emphasis on coronary vascular disease and disease of the major blood vessels within the thorax**
NHS:	Consultant Cardiothoracic Surgeon
	Guy's Hospital
	St Thomas Street
	London SE1 9RT
Tel:	0171 955 4339
Fax:	0171 922 8079
Private:	21 Upper Wimpole Street
	London W1M 7TA
Tel:	0171 486 7753
Fax:	0171 935 4416
First Qualified:	1960 – London
Major Degrees:	MB, FRCS
Academic:	Lecturer in Surgery, Guy's Hospital, London
Specialist Training:	Great Ormond Street Hospital for Children, London
USA:	Cardiovascular Research Fellow, University of Alabama

ELLIOT, Mr Martin J.

Special interests:	**Congenital heart disease; paediatric thoracic surgery especially trachea; paediatric thoracic transplantation**
NHS:	Consultant Cardiothoracic Surgeon Great Ormond Street Hospital for Children Great Ormond Street London WC1N 3JH
Tel:	0171 405 9200 Ext. 5308
Fax:	0171 813 8262
Private:	Refer to address and number above
First Qualified:	1973 – Newcastle
Major Degrees:	MD, FRCS
Academic:	Senior Lecturer, Paediatric Cardiology, Institute of Child Health, London
Specialist Training:	Regional Cardiothoracic Unit, Newcastle upon Tyne, and Great Ormond Street Hospital for Children, London
Distinctions:	Director, European Congenital Heart Defects Database Secretary, European Congenital Heart Surgeons Foundation
Research:	Pathophysiology of cardiopulmonary bypass and surgery for congenital tracheal stenosis

LINCOLN, Mr J. Christopher

NHS:	Consultant Cardiothoracic Surgeon Royal Brompton Hospital Sydney Street London SW3 6NP
Tel:	0171 351 8251
Fax:	0171 351 8099
Private:	38 Devonshire Street London W1N 1LD
Tel:	0171 935 7529
Fax:	0171 351 8214
First Qualified:	1959 – Dublin
Major Degrees:	FRCS Ed, FRCS
Academic:	Senior Lecturer in Paediatric Surgery, Heart and Lung Institute, London
Specialist Training:	Great Ormond Street Hospital for Children and Westminster Hospital, London
Distinctions:	Previously Hunterian Professor, Royal College of Surgeons
USA:	Previously Clinical and Research Fellow, Harvard Medical School and Massachusetts General Hospital

SHORE, Mr Darryl

NHS:	Consultant Cardiothoracic Surgeon Royal Brompton Hospital Sydney Street London SW3 6NP
Tel:	0171 351 8561
Fax:	0171 351 8562
Private:	Refer to address and number above
First Qualified:	1971 – Sheffield
Major Degrees:	FRCS

STANBRIDGE, Mr Rex D. L.

NHS:	Consultant Cardiothoracic Surgeon St Mary's Hospital Praed Street London W2 1NY
Tel:	0171 725 6038
Fax:	0171 725 1341
Private:	Refer to address above
Tel:	0171 725 1484
First Qualified:	1971 – London
Major Degrees:	FRCS
Academic:	Senior Lecturer, Royal Postgraduate Medical School, London
Specialist Training:	Great Ormond Street Hospital for Children, Hammersmith and The Middlesex Hospitals, London, and Harefield, Middlesex
USA:	Previously Research Fellow, Cardiac Surgery, Alabama University, Birmingham

STARK, Mr Jaroslav

Special interests:	**Congenital heart defects especially in infancy**
NHS:	Consultant Cardiothoracic Surgeon Great Ormond Street Hospital for Children Great Ormond Street London WC1N 3JH
Tel:	0171 831 7593
Fax:	0171 430 1281
Private:	Refer to address and number above
First Qualified:	1958 – Prague
Major Degrees:	FRCS, FACC, FACS
Specialist Training:	Charles University, Prague, and Great Ormond Street Hospital for Children, London
USA:	Honorary member, American Association of Thoracic Surgeons Research Fellow in Cardiology, Harvard Medical School, Boston

NORTHERN AND YORKSHIRE REGION

NEWCASTLE

HAMILTON, Mr John Robert Leslie

Special interests:	**Transplants**
NHS:	Consultant Paediatric Cardiac Surgeon
	Freeman Hospital
	Freeman Road
	High Heaton
	Newcastle upon Tyne NE7 7DN
Tel:	0191 284 3111
Fax:	0191 213 2167
Private:	Refer to address and number above
First Qualified:	1977 – Belfast
Major Degrees:	MD, FRCS Ed
Specialist Training:	Great Ormond Street Hospital for Children, London

WEST MIDLANDS

BIRMINGHAM

BRAWN, Mr William James

Special interests:	**Congenital heart disease**
NHS:	Consultant Paediatrician Cardiothoracic Surgeon
	Children's Hospital
	Ladywood Middleway
	Birmingham B16 8ET
Tel:	0121 454 4851
Fax:	0121 456 4697
Private:	Refer to address and number above
First Qualified:	1970 – London
Major Degrees:	FRCS, FRACS
Academic:	Senior Clinical Lecturer, Birmingham University

PAEDIATRIC CHEST PHYSICIANS

LONDON AND THE SOUTH EAST

BUSH, Dr Andrew

Special interests:	**Paediatric respiratory medicine**
NHS:	Consultant Paediatrician
	Royal Brompton Hospital
	Sydney Street
	London SW3 6NP
Tel:	0171 351 8232
Fax:	0171 351 8754
Private:	Private Consulting Rooms
	Royal Brompton Hospital
	Sydney Street
	London SW3 6NP
Tel:	0171 352 8121 Ext. 8830
Fax:	0171 351 8763
First Qualified:	1978 – Cambridge and London (with Honours)
Major Degrees:	MD, MRCP
Academic:	Senior Lecturer, Paediatric Respiratory Medicine, National Heart and Lung Institute, London
Specialist Training:	Royal Postgraduate Medical School and Brompton Hospitals, London
Distinctions:	Goldsmid Entrance Exhibition, University College Hospital, London
USA:	Norman A Brady Fellow, Norwalk Hospital, Yale University School of Medicine, Connecticut

DINWIDDIE, Dr Robert

Special interests:	**Respiratory disorders of children**
NHS:	Consultant Paediatrician
	Great Ormond Street Hospital for Children
	Great Ormond Street
	London WC1N 3JH
Tel:	0171 405 9200 Ext. 5453
Fax:	0171 829 8643
Private:	Refer to address and number above
First Qualified:	1969 – Aberdeen
Major Degrees:	FRCP
Specialist Training:	Aberdeen University, Scotland, Children's Hospital, Philadelphia, USA, and Great Ormond Street Hospital for Children, London
USA:	See 'Specialist Training' above

SOUTH AND WEST REGION

SOUTHAMPTON

WARNER, Professor John O.

Special interests:	**Paediatric allergies**
NHS:	Professor of Child Health
	Southampton General Hospital
	Tremona Road
	Southampton SO16 6YD
Tel:	01703 796160
Fax:	01703 796378
Private:	Refer to address and number above
First Qualified:	1968 – Sheffield
Major Degrees:	MD, FRCP
Academic:	Professor of Child Health, Southampton University
Specialist Training:	Great Ormond Street Hospital for Children, London
Distinctions:	Previously, Secretary, British Society of Allergy and Immunology

SCOTLAND

PATON, Dr James Y.

Special interests:	**Paediatric respiratory medicine**
NHS:	Honorary Consultant Paediatrician
	Department of Child Health
	Royal Hospital for Sick Children
	Yorkhill, Glasgow G3 8SJ
Tel:	0141 201 0238
Fax:	0141 201 0837
Private:	No private work
First Qualified:	1977 – Glasgow
Major Degrees:	MD, FRCP
Academic:	Senior Lecturer in Paediatric Respiratory Disease, Department of Child Health, Glasgow University
Specialist Training:	Royal Hospital for Sick Children, Edinburgh Department of Child Health University of Leicester.
USA:	MRC Travelling Fellow, Children's Hospital of Los Angeles, California

PAEDIATRIC CLINICAL ONCOLOGISTS

LONDON AND THE SOUTH EAST

MacDONALD, Dr Elizabeth Anne

Special interests:	**Breast cancer; lymphomas; children's brain tumours**
NHS:	Consultant Clinical Oncologist
	Radiotherapy Department
	Guy's Hospital
	St Thomas Street
	London SE1 9RT
Tel:	0171 955 4407
Fax:	0171 955 4828
Private:	Radiotherapy Department
	Cromwell Hospital
	Cromwell Road
	London SW5 0TU
Tel:	0171 370 4233 Ext. 5024
Fax:	0171 370 4063
First Qualified:	1969 – London
Major Degrees:	DMRT, MA (Medical Law and Ethics), FRCR
Academic:	Previously Clinical Tutor, Hammersmith Hospital, London
Specialist Training:	Westminster and Charing Cross Hospitals, London
Distinctions:	Previously Consultant, Nice Cancer Centre, France
	Founder, London Paediatric Neuro-oncology Forum
USA:	Clinical Researcher, Northern California Oncology Group, Stanford University

PLOWMAN, Dr P. Nicholas

Special interests: **Neuro-oncology; breast cancer; urological cancer; paediatric cancers**
NHS: Consultant Physician in Radiotherapy and Oncology
St Bartholomew's Hospital
West Smithfield
London EC1A 7BE
Tel: 0171 601 8351
Fax: 0171 601 8364
and: Consultant Physician in Radiotherapy and Oncology
Hospital for Sick Children
34 Great Ormond Street
London WC1N 3JH
Tel: 0171 405 9200
Fax: 0171 813 8588
Private: 14 Harmont House
20 Harley Street
London W1
Tel: 0171 631 1632
Fax: 0171 323 3487
First Qualified: 1974 – Cambridge (with Honours)
Major Degrees: MD, FRCP, FRCR
Academic: Honorary Senior Lecturer, Institute of Child Health, London
Specialist Training: St Bartholomew's Hospital, London, and Cambridge

SCOTLAND

GLASGOW

BARRETT, Professor Ann

Special interests: **Sarcomas; lymphomas**
NHS: Professor of Radiotherapy Oncology
Beatson Oncology Centre
Western Infirmary
Dumbarton Road, Glasgow G11 6NT
Tel: 0141 211 1738
Fax: 0141 337 1712
Private: Refer to address and number above
First Qualified: 1968 – London
Major Degrees: MD, FRCP, FRCR
Academic: Previously Senior Lecturer, Royal Marsden Hospital, Sutton
Specialist Training: Middlesex and Royal Marsden Hospitals, London, Villejuif, Paris
Distinctions: President of Scottish Radiological Society
President-Elect ESTRO

PAEDIATRIC COLONOSCOPISTS

LONDON AND THE SOUTH EAST

FAIRCLOUGH, Dr Peter D.

NHS:	Consultant Physician
	Department of Gastroenterology
	St Bartholomew's Hospital
	London EC1A 7BE
Tel:	0171 601 8517
Fax:	0171 982 6123
Private:	Endoscopy Unit, London Clinic
	20 Devonshire Place
	London W1N 2DH
Tel:	0171 935 4444
Fax:	0171 486 1755
First Qualified:	1969 – London
Major Degrees:	MD, FRCP
Academic:	Senior Lecturer, St Bartholomew's Medical College, London
Specialist Training:	St Mark's and St Bartholomew's Hospitals, London
Distinctions:	Lately Wellcome Senior Clinical Research Fellow, USA
USA:	See 'Distinctions' above

WILLIAMS, Dr Christopher B.

Special interests:	**Gastrointestinal endoscopy; colonoscopy and colonic medicine**
NHS:	Consultant Physician
	Endoscopy Unit
	St Mark's Hospital
	Northwich Park
	Watford Road, Harrow HA1 3UJ
Tel:	0181 235 4000
Fax:	0181 235 4001
Private:	Endoscopy Unit, London Clinic
	20 Devonshire Place
	London W1N 2DH
Tel:	0171 935 4444
Fax:	0171 486 1755
First Qualified:	1964 – Oxford
Major Degrees:	FRCP
Specialist Training:	St Mark's and St Bartholomew's Hospitals, London

PAEDIATRIC DERMATOLOGISTS

LONDON AND THE SOUTH EAST

ATHERTON, Dr David

Special interests:	**Paediatric dermatology; eczema; genetic skin disorders**
NHS:	Consultant Dermatologist
	Great Ormond Street Hospital for Children
	Great Ormond Street
	London WC1N 3JH
Tel:	0171 405 9200 Ext. 5601
Fax:	0171 813 8274
Private:	Private Consulting Rooms
	Great Ormond Street Hospital for Children
	Great Ormond Street
	London WC1N 3JH
Tel:	0171 829 8632
Fax:	0171 829 8650
First Qualified:	1974 – Cambridge
Major Degrees:	FRCP
Academic:	Senior Lecturer, Institute of Child Health, London
Specialist Training:	Guy's Hospital and Institute of Child Health, London

HARPER, Dr John I.

Special interests:	**Children**
NHS:	Consultant Paediatric Dermatologist
	Great Ormond Street Hospital for Children
	Great Ormond Street
	London WC1N 3JH
Tel:	0171 405 9200
Fax:	0171 813 8274
Private:	Refer to address and number above
First Qualified:	1973 – London
Major Degrees:	MD, MRCP
Distinctions:	Author, *Handbook of Paediatric Dermatology*

MAYOU, Dr Susan C.

Special interests: **Children's skin problems**
NHS: Consultant Paediatric Dermatologist
Chelsea and Westminster Hospital
369 Fulham Road
London SW10 9NH
Tel: 0181 746 8659
Fax: 0181 746 8221
Private: Lister Hospital
Chelsea Bridge Road
London SW1W 8RH
Tel: 0171 259 9892
Fax: 0171 259 9887
First Qualified: 1977 – London
Major Degrees: MRCP
Specialist Training: St Thomas' and St Bartholomew's Hospitals, London

PAEDIATRIC DIABETOLOGISTS AND ENDOCRINOLOGISTS

LONDON AND THE SOUTH EAST

BROOK, Professor Charles G. D.

Special interests: **Paediatric endocrinology**
NHS: Director, London Centre for Paediatric Endocrinology
Great Ormond Street Hospital for Children
Great Ormond Street
London WC1N 3JH
Tel: 0171 405 9200
Fax: 0171 829 8634
and: The Middlesex Hospital
Mortimer Street
London W1N 8AA
Tel: 0171 380 9450
Fax: 0171 636 9941
Private: Refer to address and numbers above
First Qualified: 1964 – Cambridge
Major Degrees: MD, FRCP
Academic: Professor of Endocrinology, University College London
Medical School and Royal Free Hospital School of
Medicine
Specialist Training: The Middlesex Hospital, London
Distinctions: Director, London Centre for Paediatric Endocrinology

SAVAGE, Dr Martin O.

Special interests:	**Paediatric and adolescent endocrinology, growth and development disorders; thyroid disease; paediatric neuroendocrinology**
NHS:	Honorary Consultant Paediatrician St Bartholomew's Hospital West Smithfield London EC1A 7BE
Tel:	0171 601 8888 Ext. 8953 or 0171 601 8468
Fax:	0171 601 8468
Private:	Refer to address and number above
First Qualified:	1968 – Cambridge
Major Degrees:	MD, FRCP
Academic:	Reader in Paediatric Endocrinology, St Bartholomew's Hospital, London Clinical Lecturer in Growth and Development, Institute of Child Health, London
Specialist Training:	Great Ormond Street Hospital for Children, London and Research Fellow in Paediatric Endocrinology, Hôpital St Vincent de Paul, Paris

STANHOPE, Dr Richard G.

Special interests:	**Paediatric and adolescent endocrinology with a special interest in disorders of sexual maturation**
NHS:	Consultant Paediatric Endocrinologist Great Ormond Street Hospital for Children Great Ormond Street London WC1N 3JH
Tel:	0171 405 9200 Ext. 5469
Fax:	0171 829 8841
Private:	Private Consulting Rooms 34 Great Ormond Street London WC1N 3JH
Tel:	0181 670 1957
Fax:	0181 670 1957
First Qualified:	1974 – London
Major Degrees:	MD, DCH, FRCP
Academic:	Senior Lecturer, Paediatric Endocrinology, Institute of Child Health, London
Specialist Training:	St Bartholomew's and The Middlesex Hospitals, London

ANGLIA AND OXFORD REGION

CAMBRIDGE

BARNES, Dr Nicholas D.

Special interests:	**General paediatrics including problems of growth and development in children; liver transplantation in childhood**
NHS:	Consultant Paediatrician
	Department of Paediatrics
	Addenbrooke's Hospital
	Hills Road, Cambridge CB2 2QQ
Tel:	01223 217235
Fax:	01223 216966
Private:	Refer to address and number above
First Qualified:	1963 London
Major Degrees:	FRCP
Academic:	Associated Lecturer, Cambridge University
Specialist Training:	Great Ormond Street Hospital for Children, London
Distinctions:	Honorary Consultant Endocrinologist, Great Ormond Street Hospital for Children, London
USA:	Previously Fellow, Paediatric Endocrinology, Mayo Clinic, Rochester

HUGHES, Professor Ieuan Arwel

Special interests:	**Genetics; disorder of sexual differentiation**
NHS:	Honorary Consultant Paediatrician
	Addenbrooke's Hospital
	Hills Road
	Cambridge CB2 2QQ
Tel:	01223 245151
Fax:	01223 336996
and:	Paediatric Endocrinologist
	Great Ormond Street Hospital for Children
	Great Ormond Street
	London WC1N 3JH
Tel:	0171 405 9200
Private:	No private work
First Qualified:	1968 – Wales
Major Degrees:	MD, FRCP
Academic:	Professor of Paediatrics, Cambridge University
	Previously, Senior Lecturer and Reader in Paediatric Endocrinology, Wales University
Specialist Training:	Hammersmith and University College Hospitals, London
Distinctions:	Head of Paediatric Department, Cambridge University
	Honorary Consultant in Paediatric Endocrinology, Great Ormond Street Hospital for Children, London
USA and Canada:	Dalhouse University, Nova Scotia, and Manitoba University, Winnipeg, Canada

OXFORD

DUNGER, Dr David Brian

NHS:	Consultant Paediatric Endocrinologist
	John Radcliffe Hospital
	Headley Way
	Headington, Oxford OX3 9DU
Tel:	01865 741166 or 221488
Fax:	01865 741408 or 220479
Private:	Refer to address and number above
First Qualified:	1971 – London
Major Degrees:	MD, MRCP
Specialist Training:	Great Ormond Street Hospital for Children, London

NORTHERN AND YORKSHIRE

LEEDS

HOLLAND, Dr Philip C.

Special interests:	**General paediatrics and diabetes**
NHS:	Consultant Paediatrician
	General Infirmary at Leeds
	Great George Street
	Leeds LS2 9NS
Tel:	01132 292 2840
Fax:	01132 292 6479
Private:	Refer to address and number above
First Qualified:	1973 – London
Major Degrees:	FRCP

NORTH WEST REGION

MANCHESTER

See *CLAYTON, Dr Peter Theodore* under Paediatric Metabolic Physicians

PRICE, Dr David A.

Special interests: **Growth disorders in children; growth hormone treatment; hormonal disorders in children, including precocious puberty, adrenal problems and diabetes**
NHS: Consultant Paediatric Endocrinologist
Royal Manchester Children's Hospital
Pendelbury, Manchester M27 1HA
Tel: 0161 727 2584
Fax: 0161 727 8387
Private: No private work
First Qualified: 1967 – Oxford
Major Degrees: FRCP
Academic: Senior Lecturer in Child Health, Manchester University
Specialist Training: Sophia Kinderziekenhuss, Rotterdam
Distinctions: Chairman, British Society of Paediatric Endocrinology

SOUTH AND WEST REGION

BRISTOL

BAUM, Professor J. David

Special interests: **Diabetes in children and young adults**
NHS: Professor of Child Health
Institute of Child Health
Royal Hospital for Sick Children
St Michael's Hill, Bristol BS2 8BJ
Tel: 0117 928 5383
Fax: 0117 925 5051
Private: No private work
First Qualified: 1963 – Birmingham
Major Degrees: MD, FRCP
Academic: Visiting Professor; Monahs Medical Centre, Melbourne, Australia
Sophia's Children's Hospital, Rotterdam University, The Netherlands
Dozor Visiting Professor, Ben Gurion University, Negev, Beersheva, Israel
Frohlich Visiting Professor, Royal Society of Medicine, New York, USA
Distinctions: Founding Chairman, National Association Care of Children with life-threatening disease and their families 1990–95
Founding Director , Institute of Child Health, Bristol University
Chairman, Academic Board British Paediatriac Association
Honorary Secretary, European Society of Paediatric Research
USA: Visiting Professor, University of Colorado Medical Centre

SOUTHAMPTON

BETTS, Dr Peter R.

Special interests:	**Paediatric endocrinology; diabetes in childhood**
NHS:	Consultant Paediatrician
	Southampton General Hospital
	Tremona Road
	Southampton SO9 4XY
Tel:	01703 796985
Fax:	01703 794750
Private:	Refer to address and number above
First Qualified:	1966 – London
Major Degrees:	FRCP

TRENT REGION

NOTTINGHAM

JOHNSTON, Dr Derek I.

Special interests:	**Paediatric endocrinology**
NHS:	Consultant Paediatrician
	Queen's Medical Centre
	University Hospital
	Nottingham NG7 2UH
Tel:	0115 924 9924 Ext. 43343
Fax:	0115 970 9763
Private:	The Park Hospital
	Sherwood Lodge Drive
	Burntstum Country Park
	Arnold, Nottingham NG 8RX
Tel:	0115 967 0670
First Qualified:	1967 – Cambridge and London
Major Degrees:	MD, FRCP, DCH
Academic:	Previously Lecturer, King's College Hospital, London
Specialist Training:	King's College Hospital and Great Ormond Street Hospital for Children, London
USA:	Chief Resident and Research Fellow Colorado University, Denver

LEICESTER

SWIFT, Dr Peter G.

Special interests:	**Paediatric diabetology: epidemiology; preschool; insulin therapy; paediatric endocrinology: thyroid; growth hormone; Turner's syndrome**
NHS:	Consultant Paediatrician and Endocrinologist Leicester Royal Infirmary Leicester LE1 5WW
Tel:	01162 541414
Fax:	01162 586912
Private:	No private work
First Qualified:	1968 – Cambridge
Major Degrees:	DCH, FRCP
Specialist Training:	Bristol Hospital for Sick Children, Sheffield Children's Hospital and Exeter
Distinctions:	Chairman BPA Diabetes Working Party Chairman Children's Committee BDA Council of International Society Paediatric Diabetes

SCOTLAND

DUNDEE

GREENE, Dr Stephen Allan

Special interests:	**Growth disorders in children; childhood diabetes**
NHS:	Consultant Paediatric Endocrinologist Department of Child Health Ninewells Hospital and Medical School Dundee DD1 9SY
Tel:	01382 66011
Private:	Refer to address and number above
First Qualified:	1973 – London
Major Degrees:	FRCP Ed
Academic:	Previously Wellcome Lecturer, Department of Paediatrics and Metabolic Medicine, Guy's Hospital, London; Research Fellow, John Radcliffe Hospital, Oxford; Smith and Nephew Travelling Fellowship, Zurich

PAEDIATRIC DIAGNOSTIC RADIOLOGY
See adult Diagnostic Radiology

PAEDIATRIC EAR, NOSE AND THROAT SPECIALISTS

LONDON AND THE SOUTH EAST

BAILEY, Mr C. Martin

Special interests:	**Paediatric otolaryngology and otology; management of airway obstruction in children**
NHS:	Consultant ENT Surgeon
	Great Ormond Street Hospital for Children
	Great Ormond Street, London WC1N 3JH
Tel:	0171 405 9200 Ext. 5362
Fax:	0171 829 8643
and:	Royal National Throat, Nose and Ear Hospital
	Gray's Inn Road
	London WC1X 8DA
Tel:	0171 837 8855
Private:	55 Harley Street, London WC1N 1DD
Tel:	0171 580 2426
Fax:	0171 436 1645
First Qualified:	1973 – London
Major Degrees:	FRCS
Academic:	Honorary Senior Lecturer, Institute of Child Health and Institute of Laryngology and Otology, London
Specialist Training:	Sussex Throat and Ear Hospital and Royal National Throat, Nose and Ear Hospital, London
USA:	TWJ Foundation Clinical and Research Fellow, Michigan University

---

BELLMAN, Dr Susan C.

Special interests:	**Paediatric audiological physician**
NHS:	Consultant Physician in Audiological Medicine
	Great Ormond Street Hospital for Children
	Great Ormond Street, London WC1N 3JH
Tel:	0171 405 9200 Ext. 5381
Fax:	0171 829 8643
Private:	Refer to address and number below
First Qualified:	1972 – Cambridge
Major Degrees:	FRCS
Specialist Training:	Royal National Throat, Nose and Ear Hospital, London

---

CROFT, Mr Charles B.

Special interests:	**Sleep apnoea, snoring; surgical management of head and neck tumours**
NHS:	Consultant ENT Surgeon
	Royal National Throat, Nose and Ear Hospital
	330 Gray's Inn Road
	London WC1X 8DA
Tel:	0171 837 8855
Fax:	0171 833 5518
Private:	55 Harley Street
	London W1N 1DD
Tel:	0171 580 2426
Fax:	0171 436 1645
First Qualified:	1965 – Leeds (with Honours)
Major Degrees:	FRCS
Specialist Training:	Leeds General Infirmary
Distinctions:	Civil Consultant in Laryngology to the Royal Air Force
	Examiner, Royal College of Surgeons, Edinburgh
	Consultant ENT Surgeon, National Heart and Chest Hospital, London
USA:	Previously Associate Professor, Albert Einstein Medical School, New York
	Attending Head and Neck Surgeon
	Montefiore Hospital, New York

EVANS, Mr John N. G.

Special interests:	**Paediatric otolaryngology; laryngotracheoplasty in children; management of cleft larynx and tracheo-oesophageal clefts; recurrent meningitis in children due to inner ear abnormalities**
NHS:	Consultant ENT Surgeon
	St Thomas' Hospital
	Lambeth Palace Road
	London SE1 7EH
Tel:	0171 928 9292
Fax:	0171 922 8079
and:	Consultant ENT Surgeon
	Great Ormond Street Hospital for Children
	Great Ormond Street
	London WC1N 3JH
Tel:	0171 405 9200
Fax:	0171 829 8644
Private:	55 Harley Street
	London W1N 1DD
Tel:	0171 580 1481
Fax:	0171 580 4163
First Qualified:	1559 – London
Major Degrees:	FRCS, FRCS Ed (with Honours)
Specialist Training:	Great Ormond Street Hospital for Children and St Thomas' Hospitals, London
Distinctions:	Honorary Consultant to the Army; Fellow, Royal Society of Medicine; Previously Honorary Secretary, British Association of Otolaryngology

MACKAY, Mr Ian S.

Special interests:	**Rhinoplasty; rhinosinusitis; endoscopic sinus surgery; nasal polyps**
NHS:	Consultant ENT Surgeon
	Chelsea and Westminster Hospital
	369 Fulham Road
	London SW10 9NH
Tel:	0181 746 8000
Fax:	0181 746 8111
and:	Charing Cross Hospital
	Fulham Palace Road
	London W6 8RF
Tel:	0181 846 1234
Fax:	0181 846 1111
and:	Royal Brompton Hospital
	Sydney Street
	London SW3 6NB
Tel:	0171 351 8121
Private:	55 Harley Street
	London W1N 1DD
Tel:	0171 580 5070
Fax:	0171 323 5401
First Qualified:	1968 – London
Major Degrees:	FRCS
Academic:	Senior Lecturer, Royal National Throat, Nose and Ear Hospital, London
Specialist Training:	Royal National Throat, Nose and Ear Hospital, London

NORTH WEST REGION

LIVERPOOL

SWIFT, Mr Andrew C.

Special interests:	**Paediatric ENT; infections after head and neck surgery**
NHS:	Consultant ENT Surgeon
	Walton Hospital
	Rice Lane
	Liverpool L9 1AE
Tel:	0151 529 4720
Fax:	0151 529 4033
Private:	Refer to address and number above
First Qualified:	1977 – Sheffield
Major Degrees:	ChM, FRCS, FRCS Ed
Academic:	Clinical Lecturer, Liverpool University

SOUTH AND WEST REGION

BRISTOL

MAW, Mr Richard

Special interests:	**Otolaryngology particularly related to chronic otitis media in children**
NHS:	Consultant ENT Surgeon
	Royal Hospital for Sick Children
	St Michael's Hill
	Bristol BS2 8BJ
Tel:	0117 928 5870
Fax:	0117 928 5117
and:	St Michael's Hospital
	Southwell Street
	Bristol BS2 8EG
Tel:	0117 921 5411
Fax:	0117 928 5820
and:	Bristol Royal Infirmary
	Maudlin Street
	Bristol BS2 8HW
Tel:	0117 923 0000
Fax:	0117 928 2000
Private:	Litfield House
	Litfield Place
	Clifton
	Bristol BS8 3LS
Tel:	01179 731323
Fax:	01179 733303
First Qualified:	1963 – London
Major Degrees:	FRCS
Academic:	Senior Clinical Lecturer, Otolaryngology, Bristol University
Specialist Training:	St Bartholomew's Hospital, London
Distinctions:	Wellcome Trust Travelling Research Fellow Uppsala University, Sweden

SOUTHAMPTON

HAACKE, Mr Norman P.

Special interests:	**Endoscopic sinus surgery; implants for profoundly deaf children**
NHS:	Consultant ENT and Otoneurology Surgeon Southampton University Hospital Southampton SO9 4XY
Tel:	01703 796741
Fax:	01703 283170
Private:	Refer to address and number above
First Qualified:	1977 – Cambridge
Major Degrees:	FRCS
Academic:	Senior Lecturer, Otolaryngology, Southampton University Honorary Clinical Tutor, Edinburgh University
Specialist Training:	Royal Infirmary, Edinburgh, and Royal National Throat, Nose and Ear Hospital, London
Distinctions:	Director, South England Cochlear Implant Centre, Southampton

TRENT REGION

SHEFFIELD

BULL, Mr Peter D.

Special interests:	**Paediatric Laryngology**
NHS:	Consultant Otolaryngologist Royal Hallamshire Hospital Glossop Road Sheffield S10 2JF
Tel:	0114 2711900
Fax:	0114 2712280
Private:	Consulting Rooms Thornbury Hospital 312 Fulwood Road Sheffield S10 3BR
Tel:	0114 266 1133
Fax:	0114 268 6913
First Qualified:	1967 – Wales
Major Degrees:	FRCS
Distinctions:	Editorial Representive, Laryngology Section, Royal Society of Medicine President, British Association, Paediatric Otolaryngology

WEST MIDLANDS REGION

BIRMINGHAM

PROOPS, Mr David W.

Special interests:	**Paediatric ENT**
NHS:	Consultant ENT Surgeon
	Birmingham Children's Hospital
	Ladywood Middleway
	Ladywood
	Birmingham B16 8ET
Tel:	0121 454 4851
Fax:	0121 452 1834
Private:	Refer to address and number above
First Qualified:	1975 – Birmingham
Major Degrees:	FRCS

PAEDIATRIC ENDOCRINOLOGISTS
See Diabetologists

PAEDIATRIC GASTROENTEROLOGISTS

LONDON AND THE SOUTH EAST

BRUETON, Dr Martin J.

Special interests:	**Including Tropical**
NHS:	Consultant Paediatrician
	Chelsea and Westminster Hospital
	369 Fulham Road
	London SW10 9NH
Tel:	0181 746 8000
Fax:	0181 746 8770
Private:	Refer to address and number above
First Qualified:	1967 – London
Major Degrees:	MD, FRCP
Specialist Training:	St Bartholomew's Hospital, London, and Birmingham Children's Hospital

---

MILLA, Dr Peter J.

NHS:	Honorary Consultant Paediatric Gastroenterologist
	Great Ormond Street Hospital for Children
	Great Ormond Street
	London WC1N 3JH
Tel:	0171 405 9200
Fax:	0171 404 6181
Private:	Refer to address and number above
First Qualified:	1964 – London
Major Degrees:	FRCP
Academic:	Reader in Paediatric Gastroenterology, Institute of Child Health, London
Specialist Training:	Great Ormond Street Hospital for Children and St Bartholomew's Hospital, London

WALKER-SMITH, Professor John A.

Special interests:	**Diarrhoea; Crohn's disease; ulcerative colitis; gastrointestinal food allergy**
NHS:	Professor of Paediatric Gastroenterology
	Royal Free Hospital
	Pond Street, London NW3 2QG
Tel:	0171 794 0500 Ext. 6234
Fax:	0171 830 2146
Private:	Refer to address and number below
First Qualified:	1960 – Sydney, Australia
Major Degrees:	MD, FRCAP, FRCP
Academic:	Professor of Paediatric Gastroenterology, Royal Free School of Medicine, London
Specialist Training:	Sydney, Australia, and Zurich, Switzerland
Distinctions:	Advisor to HM Government on medical aspects of food policy
	Editor, Journal Paediatric Gastroenterology and Nutrition
	Former Secretary, European Society Paediatric Gastroenterology and Nutrition

NORTH WEST REGION

MANCHESTER

MILLER, Dr Victor

Special interests:	**Inflammatory bowel disease; complex diarrhoeal disease; malabsorption; endoscopy upper and lower**
NHS:	Consultant Paediatric Gastroenterologist Booth Hall Children's Hospital Charlestown Road Blackley, Manchester M9 2AA
Tel:	0161 741 5051
Fax:	0161 741 5072
Private:	Roselands 4 Middleton Road Higher Crumpsall Manchester M8 6DS
Tel:	0161 795 9111
Fax:	0161 740 6451
First Qualified:	1961 – Glasgow
Major Degrees:	FRCP
Academic:	Honorary Lecturer, Manchester University
Specialist Training:	Great Ormond Street Hospital for Children, London, and Children's Hospital of Philadelphia, USA
USA:	Assistant Chief Resident, Children's Hospital of Philadelphia

WEST MIDLANDS

BIRMINGHAM

BOOTH, Professor Ian

Special interests:	**Paediatric gastroenterology and nutrition**
NHS:	Professor of Paediatric Gastroenterology
	Institute of Child Health
	Birmingham University
	Francis Road, Birmingham B16 8ET
Tel:	0121 454 1474
Fax:	0121 454 5383
and:	Birmingham Children's Hospital
	Ladywood Middleway
	Birmingham B16 8ET
Tel:	0121 454 4851
Fax:	0121 456 4697
Private:	Refer to address and number above
First Qualified:	1972 – London
Major Degrees:	DobstRCOG, DCH, MD, FRCP
Academic:	Professor of Paediatric Gastroenterology and Nutrition, Institute of Child Health, Birmingham University
	Previously Lecturer in Child Health, Institute of Child Health, Birmingham University
	Previously Reader in Paediatric Gastroenterology and Nutrition, Institute of Child Health, Birmingham University
Specialist Training:	Institute of Child Health and Great Ormond Street Hospital for Children, London
Distinctions:	Bohringer Prize Biochemistry, Chelsea College, London University
	President, British Society of Paediatric Gastroenterology and Nutrition

PAEDIATRIC GENERAL SURGEONS

LONDON AND THE SOUTH EAST

DRAKE, Mr David P.

Special interests:	**Neonatal, surgical and acute gastrointestinal disorders**
NHS:	Consultant Paediatric Surgeon
	Great Ormond Street Hospital for Children
	Great Ormond Street
	London WC1N 3JH
Tel:	0171 405 9200 Ext. 5592
Fax:	0171 813 8250
Private:	Refer to address and number above
First Qualified:	1970 – Cambridge
Major Degrees:	FRCS
Specialist Training:	Southampton General Hospital and Queen Mary's Children's Hospital, Carshalton

HOLMES, Mr S. J. Keith

Special interests:	**Gastroenterology, oncology, neonatology**
NHS:	Consultant Paediatric Surgeon
	St George's Hospital
	Blackshaw Road
	London SW17 0QT
Tel:	0181 725 2926
Fax:	0181 725 2926
Private:	Parkside Hospital
	London SW19 5NX
Tel:	0181 946 4202
Fax:	0181 946 7775
First Qualified:	1970 – Liverpool
Major Degrees:	FRCS
Specialist Training:	Great Ormond Street Hospital for Children, London
Distinctions:	Honorary Consultant Surgeon, Royal Marsden Hospital, Sutton, Surrey
USA:	Research Fellow, Chicago University

KIELY, Mr Edward M.

Special interests:	**Neo-natal surgery**
NHS:	Consultant Paediatric Surgeon
	Great Ormond Street Hospital for Children
	Great Ormond Street
	London WC1N 3JH
Tel:	0171 405 9200 Ext. 5592
Fax:	0171 404 6181
Private:	Refer to address and number above
First Qualified:	1968 – Ireland
Major Degrees:	FRCS
Specialist Training:	Great Ormond Street Hospital for Children, London;
	Johannesburg Hospital, South Africa
	Children's Hospital, Birmingham

MADDEN, Mr Nicholas P.

NHS:	Consultant Paediatric Surgeon
	Chelsea and Westminster Hospital
	369 Fulham Road
	London SW10 9NH
Tel:	0181 746 8000 or 0181 746 8696
Fax:	0181 746 8221
Private:	Refer to address and number above
First Qualified:	1974 – Oxford
Major Degrees:	FRCS
Specialist Training:	Leeds General Infirmary

SPITZ, Professor Lewis

Special interests:	**Paediatric surgery including neonatal surgery; special expertise in complex gastrointestinal abnormalities, oesophageal replacement; separation of Siamese twins**
NHS:	Consultant Paediatric Surgeon
	Great Ormond Street Hospital for Children
	Great Ormond Street
	London WC1N 3JH
Tel:	0171 829 8691
Fax:	0171 404 6181
e-mail:	L.spitz@ich.bpmf.ac.uk
Private:	Refer to address and number above
First Qualified:	1962 – Pretoria, South Africa
Major Degrees:	PhD, FRCS
Academic:	Nuffield Professor of Paediatric Surgery, Institute of Child Health, London University, 30 Guildford Street, London WC1N 1EH

WRIGHT, Miss Vanessa M.

NHS:	Consultant Paediatric Surgeon
	Queen Elizabeth Hospital for Children
	Hackney Road
	Bethnal Green, London E2 8PS
Tel:	0171 739 8422
Fax:	0171 608 6399
Private:	Refer to address and number above
First Qualified:	1966 – London
Major Degrees:	FRCS, FRACS
Specialist Training:	Royal Children's Hospital, Melbourne, Australia

SOUTH AND WEST REGION

BRISTOL

SPICER, Mr Richard Dudley

Special interests:	**Neonatal surgery; paediatric oncology surgery**
NHS:	Consultant Paediatric Surgeon
	Department of Paediatric Surgery
	Bristol Children's Hospital
	St Michael's Hill
	Bristol BS2 8BJ
Tel:	0117 928 5708
Fax:	0117 928 5701
Private:	BUPA Hopsital
	The Glen Hospital
	Bristol BS6 6UT
Tel:	0117 973 2562
Fax:	0117 974 3203
First Qualified:	1968 – London
Major Degrees:	DCH, FRCS
Specialist Training:	Sheffield, Manchester and Cape Town, South Africa

SOUTHAMPTON
BURGE, Mr David Michael

NHS:	Consultant Paediatric and Neonatal Surgeon
	Department of Paediatric Surgery
	Southampton General Hospital
	Tremona Road, Southampton SO16 6YD
Tel:	01703 776677
Fax:	01703 794750
Private:	Refer to address above
Tel:	01794 323063
First Qualified:	1973 – Oxford
Major Degrees:	FRCS, FRACS
Specialist Training:	Alexandra Hospital, Sydney, Australia

PAEDIATRIC HEART SURGEONS

See Paediatric Cardiothoracic Surgeons

PAEDIATRIC HEPATOLOGY

SEE *BALL, Dr Colin S.* under Paediatric HIV
CLAYTON, Dr Peter Theodore under Paediatric Metabolic Physicians
BARNES, Dr Nicholas D. under Paediatric Endocrine Physicians

PAEDIATRIC HIV/AIDS PHYSICIANS

LONDON AND THE SOUTH EAST

BALL, Dr Colin S.

Special interests:	**Hepatology**
NHS:	Consultant Paediatrician
	Department of Child Health
	King's College Hospital
	Denmark Hill, London SE5 9RS
Tel:	0171 346 3214
Fax:	0171 346 3564
Private:	Refer to address and number above
First Qualified:	1979 – London
Major Degrees:	MRCP
Academic:	Previously Lecturer, King's College School of Medicine
	and Dentistry, London

PAEDIATRIC KIDNEY SURGEONS

LONDON AND THE SOUTH EAST

FERNANDO, Mr Oswald N.

Special interests:	**Kidney transplants**
NHS:	Consultant Surgeon, Department of Nephrology and Renal Transplantation
	Royal Free Hospital
	Pond Street
	London NW3 2QG
Tel:	0171 794 0500 Ext. 4138
Fax:	0171 830 2125
Private:	Refer to address and number above
First Qualified:	1960 – Sri Lanka
Major Degrees:	FRCS
Academic:	Previously Research Fellow, Royal Free Hospital, London
Specialist Training:	Royal Free Hospital, London
Distinctions:	Honorary Consultant Surgeon, Great Ormond Street Hospital for Children, London

PAEDIATRIC MEDICAL ONCOLOGISTS

LONDON AND THE SOUTH EAST

GOLDSTONE, Dr Anthony H.

Special interests:	**Leukaemia and bone marrow transplants; paediatric cancer**
NHS:	Consultant Haematologist
	University College London
	Gower St, London WC1E 6AU
Tel:	0171 387 9300
Fax:	0171 387 9816
Private:	Private Patients Wing
	University College London
	Grafton Way, London WC1E 6AU
Tel:	0171 387 9709
Fax:	0171 387 9816
First Qualified:	1968 – Oxford
Major Degrees:	FRCP, FRCPath
Academic:	Previously Postgraduate Dean, University College Hospital Medical School, London
Specialist Training:	Addenbrooke's Hospital, Cambridge and Cancer Research Institute, London

KINGSTON, Dr Judith

Special interests:	**Tumours**
NHS and Academic:	Consultant Paediatrician and Senior Lecturer
	St Bartholomew's Hospital
	West Smithfield
	London EC1A 7BE
Tel:	0171 601 8004
Fax:	0171 601 7850
Private:	Refer to address and number above
First Qualified:	1973 – Bristol
Major Degrees:	FRCP
Specialist Training:	John Radcliffe Infirmary, Oxford, and Addenbrooke's Hospital, Cambridge

MALPAS, Professor James S.

Special interests:	**Paediatric cancer; haematological lymphomas**
NHS:	Honorary Consultant Physician
	Department of Medical Oncology
	St Bartholomew's Hospital
	West Smithfield, London EC1A 7BE
Tel:	0171 601 7456 or 0171 601 7461
Fax:	0171 796 3979
Private:	Refer to address and number above
First Qualified:	MD, FRCP, FRCR
Major Degrees:	1955 – London
Academic:	Emeritus Professor in Medical Oncology
	St Bartholomew's Hospital, London
Specialist Training:	Radcliffe Infirmary, Oxford, Royal Postgraduate Medical School and St Bartholomew's Hospital, London
Distinctions:	Examiner to the Universities of London and Oxford; Director, Imperial Cancer Research Fund; President, Association of Cancer Physicians; Lockyer Lecturer, Royal College of Physician; President, Association Cancer Physician; Ex-President St Bartholomew's Hospital Medical College

PINKERTON, Professor C. Ross

NHS:	Professor of Paediatric Oncology
	Royal Marsden Hospital
	Downs Road
	Sutton, Surrey
Tel:	0181 642 6011 Ext. 3498
Fax:	0181 770 7168
e-mail:	ross p@icr.ac.uk
Private:	Refer to address and number above
First Qualified:	1974 – Belfast
Major Degrees:	MD, FRCPI

NORTHERN AND YORKSHIRE REGION

NEWCASTLE

CRAFT, Professor A. W.

Special interests:	**Bone tumours**
NHS:	Consultant
	Royal Victoria Infirmary
	Queen Victoria Road
	Newcastle upon Tyne NE1 4LP
Tel:	0191 202 3010
Fax:	0191 202 3022
Private:	Refer to address and number above
First Qualified:	1969 – Newcastle
Major Degrees:	MR, FRCP
Academic:	Professor Paediatric Oncology, Newcastle University
Specialist Training:	Royal Marsden Hospital, London
Distinctions:	Chairman, MRC Bone Sarcoma Committee
	Chairman, European Osteosarcoma Intergroup
	Chairman, Anglo-German Ewings Sarcoma Study Group

WEST MIDLANDS

BIRMINGHAM

STEVENS, Dr Michael C. G.

NHS:	Consultant Paediatrician in Oncology
	Department of Oncology
	Birmingham Children's Hospital
	Ladywood Middleway
	Birmingham B16 8ET
Tel:	0121 454 4851
Fax:	0121 456 4697
Private:	Refer to address and number above
First Qualified:	1974 – London (with Honours)
Major Degrees:	MD, FRCP
Specialist Training:	John Radcliffe Hospital, Oxford, and Hospital for Sick Children, Toronto, Canada
Distinctions:	Secretary, UK Children's Cancer Study Group

PAEDIATRIC METABOLIC PHYSICIANS

LONDON AND THE SOUTH EAST

CLAYTON, Dr Peter Theodore

Special interests:	**Paediatric metabolic disease and hepatology**
NHS:	Honorary Consultant Physician
	Great Ormond Street Hospital for Children
	Great Ormond Street
	London WC1N 3JH
Tel:	0171 242 9789
Fax:	0171 831 0488
Private:	Refer to address and number above
First Qualified:	1974 – Cambridge
Major Degrees:	MD, FRCP
Academic:	Senior Lecturer, Institute of Child Health, London

LEONARD, Professor James V.

NHS:	Consultant Physician
	Great Ormond Street Hospital for Children
	Great Ormond Street
	London WC1N 3JH
Tel:	0171 242 9789 Ext. 2190
Fax:	0171 813 0387
Private:	Refer to address and number above
First Qualified:	1970 – Cambridge
Major Degrees:	PhD, FRCP
Specialist Training:	Great Ormond Street Hospital for Children, London

WALTER, Dr John

Special interests:	**Inherited metabolic disease**
NHS:	Consultant Paediatrician
	Royal Manchester Children's Hospital
	Pendelbury
	Manchester M27 1HA
Tel:	0161 727 2138
Fax:	0161 727 2137
Private:	Refer to address and number above
First Qualified:	1978 – London
Major Degrees:	MSc, MD
Academic:	Prevously Clinical Research Fellow, Institute of Child Health, London
Specialist Training:	Institute of Child Health, London

WRAITH, Dr James

Special interests:	**Inherited metabolic disease; lysosomal storage disease**
NHS:	Director, Willink Biochemical Genetics Unit
	Royal Manchester Children's Hospital
	Pendelbury
	Manchester M27 4HA
Tel:	0161 727 2137
Fax:	0161 727 2137
e-mail:	ed@willink.demon.co.uk
Private:	Refer to address and number above
First Qualified:	1977 – Sheffield
Major Degrees:	FRCP
Academic:	Clinical Fellow, Murdoch Institute Royal Children's Hospital, Melbourne, Australia
Specialist Training:	Melbourne and Manchester

PAEDIATRIC NEO-NATAL PHYSICIANS

LONDON AND THE SOUTH EAST

HARVEY, Professor David R.

NHS:	Honorary Consultant Paediatrician
	Queen Charlotte's and Chelsea Hospital
	Goldhawk Road
	London W6 OXG
Tel:	0181 740 3918
Fax:	0181 748 4712
Private:	Refer to address and number above
First Qualified:	1960 – London (with Honours)
Major Degrees:	FRCP
Academic:	Professor in Neo-Natal Medicine, Royal Postgraduate Medical School, London
Specialist Training:	Royal Postgraduate Medical School and Great Ormond Street Hospital for Children, London
Distinctions:	Consultant Paediatrician to the Royal Family

KOVAR, Dr Ilya

NHS:	Consultant in Paediatrics and Perinatal Medicine
	Chelsea and Westminster Hospital
	369 Fulham Road
	London SW10 9NH
Tel:	0181 846 7193/7195
Fax:	0181 846 7998
Private:	Refer to address and number above
First Qualified:	1970 – Sydney, Australia
Major Degrees:	FRCP
Academic:	Honorary Senior Lecturer in Perinatal Medicine, Charing Cross and Westminster Medical Schools, London
Specialist Training:	Toronto, Sydney and USA
USA:	Fellow, American Academy of Paediatrics

WYATT, Dr John S.

Special interests:	**Cerebral injury in the newborn**
NHS:	Consultant Paediatrician
	University College Hospital
	Gower Street
	London WC1E 6AU
Tel:	0171 209 6115
Fax:	0171 209 6103
Private:	Refer to address and number above
First Qualified:	1978 – London
Major Degrees:	FRCP
Academic:	Senior Lecturer in Neonatal Paediatrics
	University College London

ANGLIA AND OXFORD REGION

CAMBRIDGE

MORLEY, Dr Colin John

Special interests:	**Neonatology; surfactant therapy; babies' breathing problems**
NHS:	Consultant Paediatrician
	Neonatal Intensive Care Unit
	Rosie Maternity Hospital
	Addenbrooke's Hospital
	Hills Road
	Cambridge CB2 2QQ
Tel:	01223 217677
Fax:	01223 217064
e-mail:	cjm11@cus.cam.ac.uk
Private:	Refer to address and number above
First Qualified:	1968 – Cambridge
Major Degrees:	MD, FRCP, DCH
Academic:	Lecturer in Paediatrics, Cambridge University

NORTH WEST REGION

LIVERPOOL

COOKE, Professor Richard W. I.

NHS:	Professor of Paediatric Medicine
	Royal Liverpool Children's Hospital
	Eaton Road
	West Derby
	Liverpool LP12 2AP
Tel:	0151 252 5695
Fax:	0151 228 2024
Private:	Refer to address and number above
First Qualified:	1971 – London
Major Degrees:	MD, FRCP
Academic:	Professor of Paediatric Medicine, Liverpool University
	Research Fellow, Department of Paediatric, Oxford University
Distinctions:	President, British Association Perinatal Medicine

NORTHERN AND YORKSHIRE REGION

LEEDS

LEVENE, Malcolm Irvin

Special interests:	**Neonatal intensive care; neurology of the newborn; causes of damage to the developing brain**
NHS:	Professor of Paediatrics and Child Health
	University of Leeds
	D Floor, Clarendon Wing
	General Infirmary at Leeds
	Belmont Grove
	Leeds LS2 9NS
Tel:	0113 292 3905
Fax:	0113 292 3902
Private:	Refer to address and number above
First Qualified:	1974 – London
Major Degrees:	MD, FRCP
Academic:	Research Lecturer, Hammersmith Hospital, London
	Senior Lecturer and Reader, Leicester University

SOUTH AND WEST REGION

BRISTOL

SEE *BAUM, Professor J. David* under Paediatric Diabetes

PAEDIATRIC NEPHROLOGISTS

LONDON AND THE SOUTH EAST

CHANTLER, Professor Cyril

NHS:	Consultant Paediatrician
	Guy's Hospital
	London Bridge
	London SE1 9RT
Tel:	0171 955 4222
Fax:	0171 407 0082
e-mail:	C. Chantler@umds.ac.uk
Private:	Refer to address and number above
First Qualified:	1964 – Cambridge
Major Degrees:	MD, FRCP
Academic:	Professor of Paediatric Nephrology
Specialist Training:	Guy's Hospital, London
Distinctions:	Principal United Medical and Dental Schools, Guy's and St Thomas' Hospitals, London

---

DILLON, Dr Michael J.

Special interests:	**Hypertension; vasculitis; renal disease in childhood**
NHS:	Consultant Physician and Director of Clinical Nephrology
	Great Ormond Street Hospital for Children
	Great Ormond Street
	London WC1N 3JH
Tel:	0171 405 9200
Fax:	0171 829 8841
Private:	Refer to address and number above
First Qualified:	1962 – London
Major Degrees:	FRCP
Academic:	Senior Lecturer, Institute of Child Health, London
Specialist Training:	Great Ormond Street Hospital for Children and Guy's Hospital, London

---

TROMPETER, Dr Richard S.

Special interests:	**Nephrotic syndrome in children; chronic renal failure**
NHS:	Consultant Paediatric Nephrologist
	Great Ormond Street Hospital for Children
	Great Ormond Street
	London WC1N 3JH
Tel:	0171 405 9200 Ext. 8305
Fax:	0171 829 8841
Private:	Refer to address and number above
First Qualified:	1970 – London
Major Degrees:	FRCP
Academic:	Previously, Senior Lecturer in Paediatrics, Royal Free Hospital and Medical School
Specialist Training:	Guy's Hospital and Hospital for Sick Children, London

PAEDIATRIC NEUROLOGISTS

LONDON AND THE SOUTH EAST

ROSS, Professor Euan M.

Special interests:	**Epilepsy**
NHS:	Professor of Community Paediatrics
	King's College Hospital
	Mary Sheridan Centre
	405 Kennington Road
	London SE11 4QW
Tel:	0171 277 2612
Fax:	0171 346 5598
Private:	Refer to address and number above
First Qualified:	1962 – Bristol
Major Degrees:	MD, FRCP
Academic:	Professor of Community Paediatrics, King's College, London
Distinctions:	Chairman, Paediatric Surveillance Unit

WILSON, Dr John

Special interests:	**Autism**
NHS:	Consultant Neurologist
	Great Ormond Street Hospital for Children
	Great Ormond Street
	London WC1N 3JH
Tel:	0171 405 9200
Fax:	0171 829 8643
Private:	Refer to address and number above
First Qualified:	1956 – Durham (with Honours)
Major Degrees:	FRCP

NORTH WEST REGION

MANCHESTER

NEWTON, Dr Richard

NHS:	Consultant Paediatric Neurologist
	Royal Manchester Children's Hospital
	Pendlebury
	Manchester M27 1HA
Tel:	0161 794 4696
Fax:	0161 727 2185
and:	Booth Hall Children's Hospital
	Charlestown Road
	Blackley
	Manchester M9 2AA
Tel:	0161 795 7000
Fax:	0161 741 5387
Private:	Refer to address and number above
First Qualified:	1978 – London
Major Degrees:	MD, FRCP
Specialist Training:	Hull Royal Infirmary

PAEDIATRIC NEUROSURGEONS

LONDON AND THE SOUTH EAST

HAYWARD, Mr Richard D.

Special interests:	**Paediatric Neurosurgery and Craniofacial Surgery**
NHS:	Consultant Surgeon
	Great Ormond Street Hospital for Children
	Great Ormond Street
	London WC1 3JH
Tel:	0171 405 9200
Fax:	0171 242 5800
Private:	The Private Consulting Rooms
	National Hospital
	Queen Square, London WC1N 3BG
Tel:	0171 829 8792
Fax:	0171 833 8658
First Qualified:	1966 – London
Major Degrees:	FRCS
Specialist Training:	St Mary's and National Hospitals, London
Distinctions:	Honorary Consultant Neurosurgeon, King Edward VII Hospital for Officers

SOUTH AND WEST REGION

BRISTOL

COAKHAM, Professor Hugh Beresford

Special interests:	**Neuro-oncology**
NHS:	Consultant Neurosurgeon
	Department of Neurosurgery
	Frenchay Hospital
	Bristol BS16 1LE
Tel:	0117 970 1070
Fax:	0117 956 3880
Private:	Refer to address and number above
First Qualified:	1968 – London
Major Degrees:	FRCS, FRCS
Academic:	Professor of Neurosurgery, Bristol University
Specialist Training:	University College and Maudesley Hospitals, London
Distinctions:	Hunterian Professor, Royal College of Surgeons
	Director, Imperial Cancer Research Fund Brain Tumour Group
USA:	Fellow in Neurosurgery, Massachusetts General Hospital and Harvard University, Boston

NORTH WEST REGION

MANCHESTER AND SALFORD

COWIE, Mr Richard A.

Special interests:	**Spinal surgery**
NHS:	Consultant Neurosurgeon
	Neuroscience Unit
	Alexandra Hospital
	Mill Lane
	Cheadle, Cheshire SK8 2PX
Tel:	0161 491 1606
Fax:	0161 491 1645
and:	Royal Manchester Children's Hospital
	Hospital Road
	Pendlebury, Manchester M27 1HA
Tel:	0161 794 4696
Fax:	0161 794 5929
and:	Hope Hospital
	Stott Lane
	Salford 6, M6 8HD
Tel:	0161 789 7373
Fax:	0161 787 5974
Private:	Refer to address and number above
First Qualified:	1973 – Edinburgh
Major Degrees:	FRCS
Specialist Training:	Western General Hospital, Edinburgh

PAEDIATRIC OPHTHALMOLOGISTS

LONDON AND THE SOUTH EAST

LEE, Mr John P.

Special interests:	**Squint and ocular motility**
NHS:	Consultant Ophthalmic Surgeon
	Moorfields Eye Hospital
	City Road, London EC1V 2PD
Tel:	0171 253 3411
Fax:	0171 253 4696
Private:	62 Wimpole Street
	London W1M 7DE
Tel:	0171 935 5801
Fax:	0171 486 3589
First Qualified:	1971 – Oxford
Major Degrees:	FRCS, FRCP, FRCOphth
Academic:	Previously Clinical Sub-Dean, Institute of Ophthalmology
Specialist Training:	Moorfields Eye Hospital, London
USA:	Fellow in Paediatric Ophthalmology and Neurophthalmology, Bascom Palmer Eye Institute, Miami

MUSHIN, Mr Alan S.

Special interests:	**Neonatal and paediatric ophthalmology; cataracts**
NHS:	Consultant Ophthalmic Surgeon
	Royal London Hospital
	Whitechapel Road
	London E1 1BB
Tel:	0171 377 7426
Fax:	0171 377 8112
and:	Great Ormond Street Hospital for Children
	Great Ormond Street
	London WC1N 3JH
Tel:	0171 405 9200
Fax:	0171 829 8643
Private:	82 Harley Street
	London W1N 1AE
Tel:	0171 580 3116
Fax:	0171 580 6996
First Qualified:	1960 – London
Major Degrees:	FRCS, FRCOphth
Specialist Training:	Royal Postgraduate Medical School, University College and Moorfields Eye Hospitals, London

TAYLOR, Mr David S. I.

Special interests:	**Children's eye problems**
NHS:	Consultant Ophthalmologist
	Great Ormond Street Hospital for Children
	Great Ormond Street
	London WC1 3JH
Tel:	0171 405 9200
Fax:	0171 829 8643
Private:	1 Harmont House
	20 Harley Street
	London W1N 1AL
Tel:	0171 935 7916
Fax:	0171 323 5430
First Qualified:	1967 – Liverpool
Major Degrees:	FRCP, FRCS, FRCOphth
Academic:	Senior Lecturer, Institute of Child Health
Specialist Training:	National Hospital for Nervous Diseases, London
USA:	Previously, Fellow, Neuro-Ophthalmology, University of California
	Member, American Association of Paediatric Ophthalmology

PAEDIATRIC ORTHOPAEDIC SURGEONS

LONDON AND THE SOUTH EAST

CATERALL, Mr Anthony

NHS:	Consultant Orthopaedic Surgeon
	Royal National Orthopaedic Hospital
	243 Great Portland Street
	London W1N 6AD
Tel:	0171 387 5070
Fax:	0171 383 5107
Private:	149 Harley Street
	London W1N 1HG
Tel:	0171 935 4444
Fax:	0171 486 3782
First Qualified:	1961 – Cambridge
Major Degrees:	FRCS
Specialist Training:	Royal National Orthopaedic Hospital, London

EDGAR, Mr Michael A.

Special interests:	**Spine; general orthopaedics; paediatric orthopaedics**
NHS:	Consultant Orthopaedic Surgeon
	The Middlesex Hospital
	Mortimcr Street
	London WIN 8AA
Tel:	0171 636 8333
Fax:	0171 323 0397
and:	Royal National Orthopaedic Hospital
	Brockley Hill
	Stanmore
	Middlesex HA7 4LP
Tel:	0181 954 2300
Private:	149 Harley Street
	London W1N 2DE
Tel:	0171 486 0027
Fax:	0171 487 5997
First Qualified:	1964 – Cambridge
Major Degrees:	FRCS, MChir
Specialist Training:	The Orthopaedic Hospital, Oswestry, and The Middlesex Hospital, London
Distinctions:	Civilian Consultant to the Royal Air Force

FIXSEN, Mr John A.

Special interests:	**Congenital disorders in children, of feet, hips and spine**
NHS:	Consultant Orthopaedic Surgeon
	Great Ormond Street Hospital for Children
	Great Ormond Street
	London WC1N 3JH
Tel:	0171 405 9200
Fax:	0171 829 8643
Private:	Refer to address and number above
First Qualified:	1962 – Cambridge
Major Degrees:	MChir, FRCS
Specialist Training:	The Royal National Orthopaedic Hospital, London

HUNT, Mr David M.

Special interests:	**Knee injuries and paediatric orthopaedic problems**
NHS:	Consultant Orthopaedic Surgeon
	St Mary's Hospital
	Praed Street
	London W2 1NY
Tel:	0171 725 1394
Fax:	0171 725 1766
Private:	106 Harley Street
	London W1N 1AF
Tel:	0171 935 6347
Fax:	0171 935 2788
First Qualified:	1971 – London
Major Degrees:	FRCS
Specialist Training:	St Mary's Hospital, London

JACKSON, Mr Andrew M.

Special interests:	**Knee surgery including knee replacement, arthroscopy and ligament reconstruction paediatric orthopaedics excluding the spine**
NHS:	Consultant Orthopaedic Surgeon
	St George's Hospital
	Blackshaw Road
	London SW17 0QT
Tel:	0181 672 1255
Private:	107 Harley Street
	London WIN 1DG
Tel:	0171 935 9521
Fax:	0171 935 5187
First Qualified:	1969 – London
Major Degrees:	FRCS
Specialist Training:	Royal National Orthopaedic Hospital, London
Distinctions:	Honorary Consultant Surgeon, Royal National Orthopaedic Hospital

JONES, Mr David

Special interests:	**Paediatric orthopaedics**
NHS:	Consultant Orthopaedic Surgeon
	Great Ormond Street Hospital for Children
	Great Ormond Street
	London WC1N 3JH
Tel:	0171 405 9200
Fax:	0171 813 8243
Private:	Refer to address and number above
Fax:	0171 829 8650

RANSFORD, Mr Andrew O.

Special interests:	**Cervical spine problems, children's spinal deformities, low back pain and disc disease**
NHS:	Consultant Orthopaedic Surgeon
	Royal National Orthopaedic Hospital
	Brockley Hill
	Stanmore
	Middlesex HA7 4LP
Tel:	0181 954 2300 Ext. 231
Fax:	0181 420 6582
Private:	107 Harley Street
	London W1N 1DG
Tel:	0171 486 1088
Fax:	0171 935 5187
First Qualified:	1966 – Cambridge
Major Degrees:	FRCS
Specialist Training:	University College and Royal National Orthopaedic Hospitals, London
USA:	Previously Orthopaedic Fellow, Rancho Los Amigos Hospital, Downey, California

SOUTH AND WEST REGION

TAUNTON

WEBB, Mr Peter J.

Special interests:	**Scoliosis; general spine problems; general paediatric orthopaedics**
NHS:	Musgrove Park Hospital
	Taunton TA1 5DA
Tel:	01823 333444
Fax:	01823 336877
Private:	Somerset Nuffield
	Staplegrove Elm
	Taunton, Somerset TA2 6AN
Tel:	01823 286991
Fax:	01823 338951
First Qualified:	1969 – London
Major Degrees:	FRCS
Specialist Training:	Royal National Orthopaedic Hospital and Great Ormond Street Hospital for Children, London

TRENT REGION

NOTTINGHAM

COLTON, Professor Christopher L.

Special interests:	**Skeletal trauma, including reconstruction; fractures in children, skeletal infection, nonunion and malunion**
NHS:	Nottingham University Hospital
	Nottingham NG7 2UH
Tel:	0115 924 9924
Fax:	0115 942 3656
Private:	34 Regent Street
	Nottingham NG1 5BT
Tel:	0115 956 1307
Fax:	0115 942 3606
First Qualified:	1960 – London
Major Degrees:	FRCS, FRCS Ed

PAEDIATRIC PLASTIC SURGEONS

LONDON AND SOUTH EAST

COLLIN, Mr Richard

Special interests:	**Plastic and reconstructive surgery of the eyelids, including children's**
NHS:	Consultant Ophthalmic Surgeon
	Moorfields Eye Hospital
	City Road
	London EC1V 2PD
Tel:	0171 253 3411 Ext. 2577
Fax:	0171 566 2019
Private:	67 Harley Street
	London W1N 1DE
Tel:	0171 486 2699
Fax:	0171 486 8626
First Qualified:	1968 – Cambridge
Major Degrees:	FRCS
Academic:	Previously Senior Lecturer Moorfields Eye Hospital, London
Specialist Training:	Moorfields Eye Hospital, London
Distinctions:	Honorary Consultant Ophthalmic Surgeon, Hospital for Sick Children, London
	Secretary, European Society Ophthalmic Plastic and Reconstructive Surgery
USA:	Previously Fellow in Ophthalmic Plastic and Reconstructive Surgery, University of California Medical School, San Francisco

JONES, Mr Barry M.

Special interests:	**Craniofacial Surgery; aesthetic plastic surgery**
NHS:	Consultant Plastic and Reconstructive Surgeon
	Great Ormond Street Hospital for Children
	Great Ormond Street
	London WC1N 3JH
Tel:	0171 405 9200 Ext. 5292
Fax:	0171 829 8658
Private:	14a Upper Wimpole Street
	London W1M 7TB
Tel:	0171 935 1938
Fax:	0171 935 6607
First Qualified:	1974 – London
Major Degrees:	FRCS
Academic:	Honorary Senior Lecturer, Institute Child Health, London University
	Research Fellow, Hôpital des Enfants Malades, Paris, and Charing Cross Hospital Medical School, London
Specialist Training:	Mount Vernon Hospital, Middlesex, and West Middlesex University Hospital, London
Distinctions:	Honorary Consultant Plastic Surgeon, National Hospital Neurology and Neurosurgery, London; Honorary Secretary, British Association Aesthetic Plastic Surgeons
USA:	Visiting Professor, Atlanta Cleft Lip and Palate Symposium

MAYOU, Mr Brian J.

Special interests:	**Congenital melanocytic naevi and epidermolysis bullosa**
NHS:	Consultant Plastic Surgeon
	St Thomas' Hospital
	Lambeth Palace Road
	London SE1 7EH
Tel:	0171 928 9292 Ext. 2004
Fax:	0171 922 8186
Private:	Lister Hospital
	Chelsea Bridge Road
	London SW1W 8RH
Tel:	0171 824 8080
Fax:	0171 259 9887
First Qualified:	1969 – Birmingham
Major Degrees:	FRCS
Specialist Training:	Mount Vernon Hospital, Middlesex, and Hospital for Sick Children, London
Distinctions:	Treasurer, British Association of Aesthetic Plastic Surgeons

SANDERS, Professor Roy

Special interests:	**Burns; cleft lip and palate surgery**
NHS:	Consultant Plastic Surgeon
	Mount Vernon Hospital
	Rickmansworth Road
	Northwood, Middlesex HA6 2RN
Tel:	01923 844304
Fax:	01923 844408
Private:	Consulting Suite
	82 Portland Place
	London W1N 3DH
Tel:	0171 580 3541
Fax:	0171 436 2954
First Qualified:	1962 – London
Major Degrees:	FRCS
Academic:	Honorary Senior Lecturer, London University
Specialist Training:	St Bartholomew's Hospital, London
Distinctions:	President, Plastic Surgery Section, Royal Society of Medicine
	Visiting Professor, Universities of Genova, Italy, Hong Kong, and Bombay, India

SMITH, Mr Paul J.

Special interests:	**Congenital hand deformities in children, Dupuytren's contracture; rheumatoid surgery; breast surgery; rhinoplasty**
NHS:	Consultant Plastic Surgeon
	Great Ormond Street Hospital for Children
	Great Ormond Street
	London WC1N 3JH
Tel:	0171 813 8242
Fax:	0171 829 8658
Private:	The Plastic Surgery Unit
	2nd Floor, South Building
	Wellington Hospital
	London NW8 9LE
Tel:	01491 638030
Fax:	01491 638050
First Qualified:	1968 – Newcastle
Major Degrees:	FRCS
Distinctions:	1st Prize, American Association of Hand Surgery
	Pulvertaft Prize, British Society of Surgery of the Hand
	Honorary member, Australian Society for Surgery of the Hand
USA:	Visiting Professor, Plastic Surgery, Salt Lake City, Utah; Christine Kleinert Fellow, Kleinert Hand Institute, Louisville; Resident and Clinical Instructing Plastic Surgeon, Duke University; Member, American Society for Surgery of the Hand

SOMMERLAD, Mr Brian Clive

Special interests:	**Cleft palate; hypospadias; hand surgery; head and neck surgery and wound healing**
NHS:	Consultant Plastic Surgeon Great Ormond Street Hospital for Children 34 Great Ormond Street London WC1N 3JH
Tel:	01245 422477
Fax:	01245 421901
Private:	Refer to address and number above
First Qualified:	1966 – Sydney, Australia
Major Degrees:	FRCS
Specialist Training:	Sydney Hospital, Australia, University College Hospital, London
Distinctions:	Previously President, Plastic Surgery section, Royal Society of Medicine Previously Honorary Secretary, British Association Plastic Surgeons

WATERHOUSE, Mr Norman

Special interests:	**Craniofacial surgery**
NHS:	Consultant Plastic and Reconstructive Surgeon Charing Cross Hospital Fulham Palace Road London W6 8RF
Tel:	0181 846 1234 Ext. 1722
Fax:	0181 846 1719
Private:	55 Harley Street London W1N 1DD
Tel:	0171 636 4073
Fax:	0171 636 6417
First Qualified:	1978 – Birmingham
Major Degrees:	FRCS
Specialist Training:	Mount Vernon Hospital, Middlesex, West Middlesex Hospital, London, and Cranio-Facial Unit, Adelaide, Australia

NORTHERN AND YORKSHIRE REGION

LEEDS

KAY, Mr Simon P. J.

Special interests:	**Paediatric plastic surgery; trauma or congenital malformation of the hand; microsurgery**
NHS:	Consultant Plastic Surgeon
	University Hospital of St James
	Leeds LS9 7TF
Tel:	01132 836902
Fax:	01132 438162
Private:	Refer to address and number above
First Qualified:	1976 – Oxford
Major Degrees:	FRCS

PAEDIATRIC THORACIC SURGEONS

See ELLIOTT, Mr Martin J. under Paediatric Cardiothoracic Surgeons.

PAEDIATRIC TROPICAL PHYSICIAN

LONDON AND THE SOUTH EAST

TOMKINS, Professor Andrew M.

Special interests:	**Malnutrition in young children**
NHS:	Honorary Consultant Physician
	Hospital for Tropical Diseases
	4 St Pancras Way, London NW1 0PE
Tel:	0171 530 5430
Fax:	0171 530 3409 or 0171 388 7645
and:	University College Hospital
	25 Grafton Way, London WC1 6DB
Private:	Refer to address and number above
First Qualified:	1966 – London
Major Degrees:	FRCP
Academic:	Senior Lecturer, Clinical Nutrition, London School of Hygene and Tropical Medicine
	Professor of International Child Health, Institute of Child Health, London
Specialist Training:	Ahmadu Bello University, Zaria, Nigeria
	Medical Research Council Fajara, The Gambia
Distinctions:	Honorary Consultant Paediatrician, Great Ormond Street Hospital for Children, London

PAEDIATRIC UROLOGICAL SURGEONS

LONDON AND THE SOUTH EAST

DUFFY, Mr Patrick G.

Special interests:	**Reconstruction of the lower urinary tract including reconstruction of the bladder and the urethra; children with urinary tract calculi; renal transplantation**
NHS:	Paediatric Consultant Urological Surgeon
	Great Ormond Street Hospital for Children
	Great Ormond Street, London WC1N 3JH
Tel:	0171 405 9200 Ext. 5326
Fax:	0171 813 8260
Private:	234 Great Portland Street, London W1N 5PH
Tel:	0171 390 8322
First Qualified:	1973 – Belfast
Major Degrees:	FRCSI
Academic:	Senior Lecturer, Institue of Urology, London

MORGAN, Mr Robert J.

Special interests:	**General adult and paediatric urology**
NHS:	Consultant Urological Surgeon
	Royal Free Hospital
	Pond Street
	London NW3 2QG
Tel:	0171 794 0500 Ext. 3122 or 0171 830 2419
Fax:	0171 431 5245
Private:	147 Harley Street
	London W1N 1DL
Tel:	0171 935 4444 Ext. 4067
Fax:	0171 486 3782
First Qualified:	1966 – Oxford
Major Degrees:	FRCS
Specialist Training:	St Peter's Hospital, London
Distinctions:	Honorary Consultant Urologist, St Luke's Hospital for the Clergy, King Edward VII for Officers and Hospital of St John and St Elizabeth, London

RANSLEY, Mr Philip

Special interests:	**Reconstructive urology**
NHS:	Paediatric Consultant Urological Surgeon
	Great Ormond Street Hospital for Children
	Great Ormond Street
	London WC1N 3JH
Tel:	0171 405 9200 Ext. 5918
Fax:	0171 813 8260
Private:	234 Great Portland Street
	London W1N 5PH
Tel:	0171 390 8323
Fax:	0171 390 8324
First Qualified:	1966 – Cambridge
Major Degrees:	FRCS

WOODHOUSE, Mr Christopher

Special interests:	**Cancer of the bladder, kidney and prostate; reconstructive urology**
NHS:	Consultant Urologist
	Royal Marsden Hospital
	Fulham Road
	London SW3 6JJ
Tel:	0171 352 8171 Ext. 2789
Fax:	0171 376 5425
and:	The Middlesex Hospital
	Mortimer Street
	London W1N 8AA
Tel:	0171 380 9210
Fax:	0171 637 7076
Private:	Lister Hospital
	Chelsea Bridge Road
	London SW1W 8RH
Tel:	0171 730 6204
Fax:	0171 730 6204
First Qualified:	1970 – London
Major Degrees:	FRCS
Academic:	Senior Lecturer, Institute of Urology, London
Specialist Training:	St Peter's and Royal London Hospitals, London
Distinctions:	Honorary Consultant, Institute of Urology and Great Ormond Street Hospital for Children, London

NORTHERN AND YORKSHIRE REGION

LEEDS

THOMAS, Mr David F. M.

NHS:	Consultant Paediatric Urologist
	St James' University Hospital
	Leeds LS9 7TF
Tel:	01132 433144 Ext. 5114
Fax:	01132 837059
Private:	Refer to address and number above
First Qualified:	1971 – Cambridge
Major Degrees:	FRCS
Academic:	Senior Clinical Lecturer, Leeds Unversity; Wellcome Research Fellow, Institute of Child Health, London
Specialist Training:	Great Ormond Street Hospital for Children
Distinctions:	Previously Hunterian Professor, Royal College of Surgeons

SOUTH AND WEST REGION

BRISTOL

FRANK, Mr John

NHS:	Consultant Paediatric Surgeon and Urologist
	Bristol Royal Hospital for Sick Children
	St Michael's Hill
	Bristol BS2 8BJ
Tel:	0117 928 5454
Fax:	0117 928 5701
Private:	Refer to address and number above
First Qualified:	1969 – London
Major Degrees:	FRCS
Specialist Training:	St Peter's Hospital and Great Ormond Street Hospital for Children, London

WINCHESTER

ADAMSON, Mr Andrew S.

Special interests:	**Uro-oncology; incontinence; bladder outflow obstruction; paediatric urology**
NHS:	Consultant Urologist
	Royal Hampshire County Hospital
	Romsey Road
	Winchester
	Hampshire SO23
Tel:	01962 825287
Fax:	01962 824640
Private:	Sarum Road Hospital
	Sarum Road
	Winchester SO23 5HA
Tel:	01962 840142
Fax:	01962 840142
First Qualified:	1983 – London
Major Degrees:	MS, FRCS
Academic:	Lecturer, Southampton University
Specialist Training:	King's College and St Mary's Hospitals, London, and Eastbourne Hospitals
Distinctions:	Rhone–Poulenc Prize winner, Association of Surgeons in Training 1993; NATO Research Grant; Royal College of Surgeons Research Grant
USA:	North West Memorial Hospital, Chicago; Research in prostate cancer, Notre Dame University, Indiana, and Mayo Clinic, Rochester, Minnesota

PAIN RELIEF PHYSICIANS

These doctors specialise in the management of postoperative pain, chronic benign pain, pain of malignancies and the diagnosis and treatment of painful syndromes. Management takes the form of nerve block procedures, epidural and spinal opiates, local anaesthetics, drug use and patient-controlled analgesia with intravenous narcotic pumps.

Palliative care specialists provide pain relief as well as emotional support and couselling for cancer patients. This is a relatively new speciality. Clinical oncologists and medical oncologists work closely with palliative consultants who prescribe drugs and sometimes employ alternative therapies for the pain relief. Many patients still are unaware that this specialisation exists. You can seek advice from your oncologist who can often direct you to a palliative medicine specialist.

LONDON AND THE SOUTH EAST

BARANOWSKI, Dr Andrew Paul

Special interests:	**Pain management; neuropathic pain; urogenital pain; back pain; investigation of pain**
NHS:	Consultant in Pain Management and Anaesthetics
	The Middlesex Hospital
	Mortimer Street
	London W1N 8AN
Tel:	0171 380 9078
Fax:	0171 380 9076
Private:	Private Patients Unit
	University College Hospital
	25 Grafton Way
	London WC1E 6BD
Tel:	0171 380 9009
Fax:	0171 380 9076
First Qualified:	1983 – London
Major Degrees:	MD, FRCA
Academic:	Honorary Senior Lecturer, University College London
Specialist Training:	St Thomas' and National Hospital for Neurology and Neurosurgery, London

FOSTER, Dr James M. G.

Special interests:	**Spinal pain**
NHS:	Pain Clinic
	St Bartholomew's Hospital
	West Smithfield
	London EC1A 7BE
Tel:	0171 601 7518
Fax:	0171 601 7899
Private:	Private Consulting Rooms
	The Princess Grace Hospital
	42–52 Nottingham Place
	London W1M 3FD
Tel:	0171 486 1234 Ext. 4640
Fax:	0171 487 4476
First Qualified:	1974 – London
Major Degrees:	FRCA
Academic:	Honorary Senior Lecturer, St Bartholomew's Hospital
	Medical College
	Recognised Teacher, London University
Specialist Training:	St Bartholomew's and Guy's Hospitals, London
	Walton Hospital, Liverpool; Sir Charles Gairdner
	Hospital, Western Australia
Distinctions:	Visiting Consultant, St Joseph's Hospice, London;
	King's Fund Travelling Fellowship Bursary 1984

GALLAGHER, Dr Wendy Jayne

Special interests:	**Spinal pain**
NHS:	Consultant Anaesthetist
	Department of Anaesthetics
	St Bartholomew's Hospital
	West Smithfield
	London EC1A 7BE
Tel:	0171 601 7518
Fax:	0171 601 7520
Private:	Refer to address and number above
First Qualified:	1980 – London
Major Degrees:	FFARCS

JUSTINS, Dr Douglas M.

NHS:	Consultant in Pain Management and Anaesthesia
	Department of Anaesthetics
	St Thomas' Hospital
	Lambeth Palace Road
	London SE1 7EH
Tel:	0171 928 9292 Ext. 2340
Fax:	0171 922 8079
Private:	Refer to address and number above
First Qualified:	1970 – Australia
Major Degrees:	FFARCS

NAYSMITH, Dr Anne

NHS:	Consultant Physician in Palliative Medicine
	Paddington Community Hospital
	7A Woodfield Road
	London W9 2BB
Tel:	0171 451 8170
Fax:	0181 451 8245
Private:	Refer to address and number above
First Qualified:	1973 – Edinburgh
Major Degrees:	FRCP Ed
Academic:	Previously Lecturer in Medical Oncology, The Middlesex Hospital, London, and Edinburgh Royal Infirmary
Distinctions:	Chairman, Association of Palliative Medicine

PITHER, Dr Charles

Special interests:	**Especially behavioural approaches in chronic pain**
NHS:	Consultant Anaesthetist
	Medical Director, Pain Management Unit
	St Thomas' Hospital
	Lambeth Palace Road
	London SE1 7EH
Tel:	0171 922 8107 Ext. 1428
Fax:	0171 922 8229
Private:	Churchill Clinic
	80 Lambeth Road
	London SE1 7PW
Tel:	0171 633 9510
Fax:	0171 928 1702
and:	Pain Management Clinic
	Unsted Park Rehabilitation Hospital
	Munstead Heath, Godalming
	Surrey GU7 1UW
First Qualified:	1977 – London
Major Degrees:	FRCA
Specialist Training:	St Thomas' Hospital, London
Distinctions:	Honorary Consultant, National Hospital for Neurology and Neurosurgery, London
USA:	Fellow, Anaesthia and Pain Control, University of Cincinnati, Ohio

WEDLEY, Dr John R.

NHS:	Consultant Anaesthetist
	London and Pain Relief Clinic
	Guy's Hospital
	St Thomas Street
	London SE1 9RT
Tel:	0171 955 5000 Ext. 5594
Fax:	0171 955 8844
Private:	Emblem House
	London Bridge Hospital
	27 Tooley Street
	London SE1 2PR
Tel:	0171 403 3876
Fax:	0171 407 3162
First Qualified:	1968 – Liverpool
Major Degrees:	FFARCS
Academic:	Late Senior Lecturer, Guy's Hospital, London
Specialist Training:	Guy's Hospital, London

NORTH WEST REGION

LANCASTER

McILLMURRAY, Dr Malcolm B.

Special interests:	**Psycho-oncology; relaxation therapy and supportive care**
NHS:	Macmillan Consultant in Medical Oncology and Palliative Care
	Director of St John's Hospice
	Royal Lancaster Infirmary
	Ashton Road
	Lancaster LA1 4RP
Tel:	01524 583510
Fax:	01524 846346
Private:	Beech House
	Over Kellet LA6 1DL
Tel:	01524 732921
First Qualified:	1968 – London
Major Degrees:	DM, FRCP

LIVERPOOL

WELLS, Dr John Christopher Durant

Special interests:	**Rehabilitation of chronic pain suffers; especially back pain, cancer pain and neuralgia**
NHS:	Honorary Consultant in Pain Relief
	The Walton Centre for Neurosciences
	Rice Lane
	Liverpool L9 1AE
Tel:	0151 523 1486
Fax:	0151 521 6155
Private:	45a Rodney Street
	Liverpool L1 9EW
Tel:	0151 708 9344
Fax:	0151 707 0609
First Qualified:	1970 – Liverpool
Major Degrees:	LMCC, FRCA
Academic:	Honorary Senior Lecturer, Liverpool University
Specialist Training:	Liverpool Pain Relief Centre

PLASTIC SURGEONS

Plastic surgeons repair damage to the skin, musculoskeletal system, extremities, breast and trunk. Some do only 'cosmetic' or aesthetic surgery which deals with problems of appearance, and others do reconstructive surgery following accidents or disfigurement following disease such as skin cancer. Different sub-specialisations require team work with other disciplines, especially where specialist reconstruction skills are required. See appendix 1(iv) for specialist burns and plastic surgery units. The main sections of plastic surgery are:

Burns and injury
The treatment of burns is a significant part of the plastic surgeon's work. This involves the excision of the burnt tissue and reconstruction of the area.

Hand Surgery
In addition to treating congenitally deformed hands, the surgeon treats crippling hand deformities such as Dupuytren's disease and arthritis. Hand surgeons work in conjunction with orthopaedic surgeons and hand therapists.

Congenital Abnormalities
These abnormalities often involve skin, muscle and bone and often require several operations. Common examples include the treatment of cleft lip and palate and their associated speech defects and growth abnormalities of the lip, nose and jaw; the treatment of birthmarks by surgery or laser; and the treatment of malformed fingers, external genitals etc. Other medical specialists are often called upon, such as paediatricians, speech therapists and orthodontists.

Cancer
The surgery of cancerous or non-cancerous tumours of the skin and subcutaneous tissues.

Aesthetic Surgery
This section of plastic surgery constitutes the smallest proportion of the total work load in plastic surgery and is rarely carried out under the NHS. The majority of patients who receive this surgery under the National Health Service are children or young adults with protuberant ears, misshapen noses, unsightly scars or abnormal breasts.

LONDON AND THE SOUTH EAST

BOWEN, Mr John E.

Special interests:	**Paediatrics**
NHS:	No NHS work
Private:	30 Harley Street
	London W1N 1AB
Tel:	0171 636 0955
Fax:	0171 636 3497
First Qualified:	1962 – Cambridge
Major Degrees:	FRCS
Specialist Training:	Great Ormond Street Hospital for Children, London, and Queen Victoria Hospital, East Grinstead

BREACH, Mr Nicholas M.

Special interests:	**Reconstruction of head and neck; facial and oral cancer; breast surgery and reconstruction**
NHS:	Consultant Plastic and Reconstructive Surgeon
	Head and Neck Unit
	Royal Marsden Hospital
	Fulham Road
	London SW3 6JJ
Tel:	0171 352 8171 Ext. 2732
Fax:	0171 376 4809 or 0171 351 3785
NHS:	Consultant Plastic and Reconstructive Surgeon
	Charing Cross Hospital
	Fulham Palace Road
	London W6 8RF
Tel:	0181 846 1234
Fax:	0181 846 1111
Private:	The Consulting Suite
	82 Portland Place
	London W1N 3DH
Tel:	0171 636 1298
Fax:	0171 436 2954
First Qualified:	1970 – London
Major Degrees:	FRCS, FDS RCS
Specialist Training:	Queen Victoria Hospital, East Grinstead
Distinctions:	Honorary Consultant Plastic Surgeon, Royal Brompton Hospital
	Honorary Consultant Plastic Surgeon, Hospital for Sick Children
	Previously Director, McIndoe Burns Centre, Queen Victoria Hospital, East Grinstead

BROUGH, Mr Michael D.

Special interests:	**Reconstructive surgery**
NHS:	Consultant Plastic Surgeon
	University College Hospital
	Gower Street
	London WC1E 6AU
Tel:	0171 636 1298
Fax:	0171 436 2954
and:	Royal Free Hospital
	Pond Street
	London NW5
Tel:	0171 794 0500
Fax:	0171 830 2468
and:	Whittington Hospital
	Highgate Hill, London N19 5NF
Private:	The Consulting Suite,
	82 Portland Place
	London W1N 3DH
Tel:	0171 935 8910
Fax:	0171 436 2954
and:	King Edward VII Hospital For Officers
	Beaumont Street, London W1N 2AA
Tel:	0171 486 4411
Fax:	0171 935 6770
First Qualified:	1969 – Cambridge
Major Degrees:	FRCS
Specialist Training:	Queen Elizabeth Hospital for Children and Whipps Cross Hospitals, London
Distinctions:	Previously President, Plastic Surgeons Section, Royal Society of Medicine
	Honorary Consultant, Plastic Surgeon, St Luke's Hospital for Clergy

CLARKE, Mr John A.

Special interests:	**Burns**
NHS:	Consultant Plastic Surgeon
	Queen Mary's Hospital
	Roehampton Lane
	London SW15 5PN
Tel:	0181 789 6611
Fax:	0181 780 1089
Private:	Refer to address and number above
First Qualified:	1963 – London
Major Degrees:	FRCS
Specialist Training:	Queen Mary's Hospital, Roehampton, London and Hospital for Sick Children, Toronto, Canada
Distinctions:	Handcock Prize, Royal College of Surgeons

COLLIN, Mr Richard

Special interests:	**Plastic and reconstructive surgery of the eyelids, including children's**
NHS:	Consultant Ophthalmologist
	Moorfields Eye Hospital
	City Road
	London EC1V 2PD
Tel:	0171 253 3411
Fax:	0171 566 2019
Private:	67 Harley Street
	London W1N 1DE
Tel:	0171 486 2699
Fax:	0171 486 8626
First Qualified:	1968 – Cambridge
Major Degrees:	FRCS
Academic:	Previously Senior Lecturer Moorfields Eye Hospital, London
Specialist Training:	Moorfields Eye Hospital, London
Distinctions:	Honorary Consultant Ophthalmic Surgeon, Hospital for Sick Children, London
	Secretary, European Society Ophthalmic Plastic and Reconstructive Surgery
USA:	Previously Fellow in Ophthalmic Plastic and Reconstructive Surgery, University of California Medical School, San Francisco

DAVIES, Mr Dai

Special interests:	**Aesthetic; endoscopic carpal tunnel decompression; breast aesthetic and reconstruction**
NHS:	Consultant Plastic Surgeon
	Charing Cross Hospital
	Fulham Palace Road
	London W6 8RF
Tel:	0181 846 1720
Fax:	0181 846 1719
Private:	55 Harley Street
	London W1N 1DD
Tel:	0171 631 3927
Fax:	0171 636 6573
First Qualified:	1970 – London
Major Degrees:	FRCS
Academic:	Senior Lecturer, Royal Postgraduate Medical School, and Charing Cross Hospital, London
	Previously Research Fellow, Queen Victoria Hospital, East Grinstead, and The Royal Melbourne, Australia
Specialist Training:	London, Bristol and Melbourne, Australia

DAVIS, Mr Peter K. B.

NHS:	Emeritus Consultant
	St Thomas' Hospital
	Lambeth Palace Road
	London SE1 7EH
Tel:	0171 928 9292
Fax:	0171 922 8079
Private:	97 Harley Street
	London W1N 1DF
Tel:	0171 486 4976
First Qualified:	1959 – London
Major Degrees:	MS, FRCS, T(S)Plast
Specialist Training:	Leicester General Hospital and Oxford
Distinctions:	Previously President, British Association of Aesthetic Plastic Surgeons

EVANS, Mr David M.

Special interests:	**Hand surgery**
NHS:	Consultant Hand Surgeon
	Royal National Orthopaedic Hospital
	Brockley Hill
	Stanmore, Middlesex HA7 4LP
Tel:	0171 954 2300
Fax:	0181 954 7249
Private:	Hand Clinic
	Oakley Green
	Windsor, Berkshire SL4 4LH
Tel:	01753 831333
Fax:	01753 832109
First Qualified:	1965 – London
Major Degrees:	FRCS
Specialist Training:	Churchill Hospital, Oxford

GAULT, Mr David T.

Special interests:	**Ear reconstruction and any unusual deformities of the ear; laser surgery for removal of portwine stains, pigmented lesions and tattoos**
NHS:	Consultant Plastic Surgeon
	Mount Vernon Hospital
	Rickmansworth Road
	Northwood, Middlesex HA6 2RN
Tel:	01628 524978
Fax:	01628 525188
Private:	Department of Plastic and Reconstructive Surgery
	Wellington Hospital
	Wellington Place
	London NW8 9LE
Tel:	0171 586 5959
Fax:	0171 586 1960
First Qualified:	1977 – Edinburgh
Major Degrees:	FRCS
Specialist Training:	St Thomas' Hospital and Hospital for Sick Children, London, and Paris and San Francisco
USA:	See 'Specialist Training' above

HARRISON, Mr Douglas H.

Special interests:	**Correction of facial paralysis; hand, microvascular and aesthetic surgery**
NHS:	Consultant Plastic Surgeon
	Mount Vernon Hospital
	Rickmansworth Road
	Northwood, Middlesex HA6 2RN
Tel:	01923 844412
Fax:	01923 844408
Private:	Flat 33, Harmont House
	20 Harley Street
	London W1N 1AA
Tel:	0171 935 6184
Fax:	0171 436 1178
First Qualified:	1967 – London
Major Degrees:	FRCS
Specialist Training:	Edinburgh, and Mount Vernon Hospital, Middlesex
Distinctions:	Previously Hunterian Professor, Royal College of Surgeons

JONES, Mr Barry M.

Special interests:	**Craniofacial surgery; aesthetic plastic surgery**
NHS:	Consultant Plastic and Reconstructive Surgeon
	Great Ormond Street Hospital for Children
	34 Great Ormond Street
	London WC1N 3JH
Tel:	0171 405 9200
Fax:	0171 829 8643
Private:	14a Upper Wimpole Street
	London W1M 7TB
Tel:	0171 935 1938
Fax:	0171 935 6607
First Qualified:	1974 – London
Major Degrees:	FRCS
Academic:	Honorary Senior Lecturer, Institute Child Health, London University
	Research Fellow, Hôpital des Enfants Malades, Paris, and Charing Cross Hospital Medical School, London
Specialist Training:	Mount Vernon Hospital, Northwood, and West Middlesex University Hospital, London
Distinctions:	Honorary Consultant Plastic Surgeon, National Hospital of Neurology and Neurosurgery, London; Honorary Secretary, British Association Aesthetic Plastic Surgeons
USA:	Visiting Professor, Atlanta Cleft Lip and Palate Symposium

MATTI, Mr Basim

Special interests:	**Facelift; rhinoplasty; collagen injection and liposuction; endoscopic browlifts/breasts**
NHS:	None
Private:	30 Harley Street
	London W1N 1AB
Tel:	0171 637 9595
Fax:	0171 636 1639
First Qualified:	1973 – Mosul, Iraq
Major Degrees:	FRCS Ed
Specialist Training:	West Middlesex, Hammersmith and St Mary's Hospitals, London

MAYOU, Mr Brian J.

Special interests:	**Aesthetic surgery including endoscopic surgery and liposuction**
NHS:	Consultant Plastic Surgeon
	St Thomas' Hospital
	Lambeth Palace Road
	London SE1 7EH
Tel:	0171 928 9292
Fax:	0171 922 8186
Private:	Lister Hospital
	Chelsea Bridge Road
	London SW1W 8RH
Tel:	0171 824 8080
Fax:	0171 259 9887
First Qualified:	1969 – Birmingham
Major Degrees:	FRCS
Specialist Training:	Mount Vernon Hospital, Northwood, and Hospital for Sick Children, London
Distinctions:	Treasurer, British Association of Aesthetic Plastic Surgeons

MORGAN, Mr Brian D. G.

Special interests:	**Melanoma**
NHS:	Consultant Plastic Surgeon
	University College Hospital
	Grafton Way, London WC1E 6AU
Tel:	0171 383 7395
Fax:	0171 380 9816
Private:	Consulting Rooms
	University College Hospital
	Grafton Way
	London WC1E 6AU
Tel:	0171 383 7395
Fax:	0171 380 9816
First Qualified:	1959 – London
Major Degrees:	FRCS
Specialist Training:	Mount Vernon Hospital, Northwood
Distinctions:	Chairman, Court of Examiners, Royal College of Surgeons

PARKHOUSE, Mr Nicholas

Special interests:	**Scarring; burn reconstruction; microsurgical salvage and inflammation**
NHS:	Consultant Plastic Surgeon
	Queen Victoria Hospital
	Holtye Road
	East Grinstead
	West Sussex RH19 3DZ
Tel:	01342 410210
Fax:	01342 317907
Private:	149 Harley Street
	London W1N 2DH
Tel:	0171 224 0864
Fax:	0171 224 0864
First Qualified:	1981 – London
Major Degrees:	DM, FRCS
Academic:	Hunterian Professor, Royal College of Surgeons 1989–90
	Previously Clinical Lecturer, The Middlesex Hospital, London
Specialist Training:	Queen Victoria Hospital, East Grinstead and Basildon Hospital
Distinctions:	Director, Rainsford Burns Unit
	Honorary Consultant, St Luke's Hospital for the Clergy

SANDERS, Professor Roy

Special interests:	**Burns; cleft lip and palate surgery**
NHS:	Consultant Plastic Surgeon
	Mount Vernon Hospital
	Rickmansworth Road
	Northwood, Middlesex HA6 2RN
Tel:	01923 844304
Fax:	01923 835803
Private:	Consulting Suite
	82 Portland Place
	London W1N 3DH
Tel:	0171 580 3541
Fax:	0171 436 2954
First Qualified:	1962 – London
Major Degrees:	FRCS
Academic:	Honorary Senior Lecturer, London University
Specialist Training:	St Bartholomew's Hospital, London
Distinctions:	President, Plastic Surgery Section, Royal Society of Medicine
	Visiting Professor, Universities of Genova, Italy, Hong Kong, and Bombay, India

---

SINNETT, Mr Hugh Dudley

Special interests:	**Breast diseases; soft tissue tumours**
NHS:	Consultant in Breast Surgery
	Department of Surgery
	Charing Cross Hospital
	Fulham Palace Road
	London W6 8RF
Tel:	0181 846 7303
Fax:	0181 846 1617
Private:	Refer to address and number above
First Qualified:	1972 – London
Major Degrees:	FRCS
Academic:	Senior Lecturer, Royal Marsden Hospital, London
Specialist Training:	St Bartholomew's Hospital, London
Distinctions:	Member, Court of Examiners, Royal College of Surgeons
	Honorary Consultant Surgeon, Royal Marsden Hospital, London

SMITH, Mr Paul J.

Special interests:	**Congenital hand deformities in children; Dupuytren's contracture and rheumatoid surgery; breast surgery; rhinoplasty**
NHS:	Consultant Plastic Surgeon
	Great Ormond Street Hospital for Children
	Great Ormond Street
	London WC1N 3JH
Tel:	0171 405 9200
Fax:	0171 829 8643
Private:	The Plastic Surgery Unit
	2nd Floor, South Building
	Wellington Hospital
	London NW8
Tel:	01491 638030
Fax:	01491 638050
First Qualified:	1968 – Newcastle
Major Degrees:	FRCS
Distinctions:	1st Prize, American Association of Hand Surgery
	Pulvertaft Prize, British Society of Surgery of the Hand
	Honorary Member, Australian Society for Surgery of the Hand
USA:	Visiting Professor, Plastic Surgery, Salt Lake City, Utah
	Christine Kleinert Fellow, Kleinert Hand Institute, Louisville
	Resident and Clinical Instructing Plastic Surgeon, Duke University
	Member, American Society for Surgery of the Hand

SOMMERLAD, Mr Brian Clive

Special interests:	**Cleft palate; hypospadias; hand surgery; head and neck surgery and wound healing**
NHS:	Consultant Plastic Surgeon Great Ormond Street Hospital for Children 34 Great Ormond Street London WC1N 3JH
Tel:	01245 422477
Fax:	01245 421901
Private:	Refer to address and number above
First Qualified:	1966 – Sydney, Australia
Major Degrees:	FRCS
Specialist Training:	Sydney Hospital, Australia, University College Hospital, London
Distinctions:	Previously President, Plastic Surgery Section, Royal Society of Medicine Previously Honorary Secretary, British Association Plastic Surgeons

WARD, Mr Christopher

Special interests:	**Reconstructive surgery of the breast following mastectomy and aesthetic breast surgery**
NHS:	Retired from the NHS
Private:	15 Cumberland Road Kew Gardens Richmond Surrey TW9 3HJ
Tel:	0181 948 4990
Fax:	0181 332 7770
First Qualified:	1965 – London
Major Degrees:	FRCS
Academic:	Hunterian Professor, Royal College of Surgeons
Specialist Training:	Toronto, Canada, and Royal Postgraduate Medical School, London
Distinctions:	Honorary Consultant Plastic and Reconstructive Surgeon, Charing Cross and West Middlesex Hospitals

WATERHOUSE, Mr Norman

Special interests:	**Craniofacial surgery**
NHS:	Consultant Plastic and Reconstructive Surgeon
	Charing Cross Hospital
	Fulham Palace Road
	London W6 8RF
Tel:	0181 846 1234
Fax:	0181 846 1111
Private:	55 Harley Street
	London W1N 1DD
Tel:	0171 636 4073
Fax:	0171 636 6417
First Qualified:	1978 – Birmingham
Major Degrees:	FRCS
Specialist Training:	Mount Vernon Hospital, Northwood, West Middlesex Hospital, London, and Cranio-Facial Unit, Adelaide, Australia

WHITFIELD, Mr Patrick J.

Special interests:	**Especially remodelling of professional models and actresses**
NHS:	Retired from the NHS
Private:	17 Harley Street
	London W1N 1DA
Tel:	0171 580 6283
First Qualified:	1958 – London
Major Degrees:	FRCS
Specialist Training:	Queen Mary's Hospital, London, and in Paris, Rome and New York
Distinctions:	Founder, British Association of Aesthetic Plastic Surgeons

ANGLIA AND OXFORD REGION

BERKSHIRE

KHOO, Mr Christopher

Special interests:	**Hand surgery; breast reconstruction; microsurgical reconstructive surgery**
NHS:	Consultant Plastic Surgeon
	Wexham Park Hospital
	Slough
	Berkshire SL2 4HL
Tel:	01753 633052
Fax:	01753 634848
and:	St Mark's Hospital
	St Mark's Road
	Maidenhead
	Berkshire SL6 6DU
Tel:	01628 32012
Fax:	01753 638399
and:	Heatherwood Hospital
	Ascot
	Berkshire SL5 8AA
Tel:	01344 23333
Fax:	01344 874340
Private:	Refer to address and number above
First Qualified:	1973 – Cambridge
Major Degrees:	FRCS
Distinctions:	Previously Consultant Plastic Surgeon and Director, Burns Unit, Stoke Mandeville Hospital, Aylesbury

NORTH WEST REGION

MANCHESTER

DAVENPORT, Mr Peter James

Special interests:	**Burns**
NHS:	Consultant Plastic Surgeon
	Wythenshawe Hospital
	Southmoor Road
	Manchester M23 9LT
Tel:	0161 998 7070
Fax:	0161 946 2037
Private:	The Consultant Suite
	BUPA Hospital
	Russell Rd
	Whalley Range, Manchester M16 8AJ
Tel:	0161 862 9563
Fax:	0161 227 9405
First Qualified:	1969 – London
Major Degrees:	FRCS
Specialist Training:	Queen Victoria Hospital, East Grinstead

WATSON, Mr Stewart

Special interests:	**Hand surgery**
NHS:	Consultant Plastic and Hand Surgeon
	Plastic Unit
	Withington Hospital
	West Didsbury
	Manchester M20 2LR
Tel:	0161 447 4075
Fax:	0161 447 4077
Private:	Refer to address and number above
First Qualified:	1971 – Cambridge
Major Degrees:	FRCS
Specialist Training:	Withington Hospital, Manchester

NORTHERN AND YORKSHIRE REGION

BRADFORD

SHARPE, Mr David Thomas, OBE

Special interests:	**Breast surgery; aesthetics; tissue expansion**
NHS:	Consultant Plastic Surgeon
	Bradford Royal Infirmary
	Duckworth Lane
	Bradford BD9 6RJ
Tel:	01274 364608
Fax:	01274 366593
Private:	The Yorkshire Clinic
	Bradford Road
	Bingley BD16 ITW
Tel:	01274 560311
Fax:	01274 510760
First Qualified:	1970 – Cambridge
Major Degrees:	FRCS
Academic:	Director, Plastic Surgery and Burns Unit, Bradford University and Welsh, Scottish and West Yorkshire Plastic Surgery Units
Specialist Training:	Canniesburn Hospital, Glasgow; Royal United Hospital, Bath and Mayo Clinic, USA
USA:	See 'Specialist Training' above

LEEDS

KAY, Mr Simon Peter J.

Special interests:	**Children's hand surgery; brachial plexus injury and major nerve injury; aesthetic surgery**
NHS:	Consultant Plastic Surgeon
	University Hospital of St James
	Leeds LS9 7TF
Tel:	01132 836902
Fax:	01132 438162
Private:	BUPA Hospital
	Jackson Avenue
	Leeds LS8 1NT
Tel:	0113 2688788
Fax:	0113 2690003
First Qualified:	1976 – Oxford
Major Degrees:	FRCS
Academic:	Senior Clinical Lecturer, Leeds University
Specialist Training:	Manchester, Adelaide, Australia, and Louisville, USA
USA:	Christine Keinert Fellow, Kleinert Hand Institute, Louisville, Kentucky

NEWCASTLE

McLEAN, Mr Neil

Special interests: **The excision and reconstruction of head and neck cancers; the management of sarcomas; reconstructive breast surgery and microsurgery**
NHS: Consultant Plastic and Reconstructive Head and Neck Surgeon
Neck Unit
Department of Plastic Surgery
Newcastle General Hospital
Westgate Road
Newcastle upon Tyne NE4 6BE
Tel: 0191 273 8811
Fax: 0191 273 3534
Private: Refer to address and number above
First Qualified: 1976 – Glasgow
Major Degrees: MD, FRCS
Academic: Lecturer in Anatomy and Surgery, University of Newcastle upon Tyne
Specialist Training: Queen Mary's Hospital, Roehampton, London

SOUTH AND WEST REGION

PLYMOUTH

HARRIS, Mr David Leslie

Special interests: **Breast reconstruction**
NHS: Consultant Plastic Surgeon
Derriford Hospital
Derriford Road
Plymouth PL6 8DH
Tel: 01752 777111
Fax: 01752 763185
Private: The Nuffield Hospital
Derriford Road
Plymouth PL6 8BG
Tel: 01752 707345 or 775861
Fax: 01752 778421
First Qualified: 1961 – London
Major Degrees: FRCS
Specialist Training: University Hospital, South Manchester, and Royal Marsden Hospital, London
Distinctions: Senior Consultant Plastic Surgeon, Plymouth and Torbay Health Districts and Cornwall Health Authority
Civilian Consultant Plastic Surgeon to the Royal Navy
President, British Association Aesthetic Plastic Surgeons
Previously Honorary Lecturer, Makerere University, Kampala, Uganda

WEST MIDLANDS

BRACKA, Mr Aivar

Special interests: **Male genital surgery**
NHS: Consultant Genital and Plastic Surgeon
Department of Plastic Surgery
Wordsley Hospital
Stourbridge
West Midlands DY8 5QX
Tel: 01384 244451
Fax: 01384 244436
and: Queen Elizabeth Hospital
Birmingham B15 2TH
Tel: 0121 472 1311
Fax: 0121 627 2202
Private: Refer to address and number above
First Qualified: 1972 – Sheffield
Major Degrees: FRCS
Specialist Training: Wordsley Hospital, Stourbridge, and Septon General
Hospital, Liverpool

WALES

SWANSEA

SYKES, Mr Philip

Special interests: **Hand surgery and microsurgery**
NHS: Consultant Plastic Surgeon
Welsh Centre for Burns, Plastic and Maxillofacial
Surgery
Morriston Hospital
Swansea
West Glamorgan SA6 6NL
Tel: 01792 702222
Fax: 01792 703875
Private: Refer to address and number above
First Qualified: 1964 – Cambridge
Major Degrees: FRCS, T(S)
Academic: Honorary Clinical Teacher, University Hospital, Wales
Specialist Training: Stoke Mandeville Hospital, Aylesbury, and
Northampton General Hospital

PSYCHIATRISTS

Psychiatrists treat mental and emotional disorders, including depression, anxiety and psychoses. Drug misuse and sleep disorders are also treated by Psychiatrists. Psychiatrists are trained in medicine and treat patients with a serious mental disorder by prescribing drugs. Many Psychiatrists use various forms of therapy including psychotherapy (see below). (See appendix 1(vi) for a list of specialist psychiatry and psychotherapy centres/hospitals.)

Psychotherapy
This is the area within psychiatry which offers talking treatments either individually or in groups. Since 1975 it has been formally recognised as a separate speciality. Roughly one third of all the patients visiting GPs have primarily emotional problems and need some Psychotherapy. Many GP practices employ a councillor or psychotherapist. The term psychotherapist which does not necessarily imply any formal training has to date been unregulated, giving rise to many charlatans offering therapy. The medical establishment, in its endeavours to rectify this situation, has called for a drive towards formal qualifications and training. All the psychiatrists who use psychotherapy in this section are trained in medicine.

Old Age Psychiatry
Britain has led the world in the development of Psychiatric services for elderly people. With 15% of the UK population now over 65, necessary advances in geriatric medicine have had to take place. Old Age Psychiatry as a medical speciality was formally recognised by the Department of Health around 1990. A good Old Age Psychiatry service would be regarded as community oriented and involving multi-disciplinary teamwork; it generally accepts referrals for people who have developed a mental illness in old age and this most commonly means dementia or depression. Five per cent of those over 65 and 20% of those over 80 suffer from dementia, mainly in the form of Alzheimer's disease.

LONDON AND THE SOUTH EAST

BATEMAN, Dr Anthony W.

Special interests:	**Borderline personality disorders**
NHS:	Consultant Psychotherapist
	St Ann's Hospital
	St Ann's Road
	South Tottenham
	London N15 3TH
Tel:	0181 442 6000
Fax:	0181 442 6545
Private:	3 Beech Drive
	London N2 9NX
Tel:	0181 442 1291
First Qualified:	1978 – London
Major Degrees:	MRCPsych
Specialist Training:	Tavistock Clinic and Royal Free Hospital, London
Distinctions:	Editor, University College Hospital textbook of Psychiatry

BLANCHARD, Dr Martin R.

Special interests:	**Management of depression in older people**
NHS:	Consultant in Old Age Psychiatry
	Royal Free Hospital
	Pond Street
	London NW3 2QG
Tel:	0171 749 0500 Ext. 2014
Fax:	0171 830 2139
Private:	Refer to address and number above
First Qualified:	1982 – London
Major Degrees:	MRCPsych
Academic:	Senior Lecturer, Old Age Psychiatry, Royal Free Hospital School of Medicine, London
Specialist Training:	Maudsley and Royal Free Hospitals, London

BOWDEN, Dr Paul M. A.

Special interests:	**Forensic psychiatry: for mentally abnormal offenders**
NHS:	Consultant Forensic Psychiatrist
	Maudsley Hospital
	Denmark Hill
	London SE5 8AZ
Tel:	0171 703 6333 Ext. 2327
Fax:	0171 919 2382
Private:	No private work
First Qualified:	1965 – London
Major Degrees:	MPhil, FRCP, FRCPsych
Academic:	Senior Lecturer, St George's Hospital, London
Specialist Training:	Royal Postgraduate Medical School, London
Distinctions:	Editor, Journal of Forensic Psychiatry
	Consultant Forensic Psychiatrist to the Home Office

BRIDGETT, Dr Christopher K.

Special interests:	**Psychological effects of skin diseases and eczema**
NHS:	Consultant Psychiatrist
	Chelsea and Westminster Hospital
	369 Fulham Road
	London SW10 9NH
Tel:	0181 846 6053
Fax:	0181 846 6119
Private:	Refer to address and number above
First Qualified:	1969 – Oxford
Major Degrees:	FRCPsych
Specialist Training:	Oxford, and Addenbrooke's Hospital, Cambridge

CHRISTIE-BROWN, Dr Jeremy R. W.

Special interests:	**Including psychiatric aspects of transsexualism**
NHS:	No NHS Work
Private:	130 Harley Street
	London W1N 1AH
Tel:	0171 935 2190
Fax:	0181 265 2026
First Qualified:	1960 – Oxford
Major Degrees:	FRCP, FRCPsych
Specialist Training:	Maudsley Hospital, London

COX, Dr Murray

Special interests:	**Psychotherapy in forensic treatment**
NHS:	Consultant Psychotherapist
	Broadmoor Hospital
	Crowthorne, Berks RG11 7EG
Tel:	01344 773111
Fax:	01344 754179 or 01344 754334
Private:	London Independent Hospital
	Beaumont Square
	Stepney Green, London E1
Tel:	0171 790 7845
Fax:	0171 265 9032
First Qualified:	1956 – Cambridge
Major Degrees:	FRCPsych
Academic:	Previously Honorary Lecturer, London Hospital
	Medical College
Specialist Training:	Royal London Hospital
Distinctions:	Honorary Research Fellow Shakespeare Institute,
	Birmingham University
	Honorary Consultant Psychotherapist, Inner London
	Probation Service
USA:	Member, American Psychotherapy Association

COXON, Dr Ann Y.

Special interests:	**Body-mind interactions (behavioural disorders, psychosomatic disorders, eating problems and addiction)**
NHS:	Refer to address and number below
Private:	78 Harley Street
	London W1N 1AE
Tel:	0171 486 2534
Fax:	0171 637 1665
First Qualified:	1963 – London
Major Degrees:	DCH, MRCP
Academic:	Consultant Physician, Portman Clinic, London
Specialist Training:	National Hospital for Nervous Diseases and
	St Bartholomew's Hospital, London
Distinctions:	Previously Research Director Howard Foundation,
	Cambridge
USA:	Paediatric Neurology, Johns Hopkins University,
	Baltimore

CROWN, Dr Sidney

Special interests:	**Psychotherapy; psychosexual problems; liaison psychiatry**
NHS:	Retired from the NHS
Private:	14 Devonshire Place, London W1N 1PB
Tel:	0171 935 0640
Fax:	0171 224 6256
First Qualified:	1959 – London
Major Degrees:	PhD, FRCP, FRCPsych
Specialist Training:	The Middlesex and National Hospitals, London
Distinctions:	Editor, *Contemporary Psychiatry*

DAVIES, Dr Sheilagh

Special interests:	**Adult psychotherapy; psychiatry**
NHS:	Consultant Psychotherapist
	Department of Psychiatry
	Royal Free Hospital
	Pond Street
	London NW3 2QG
Tel:	0171 794 0500 Ext. 3617
Fax:	0171 830 2139
Private:	90 Liverpool Road
	London N1 0RD
Tel:	Refer to numbers above
First Qualified:	1970 – London
Major Degrees:	DPM, FRCPsych
Academic:	Honorary Senior Lecturer, Royal Free Hospital, London
Specialist Training:	The Maudsley, National Hospital for Nervous Diseases and University College Hospitals, London
Distinctions:	Member, British Psychoanalytical Society

FRY, Dr Anthony H.

Special interests:	**Post traumatic stress disorder; reactive depression; problems due to work stress**
NHS:	No NHS work
Private:	Service Director and Consultant Psychiatrist
	Charter Nightingale Hospital
	11–19 Lisson Grove
	London NW1 6SH
Tel:	0171 258 3828 Ext. 2035
Fax:	0171 724 8294
Private:	Consultant Psychiatrist and Medical Director
	Stress Management Unit
	Emblem House
	London Bridge Hospital
	27 Tooley Street
	London SE1 2PR
Tel:	0171 607 3937
Fax:	0171 607 3815
First Qualified:	1966 – London
Major Degrees:	FRCPsych
Academic:	Author, *Safe Space: An Ecological Approach to Psychiatry*
Specialist Training:	Middlesex and Maudsley Hospitals, London
Distinctions:	Previously Medical Adviser, National Marriage Guidance Council
	Examiner, Royal College of Psychiatrists
	Previously Consultant Psychiatrist, Guy's Hospital, London

GOLDBERG, Professor David P. B.

Special interests:	**Mental disorders**
NHS:	Professor of Psychiatry
	Institute of Psychiatry
	De Crespigny Park
	Denmark Hill
	London SE5 8AF
Tel:	0171 703 5411 Ext. 3100
Fax:	0171 277 1586
Private:	No private work
First Qualified:	1959 – London (with Honours)
Major Degrees:	FRCP, FRCP Ed, FRCPsych
Academic:	Professor of Psychiatry, Institute of Psychiatry, London; Previously Professor of Psychiatry, Manchester University
	Lecturer in Psychiatry, Institute of Psychiatry, London
Specialist Training:	St Thomas' Hospital and National Hospital for Nervous Diseases, London
Distinctions:	Gaskell Gold Medal & Prize, Royal Medicine Psychiatry Association; Doris Odlum Prize, Research in Psychiatry, BMA; Mental Health Research Fund Prize

GRAHAM, Dr Nori

Special interests:	**Mental health problems in people over 65**
NHS:	Consultant in Old Age Psychiatry
	Royal Free Hospital
	Pond Street
	London NW3 2QG
Tel:	0171 830 2400/2401 or 0171 792 0500 Ext. 3662
Fax:	0171 830 2139
Private:	Refer to address and number above
First Qualified:	1961 – Oxford and London
Major Degrees:	FRCPsych
Academic:	Honorary Senior Lecturer, Royal Free Hospital School of Medicine, London
Specialist Training:	Royal Free Hospital, London
Distinctions:	Chairman, Alzheimer's Disease International; Former National Chairman, Alzheimer's Disease Society, UK Honorary Doctorate, Open University

GREENBERG, Dr Maurice Philip

Special interests:	**Incest**
NHS:	No NHS work
Private:	Private Patients Wing
	University College Hospital
	25 Grafton Way
	London WC1E 6DB
Tel:	0171 387 9300
Fax:	0171 380 9816
First Qualified:	1971 – London
Major Degrees:	MPhil, FRCPsych
Academic:	Previously Lecturer, St Bartholomew's Hospital, London
Specialist Training:	Bethlem Royal and Maudsley Hospitals, London
Distinctions:	Previously, Psychiatric Adviser, University College London

GREENWOOD, Dr Monica H.

Special interests:	**Old Age Psychiatry**
NHS:	Consultant Psychiatrist
	Middlesex Hospital
	Mortimer Street
	London W1N 8AA
Tel:	0171 636 8333
Fax:	0171 637 0545
Private:	144 Harley Street
	London W1N 1AH
Tel:	0171 380 9186
Fax:	0171 637 0545
First Qualified:	1967 – London
Major Degrees:	FRCPsych
Specialist Training:	Royal Free and Institute of Psychiatry, London

GUNN, Professor John, CBE

Special interests:	**Psychiatric aspects of imprisonment**
NHS:	Professor of Forensic Psychiatry
	Department of Forensic Psychiatry
	Institute of Psychiatry
	De Crespigny Park
	Denmark Hill
	London SE5 8AF
Tel:	0171 703 5411
Fax:	0171 703 5796
Private:	Refer to address and number above
First Qualified:	1961 – Birmingham
Major Degrees:	FRCPsych
Academic:	Professor of Forensic Psychiatry, Institute of Psychiatry, London
Specialist Training:	Maudsley Hospital, London, and Queen Elizabeth Hospital, Birmingham
Distinctions:	Director, Special Hospitals Research Unit DHSS, London
	Honorary Consultant Bethlem Royal and Maudsley Hospitals, London

HIRSCH, Professor Stephen R.

Special interests:	**Schizophrenia; autism**
NHS:	Consultant Psychiatrist
	Lorna Wing
	Charing Cross Hospital
	Fulham Palace Road
	London W6 8RF
Tel:	0181 846 7390 or 0181 846 1234
Fax:	0181 846 7372
Private:	No private work
First Qualified:	1963 – Baltimore, USA
Major Degrees:	MD, FRCP, FRCPsych
Academic:	Professor of Psychiatry and Honorary Consultant, Charing Cross and Westminster Medical Schools, London
Specialist Training:	John Hopkins, Baltimore, USA, and Westminster Hospital, London
Distinctions:	Previously President, Psychiatric Section, Royal Society of Medicine; Author, *Psychopharmacology and Treatment of Schizophrenia*
USA:	See 'Specialist Training' above

ISAACS, Dr Anthony D.

Special interests:	**General psychiatry**
NHS:	Retired from NHS
Private:	138 Harley Street
	London W1N 1AH
Tel:	0171 935 1963
Fax:	0171 724 2505 or 0171 724 8294
First Qualified:	1954 – London
Major Degrees:	FRCP, FRCPsych
Academic:	Previously Sub-Dean, Institute of Psychiatry, London
Specialist Training:	Maudsley Hospital, London
Distinctions:	Emeritus Consultant Psychiatrist

KERWIN, Dr Robert William

Special interests:	**Management of psychosis**
NHS:	Honorary Consultant Psychiatrist
	Institute of Psychiatry
	De Crespigny Park
	London SE5 8AF
Tel:	0171 703 5411
Fax:	0171 703 5796
Private:	Refer to address and number above
First Qualified:	1984 – Cambridge
Major Degrees:	PhD, MRCPsych
Academic:	Reader in Clinical Neuropharmacology, Institute of Psychiatry, London

KING, Professor Michael B.

Special interests:	**Psychological aspects of AIDS and of male victims of sexual abuse; effects of sexual orientation and sexual habits of parents on children in their care, either their own or adopted**
NHS:	Reader and Honorary Consultant Psychiatrist Royal Free Hospital School of Medicine Rowland Hill Street London NW3 2PF
Tel:	0171 830 2397
Fax:	0171 830 2808
and:	Director, Psychosexual Clinic Royal Free Hospital Pond Street London NW3 2QG
Tel:	0171 794 0500 Ext. 4502
Fax:	0171 830 2808
Private:	Refer to address and number above
First Qualified:	1976 – New Zealand
Major Degrees:	MD, FRCPsych
Academic:	Head Department of Psychiatry, London University
Specialist Training:	Auckland, New Zealand, and Royal Free Hospital, London

KNOWLES, Dr L. Jane: See Anglia and Oxford Region below

LADER, Professor Malcolm H.

Special interests:	**Pharmaceutical treatment of mental illness; treatment of patients who fail to respond to usual medication**
NHS:	Consultant Psychiatrist Maudsley Hospital Denmark Hill, London SE5 8AF
Tel:	0171 703 6333
Fax:	0171 252 5437
Private:	Refer to address and number below
First Qualified:	1959 – London
Major Degrees:	MD, FRCPsych
Academic:	Professor of Clinical Psychopharmacology, Institute of Psychiatry, London
Specialist Training:	Maudsley Hospital, London

LEVY, Professor Raymond

Special interests:	**Alzheimer's disease; dementia, depression and hysteria; obsessional disorders**
NHS:	Consultant Psychiatrist Maudsley Hospital Denmark Hill, London SE5 8AZ
Tel:	0171 703 6333
Fax:	0171 701 0167
Private:	Refer to address and number above
First Qualified:	1957 – Edinburgh
Major Degrees:	FRCP Ed, FRCPsych
Academic:	Professor of Old Age Psychiatry, Institute of Psychiatry, London
Specialist Training:	Maudsley Hospital, London, and Royal Infirmary, Edinburgh

LIBBY, Mr Gerald William

Special interests:	**Psychosomatics; gastroenterology and psychological aspects of functional bowel disorders**
NHS:	Consultant Psychiatrist in Gastroenterology St Bartholomew's Hospital West Smithfield London EC1A 7BE
Tel:	0171 601 8517
Fax:	0171 982 6121
Private:	17 Harley Street London W1N 1DA
Tel:	0171 636 7916
Fax:	0171 637 2373
and:	Wellington Hospital 8a Wellington Place London NW8 9LE
Tel:	0171 586 5959
Fax:	0171 586 3869
First Qualified:	1967 – London
Major Degrees:	DPM, FRCPsych
Academic:	Honorary Senior Lecturer, St Bartholomew's and London School of Medicine and Dentistry
Distinctions:	Member, British Society of Gastroenterology

LIPSEDGE, Dr Maurice S.

Special interests:	**Cross-cultural problems; behaviour therapy and drug treatment of phobic and obsessional disorders**
NHS:	Consultant in Psychological Medicine
	Guy's Hospital
	St Thomas Street
	London SEI 9RT
Tel:	0171 955 5000 Ext. 4951
Fax:	0171 955 4059
Private:	Keats House
	24–26 St Thomas Street
	London SE1 9RT
Tel:	0171 407 7517
Fax:	0171 378 0931
First Qualified:	1966 – London
Major Degrees:	FRCP, FRCPsych
Specialist Training:	St Bartholomew's Hospital, London
Distinctions:	Councillor, Association of University Teachers in Psychiatry; Previously Psychiatric Adviser, Alcoholics Recovery Project

LLOYD, Dr Geoffrey G.

Special interests:	**Psychosomatic disorders and psychiatric conditions associated with physical illness**
NHS:	Consultant Psychiatrist
	Royal Free Hospital
	Pond Street, London NW2 2QG
Tel:	0171 794 0500 Ext. 3589
Fax:	0171 830 2876
Private:	148 Harley Street
	London WIN IAH
Tel:	0171 935 1207
Fax:	0171 224 1528
First Qualified:	1967 – Cambridge
Major Degrees:	MPhil, MD, FRCP, FRCPsych
Specialist Training:	Maudsley Hospital, London
Distinctions:	President, Section of Psychiatry, Royal Society of Medicine
	Previously Editor, *Journal of Psychosomatic Research*

MACKEITH, Dr James A. C.

Special interests:	**Forensic psychiatry, for mentally abnormal offenders**
NHS:	Consultant Forensic Psychiatrist
	Denis Hill Unit
	Bethlem Royal Hospital
	Monks Orchard
	Beckenham, Kent BR3 3BX
Tel:	0181 776 4242
Fax:	0181 777 4933
Private:	Refer to address and number above
First Qualified:	1965 – Dublin
Major Degrees:	DPM, FRCPsych
Specialist Training:	Maudsley Hospital, London

MONTGOMERY, Professor Stuart A.

Special interests:	**Depression; suicide**
NHS:	Honorary Consultant Psychiatrist
	St Mary's Hospital
	Praed Street, London W2 1NY
Tel:	0171 725 6666
Fax:	0171 725 6609
Private:	Refer to address and number above
First Qualified:	1963 – London
Major Degrees:	MD (Stockholm), FRCP, FRCPsych
Academic:	Professor of Psychiatry, St Mary's Hospital Medical School; Editor, *International Clinical Psychopharmacology and European Neuropsychopharmacology*; Previously Senior Lecturer and Honorary Consultant, Guy's Hospital, London, and Oakwood Hospital, Maidstone;
Specialist Training:	Stockholm, Sweden
	Guy's and St Mary's Hospitals, London
Distinctions:	President, British Association of Psychopharmacology

MURRAY, Professor Robin MacGregor

Special interests:	**Schizophrenia**
NHS:	King's College Hospital
	Institute of Psychiatry
	De Crespigny Park
	London SE5 8AF
Tel:	0171 703 6091
Fax:	0171 701 9044
Private:	Refer to address and number above
First Qualified:	1968 – Glasgow
Major Degrees:	FRCP Glas, DSc, FRCPsych
Academic:	Professor Psychology, Institute of Psychiatry, King's College Hospital Medical School, London
	Previously Dean, Institute of Psychiatry
Distinctions:	President, European Psychiatrists Association
USA:	Lilly International Fellowship, National Institute of Mental Health, Bethesda

NOBLE, Dr Peter J.

Special interests:	**Affective disorders; medico-legal reports**
NHS:	Emeritus Consultant Psychiatrist
	Maudsley Hospital
	Denmark Hill
	London SE5 8AZ
Tel:	0171 703 6333
Fax:	0171 703 0179
Private:	7 Devonshire Place
	London W1N 1PA
Tel:	0171 935 4688
First Qualified:	1961 – Cambridge
Major Degrees:	MD, FRCP, FRCPsych
Academic:	Honorary Senior Lecturer, Institute of Psychiatry, London
Specialist Training:	Maudsley Hospital, London

PFEFFER, Dr Jeremy M.

Special interests:	**General psychiatry**
NHS:	Consultant Psychiatrist
	Royal London Hospital
	Whitechapel, London E1 1BB
Tel:	0171 377 7000 Ext. 7729
Fax:	0171 377 7316
Private:	97 Harley Street
	London WIN IDF
Tel:	0171 935 3878
Fax:	0171 935 3865
First Qualified:	1971 – London (with Honours)
Major Degrees:	FRCP, FRCPsych
Academic:	Honorary Senior Lecturer, Royal London Hospital
Specialist Training:	Maudsley Hospital, London

PITT, Professor Brice M. N.

Special interests:	**Psychiatry of old age and childbearing**
NHS:	Retired from the NHS
Private:	The Maltings
	Palmers Hill
	Epping
	Essex CM16 6SG
Tel:	01992 574748
First Qualified:	1955 – London
Major Degrees:	MD, FRCPsych
Academic:	Professor in Psychiatry of the Elderly, St Mary's Hospital and Royal Postgraduate Medical School, London
Specialist Training:	St Bartholomew's and Royal London
Distinctions:	President, Marce Society
	Chairman, Association of Postnatal Illness

RUTTER, Professor Sir Michael L., CBE

Special interests:	**Problems of adolescence; child psychiatry**
NHS:	Honorary Director
	MRC Child Psychiatry Unit
	Institute of Psychiatry
	De Crespigny Park
	Denmark Hill
	London SE5 8AF
Tel:	0171 703 5411 Ext. 3465
Fax:	0171 708 5800
Private:	Refer to address and number above
First Qualified:	1955 – Birmingham (with Distinction)
Major Degrees:	MD, FRCPsych, DPM
Academic:	Professor, Child Psychiatry, Institute of Psychiatry, London University
Specialist Training:	Queen Elizabeth Hospital, Birmingham, and Maudsley Hospital, London
Distinctions:	Fellow, Royal Society
	Honorary Fellow, British Psychological Society
USA:	Previously Fellow in Paediatric Psychiatry Albert Einstein College of Medicine, New York.

SEIFERT, Dr Ruth

NHS:	Consultant Psychiatrist
	St Bartholomew's Hospital
	West Smithfield
	London EC1A 7BE
Tel:	0171 601 8106
Private:	No private work
First Qualified:	1968 – London
Major Degrees:	FRCPsych
Specialist Training:	Guy's and Maudsley Hospitals, London
Academic:	Honorary Senior Lecturer and Regional Advisor, North Thames Region (East)

SHUR, Dr Eric

NHS:	No NHS work
Private:	Priory Hospital
	Priory Lane
	Roehampton Hospital
	London SW15 5JJ
Tel:	0181 876 8261
Fax:	0181 876 4015
First Qualified:	1973 – Witwatersand, South Africa
Major Degrees:	MPhil, MRCPsych
Distinctions:	Deputy Medical Director, Priory Hospital
	Honorary Senior Research Fellow, Charing Cross
	Medical School, London

STONEHILL, Dr Edward

Special interests:	**Eating disorders and psychosomatic illness**
NHS:	No NHS work
Private:	Executive Medical Director
	Charter Nightingale Hospital
	11–19 Lisson Grove
	London NW1 6SH
Tel:	0171 258 3828 Ext. 2035
Fax:	0171 724 1016
Private:	Charter Clinic,
	1–5 Radnor Walk
	London SW3 4PB
Tel:	0171 351 1272
Fax:	0171 351 7098
Private:	138 Harley Street
	London W1N 1AH
Tel:	0171 935 0554
First Qualified:	1961 – London
Major Degrees:	MD, FRCPsych
Specialist Training:	The Middlesex and St George's Hospitals, London
Distinctions:	Emeritus Consultant Psychiatrist, Central Middlesex
	Hospital, London
	Research Fellow, Department of Psychiatry,
	St George's Hospital, London

TROWELL, Dr Judith Ann

Special interests: **Child psychotherapy**
NHS: Consultant Psychiatrist
Child and Family Department
Tavistock Clinic
120 Belsize Lane
London NW3 5BA
Tel: 0171 435 7111
Fax: 0171 447 3733
Private: Refer to address and number above
First Qualified: 1965 – London
Major Degrees: FRCPsych
Academic: Honorary Senior Lecturer, Royal Free Hospital Medical School, London; Honorary Senior Lecturer, Institute of Psychiatry, Maudsley Hospital, London
Distinctions: Chairperson: Young Minds; Co-Author, *Children's Welfare and the Law: The Limits of Legal Intervention*

WELLDON, Dr Estela V.

Special interests: **Sexual and social deviancy in women**
NHS: Consultant Psychotherapist and Clinical Tutor
Portman Clinic
8 Fitzjohn's Avenue
London NW3 5NA
Tel: 0171 794 8262
Fax: 0171 447 3748
Private: 121 Harley Street, London W1N 1DH
Tel: 0171 935 9076
Fax: 0171 586 0173
First Qualified: 1962 – Argentina
Major Degrees: MD, FRCPsych
Academic: Honorary Senior Lecturer, University College London
Specialist Training: Cuyo University, Argentina, and Henderson Hospital, Sutton
Distinctions: Director, 1st Diploma course in Forensic Physcotherapy, London University
Author, Mother Madonna Whore: The Idealization and Denigration of Motherhood
Honorary Life President, International Association for Forensic Psycotherapy
Director of Studies in Forensic Psychiatry, London University
Co-Editor, Revised Applications of Group Analysis and Psychotherapy in Great Britain
USA: Postgraduate Fellow, Menninger Clinic, Topeka

WOOLFSON, Dr Gerald

Special interests:	**Psychotic illness, personality disorders, anxiety states and depressive illness**
NHS:	Honorary Consultant Psychiatrist
	Hammersmith Hospital
	Du Cane Road
	London W12 0HS
Tel:	0181 743 2030
Fax:	0181 740 3139
Private:	97 Harley Street
	London W1N 1DF
Tel:	0171 935 3400
Fax:	0171 487 3834
First Qualified:	1954 – Cape Town
Major Degrees:	FRCP, FRCPsych
Academic:	Senior Lecturer, Royal Postgraduate Medical School, London
Specialist Training:	Groote Schuur Hospital, Cape Town and St George's Hospital, London
Distinctions:	Gaskell Gold Medal

ANGLIA AND OXFORD REGION

READING

KNOWLES, Dr L. Jane

Special interests:	**Psychological experiences of women with young children; post traumatic stress disorder – particularly after childhood abuse; psychotherapy: group analysis**
NHS:	Consultant Psychotherapist
	West Berkshire Psychotherapy Service
	Winterbourne House
	53–55 Argyle Road, Reading RG1 7YL
Tel:	01734 561250
Fax:	01734 561251
Private:	The Group Analytic Practice
	88 Montague Mansions
	London W1H 1LF
Tel:	0171 935 3085 /3103
Fax:	0171 935 1397
and:	7 Albert Road
	Caversham Road
	Reading DG4 7AN
Tel:	01734 478872
First Qualified:	1974 – London
Major Degrees:	MRCPsych
Academic:	Senior Tutor, Psychodynamic Psychotherapy, Oxford University
	External Examiner, Goldsmith's College, London University
Distinctions:	Author, *Motherhood: What it does to your mind*, *Know your own Mind*, and *Love: a user's guide*
USA:	Editorial Board, 'Women and Therapy'

NORTH WEST REGION

MANCHESTER

Baldwin, Dr Robert Charles

Special interests:	**Old Age Psychiatry**
NHS:	Consultant in Old Age Psychiatry
	Manchester Royal Infirmary
	York House
	Oxford Road
	Manchester M13 9BX
Tel:	0161 276 5317
Fax:	0161 276 5303
Private:	The Manchester Clinic
	Manchester Royal Infirmary
Tel:	0161 276 5317
Fax:	0161 276 5303
First Qualified:	1976 – Southampton
Major Degrees:	DM, MRCPsych
Academic:	Honorary Consultant Lecturer, Manchester University

BENBOW, Dr Susan M.

Special interests:	**Old Age Psychiatry**
NHS:	Consultant Psychiatrist
	SCOPE, Carrisbrooke Resource Centre
	Wenlock Way
	Gorton
	Manchester M12 5LF
Tel:	0161 273 4383 or 0161 274 4173
Fax:	0161 273 3818
Private:	Refer to address and number above
First Qualified:	1977 – Manchester (with Honours)
Major Degrees:	MSc, MRCPsych
Specialist Training:	Withington Hospital, Manchester

BURNS, Professor Alistair S.

Special interests:	**Old Age Psychiatry; dementia syndromes; confusional states**
NHS:	Professor of Old Age Psychiatry
	Withington Hospital
	West Didsbury
	Manchester M20 2LR
Tel:	0161 445 8111
Fax:	0161 447 3316
Private:	Refer to address and number above
First Qualified:	1980 – Glasgow
Major Degrees:	FRCP, MRCPsych, T(Psych)
Academic:	Professor of Old Age Psychiatry, Manchester University
Specialist Training:	Institute of Psychiatry and Maudsley Hospital, London

JOLLEY, Professor David

Special interests:	**Old Age Psychiatry**
NHS:	Honorary Professor
	Consultant in Old Age Psychiatry
	Withington Hospital
	West Didsbury
	Manchester M20 2LR
Tel:	0161 447 4390
Fax:	0161 448 1348
Private:	Refer to address and number above
First Qualified:	1969 – London
Major Degrees:	FRCPsych
Academic:	Honorary Reader, Manchester University
	Honorary Professor, Wolverhampton
Specialist Training:	Manchester
Distinctions:	Previously Chairman, Old Age Psychiatry, Royal College of Psychiatrists

LENNON, Dr Sean P.

Special interests:	**Old Age Psychiatry**
NHS:	Consultant in Old Age Psychiatry
	Withington Hospital
	West Didsbury
	Manchester M20 2LR
Tel:	0161 447 4390
Fax:	0161 448 1348
Private:	Refer to address and number above
First Qualified:	1978 – Southampton
Major Degrees:	MRCPsych
Academic:	Honorary Clinical Lecturer, Manchester University
Specialist Training:	Manchester

NORTHERN AND YORKSHIRE REGION

NEWCASTLE

FAIRBAIRN, Dr Andrew F.

Special interests:	**Old Age Psychiatry**
NHS:	Brighton Clinic
	Newcastle General Hospital
	Newcastle upon Tyne NE4 6BE
Tel:	0191 273 6666 Ext. 22560
Fax:	0191 272 0816
Private:	No private work
First Qualified:	1974 – Newcastle
Major Degrees:	MB, BS, FRCPsych
Academic:	Clinical Lecturer, Newcastle Univesity

SOUTH AND WEST REGION

BRISTOL

EAMES, Dr Peter G.

Special interests:	**Rehabilitation after head injuries; post traumatic behavioural disorders**
NHS:	No NHS work
Private:	Consultant Neuropsychiatrist
	2 Clifton Park
	Clifton
	Bristol BS8 3BS
Tel:	0117 973 2350
Fax:	0117 973 0887
Private:	Refer to address and number above
First Qualified:	1965 – Cambridge
Major Degrees:	MRCP, MRCPsych
Distinctions:	Previously Consultant to the Royal Air Force

NUTT, Professor David John

Special interests:	**Anxiety, depression, sleep and addiction**
NHS:	Professor of Psychopharmacology
	Department of Mental Health
	Bristol University
	41 St Michael's Hill
	Bristol BS2 8DZ
Tel:	01179 253066
Fax:	01179 277057
Private:	No private work
First Qualified:	1975 – Cambridge and London
Major Degrees:	DM, FRCPsych
Academic:	Wellcome Senior Fellow, Warneford Hospital, Oxford
Specialist Training:	Oxford
USA:	Head, Section of Clinical Science, National Institute of Alcohol Abuse and Alcoholism, National Institute of Health, Bethesda, Maryland

SOUTHAMPTON

ASHURST, Dr Pamela Margaret

Special interests:	**Brief psychotherapy; bereavement and loss; women's issues**
NHS:	Retired from the NHS
Private:	130 Highfield Lane
	Southampton SO17 1NR
Tel:	01703 553773
First Qualified:	1964 – Bristol
Major Degrees:	FRCPsych
Academic:	Honorary Clinical Teacher, Southampton University
Specialist Training:	Bristol and London
Distinctions:	Previously Head of Psychotherapy Department, Southampton Health District
	Co-Author: Understanding Women in Distress

GODBER, Dr Colin

Special interests:	**Old Age Psychiatry**
NHS:	Consultant in Old Age Psychiatry
	Moorgreen Hospital
	Botley Road
	West End, Southampton SO3 3JB
Tel:	01703 477165
Fax:	01703 465014
Private:	No private work
First Qualified:	1964 – Oxford
Major Degrees:	MPhil, FRCP, FRCPsych
Academic:	Honorary Clinical Teacher, Southampton University
Specialist Training:	Maudlsey, London

ROSENVINGE, Dr Henry P.

Special interests:	**Old Age Psychiatry**
NHS:	Consultant in Old Age Psychiatry
	Thornhill House
	Moorgreen Hospital
	Westend, Southampton SO3 3JB
Tel:	01703 477165
Fax:	01703 465014
Private:	Refer to address and number above
First Qualified:	1972 – London
Major Degrees:	FRCPsych
Specialist Training:	Newcastle

WILKINSON, Dr David George

Special interests:	**Old Age Psychiatry**
NHS:	Consultant in Old Age Psychiatry
	Western Community Hospital
	Walnut Grove
	Millbrook, Southampton S016 4XE
Tel:	01703 475446
Fax:	01703 475402
Private:	Refer to address and number above
First Qualified:	1975 – Birmingham
Major Degrees:	FRCPsych
Specialist Training:	Moorgreen Hospital, Southampton

TRENT REGION

NOTTINGHAM

JONES, Dr Robert

Special interests:	**Old Age Psychiatry**
NHS:	Consultant Psychiatrist
	Queen's Medical Centre
	Clifton Boulevard
	Nottingham NG7 2UH
Tel:	0115 924 9924 Ext. 41409
Fax:	0115 942 3618

WEST MIDLANDS

BIRMINGHAM

CALDICOTT, Dr Fiona

Special interests:	**Group psychotherapy**
NHS:	Consultant Psychiatrist
	Uffculme Clinic
	Queensbridge Road
	Birmingham B13 8QB
Tel:	0121 442 4545
Fax:	0121 442 4541
and:	Queen Elizabeth Psychiatric Clinic
	South Birmingham Mental Health Trust
	Vincent Drive, Edgbaston
	Birmingham B15 2TZ
Tel:	0121 627 2972
Fax:	0121 627 2972
Private:	Refer to address and number above
First Qualified:	1966 – Oxford
Major Degrees:	FRCPsych
Academic:	Senior Clinical Lecturer, University of Birmingham Medical School
	Previously, Consultant Psychiatrist, Warwick University
Specialist Training:	Uffculme Clinic, Birmingham and Walsgrave Hospital, Coventry
Distinctions:	President, Royal College Psychiatrists
	Clinical Director in Adult Psychiatry and Psychotherapy, Mental Health Unit, South Birmingham Health Authority

SCOTLAND

EDINBURGH

FREEMAN, Dr Christopher P. L.

Special interests:	**Affective disorders; depression; eating disorders; post traumatic stress disorders**
NHS:	Consultant Psychotherapist Royal Edinburgh Hospital Morningside Edinburgh EH10 5HF
Tel:	0131 537 6599
Fax:	0131 537 6104
Private:	The Consulting Rooms 14 Moray Place Edinburgh EH3 6DT
Tel:	0131 225 5320
Fax:	0131 225 6749
First Qualified:	1971 – Edinburgh
Major Degrees:	MPhil, FRCPsych
Academic:	Honorary Senior Lecturer, Edinburgh University
Specialist Training:	Edinburgh
Distinctions:	Gaskell Gold Medal, Royal College of Psychiatrists Chairman, Royal College Psychiatrists Research Committee

CHISWICK, Dr Derek

Special interests:	**Forensic psychiatry; mentally abnormal offenders**
NHS:	Consultant Forensic Psychiatrist Royal Edinburgh Hospital Morningside Edinburgh EH10 5DT
Tel:	0131 537 6000
Fax:	0131 447 7314
Private:	Refer to address and number above
First Qualified:	1969 – Liverpool
Major Degrees:	FRCPsych
Academic:	Honorary Senior Lecturer in Forensic Psychiatry, Edinburgh University
Distinctions:	Previously Chairman, Working Group HM Detention Centre and HM Young Offenders Institute, Glenochil Vice-Chairman, Parole Board for Scotland

GLASGOW

GRANT, Dr Sandra M.

NHS:	Consultant Psychotherapist
	Shaw Park Resource Centre
	41 Shaw Park Road
	Glasgow
Tel:	0141 531 8770 or 0141 211 3543
Fax:	0141 337 2408
Private:	Refer to address and number above
First Qualified:	1971 – Edinburgh
Major Degrees:	FRCPsych
Specialist Training:	Royal Edinburgh Hospital
Distinctions:	Member of Scottish Association of Psychoanalytical Psychotherapists
USA:	Resident Research Fellow, Denver General Hospital, Denver

---

HUNTER, Dr Robert

Special interests:	**Depressive illness, memory problems and dementia**
NHS:	Consultant Psychiatrist and Clinical Director of Research and Development
	Gartnavel Royal Hospital
	1055 Great Western Road
	Glasgow G12 0XH
Tel:	0141 211 3600
Fax:	0141 337 2408
Private:	Glasgow Nuffield Hospital
	25 Beaconsfield Road
	Glasgow G12 0PJ
Tel:	0141 334 9441
Fax:	0141 339 1352
First Qualified:	1980 – Glasgow
Major Degrees:	MD, MRCPsych
Academic:	Honorary Senior Lecturer in Psychological Medicine, Glasgow University; Director of Research and Development, Community Mental Health Trust, Glasgow; Previously Clinical Scientist and Lecturer, Medical Research Council, Brain Metabolism Unit, Royal Edinburgh Hospital, Edinburgh
Specialist Training:	Royal Edinburgh Hospital
Distinctions:	Cullen Medal, University of Glasgow
	McHarg Prize in Psychological Medicine, Royal College of Psychiatrists
USA:	Researcher at Marine Biological Laboratory, Massachusetts

---

RHEUMATOLOGISTS

Rheumatologists treat diseases of the joints, muscles, bones and tendons including arthritis, back pain, sports injuries and autoimmune diseases such as lupus.

Ten per cent of the population suffers from a rheumatic disorder and over half of the six million disabled adults in Britain are disabled by musculoskeletal disease. Arthritis and rheumatism are the most frequently self-reported conditions in the UK. It is estimated that the total cost of arthritis in 1990 in the UK was £1,200m.

The most common musculoskeletal diseases can be divided up into:
1. Inflammatory joint disease such as rheumatoid arthritis which affects nearly 8 million people in Britain, ankylosing spondylitis and gout.
2. Degenerative joint disease (joint failure) such as osteoarthritis.
3. Connective tissue disorders such as systemic lupus erythematosus (SLE), myositis, systemic vasculitis and scleroderma.
4. Metabolic bone disorders such as osteoporosis and osteomalacia.

Non articular conditions:
5. Soft tissue rheumatism such as frozen shoulder and repetitive strain syndrome.
6. Spinal disorders such as prolapsed disc and non specific back pain.

Due to the nature of the diseases, rheumatologists work in a multidisciplinary team and a close working relationship with doctors in other specialities is often essential. The rheumatologist is primarily concerned with the medical treatment while the orthopaedic surgeon with a special interest in rheumatological surgery may be involved with the surgical treatment (see Orthopaedic Section). A gastroenterologist may be called upon for advice as anti-arthritis medications often cause problems in the gut. Diagnostic radiologists help with the diagnosis by using X-rays, bone scans, CT and MRI equipment.

LONDON AND THE SOUTH EAST

BARNES, Dr Colin G.

Special interests:	*Behcet's* **Disease;** *Felty's* **syndrome**
NHS:	Consultant Rheumatologist
	Department of Rheumatology
	Royal London Hospital
	Whitechapel Road
	London E1 1BB
Tel:	0171 377 7810
Fax:	0171 377 7807
Private:	96 Harley Street
	London W1N 1AF
Tel:	0171 486 0967
Fax:	0171 935 1107
First Qualified:	1961 – London
Major Degrees:	FRCP
Specialist Training:	Royal London Hospital
Distinctions:	Editor, Rheumatology Europe
	Member, Editorial Board: The Foot
	Honorary Consultant Rheumatologist, St Luke's Hospital for the Clergy, London
	Previously President, European League against Rheumatism

BERRY, Dr Hedley

Special interests:	**Arthritis**
NHS:	Consultant Rheumatologist
	King's College Hospital
	Denmark Hill
	London SE5 9RS
Tel:	0171 346 6194
Fax:	0171 346 6475
Private:	96 Harley Street
	London W1N 1AF
Tel:	0171 486 0967
Fax:	0171 935 1107
First Qualified:	1967 – Oxford
Major Degrees:	DM, FRCP
Specialist Training:	Royal London and St Bartholomew's Hospitals, London
Distinctions:	Honorary Secretary, Rheumatology Section, Royal Society Medicine

HUGHES, Dr Graham R. V.

Special interests:	**Lupus; connective-tissue disorders**
NHS:	Consultant Physician
	Department of Rheumatology
	St Thomas' Hospital
	Lambeth Palace Road
	London SE1 7EH
Tel:	0171 928 9292 Ext. 3682
Fax:	0171 633 9422
Private:	Refer to address above
Tel:	0171 928 9292 Ext. 2888
Fax:	0171 633 9422
First Qualified:	1964 – London
Major Degrees:	MD, FRCP
Academic:	Previously Reader and Head of Rheumatology
	Royal Postgraduate Medical School, London
Specialist Training:	Royal Postgraduate Medical School, London
Distinctions:	Life President, Lupus UK; Winner ILAR International
	Research Prize, 1993, for his description of the
	antiphospholipid syndrome
USA:	Member, American Lupus 'Hall of Fame'

HUSKISSON, Dr Edward C.

NHS:	Retired from the NHS
Private:	14a Milford House
	7 Queen Anne Street
	London W1M 9FD
Tel:	0171 636 4278
Fax:	0171 323 6829
First Qualified:	1964 – London
Major Degrees:	MD, FRCP
Academic:	Senior Lecturer, St Bartholomew's Hospital, London
Specialist Training:	St Bartholomew's Hospital, London

MACKWORTH-YOUNG, Dr Charles G.

Special interests:	**Connective tissue diseases; antiphospholipid syndrome; soft tissue rheumatism**
NHS:	Consultant Physician in Rheumatology and General Medicine
	Charing Cross Hospital
	Fulham Palace Road
	London W6 8RF
Tel:	0181 746 8442
Fax:	0181 746 8440
Private:	134 Harley Street
	London W1N 1AH
Tel:	0171 486 2622
First Qualified:	1978 – Cambridge and London
Major Degrees:	MD, FRCP
Academic:	Honorary Senior Lecturer, Charing Cross and Westminster Medical Schools, London
Specialist Training:	Hammersmith Hospital, London
Distinctions:	Michael Mason Prize for Rheumatology Research
USA:	Previously Research Fellow, New England Medical Centre, Boston

PERRY, Dr Jeremy D.

Special interests:	**Especially relating to sporting injuries**
NHS:	Consultant Rheumatologist
	Royal London Hospital
	Whitechapel Road
	London E1 1BB
Tel:	0171 377 7859
Fax:	0171 377 7807
Private:	The London Independent
	1 Beaumont Square
	Stepney E1 4NL
Tel:	0171 790 0990 Ext. 2264 or 0171 790 4405
Fax:	0171 790 4405
First Qualified:	1970 – London
Major Degrees:	FRCP
Academic:	Teacher, London University
Specialist Training:	Royal London
Distinctions:	Consultant Adviser, Crystal Palace National Sports Centre

SEIFERT, Dr Martin H.

Special interests:	**Inflammatory joint disease; arthritis of AIDS and other infectious diseases**
NHS:	Consultant Physician in Rheumatology
	St Mary's Hospital
	Praed Street, London W2 1NY
Tel:	0171 262 1066
Fax:	0171 725 6200
Private:	Private Consulting Rooms,
	The Hospital of St John and St Elizabeth
	60 Grove End Road
	London NW8 9NH
Tel:	0171 286 5126 Ext. 361
Fax:	0171 266 2316
First Qualified:	1964 – London
Major Degrees:	FRCP
Specialist Training:	The Middlesex and St Thomas' Hospitals, London
Distinctions:	Heberden Roundsman, British Society for Rheumatology
	Previously President, Rheumatology and Rehabilitation Section, Royal Society of Medicine
USA:	Previously Fellow in Rheumatology, Colorado University, Denver

WHITE, Dr Anthony G.

Special interests:	**Electrodiagnosis**
NHS:	Consultant Rheumatologist
	Royal Free Hospital
	Pond Street, London NW3 2QG
Tel:	0171 794 0500 Ext. 4048
Fax:	0171 435 0143
Private:	152 Harley Street
	London W1N 1HH
Tel:	0171 935 8868
Fax:	0171 224 2574
First Qualified:	1959 – Bristol
Major Degrees:	FRCP
Academic:	Honorary Senior Lecturer, Clinical Medicine, University College London
Specialist Training:	Royal Free Hospital
Distinctions:	Honorary Medical Director, North London School of Physiotherapy

YATES, Dr D. Anthony

Special interests:	**Arthritis of the joints and spine**
NHS:	Retired from the NHS
Private:	26 Devonshire Place
	London W1N 1PD
Tel:	0171 935 8917
Fax:	0171 935 7185
First Qualified:	1953 – London (with Honours)
Major Degrees:	MD, FRCP
Specialist Training:	Hammersmith and St Thomas' Hospitals, London and in the Royal Army Medical Corps
Distinctions:	Consultant Rheumatologist to the Army and King Edward VII Hospital for Officers; Previously President, British Society of Rheumatology; Honorary Physician, St Thomas' Hospital, London

ANGLIA AND OXFORD REGION

ASCOT – BERKSHIRE

LIYANAGE, Dr. Sunil P.

NHS:	Consultant Rheumatologist
	Heatherwood Hospital
	London Road
	Ascot SL5 8AA
Tel:	01344 877185
Fax:	01344 877620
Private:	The Consulting Rooms
	Princess Margaret Hospital
	Windsor SL4 3SJ
Tel:	01753 856743
Fax:	01753 853211 or 01753 851749
First Qualified:	1965 – Ceylon
Major Degrees:	FRCP
Specialist Training:	London Hospital and St Ann's General Hospital, London
Distinctions:	Medical Director, Heatherwood and Wrexham Park Hospitals Trust

CAMBRIDGE

CRISP, Dr Adrian James

Special interests:	**Metabolic bone diseases: Paget's disease and steroid induced osteoporosis**
NHS:	Consultant Rheumatologist
	Addenbrooke's Hospital
	Hills Road
	Cambridge CB2 2QQ
Tel:	01223 216254
Fax:	01223 217316
Private:	Evelyn Hospital
	Trumpington Road
	Cambridge CB2 2AF
Tel:	01223 303336
First Qualified:	1974 – Cambridge and London
Major Degrees:	MD, FRCP
Academic:	Director of Studies in Clinical Medicine and Fellow of Churchill College, Cambridge
Specialist Training:	University College and Guy's Hospital, London
USA:	Previously Research Fellow, Massachusetts General Hospital and Harvard Medical School, Boston

HAZLEMAN, Dr Brian Leslie

Special interests:	**Inflammatory joint disease; connective tissue disorders; soft tissue rheumatism**
NHS:	Consultant Rheumatologist
	Addenbrooke's Hospital
	Hills Road
	Cambridge CB2 2QQ
Tel:	01223 217457
Fax:	01223 217838
Private:	Evelyn Hospital
	4 Trumpington Road
	Cambridge CB2 2AF
Tel:	01223 303336
Fax:	01223 316068
First Qualified:	1965 – London
Major Degrees:	FRCP
Academic:	Associate Lecturer, Cambridge University
	Director, Rheumatology Research Unit
Specialist Training:	London Hospital and Radcliffe Infirmary, Oxford
Distinctions:	Begley Prize, Royal College of Surgeons; Heberden Roundsman, British Society for Rheumatology; Margaret Holyrode Prize, Heberden Society

OXFORD

MOWAT, Dr Alastair G.

Special interests:	**Rheumatoid arthritis**
NHS:	Consultant Rheumatologist
	Nuffield Orthopaedic Centre
	Windmill Road
	Headington, Oxford OX3 7LD
Tel:	01865 227527
Fax:	01865 742348
Private:	Refer to address and number above
First Qualified:	1962 – Edinburgh
Major Degrees:	FRCP, FRCP Ed
Academic:	Clinical Lecturer, Oxford University
Specialist Training:	Edinburgh
Distinctions:	President, British Society for Rheumatology
	Member Editorial Committee and Board, British Journal of Rheumatology
USA:	Member of American Rheumatology Association
	Previously Instructor in Medicine, University of Rochester, New York
	Previously Instructor in Medicine, University of Rochester, New York

NORTH WEST REGION

MANCHESTER

HOLT, Dr Lennox P. J.

Special interests:	**Immunology and inflammation; paediatric rheumatology; connective tissue disorders**
NHS:	Consultant Rheumatologist
	Manchester Royal Infirmary
	Oxford Road
	Manchester M13 9WL
Tel:	0161 276 4272
Fax:	0161 276 8690
and:	Booth Hall Children's Hospital
	Charlestown Road
	Blackley, Manchester M9 2AA
Tel:	0161 795 7000
Fax:	0161 741 5387
Private:	Refer to address and number above
First Qualified:	1957 – Manchester
Major Degrees:	FRCP Ed
Academic:	Reader in Rheumatology, Manchester Medical School
USA:	Member of American Rheumatology Association

NORTHERN AND YORKSHIRE REGION

NEWCASTLE

FRANCIS, Dr Roger M.

Special interests:	**Osteoporosis in men; all secondary causes of osteoporosis**
NHS:	Consultant Physician Bone Clinic, Musculoskeletal Unit Freeman Hospital Newcastle upon Tyne NE7 7DN
Tel:	0191 284 3111 Ext. 26975
Fax:	0191 223 1161
Private:	Refer to address and number above
First Qualified:	1975 – Leeds
Major Degrees:	FRCP
Academic:	Senior Lecturer, Newcastle University
Specialist Training:	University College Hospital, London and General Infirmary, Leeds
Distinctions:	Editor, Osteoporosis: Pathogenesis and Management Smith and Nephew Research Fellowship
USA:	Research Fellow, Jewish Hospital, St Louis, Missouri

GRIFFITHS, Dr Ian David

Special interests:	**Genetic aspects of rheumatic disease; connective tissue disorders**
NHS:	Consultant Rheumatologist Department of Rheumatology Freeman Hospital Newcastle upon Tyne NE7 7DN
Tel:	0191 284 3111
Fax:	0191 213 1968
and:	Royal Victoria Infirmary Queen Victoria Road Newcastle upon Tyne NE1 4LP
Private:	Refer to address and number above
First Qualified:	1969 – London
Major Degrees:	FRCP
Academic:	Honorary Clinical Lecturer, Newcastle University
Specialist Training:	Charing Cross Hospital, London, and Southampton General Hospital; Research Fellow, Kennedy Institute of Rheumatology, London
Distinctions:	Chairman, Clinical Affairs Committee, British Rheumatology Society

SOUTH AND WEST REGION

BATH

MADDISON, Professor Peter J.

Special interests:	**Systemic lupus erythematosus**
NHS:	Professor of Bone and Joint Medicine
	Royal National Hospital for Rheumatic Diseases
	Upper Borough Walls
	Bath BA1 1RL
Tel:	01225 465941 Ext. 282
Fax:	01225 421202
Private:	Refer to address and number above
First Qualified:	1971 – Cambridge
Major Degrees:	MD, FRCP
Academic:	Professor of Bone and Joint Medicine, Bath University
Distinctions:	Heberden Roundsman, 1994
USA:	Assistant Professor and Fellow in Rheumatology and Immunology, Buffalo School of Medicine, New York State University

BRISTOL

DIEPPE, Professor Paul Adrian

Special interests:	**Osteoarthritis; rheumatological disease**
Academic:	Dean of the Faculty of Medicine
	Bristol University
Tel:	01179 288333
Fax:	01179 349854
Private:	No private work
First Qualified:	1970 – London
Major Degrees:	MD, FRCP
Academic:	Professor in Rheumatology, Bristol University

SOUTHAMPTON

CAWLEY, Dr Michael I. D.

Special interests:	**Inflammation; clinical and pathological aspects of rheumatic disease**
NHS:	Consultant Rheumatologist
	Southampton General Hospital
	Tremona Road
	Southampton SO16 6YD
Tel:	01703 796770
Fax:	01703 798529
Private:	Refer to address and number above
First Qualified:	1958 – London
Major Degrees:	MD, FRCP
Academic:	Honorary Lecturer in Medicine, Southampton University
Distinctions:	Civilian Consultant Rheumatologist to the Royal Navy
	Heberden Roundsman – 1992
	Previously Councillor, British Society for Rheumatology
USA:	Member, American College of Rheumatology

TRENT REGION

SHEFFIELD

SNAITH, Dr Michael Linton

Special interests:	**Connective tissue disease; sytemic lupus erythematosis; Sjogren's syndrome; vasculitis**
NHS:	Senior Lecturer in Rheumatology
	The Sheffield Centre for Rheumatic Diseases
	Nether Edge Hospital
	Osborne Road
	Sheffield S11 9EL
Tel:	0114 271 1800 Ext. 1939
Fax:	0114 271 3781
Private:	No private work
First Qualified:	1965 – Newcastle
Major Degrees:	MD, FRCP
Academic:	Honorary Senior Lecturer, University College and Middlesex School of Medicine, London
Specialist Training:	Nuffield Orthopaedic Centre, Oxford
Distinctions:	Previous Consultant Rheumatologist, St Stephen's and Westminster Hospitals, London

STOKE-ON-TRENT

HOTHERSALL, Dr Thomas Edward

Special interests:	**Ankylosing spondylitis; nature of anaemia and urinary infection in rheumatoid arthritis**
NHS:	Consultant Rheumatologist
	Department of Rheumatology and Remedial Services
	North Staffordshire Hospital
	Newcastle Road
	Stoke-on-Trent
	ST4 6QG
Tel:	01782 614419
Fax:	01782 630270
Private:	Refer to address and number above
First Qualified:	1963 – Edinburgh
Major Degrees:	FRCP
Academic:	Senior Clinical Lecturer, Department of Postgraduate Medicine, Keele University
Specialist Training:	Edinburgh Royal Infirmary
Distinctions:	West Midlands, Regional Advisor in Medicine
	Royal College of Physicians, Edinburgh

WARD, Dr Anthony B.

Special interests:	**Rehabilitation after trauma**
NHS:	Consultant in Rehabilitation Medicine
	Hayward Hospital
	High Lane, Burslem
	Stoke-on-Trent, Staffordshire ST6 7AG
Tel:	01782 835 721
Fax:	01782 838 721
Private:	Refer to address and number above
First Qualified:	1975 – Dundee
Major Degrees:	FRCP Ed, FRCP
Academic:	Senior Lecturer, Postgraduate Medical School, Keele University
Specialist Training:	St Thomas' Hospital, London
Distinctions:	President, British Society Rehabilitation Medicine

SCOTLAND

ABERDEEN

REID, Dr David Macauley

Special interests:	**Osteoporosis in rheumatic diseases; corticosteroid osteoporosis**
NHS:	Honorary Consultant Rheumatologist Rheumatology Department City Hospital Urquhart Road, Aberdeen AB9 8AU
Tel:	01224 681818
Fax:	01224 404904
Private:	No private work
First Qualified:	1975 – Aberdeen
Major Degrees:	MD, FRCP
Academic:	Senior Lecturer, Rheumatology, Aberdeen University
Specialist Training:	Aberdeen
Distinctions:	Honorary Secretary, British Society of Rheumatology

EDINBURGH

NUKI, Professor George

Special interests:	**Rheumatic disease; purine metabolism**
NHS:	Honorary Consultant Physician Rheumatic Diseases Unit Northern General Hospital Ferry Road Edinburgh EH5 2DQ
Tel:	0131 537 1796
Fax:	0131 537 1016
Private:	Refer to address and number above
First Qualified:	1960 – London
Major Degrees:	FRCP Ed, FRCP
Academic:	Professor of Rheumatology, Edinburgh University Previously Reader and Honorary Consultant, Welsh National School of Medicine, Cardiff

GLASGOW

STURROCK, Professor Roger D.

Special interests:	**Ankylosing spondylitis**
NHS:	Consultant Rheumatologist
	Centre for Rheumatic Diseases
	Department of Medicine
	Royal Infirmary
	10 Alexandra Parade
	Glasgow G31 2ER
Tel:	0141 211 4688
Fax:	0141 211 4878
e-mail:	R.Sturrock@udcf.gla.ac.uk
Private:	No private work
First Qualified:	1969 – London
Major Degrees:	MD, FRCP
Academic:	Professor of Rheumatology, Glasgow
Distinctions:	Editor, Recent Advances in Rheumatology

THORACIC SURGEONS

(Lung surgeons)

Thoracic surgeons operate on chest structures treating problems such as abnormalities of the major arteries and veins, airway problems, cancer and chest injuries. These surgeons often work in conjunction with a cardiologist. (See appendix 1(ii) for list of specialist cardiac units.)

LONDON AND THE SOUTH EAST

DUSSEK, Mr Julian E.

NHS:	Consultant Thoracic Surgeon
	Guy's Hospital
	St Thomas Street
	London SE1 9RT
Tel:	0171 955 5000 Ext. 4322
Fax:	0171 955 4858
Private:	Refer to address and number above
First Qualified:	1967 – London
Major Degrees:	FRCS
Specialist Training:	National Heart, Guy's and St Thomas' Hospitals, London

GOLDSTRAW, Mr Peter

Special interests:	**Thoracic oncology; oesophageal surgery; airways problems including tracheal surgery and chest wall reconstruction**
NHS:	Consultant Thoracic Surgeon
	Royal Brompton Hospital
	Sydney Street
	London SW3 6NP
Tel:	0171 351 8559
Fax:	0171 351 8560
Private:	Refer to address above
Tel:	0171 351 8558
First Qualified:	1968 – Birmingham
Major Degrees:	FRCS
Specialist Training:	Royal Infirmary, Edinburgh, and University Medical College, Glasgow

LEWIS, Mr C. Terence

Special interests:	**General thoracic surgery; oesophageal surgery**
NHS:	Consultant Cardiothoracic Surgeon
	St Bartholomew's Hospital
	West Smithfield
	London EC1A 7BE
Tel:	0171 601 7118
Fax:	0171 601 7117
Private:	149 Harley Street
	London W1N 2DE
Tel:	0171 935 6397
Fax:	0171 486 4578
First Qualified:	1968 – London
Major Degrees:	FRCS
Specialist Training:	Royal Brompton, National Heart and Royal London
	Hospitals, London

PATTISON, Mr Charles W.

NHS:	Consultant Cardiothoracic Surgeon
	Middlesex Hospital
	Mortimer Street
	London W1N 8AA
Tel:	0171 636 8333
Fax:	0171 436 1755
Private:	81 Harley Street
	London W1N 1DE
Tel:	0171 486 7416
Fax:	0171 487 2569
First Qualified:	1980 – Birmingham
Major Degrees:	FRCS
Academic:	Clinical Lecturer in Cardiac Surgery, National Heart
	and Lung Institute, London
Specialist Training:	Royal Brompton and St Thomas' Hospitals, London,
	and Harefield, Middlesex

WALESBY, Mr Robin K.

Special interests:	**Adult cardiac and thoracic surgery**
NHS:	Consultant Cardiothoracic Surgeon
	London Chest Hospital
	Bommer Road
	Bethnal Green
	London E2 9JX
Tel:	0181 983 2323
Fax:	0181 983 2331
and:	St Bartholomew's Hospital
	West Smithfield
	London EC1 7BE
Tel:	0171 601 7119
and:	Royal Free Hospital
	Pond Street
	London NW3 2QG
Tel:	0171 794 0500 Ext. 4652
Fax:	0171 830 2198
Private:	81 Harley Street
	London W1N 1DE
Tel:	0171 486 4617
Fax:	0171 935 0896
First Qualified:	1970 – London
Major Degrees:	FRCS
Specialist Training:	Hammersmith Hospital and Great Ormond Street Hospital for Children, London, and Harefield, Middlesex

ANGLIA AND OXFORD REGION

CAMBRIDGE

WALLWORK, Mr John

Special interests:	**Transplantation of heart and lungs; cardiac surgery in the elderly**
NHS:	Consultant Cardiothoracic Surgeon and Director of Transplant Services Papworth Hospital Papworth Everard Cambridge CB3 8RE
Tel:	01480 830541
Fax:	01480 831281
Private:	Refer to address and number above
First Qualified:	1970 – Edinburgh
Major Degrees:	MA, FRCS Ed
Academic:	Associate Lecturer, Edinburgh University Director of Transplant Unit
Specialist Training:	Stanford University, California
USA:	Association of Cardiothoracic Surgeons and see 'Specialist Training' above

---

NORTH WEST REGION

MANCHESTER

JONES, Mr Mark T.

Special interests:	**General adult cardiac and thoracic surgery**
NHS:	Consultant Cardiothoracic Surgeon Wythenshaw Hospital Southmoor Road Wythenshaw, Manchester M23 9LT
Tel:	0161 946 2513
Fax:	0161 946 2530
Private:	Consulting Suite Alexandra Hospital Mill Lane, Cheadle SK8 2PX
Tel:	0161 428 3656
Fax:	0161 491 3867
First Qualified:	1977 – Manchester
Major Degrees:	FRCS
Specialist Training:	Manchester University, London University, and Toronto University, Ontario, Canada
Distinctions:	Douglas Prize, Manchester University

WEST MIDLANDS

BIRMINGHAM

BONSER, Mr Robert Stuart

Special interests:	**Coronary artery surgery; thoracic aortic surgery; transplantation; Marfan's syndrome**
NHS:	Consultant Cardiothoracic Surgeon
	Queen Elizabeth Hospital
	Edgbaston
	Birmingham B15 2TH
Tel:	0121 627 2559
Fax:	0121 627 2542
Private:	Priory Hospital
	Edgbaston
	Birmingham
Tel:	0121 440 2323
Fax:	0121 446 5686
First Qualified:	1977 – Wales
Major Degrees:	FRCS
Academic:	Honorary Senior Lecturer, Queen Elizabeth Hospital, Birmingham
Specialist Training:	Royal Brompton and National Heart Hospitals, London
USA:	British Heart Foundation in America
	Fellow, Heart Association Reciprocal, Minnesota University

TROPICAL MEDICINE PHYSICIANS

Tropical medicine deals with diseases associated with tropical climates. Nearly all tropical diseases are infectious and most are curable. In the UK there are two centres of expertise, one in Liverpool and the other in London.

LONDON AND THE SOUTH EAST

BRYCESON, Dr Anthony D. M.

Special interests:	**Leishmaniasis; malaria and infectious diseases including leprosy**
NHS:	Consultant Physician Hospital for Tropical Diseases 4 St Pancras Way London NW1 0PE
Tel:	0171 530 5402
Fax:	0171 388 7645
Private:	No private work
First Qualified:	1960 – Cambridge
Major Degrees:	FRCP
Academic:	Senior Lecturer, London School of Hygiene and Tropical Medicine
Specialist Training:	Kenya, Nigeria, and at the London School of Hygiene and Tropical Medicine

CHIODINI, Dr Peter

Special interests:	**Parasites**
NHS:	Consultant Parasitologist Hospital for Tropical Diseases 4 St Pancras Way London NW1 0PE
Tel:	0171 530 3450
Fax:	0171 383 0041
Private:	Refer to address and number above
First Qualified:	1978 – London
Major Degrees:	PhD, FRCP
Academic:	Honorary Senior Lecturer, London School of Hygiene and Tropical Medicine
Specialist Training:	Birmingham and St George's Hospital, London
USA:	Previously Visiting Professor in Parasitology, Chicago University

COOK, Dr Gordon C.

Special interests:	**Tropical gastroenterology; clinical parasitology; communicable diseases**
NHS:	Honorary Consultant Physician
	Department of Clinical Sciences
	Hospital for Tropical Diseases
	4 St Pancras Way
	London NW1 0PE
Tel:	0171 530 3419
Fax:	0171 388 7645
Private:	Refer to address and number above
First Qualified:	1957 – London
Major Degrees:	MD, FRCP
Academic:	Senior Lecturer, London School of Hygiene and Tropical Medicine
	Honorary Senior Lecturer, University College London
	Honorary Lecturer in Clinical Parasitology, St Bartholomew's Hospital Medical College, London
Specialist Training:	Papua New Guinea, Zambia and Saudi Arabia
Distinctions:	Examiner in Tropical Medicine to London University, Makerere University, Kampala, and Royal College of Physicians

TOMKINS, Professor Andrew M.

Special interests:	**Malnutrition in young children**
NHS:	Honorary Consultant Physician
	Hospital for Tropical Diseases
	4 St Pancras Way
	London NW1 0PE
Tel:	0171 530 3420
Fax:	0171 530 3409 or 0171 388 7645
and:	University College Hospital
	Gower St, London WC1E 6AU
Private:	Refer to address and number above
First Qualified:	1966 – London
Major Degrees:	FRCP
Academic:	Senior Lecturer, Clinical Nutrition, London School of Hygene and Tropical Medicine
	Professor of International Child Health, Institute of Child Health, London
Specialist Training:	Ahmadu Bello University, Zaria, Nigeria
	Medical Research Council, Fajara, The Gambia
Distinctions:	Honorary Consultant Paediatrician, Great Ormond Street Hospital for Children, London

WRIGHT, Dr Stephen G.

Special interests:	**Tropical gastrointestinal infections; brucellosis**
NHS:	Honorary Consultant Physician
	Hospital for Tropical Diseases
	4 St Pancras Way
	London NW1 0PE
Tel:	0171 530 3420
Fax:	0171 388 7645
Private:	Refer to address and number above
First Qualified:	1968 – London
Major Degrees:	FRCP
Academic:	Senior Lecturer in Clinical Science, London School of Hygiene and Tropical Medicine
Specialist Training:	Hospital for Tropical Diseases, London, and in Nigeria, Nepal and Saudi Arabia

NORTH WEST REGION

LIVERPOOL

BEECHING, Mr Nicholas John

Special interests:	**General infectious diseases; infections of returned travellers; hydatid disease; brucellosis; salmonellosis; viral hepatitis; HIV; infections related to drug abuse**
NHS:	Honorary Consultant Physician
	Infectious Diseases Unit
	Fazakerley Hospital
	Liverpool L9 7AL
Tel:	0151 529 3833
Fax:	0151 529 3762
also at:	Liverpool School of Tropical Medicine
	Pembroke Place
	Liverpool L3 5QA
Tel:	0151 708 9393
Fax:	0151 708 8733
First Qualified:	1977 – Oxford
Major Degrees:	FRCP, FRACP, DCH, DTM&H
Academic:	Senior Clinical Lecturer in Infectious Diseases Liverpool School of Tropical Medicine
Specialist Training:	Liverpool, Birmingham and Auckland, New Zealand

SQUIRE, Dr S. Bertel

Special interests:	**Lung complications in immunocompromised individuals; tuberculosis, especially in relation to HIV infection; clinical management of HIV/AIDS; schistosomiasis**
NHS:	Honorary Consultant Physician Liverpool School of Tropical Medicine Pembroke Place Liverpool L36 5QA
Tel:	0151 708 9393 Ext. 2111 or 2223
Fax:	0151 708 8733
Private:	Refer to address and number above
First Qualified:	1984 – Cambridge
Major Degrees:	MD, MRCP
Academic:	Senior Lecturer in Tropical Medicine, Liverpool University Previously Lecturer in Medicine, College of Medicine, Malawi, Africa
Specialist Training:	Royal Free Hospital, London

WYATT, Dr George B.

NHS:	Honorary Consultant Physician Liverpool School of Tropical Medicine Pembroke Place Liverpool L36 5QA
Tel:	0151 708 9393
Fax:	0151 707 2052
Private:	Refer to address and number above
First Qualified:	1957 – London
Major Degrees:	FRCP
Academic:	Senior Lecturer in Tropical Medicine, Liverpool School of Tropical Medicine Professor of Community Medicine, University of Papua New Guinea, Port Moresby
Specialist Training:	University College Hospital, Ibadan, Nigeria
Distinctions:	Civilian Consultant in Tropical Medicine to the Royal Air Force Clinical Director, Royal Liverpool University Hospital

WEST MIDLANDS

BIRMINGHAM

ELLIS, Dr Christopher John

NHS:	Consultant Physician in Communicable and Tropical Disease
	Birmingham Heartlands Hospital
	Birmingham B9 5SS
Tel:	0121 766 6611
Fax:	0121 766 8752
Private:	Refer to address and number above
First Qualified:	1971 – London
Major Degrees:	FRCP
Academic:	Previously Lecturer in Medicine, London University
Specialist Training:	University College Hospital, London, and Ibadan, Nigeria

SCOTLAND

EDINBURGH

WELSBY, Dr Philip Douglas

Special interests:	Infectious diseases
NHS:	Consultant Physician in Communicable Diseases
	City Hospital
	51 Greenbank Drive
	Edinburgh EH10 5SB
Tel:	0131 536 6000
Fax:	0131 536 6749
Private:	Refer to address and number above
First Qualified:	1970 – London
Major Degrees:	FRCP Ed
Specialist Training:	Royal Free Hospital, London

UROLOGISTS

Urologists treat benign and malignant problems of the genito-urinary system. Some subspecialise in prostate, impotence, male infertility and female urological problems. Surgery is performed in conjunction with genito-urinary physicians.

LONDON AND THE SOUTH EAST

BADENOCH, Mr David Fraser

Special interests:	**Stone disease; prostate diseases; male infertility**
NHS:	Consultant Urological Surgeon
	Royal London Hospital
	Whitechapel Road
	London E1 1BB
Tel:	0171 377 7261 or 0171 601 8391
Private:	123 Harley Street
	London W1N 1HE
Tel:	0171 935 3881
Fax:	0171 224 6481
First Qualified:	1975 – Oxford
Major Degrees:	DM, MCh, FRCS
Academic:	Senior Lecturer, London Hospital Medical College
	Honorary Senior Lecturer, St Bartholomew's Hospital Medical School, London
Specialist Training:	London and St Bartholomew's Hospitals, London
Distinctions:	Grand Prix 1988, European Association of Urology
USA:	Surgitek Travelling Fellowship 1987

CARTER, Mr Simon St Clair

Special interests:	**'World expert on minimally invasive treatments for benign prostatic hyperplasia'**
NHS:	Consultant Urologist
	Charing Cross Hospital
	Fulham Palace Road
	London W6 8RF
Tel:	0181 846 1766
Fax:	0181 846 1757
Private:	147 Harley Street
	London W1N 1DL
Tel:	0171 487 4426
Fax:	0171 935 5608
First Qualified:	1976 – London
Major Degrees:	FRCS
Academic:	Lecturer, Institute of Urology, London
Specialist Training:	St Peter's Hospital, London
Distinctions:	Councillor, Clinical Section, Royal Society of Medicine

CHRISTMAS, Mr Timothy

Special interests:	**Genito-urinary cancer, particularly cancer for metastatic carcinoma of the testis, radical prostatectomy for prostate cancer and cystectomy and bladder reconstruction for cancer**
NHS:	Consultant Urological Surgeon
	Charing Cross Hospital
	Fulham Palace Road
	London W6 8RF
Tel:	0181 846 1966
Fax:	0181 846 1757
and:	Chelsea and Westminster Hospital
	369 Fulham Road
	London SW10 9NH
Tel:	0181 746 8000
Fax:	0181 746 8111
Private:	Refer to address and number above
First Qualified:	1980 – London
Major Degrees:	MD, FRCS, FRCS (Urol)
Specialist Training:	Addenbrooke's Hospital, Cambridge, and Royal London, The Middlesex and St Bartholomew's Hospitals, London, and University of Southern California, Los Angeles
USA:	See 'Specialist Training' above

COWIE, Mr Alfred G. A.

Special interests:	**Urological aspects of tropical diseases; tropical surgery**
NHS:	Consultant Urologist
	District General Hospital
	Kings Drive
	Eastbourne BN201 2UD
Tel:	01323 417400 Ext. 4838
Fax:	01323 414954
Private:	Esperance Private Hospital
	Hartington Place
	Eastbourne BN21 3BG
Tel:	01323 410717
Fax:	01323 730313
First Qualified:	1963 – Cambridge
Major Degrees:	FRCS, FICS
Academic:	Previously Honorary Senior Lecturer, Institute of Urology, London
Specialist Training:	Brompton and University College Hospitals, London
Distinctions:	Member, Court of Examiners, Royal College of Surgeons, England

See *FERNANDO, Mr Oswald* under General Surgeons.

HENDRY, Mr William F.

Special interests:	**Male infertility; cancer of the testicles and bladder**
NHS:	Consultant Urological Surgeon
	St Bartholomew's Hospital
	West Smithfield
	London EC1A 7BE
Tel:	0171 601 8888 Ext. 8394
Fax:	0171 601 7560
and:	Royal Marsden Hospital
	Fulham Road
	London SW3 6JJ
Tel:	0171 352 8171
Private:	149 Harley Street
	London W1N 2DE
Tel:	0171 636 7426
Fax:	0171 935 5765
First Qualified:	1961 – Glasgow
Major Degrees:	MD, FRCS Ed, FRCS
Specialist Training:	St Peter's Hospital, London, and Royal Infirmary, Glasgow
Distinctions:	President, Urology Section, Royal Society of Medicine
	Vice-President, British Association of Urological Surgeons
USA:	Assistant Resident, Mallory Institute of Pathology, Boston

KIRBY, Mr Roger S.

Special interests:	**Impotence, reconstruction of male genitals; minimally interventionist surgery of prostate**
NHS:	Consultant Urologist
	St George's Hospital
	Blackshaw Road
	London SW17 0QT
Tel:	0181 672 1255 Ext. 3203 or 0181 725 3203
Fax:	0181 725 2915
Private:	95 Harley Street
	London W1N 1DF
Tel:	0171 935 9720
Fax:	0171 224 5706
First Qualified:	1976 – Cambridge
Major Degrees:	MD, FRCS, FEBU
Specialist Training:	St Thomas' and Middlesex Hospitals, London
Distinctions:	Previously Hunterian Professor, Royal College of Surgeons

---

LLOYD-DAVIES, Mr Reginald Wyndham

Special interests:	**Urological oncology**
NHS:	Senior Consultant Urologist
	St Thomas' Hospital
	Lambeth Palace Road
	London SE1 7EH
Tel:	0171 928 9292
Fax:	0171 922 8354
Private:	53 Harley Street
	London W1N 1DD
Tel:	0171 637 9411
Fax:	0171 636 4596
First Qualified:	1958 – London
Major Degrees:	FRCS, MS, FEBU
Academic:	Fellow, Medical Research Council, St Thomas' Hospital, London
Specialist Training:	St Thomas' Hospital, London
Distinctions:	Consultant Surgeon to the Metropolitan Police
	Previously President, Urology Section, Royal Society of Medicine
USA:	Previously, Research Fellow, San Francisco Medical Centre, University of California

---

MILROY, Mr Euan

Special interests:	**General urology including urine infections, prostate, stones, urological tumours and impotence with particular expertise in new and alternative treatments for prostate disease and urethral strictures, prostate and bladder cancer, urodynamics and urinary incontinence**
NHS:	No NHS urology work
Private:	77 Harley House
	Marylebone Road
	London NW1 5HN
Tel:	0171 486 6886
Fax:	0171 487 4650
First Qualified:	1963 – London
Major Degrees:	FRCS
Academic:	Senior Lecturer, Institute of Urology, London
Specialist Training:	St Mary's Hospital, London, University College of the West Indies, Jamaica, and Department of Urology, University of Rochester, New York State
USA:	See 'Specialist Training' above

MORGAN, Mr Robert J.

Special interests:	**General adult and paediatric urology**
NHS:	Consultant Urological Surgeon
	Royal Free Hospital
	Pond Street
	London NW3 2QG
Tel:	0171 830 2419
Fax:	0171 431 5245
Private:	147 Harley Street
	London W1N 1DL
Tel:	0171 935 4444 Ext. 4067
Fax:	0171 486 3782
First Qualified:	1966 – Oxford
Major Degrees:	FRCS
Specialist Training:	St Peter's Hospitals, London
Distinctions:	Honorary Consultant Urologist, St Luke's Hospital for the Clergy, King Edward VII for Officers and Hospital of St John and St Elizabeth, London

MUNDY, Professor Anthony R.

Special interests:	**Reconstructive urology and treatment of urinary incontinence**
NHS:	Professor of Urology and Consultant Urological Surgeon
	Guy's Hospital
	St Thomas Street
	London SE1 9RT
Tel:	0171 955 5000 Ext. 4659
Fax:	0171 955 4675
Private:	Emblem House
	London Bridge Hospital
	27 Tooley Street
	London SE1 2PR
Tel:	0171 403 1221
Fax:	0171 403 1664
First Qualified:	1971 – London (with Honours)
Major Degrees:	FRCS, MS
Academic:	Professor of Urology, Guy's Hospital United Medical and Dental School and Institute of Urology, London
Specialist Training:	Guy's Hospital, London
Distinctions:	Visiting Consultant, St Luke's Hospital, Malta
	Consultant Surgeon, Force Base Hospital, Muscat, Oman

PACKHAM, Mr Derek A.

Special interests:	**General urology**
NHS:	No NHS work
Private:	Consultant Urologist
	Cromwell Hospital
	18 Pennant Mews
	London W8 5JN
Tel:	0171 935 1286
Fax:	0171 935 1286
First Qualified:	1956 – London
Major Degrees:	FRCS
Specialist Training:	St Peter's and King's College Hospitals, London

PARIS, Mr Andrew M. I.

Special interests:	**General urology**
NHS:	Consultant Urological Surgeon
	Royal London Hospital
	Whitechapel Road
	London E1 1BB
Tel:	0171 377 7262
Fax:	0171 377 7292
Private:	121 Harley Street
	London W1N 1DM
Tel:	0171 486 6324
Fax:	0171 935 5333
First Qualified:	1964 – London
Major Degrees:	FRCS
Specialist Training:	St Peter's and London Hospitals, London
Distinctions:	Fellow and Vice-President, Urology Section,
	Royal Society of Medicine

RAMSAY, Mr Jonathan W. A.

Special interests:	**Minimally invasive and endoscopic treatment of urinary tract stones; treatment of male infertility**
NHS:	Consultant Urologist
	Charing Cross Hospital
	Fulham Palace Road
	London W6 8RF
Tel:	0181 846 1146
Fax:	0181 846 7696
Private:	15th Floor
	Charing Cross Hospital
	Fulham Palace Road
	London W6 8RF
Tel:	0181 846 7669
Fax:	0181 846 7696
and:	149 Harley Street
	London W1N 1HG
Tel:	0171 935 4444
First Qualified:	1977 – London
Major Degrees:	FRCS
Specialist Training:	St Paul's and St Bartholomew's Hospitals, London
Distinctions:	President, Clinical Section, Royal Society of Medicine

SHEARER, Mr Robert J.

Special interests:	**Bladder cancer; prostate cancer**
NHS:	Consultant Urologist
	Royal Marsden Hospital
	Fulham Road
	London SW3 6JJ
Tel:	0171 352 8171 Ext. 2788
Fax:	0171 376 7163
Private:	Consultant Urologist
	Parkside Hospital
	53 Parkside
	Wimbledon, London SW19 5NX
Tel:	0181 946 4202
Fax:	0181 946 7775
and:	Royal Marsden Hospital
	Fulham Road
	London SW3 6JJ
Tel:	0171 351 2166
Fax:	0171 376 5424
First Qualified:	1962 – London
Major Degrees:	FRCS
Academic:	Senior Lecturer, Institute of Cancer Research, London
Specialist Training:	St Peter's and Royal Marsden Hospitals, London
Distinctions:	Member (Immediate Past Chairman), MRC Prostate Cancer Working Party
	Previously Chairman, British Prostate Group

TIPTAFT, Mr Richard C.

Special interests:	**The urinary tract, including cancer**
NHS:	Consultant Urologist and Director of Stone Surgery
	St Thomas' Hospital
	Lambeth Palace Road
	London SE1 7EH
Tel:	0171 922 8012
Fax:	0171 928 8454
Private:	134 Harley Street
	London W1N 1AH
Tel:	0171 935 0711
Fax:	0171 486 1042
First Qualified:	1972 – London
Major Degrees:	FRCS
Specialist Training:	Royal London Hospital
USA:	Previously Resident Urologist, Yale University Medical Centre

WHITFIELD, Mr Hugh N.

Special interests:	**Minimally invasive treatment of urinary tract stones; laser prostatectomy**
NHS:	Director Stone Unit, Institute of Urology Middlesex Hospital Mortimer Street London W1N 8AA
Tel:	0171 380 9372
Fax:	0171 637 7076
and:	Consultant Urologist Central Middlesex Hospital Acton Lane, Park Royal London NW10 7NS
Tel:	0181 965 5733
Fax:	0181 453 2439
Private:	43 Wimpole Street London W1M 7AF
Tel:	0171 935 3095
Fax:	0171 935 3147
First Qualified:	1969 – Cambridge
Major Degrees:	FRCS, MS
Specialist Training:	Institute of Urology and St Bartholomew's Hospitals, London
Distinctions:	Honorary Consultant Urologist, St Mark's Hospital, Northwick Park, Middlesex

WILLIAMS, Mr Gordon J.

Special interests:	**Urological cancers; impotence; renal transplantation**
NHS:	Consultant Urological Surgeon Urological and Transplantation Unit Hammersmith Hospital Du Cane Road London W12 0HS
Tel:	0181 740 3218
Fax:	0181 740 3443
Private:	Refer to address and number above
First Qualified:	1968 – London
Major Degrees:	FRCS, MS
Specialist Training:	Hammersmith Hospital, London, and Norfolk and Norwich Hospital, Norwich
Distinctions:	Co-Editor, Urological Oncology

WITHEROW, Mr Ross O'N.

Special interests:	**General urology; prostastic disease; impotence**
NHS:	Consultant Urologist
	St Mary's Hospital
	Praed Street
	London W2 1NY
Tel:	0171 725 1033
Fax:	0141 725 1546
Private:	26 Harmont House
	20 Harley Street
	London W1N 1AN
Tel:	0171 935 1252
Fax:	0171 637 5373
First Qualified:	1968 – London
Major Degrees:	FRCS, MS
Academic:	Senior Clinical Lecturer, London University
Specialist Training:	St Peter's and Royal London Hospitals, London
USA:	Research Fellow in Urology, San Francisco Medical Centre, California University

WOODHOUSE, Mr Christopher

Special interests:	**Cancer of the bladder, kidney and prostate; reconstructive urology**
NHS:	Consultant Urologist
	Royal Marsden Hospital
	Fulham Road
	London SW3 6JJ
Tel:	0171 352 8171 Ext. 2789
Fax:	0171 376 5425
and:	Middlesex Hospital
	Mortimer Street
	London W1N 8AA
Tel:	0171 380 3210
Fax:	0171 637 7076
Private:	Lister Hospital
	Chelsea Bridge Road
	London SW1W 8RH
Tel:	0171 730 6204
Fax:	0171 730 6204
First Qualified:	1970 – London
Major Degrees:	FRCS
Academic:	Senior Lecturer, Institute of Urology, London
Specialist Training:	St Peter's and Royal London Hospitals, London
Distinctions:	Honorary Consultant, Institute of Urology and Great Ormond Street Hospital for Children, London

WORTH, Mr Peter

Special interests:	**Incontinence**
NHS:	Consultant Urological Surgeon
	The Middlesex Hospital
	Mortimer Street
	London W1N 8AA
Tel:	0171 380 9339
Fax:	0171 380 9062
Private:	31 Wimpole Street
	London W1M 7AE
Tel:	0171 935 3593
Fax:	0171 224 1957
First Qualified:	1961 – London
Major Degrees:	FRCS
Academic:	Senior Lecturer, Institute of Urology, London
Specialist Training:	St Paul's and The Middlesex Hospitals, London

ANGLIA AND OXFORD REGION

READING

PENGELLY, Mr Andrew W.

Special interests:	**Treatment of incontinence of urine; prostatic disorders**
NHS:	Consultant Urologist
	Battle Hospital
	Oxford Road
	Reading, Berks RG3 1AG
Tel:	01734 583666
Fax:	01734 878706
Private:	72 Berkeley Avenue
	Reading, Berks RG1 6HY
Tel:	01734 584711
Fax:	01734 588110
First Qualified:	1969 – Oxford
Major Degrees:	FRCS, FEBU
Specialist Training:	The Middlesex Hospital, London

NORTH WEST REGION

MANCHESTER

GEORGE, Mr Nicholas J. R.

NHS:	Consultant Urologist
	Department of Urology
	University Hospital of South Manchester
	Nell Lane
	West Didsbury
	Manchester M20 8LR
Tel:	0161 447 3766
Fax:	0161 447 3767
Private:	Refer to address and number above
First Qualified:	1970 – London
Major Degrees:	MD, FRCS
Academic:	Senior Lecturer, Manchester University

NORTHERN AND YORKSHIRE REGION

NEWCASTLE

HALL, Dr Reginald R.

Special interests:	**Urological oncology**
NHS:	Consultant Urologist
	Freeman Hospital
	High Heaton
	Newcastle upon Tyne NE7 7DN
Tel:	0191 284 3111 Ext. 26138
Fax:	0191 213 0205
Private:	Refer to address and number above
First Qualified:	1962 – London
Major Degrees:	FRCS, MS
Academic:	Senior Lecturer, Newcastle University
Distinctions:	Chairman, European Organisation for Research and Treatment of Genito-urinary Cancer Group; Previously Vandervell Research Fellow, Institute of Cancer Research; Honorary Senior Registrar, Royal Marsden Hospital, London; Tudor Edwards Research Fellow, Department of Surgery, Royal College of Surgeons

RAMSDEN, Mr Peter David

NHS:	Consultant Urologist
	Freeman Hospital
	High Heaton
	Newcastle upon Tyne NE7 7DN
Tel:	0191 284 3111
Fax:	0191 213 0205
Private:	Refer to address and number above
First Qualified:	1968 – London
Major Degrees:	FRCS

SOUTH AND WEST REGION

BRISTOL

FENELEY, Mr Roger C. L.

Special interests:	**Urinary incontinence**
NHS:	Consultant Urologist
	Bristol Royal Infirmary
	Marlborough Street
	Bristol BS2 8HW
Tel:	0117 923 0000 Ext. 2364
Fax:	0117 928 2000
Private:	Refer to address and number above
First Qualified:	1958 – Cambridge
Major Degrees:	FRCS
Academic:	Senior Clinical Lecturer, Bristol University
Specialist Training:	Bristol Royal Infirmary

WINCHESTER

ADAMSON, Mr Andrew S.

Special interests:	**Uro-oncology; incontinence; bladder outflow obstruction**
NHS:	Consultant Urologist
	Royal Hampshire County Hospital
	Romsey Road
	Winchester
	Hampshire SO23
Tel:	01962 825287
Fax:	01962 824640
Private:	Sarum Road Hospital
	Sarum Road
	Winchester SO23 5HA
Tel:	01962 840142
Fax:	01962 840142
First Qualified:	1983 – London
Major Degrees:	MS, FRCS
Academic:	Lecturer, Southampton University
Specialist Training:	King's College and St Mary's Hospitals, London, and Eastbourne Hospitals
Distinctions:	Rhone–Poulenc Prize Winner, Association of Surgeons in Training 1993; NATO Research Grant; Royal College of Surgeons Research Grant.
USA:	North West Memorial Hospital, Chicago; Research in Prostate Cancer, Notre Dame University, Indiana, and Mayo Clinic, Rochester, Minnesota

TRENT REGION

DERBY

CHILTON, Mr Christopher Paul

NHS:	Consultant Urologist
	Derby City General Hospital
	Uttoxeter Road
	Derby DE22 2NE
Tel:	01332 340131
Fax:	01332 290559
Private:	Refer to address and number above
First Qualified:	1971 – London
Major Degrees:	FRCS
Specialist Training:	St Peter's Hospital, London
Distinctions:	Hunterian Professor, Royal College of Surgeons

MUNSON, Mr Kenneth

NHS:	Consultant Urologist
	Derby City General Hospital
	Uttoxeter Road
	Derby DE22 2NE
Tel:	01332 340131
Fax:	01332 290559
Private:	Refer to address and number above
First Qualified:	1965 – London
Major Degrees:	FRCS
Specialist Training:	King's College Hospital, London

SCOTLAND

EDINBURGH

HARGREAVE, Mr Timothy Bruce

Special interests:	**Prostate disease; renal cancer; cancer of the testes; impotence; male infertility**
NHS:	Consultant, Urology and Renal Transplant
	Western General Hospital
	Crewe Road
	Edinburgh EH4 2XU
Tel:	0131 537 1580
Fax:	0131 537 1019
Private:	Murrayfield Hospital
	122 Corstorphine Road
	Edinburgh EH12 6UD
Tel:	0131 334 0363
Fax:	0131 334 7338
First Qualified:	1967 – London
Major Degrees:	MS, FRCS, FRCS Ed
Academic:	Part-time Senior Lecturer, Edinburgh University
Specialist Training:	Western Infirmary, Glasgow, and University College Hospital, London
Distinctions:	Member, Scientific and Ethical review group Human Reproduction Programme, World Health Organisation
	Member, Prostate Guidelines Group, British Association of Urology Surgeons

GLASGOW

DEANE, Mr Robert Fletcher

Special interests:	**Bladder disease surgery; bladder cancer**
NHS:	Consultant Urologist
	Western Infirmary
	Glasgow G11 6NT
Tel:	0141 211 2000
Fax:	0141 337 6010
Private:	Refer to address and number above
First Qualified:	1962 – Glasgow
Major Degrees:	FRCS Glas, FRCS Ed

KIRK, Professor David

Special interests:	**Prostatic cancer**
NHS:	Consultant Urologist
	Western Infirmary
	Glasgow G11 6NT
Tel:	0141 211 2000
Fax:	0141 337 6010
Private:	Refer to address and number above
First Qualified:	1968 – Oxford
Major Degrees:	DM, FRCS
Academic:	Honorary Clinical Lecturer, Glasgow University
	Arris and Gale Lecturer, Royal College of Surgeons
Specialist Training:	Sheffield University; Royal Infirmary and Children's
	Hospital, Sheffield
Distinctions:	Chairman, Intercollegiate Board in Urology
	Previously Councillor, Urology Section, Royal Society of
	Medicine

APPENDIX 1

(i) TOP CANCER UNITS

Recent advances in the fight against cancer have been supported by the development of 'Centres of Excellence' throughout the UK. This section lists such centres.

Cancer diagnosis and treatment involves complex and expensive technology as well as specialist services drawing on a number of different disciplines which cannot be provided in all major hospitals. Cross-fertilization of such disciplines working together in specialist centres maximises the chances for a patient's survival. It has been estimated that the survival rate of patients treated at these specialist centres could increase by as much as 10% and at present around 16,000 lives a year could be saved if the quality of cancer services was consistently high and the best treatment applied to all.

The following list of centres are all equipped with full radiotherapy equipment; day care chemotherapy; counselling; nurse specialists; active research programmes; tumour site specialization; medical oncologists.

LONDON AND THE SOUTH EAST

	TEL	FAX
Charing Cross Hospital, Fulham Palace Road, London W6 8RF	0181 846 1234	0181 846 1111
Guy's Hospital, St Thomas Street, London SE1 9RT	0171 955 5000	0171 955 4939
Hammersmith Hospital NHS Trust, 150 Du Cane Road, London W12 0HS	0181 743 2030	0181 740 3212
Middlesex Hospital, Mortimer Street, London W1N 8AA	0171 636 8333	0171 436 0160
Royal Marsden Hospital, Fulham Road, London SW3 6JJ	0171 352 8171	0171 351 3785
Royal Marsden Hospital, Downs Road, Sutton, Surrey SM2 5PT	0181 642 6011	0181 770 9297
St Bartholomew's Hospital, West Smithfield, London EC1A 7BE	0171 601 8888	0171 796 3979
St Luke's Hospital, Warren Road, Guildford, Surrey GU2 5XX	01483 571122	01483 39106
St Thomas' Hospital, Lambeth Palace Road, London SE1 7EH	0171 928 9292	0171 922 8079
Mid Kent Oncology Centre, Maidstone Hospital, Hermitage Lane, Maidstone, Kent ME16 9QQ	01622 729000	01622 721303
Mount Vernon Hospital, Rickmansworth Road, Northwood, Middlesex HA6 2RN	01923 844469	01923 835803
Kent & Canterbury Hospital, Ethelbert Road, Canterbury, Kent CT1 3NG	01227 766877	01227 783095

* Denotes independent hospitals

ANGLIA AND OXFORD REGION

	TEL	FAX
Addenbrooke's Hospital, Hills Road, Cambridge CB2 2QQ	01223 245151	01223 217094
Churchill Hospital, Headington, Oxon OX3 7LJ	01865 741841	01865 225660

NORTH WEST REGION

Christie Hospital, Wilmslow Road, Withington, Manchester M20 9BX	0161 446 3000	0161 446 3977
Clatterbridge Centre for Oncology, Clatterbridge Road, Bebington, Wirral L63 4JY	0151 334 1155	0151 334 0882

NORTHERN AND YORKSHIRE REGION

St James University Hospital, Beckett Street, Leeds, West Yorkshire LS9 7TF	01132 602528	01132 426496
Newcastle General Hospital, Westgate Road, Newcastle upon Tyne NE4 6BE	0191 273 8811	0191 272 4236

SOUTH AND WEST REGION

Bristol Oncology Centre, Horfield Road, Bristol, Avon BS2 8ED	0117 923 0000	0117 928 5329
Southampton General Hospital, Tremona Road, Southampton SO16 6YD	01703 634288	01703 825441

TRENT REGION

University Hospital, Queen's Medical Centre, Nottingham NG7 2UH	0115 942 1421	01602 709196
Weston Park Hospital, Whitham Road, Sheffield S10 2SJ	0114 267 022	0114 268 4193

WEST MIDLANDS

Queen Elizabeth Hospital, Edgbaston, Birmingham B12 2TH	0121 472 1311	0121 627 2026

SCOTLAND

	TEL	FAX
Ninewells Hospital, Ninewells, Dundee, DD1 9SY	01382 660111	01382 632885
Western General Hospital, Crewe Road, Edinburgh, Lothian EH4 2XU	0131 537 1000	0131 537 1007
Western Infirmary, Dumbarton Road, Glasgow G11 6NT	0141 211 2000	0141 357 4732

WALES

	TEL	FAX
Velindre Hospital, Whitchurch, Cardiff, South Glamorgan CF4 7XL	01222 615888	01222 522694

NORTHERN IRELAND

	TEL	FAX
Belvoir Park Hospital, Hospital Road, Belfast, Co. Antrim BT8 8JR	01232 491942	01232 492554

PAEDIATRIC ONCOLOGY CENTRES

LONDON AND THE SOUTH EAST

	TEL	FAX
Great Ormond Street Hospital for Children, Great Ormond Street, London WC1N 3JH	0171 405 9200	0171 829 8643
Royal Marsden Hospital, Downs Road, Sutton, Surrey SM2 5PT	0181 642 6011	0181 770 9297
St Bartholomew's Hospital, West Smithfield, London EC1A 7BE	0171 601 8888	0171 796 3979
University College London, Mortimer Street, London W1N 8AA	0171 387 9300	0171 380 9977

ANGLIA AND OXFORD REGION

	TEL	FAX
Addenbrooke's Hospital, Hills Road, Cambridge CB2 2QQ	01223 245151	01223 216149
John Radcliffe, Headington, Oxford OX3 9DU	01865 741166	01865 741408

NORTH WEST REGION

	TEL	FAX
Alder Hey Children's Hospital, Eaton Road, Liverpool L12 2AP	0151 228 4811	0151 228 0328
Royal Manchester Children's Hospital, Pendelbury, Manchester M27 1HA	0161 794 4696	0161 994 5929

NORTHERN AND YORKSHIRE REGION

	TEL	FAX
St James's University Hospital, Beckett Street, Leeds, West Yorkshire LS9 7TF	01132 602528	01132 426496
Royal Victoria Infirmary, Queen Victoria Road, Newcastle upon Tyne NE1 4LP	0191 232 5131	0191 201 0155

SOUTH AND WEST REGION

Royal Hospital for Sick Children, St Michael's Hill, Bristol BS2 8BJ	0117 921 5411	0117 928 5820
Southampton General Hospital, Tremona Road, Southampton SO16 6YD	01703 777222	01703 783839

TRENT REGION

Leicester Royal Infirmary, Infirmary Square, Leicester LE1 5WW	0116 254 1414	0116 258 5631
Sheffield Children's Hospital, Western Bank, Sheffield S10 2TH	0114 271 7000	0114 272 3418
University Hospital, Queen's Medical Centre, Nottingham NG7 2UH	0115 924 9924	0115 970 9196

WEST MIDLANDS

Birmingham Children's Hospital, Ladywood Middleway, Birmingham B16 8ET	0121 454 4851	0121 456 4697

SCOTLAND

Royal Aberdeen Children's Hospital, Cornhill Road, Aberdeen AB9 2ZB	01224 681818	01224 840597
Royal Hospital for Sick Children, Millerfield Place, Edinburgh EH9 1LF	0131 536 0421	0131 536 0001
Royal Hospital for Sick Children, Yorkhill, Glasgow G3 8SJ	0141 339 8888	0141 201 0836

WALES

Llandough Hospital, Llandough, Nr Penarth, South Glamorgan DF6 1XX	01222 711711	01222 708973

NORTHERN IRELAND

Royal Hospital for Sick Children, 180 Falls Road, Belfast BT 6BE	01232 240503	01232 240899

(ii)SPECIALIST CARDIAC UNITS – LONDON

LONDON AND THE SOUTH EAST

	TEL	FAX
Cromwell Hospital, Cromwell Road, London SW5 0TU*	0171 370 4233	0171 460 5555
Guy's Nuffield House, Newcomen Street, London SE1 1YR*	0171 955 4257	0171 955 4754
Harefield Hospital, Harefield, Uxbridge, Middlesex UB9 6JH	01895 823737	01895 822870
Harley Street Clinic (The), 35 Weymouth Street, London W1N 4BJ*	0171 935 7700	0171 487 4415
London Bridge Hospital, 27 Tooley Street, London SE1 2PR*	0171 407 3100	0171 407 3162
London Chest Hospital, Bonner Road, London E2 9JX	0181 980 4433	0181 983 2402
Royal Brompton Hospital, Sydney Street, London SW3 6NB	0171 352 8121	0171 351 8473
St Anthony's Hospital, London Road, North Cheam, Sutton, Surrey SM3 9DW*	0181 337 6691	0181 335 3325
Wellington Hospital, 8a Wellington Place, London NW8 9LE*	0171 586 5959	0171 586 1960

The National Heart Hospital, a specialist heart hospital, was not operational at the time of going to press.

(iii) CHILDREN'S HOSPITALS

LONDON AND THE SOUTH EAST

	TEL	FAX
Great Ormond Street Hospital for Children, Great Ormond Street, London WC1N 3JH	0171 405 9200	0171 829 8643
Portland Hospital (The), 209 Great Portland St., London W1N 6AH*	0171 580 4400	0171 631 1170
Queen Charlotte's Hospital, Goldhawk Road, London W6 0XG	0181 748 4666	0181 740 3588
Queen Elizabeth Hospital for Children, Hackney Road, Bethnal Green, London E2 8PS	0171 739 8422	0171 608 6399
Queen Mary's Hospital for Children, Hackney Road, Bethnal Green, London E2 8PS	0171 739 8422	0171 608 6399
Royal Alexandra Hospital for Sick Children, Dyke Road, Brighton BN1 3JN	01273 328145	01273 736685
Tadworth Court Children's Hospital, Wexham Street, Slough SL3 6NH	01737 357171	01737 373848

ANGLIA AND OXFORD REGION

	TEL	FAX
Park Hospital for Children, Old Road, Headington, Oxford OX3 7LQ	01865 741717	01865 226276

NORTH WEST REGION

Alder Hey Children's Hospital, Eaton Road, Liverpool L12 2AP	0151 228 4811	0151 228 0328
Booth Hall Children's Hospital, Charlestown Road, Blackley, Manchester M9 2AA	0161 795 7000	0161 741 5387
Derby Children's Hospital, North Steeet, Derby DE1 3BA	01332 340131	01332 200857
Royal Liverpool Children's Hospital, Eaton Rd, West Derby, Liverpool LP12 2AP	0151 252 5695	0151 228 0328
Royal Manchester Children's Hospital, Pendelbury, Manchester M27 1HA	0161 794 4696	0161 994 5929
St Mary's Hospital for Women and Children, Hathersage Road, Manchester M13 0JH	0161 276 1234	0161 276 6107

SOUTH AND WEST REGION

Marlborough Children's Hospital, Okus Road, Swindon SN1 4JU	01793 536231	01793 480817
Royal Hospital for Sick Children, St Michael's Hill, Bristol BS2 8BJ	0117 921 5411	0117 928 5820

TRENT REGION

Sheffield Children's Hospital, Western Bank, Sheffield S10 2TH	0114 271 7000	0114 272 3418

WEST MIDLANDS

Birmingham Children's Hospital, Ladywood Middleway, Birmingham B16 8ET	0121 454 4851	0121 456 4697

SCOTLAND

Royal Aberdeen Children's Hospital, Cornhill Road, Aberdeen AB9 2ZA	01224 681818	01224 840704
Royal Hospital for Sick Children, Yorkhill, Glasgow G3 8SJ	0141 201 0000	0141 201 0836

(iv) SPECIALIST BURNS and PLASTIC SURGERY UNITS

LONDON AND THE SOUTH EAST

	TEL	FAX
Belverdere Private Clinic, Knee Hill, Abbeywood, London SE2 0AT	0181 311 4464	0181 311 8249
Charing Cross Hospital, Fulham Palace Road, London W6 8RF	0181 846 1234	0181 846 1111
Great Ormond Street Hospital for Children, Great Ormond Street, London WC1N 3JH	0171 405 9200	0171 829 8643
Harley Street Clinic (The), 35 Weymouth Street, London W1N 4BJ*	0171 935 7700	0171 487 4415
Mount Vernon Hospital, Rickmansworth Road, Northwood, Middlesex HA6 2RN	01923 826111	01923 835803
Queen Mary's University Hospital, Roehampton, London SW15 5PN	0181 789 6611	0181 788 8417
Queen Victoria Hospital, Holtye Road, East Grinstead, West Sussex RH19 3DZ	01342 410210	01342 317907
Royal London Hospital, Whitechapel, London E1 1BB	0171 377 7000	0171 377 7666
St Andrew's Hospital Hospital, Stock Road, Billericay, Essex, CM12 0BH	01277 622611	01268 594137
St Thomas' Hospital, Lambeth Palace Road, London SE1 7EH	0171 928 9292	0171 922 8079
Wellington Hospital, 8a Wellington Place, London NW8 9LE *	0171 586 5959	0171 586 1960

ANGLIA AND OXFORD REGION

Addenbrooke's Hospital, Hills Road, Cambridge CB2 2QQ	01223 245151	01223 217094
Radcliffe Infirmary, Woodstock Road, Oxford OX2 6HE	01865 311188	01865 311673
Stoke Mandeville Hospital, Mandeville Road, Aylesbury, Bucks, HP21 8AL	01296 315000	01296 315183
West Norwich Hospital, Bowthorpe Road, Norwich NR2 3TU	01603 286286	01603 288545
Wexham Park Hospital, Slough, Berkshire SL2 4HL	01753 633000	01753 691343

NORTH WEST REGION

	TEL	FAX
Royal Preston Hospital, Sharoe Green Lane North, Fulwood, Preston, Lancashire PR2 4HT	01772 716565	01772 710162
Whiston Hospital, Whiston, Prescot, Merseyside L35 5DR	0151 426 1600	0151 430 1855
Withington Hospital, West Didsbury, Manchester M20 2LR	0161 445 8111	0161 445 5631

NORTHERN AND YORKSHIRE REGION

Bradford Royal Infirmary, Duckworth Lane, Bradford BD9 6RJ	01274 542200	01274 364026
Kingston General Hospital, Beverley Road, Hull HU3 1UR	01482 28631	01482 589002
Leeds General Infirmary, Great George Street, Leeds LS1 3EX	0113 243 2799	0113 292 6336
Middlesbrough General Hospital, Green Lane, Middlesbrough TS5 5AZ	01642 850222	01642 854136
Pinderfields General Hospital, Aberford Road, West Yorkshire WF1 4DF	01924 201688	01924 814864
Royal Victoria Infirmary, Queen Victoria Road, Newcastle upon Tyne NE1 4LP	0191 227 5002	0191 201 0155

SOUTH AND WEST REGION

Derriford Hospital, Derriford Road, Plymouth PL6 8DH	01752 777111	01752 768976
Frenchay Hospital, Frenchay Park Road, Bristol BS16 1LE	0117 970 1212	0117 975 3761
New Hall Hospital, Bodenham, Salisbury SP5 4EY*	01722 422333	01722 435158
Royal Devon and Exeter Hospital Wonford, Barrack Road, Exeter, Devon EX2 5DW	01392 402632	01392 402820
Salisbury District Hospital, Salisbury, Wiltshire SP2 8BJ	01722 336262	01722 330221

TRENT REGION

Leicester Royal Infirmary, Infirmary Square, Leicester LE1 5WW	0116 254 1414	0116 258 5631
Northern General Hospital, Herries Road, Sheffield S5 7AU	0114 243 4343	0114 256 0472
Nottingham City Hospital, Hucknall Road, Nottingham NG5 1PB	0115 969 1169	0115 962 7788

WEST MIDLANDS

	TEL	FAX
George Eliot Hospital, College Street, Nuneaton, Warks CV10 7BL	01203 351351	01203 865058
Selly Oak Hospital, Raddlebarn Road, Birmingham B29 6JD	0121 236 8611	0121 233 2189
Wordsley Hospital, Near Stourbridge, DY8 5QX	01384 401401	01384 244436

SCOTLAND

Aberdeen Royal Infirmary, Foresterhill, Aberdeen AB9 2ZB	01224 681818	01224 840582
Dundee Royal, Barrack Rd, Dundee DD1 9ND	01382 660111	01382 660445
Canniesburn Hospital, Glasgow G61 1QL	0141 211 5600	0141 211 5652
St John's Hospital at Howden, Howden West Road, Livingston, West Lothian EH54 6PP	01506 419666	01506 416484

WALES

Morriston Hospital, Swansea, West Glamorgan SA6 6NL	01792 702222	01792 796907

(v) SPECIALIST HIV/AIDS UNITS

LONDON AND THE SOUTH EAST

	TEL	FAX
Kobler Centre, Chelsea and Westminster Hospital, 369 Fulham Road, London SW10 9NH	0181 846 6161	0181 746 8111
Ealing Hospital, Uxbridge Road, Southall, Middlesex UB1 3HW	0181 967 5555	0181 967 5552
Royal Free Hospital, Pond Street, London NW3 2QG	0171 794 0500	0171 830 2468
Harrison Wing, St Thomas' Hospital, Lambeth Palace Road, London SE1 7EH	0171 928 9292	0171 922 8079
Kent & Canterbury Hospital, Ethelbert Road, Canterbury, Kent CT1 3NG	01227 766877	01227 783017
St George's Hospital, Blackshaw Road, London SW17 0QT	0181 672 1255	0181 672 5304
St Mary's Hospital, Praed Street, London W2 1NY	0171 725 6666	0171 725 6200
Middlesex Hospital (The), Mortimer Street, London W1N 8AA	0171 636 8333	0171 380 9205

ANGLIA AND OXFORD REGION

	TEL	FAX
John Warin Ward, Churchill Hospital, Headington, Oxford OX3 7LJ	01865 225218	01865 225219

NORTH WEST REGION

	TEL	FAX
Royal Liverpool Hospital, Prescot Street, Liverpool L7 8XP	0151 706 2000	0151 706 5806
Fazakerley Hospital, Longmoor Lane, Liverpool L9 7AL	0151 525 3622	0151 252 6086
North Manchester General Hospital, Delaunays Road, Crumpsall, Manchester M8 5RB	0161 795 4567	0161 740 4450

SCOTLAND

	TEL	FAX
King's Cross Hospital Immunodeficiency Unit, Clepington Road, Dundee DD3 8EA	01382 596951	01382 816178
Edinburgh Royal Infirmary, 1 Lauriston Place, Edinburgh EH3 9YW	0131 536 6404	0131 452 9720
Ruchill Hospital, Bilsland Drive, Glasgow G20 9NB	0141 946 7120	0141 946 7094

(vi) SPECIALIST PSYCHIATRY and PSYCHOTHERAPY UNITS

LONDON AND THE SOUTH EAST

	TEL	FAX
Bethlem Royal Hospital, Monks Orchard Rd., Beckenham, Kent BR3 3BX	0181 777 6611	0181 777 1668
Charter Clinic Chelsea, 1–5 Radnor Walk, London SW3 4PB *	0171 351 1272	0171 351 7098
Charter Nightingale Hospital, 11-19 Lisson Grove, London NW1 6SH *	0171 258 3828	0171 724 8294
Institute of Psychiatry, De Crespigny Park, Denmark Hill, London SE5 8AF	0171 703 5411	0171 277 1586
Maudesley Hospital, Denmark Hill, London SE5 8AZ	0171 703 6333	0171 919 2171
Portman Clinic, 8 Fitzjohn's Avenue, London NW3 5NA	0171 794 8262	0171 447 3748
Priory Hospital (The), Priory Lane, Roehampton Hospital, London SW15 5JJ	0181 876 8261	0181 392 2632
St Ann's Hospital, St Ann's Road, South Tottenham, London N15 3TH	0181 442 6000	0181 442 6567
Tavistock Clinic, 120 Belsize Lane, London NW3 5BA	0171 435 7111	0171 435 8855

ANGLIA AND OXFORD REGION

	TEL	FAX
Broadmoor Hospital, Crowthorne, Berks RG11 7EG	01344 773111	01344 754179
Eldon Day Hospital, Reading RG1 4DL	01734 586885	01734 561226
FairMile Hospital, Cholsey Wallingford, Oxfordshire OX10 9HH	01491 651281	01491 651128
Fulbourn Hospital, Robinson Way, Cambridge CB2 5EF	01223 248074	01223 410471
Prospect Park Hospital, Honey End Lane, Tilehurst, Reading RG3 4EJ	01734 586161	01734 591135

NORTH WEST REGION

Ashworth Hospital North and South, Maghull, Liverpool L31 1HW	0151 473 0303	0151 526 6603

SOUTH AND WEST REGION

Broadreach House, 465 Tavistock Road, Plymouth PL6 7HE *	01752 790000	01752 785750
Broadway Lodge, Totterdown Lane, off Oldmixon Rd, Weston Super Mare, Avon BS24 9NN *	01934 815515	01934 815381
Clouds House, East Knoyle, Salisbury, Wiltshire SP3 6BE *	01747 830733	01747 830783

TRENT REGION

Rampton Hospital, Retford, Nottingham DN22 OPD	01777 248321	01777 247316

WEST MIDLANDS

Parkview Clinic, 60 Queensbridge Road, Mosley, Birmingham B13 8QE	0121 243 2000	0121 243 2010
Queen Elizabeth Psychiatric Hospital, Mindelsohn Way, Edgbaston, Birmingham B15 2QZ	0121 627 2999	0121 627 2810
Reaside Clinic, Bristol Road South, Rednall, Birmingham B45 9BD	0121 453 3771	0121 452 7181
Uffculme Clinic, Queensbridge, Birmingham B13 8BQ	0121 442 4545	0121 442 4541

SCOTLAND

	TEL	FAX
Gartnavel Royal Hospital, 1055 Great Western Road, Glasgow G12 0XH	0141 211 3600	0141 337 2408

WALES

Whitchurch Hospital, Whitchurch, Cardiff, South Glamorgan CF4 7XB	01222 693191	01222 614799

APPENDIX 2

HOSPITAL DIRECTORY

LONDON AND THE SOUTH EAST

	TEL	FAX
Atkinson Morley's Hospital, 31 Copse Hill, London SW20 0NE	0181 946 7711	0181 947 8389
Barnet General Hospital, Wellhouse Lane, Barnet, Hertfordshire EN5 3DJ	0181 440 5111	0181 732 4353
Bethlem Royal Hospital, Monks Orchard Rd., Beckenham, Kent BR3 3BX	0181 777 6611	0181 777 1668
Bromley Hospital, 17 Cromwell Avenue, Bromley Kent BR2 9AJ	0181 289 7000	0181 289 7127
BUPA Hospital, Heathbourne Road, Bushey, Herts WD2 1RD*	0181 950 9090	0181 950 7556
Central Middlesex Hospital, Acton Lane, Park Royal, London NW10 7NS	0181 965 5733	0181 961 0012
Charing Cross Hospital, Fulham Palace Road, London W6 8RF	0181 846 1234	0181 846 1773
Charter Clinic Chelsea, 1–5 Radnor Walk, London SW3 4PB*	0171 351 1272	0171 351 7098
Charter Nightingale Hospital, 11–19 Lisson Grove, London NW1 6SH*	0171 258 3828	0171 724 8294
Chase Farm Hospital, The Ridgeway, Enfield, Middlesex EN2 8JL	0181 366 6600	0181 363 3485
Chelsea and Westminster Hospital, 369 Fulham Road, London SW10 9NH	0181 746 8000	0181 746 8111
Churchill Clinic, 80 Lambeth Road, London SE1 7PW*	0171 928 5633	0171 928 1702
Clementine Churchill Hospital (The), Sudbury Hill, Harrow, Middlesex HA1 3RX*	0181 422 3464	0181 864 1747
Cromwell Hospital, Cromwell Road, London SW5 0TU*	0171 370 4233	0171 460 5555
Edgware General Hospital, Edgware, Middlesex HA8 0AD	0181 952 2381	0181 732 6615
Epsom General Hospital, Dorking Rd, Epsom, Surrey KT18 7EG	01372 735735	01372 735159
Great Ormond Street Hospital for Children, Great Ormond Street, London WC1N 3JH	0171 405 9200	0171 829 8643
Guy's Hospital, St Thomas Street, London SE1 9RT	0171 955 5000	0171 955 4844

LONDON AND THE SOUTH EAST *contd*

	TEL	FAX
Hackney Hospital, Homerton High Street, London E9 6BE	0181 919 5555	0181 919 7777
Hammersmith Hospital, 150 Du Cane Road, London W12 0HS	0181 743 2030	0181 740 3212
Harefield Hospital, Harefield, Uxbridge, Middlesex UB9 6JH	01895 823737	01895 822870
Harley Street Clinic (The), 35 Weymouth Street, London W1N 4BJ*	0171 935 7700	0171 487 4415
Hillingdon Hospital, Pield Health Road, Uxbridge, Middlesex UB8 2NN	01895 238282	01895 811687
Hospital of St John & St Elizabeth, 60 Grove End Road, St John's Wood, London NW8 9NH*	0171 286 5126	0171 266 4813
Holly House Hospital, High Road, Buckhurst Hill, Essex IG9 5HX*	0181 505 3311	0181 506 1013
Hospital for Tropical Diseases, 4 St Pancras Way, London NW1 0PE	0171 530 3500	0171 388 7645
Kent & Canterbury Hospital, Ethelbert Road, Canterbury, Kent CT1 3NG	01227 766877	01227 783017
King's College Hospital, Denmark Hill, London SE5 9RS	0171 737 4000	0171 346 3445
King Edward VII Hospital For Officers, Beaumont Street, London W1N 2AA*	0171 486 4411	0171 935 6770
Kingston Hospital, Galsworthy Road, Kingston upon Thames, Surrey	0181 546 7711	0181 547 2182
Lewisham Hospital, High Street, Lewisham, London SW13 6LH	0181 333 3000	0181 333 3333
London Bridge Hospital, 27 Tooley Street, London SE1 2PR*	0171 407 3100	0171 407 3162
London Chest Hospital, Bonner Road, London E2 9JX	0181 980 4433	0181 983 2402
London Clinic (The), 20 Devonshire Place, London W1N 2DH*	0171 935 4444	0171 486 3782
London Independent Hospital, 1 Beaumont Square, Stepney Green, London E1 4NL*	0171 790 0990	0171 265 9032
Lister Hospital, Chelsea Bridge Road, London SW1W 8RH*	0171 730 3417	0171 824 8867
Maidstone Hospital, Hermitage Lane, Maidstone, Kent ME16 9QQ	01622 729000	01622 720807
Maudesley Hospital, Denmark Hill, London SE5 8AZ	0171 703 6333	0171 919 2171
Middlesex Hospital (The), Mortimer Street, London W1N 8AA	0171 636 8333	0171 380 9205

LONDON AND THE SOUTH EAST *contd*

	TEL	FAX
Moorfields Eye Hospital, City Road, London EC1V 2PD	0171 253 3411	0171 253 4696
Mount Vernon Hospital, Rickmansworth Road, Northwood, Middlesex HA6 2RN	01923 826111	01923 835803
National Hospital for Neurology and Neurosurgery, Queen Square, London WC1N 3BG	0171 837 3611	0171 829 8720
New Victoria Hospital, 184 Coombe Lane West, Kingston, Surrey KT2 7EG*	0181 949 9000	0181 949 9099
Northwick Park and St Mark's Hospital, Watford Road, Harrow, Middlesex HA1 3UJ	0181 864 3232	0181 869 2009
Orpington Hospital, Sevenoaks Road, Orpington, Kent BR6 9JU	01689 815000	01689 815127
Parkside Hospital, 53 Parkside, Wimbledon, London SW19 5NX*	0181 946 4202	0181 946 7775
Portland Hospital (The), 209 Great Portland St., London W1N 6AH*	0171 580 4400	0171 631 1170
Portman Clinic, 8 Fitzjohn's Avenue, London NW3 5NA	0171 794 8262	0171 447 3748
Princess Grace Hospital, 42–52 Nottingham Place, London W1M 3FD	0171 486 1234	0171 935 2198
Priory Hospital, Priory Lane, Roehampton, London SW15 5JJ*	0181 876 8261	0181 392 2632
Queen Charlotte's Hospital, Goldhawk Road, London W6 0XG	0181 748 4666	0181 740 3588
Queen Elizabeth Hospital for Children, Hackney Road, London E2 8PS	0171 739 8422	0171 608 6399
Queen Mary's University Hospital, Roehampton, London SW15 5PN	0181 789 6611	0181 788 8417
Queen Victoria Hospital, Holtye Road, East Grinstead, West Sussex RH19 3DZ	01342 410210	01342 317907
Royal Brompton Hospital, Sydney Street, London SW3 6NB	0171 352 8121	0171 351 8473
Royal Free Hospital, Pond Street, London NW3 2QG	0171 794 0500	0171 830 2468
Royal London Hospital, Whitechapel, London E1 1BB	0171 377 7000	0171 377 7666
Royal Marsden Hospital, Fulham Road, London SW3 6JJ	0171 352 8171	0171 351 3785
Royal Marsden Hospital, Downs Road, Sutton, Surrey SM2 5PT	0181 642 6011	0181 770 9297

LONDON AND THE SOUTH EAST *contd*

	TEL	FAX
Royal Masonic Hospital, Ravenscourt Park, London W6 OTN*	0181 748 4611	0181 748 3817
Royal National Throat, Nose and Ear Hospital, Gray's Inn Road, London WC1X 8DA	0171 837 8855	0171 833 5518
Royal National Orthopaedic Hospital, Brockley Hill, Stanmore, Middlesex HA7 4LP	0181 954 2300	0181 954 9133
Royal Sussex County Hospital, Eastern Road, Brighton, Sussex BN2 5BE	01273 696955	01273 690919
St Ann's Hospital, St Ann's Road, South Tottenham, London N15 3TH	0181 442 6000	0181 442 6567
St Anthony's Hospital, London Road, North Cheam, Sutton, Surrey SM3 9DW*	0181 337 6691	0181 335 3325
St Bartholomew's Hospital, West Smithfield, London EC1A 7BE	0171 601 8888	0171 601 7656
St George's Hospital, Blackshaw Road, London SW17 0QT	0181 672 1255	0181 672 5304
St John and St Elizabeth, 60 Grove End Road, London NW8 9NH	0171 286 5126	0171 266 4813
St Luke's Hospital, Warren Road, Guildford, Surrey GM2 5XX	01483 571122	01483 39106
St Richard's Hospital, Chichester, West Sussex	01243 788122	01243 531269
St Mary's Hospital, Praed Street, London W2 1NY	0171 725 6666	0171 725 6200
St Thomas' Hospital, Lambeth Palace Road, London SE1 7EH	0171 928 9292	0171 922 8079
Samaritan's Hospital, 171 Marylebone Road, London NW1 5YE	0171 402 4211	0171 723 8726
Sherbourne Hospital, Broyle Road, Chichester, West Sussex PO19 4BE*	01243 530600	01243 532244
Sussex Nuffield Hospital, 55 New Church Rd, Hove, East Sussex BN3 4BG*	01273 779471	01273 220919
Tavistock Clinic, 120 Belsize Lane, London NW3 5BA	0171 435 7111	0171 435 8855
University College Hospital, Gower St, London WC1E 6AU	0171 387 9300	0171 380 9977
Wellington Hospital, 8a Wellington Place, London NW8 9LE *	0171 586 5959	0171 586 1960
West Middlesex University Hospital, Twickenham Road, Isleworth, Middlesex TW7 6AF	0181 560 2121	0181 560 5425
Western Eye Hospital (The), 171 Marylebone Road, London NW1 5YE	0171 402 4211	0171 723 8726

LONDON AND THE SOUTH EAST *contd*

	TEL	FAX
Whittington Hospital, Highgate Hill, Archway, London N19 5NF	0171 272 3070	0171 288 5930

ANGLIA AND OXFORD REGION

Addenbrooke's Hospital, Hills Road, Cambridge CB2 2QQ	01223 245151	01223 217094
Battle Hospital, Oxford Road, Reading, Berks RG3 1AG	01734 583666	01734 636503
Broadmoor Hospital, Crowthorne, Berks RG11 7EG	01344 773111	01344 754179
BUPA Cambridge Lea Hospital, 30 New Road, Impington, Cambridge CB4 4EL*	01223 237474	01223 233421
Churchill Hospital, Headington, Oxon OX3 7LJ	01865 741841	01865 225660
Evelyn Hospital, Trumpington Road, Cambridge CB2 2AF	01223 303336	01223 316068
Heatherwood Hospital, Ascot, Berkshire SL5 8AA	01344 23333	01344 874340
Ipswich Hospital (The), Heath Road Wing, Ipswich IP4 5PD	01473 712233	01473 703400
John Radcliffe Hospital, Headley Way, Headington, Oxford OX3 9DU	01865 741166	01865 741408
Norfolk and Norwich Hospital, Brunswick Road, Norwich, Norfolk NR1 2BB	01603 286286	01603 287211
Nuffield Orthopaedic Centre, Windmill Road, Headington, Oxford OX3 7LD	01865 741155	01865 742348
Papworth Hospital, Papworth Everard, Cambridge CB3 8RE	01480 830541	01480 831147
Princess Margaret Hospital, Windsor SL4 3SJ	01753 856743	01753 851749
Radcliffe Infirmary, Woodstock Road, Oxford OX2 6HE	01865 311188	01865 224566
St Mark's Hospital, St Mark's Road, Maidenhead, Berkshire SL6 6DU	01628 32012	01753 638399
Thames Valley Nuffield Hospital, Wexham, Slough, Berkshire SL3 6NH*	01753 662241	01753 662129
Wexham Park Hospital, Slough, Berkshire SL2 4HL	01753 633052	01753 634848

NORTH WEST REGION

	TEL	FAX
Alder Hey Children's Hospital, Eaton Road, Liverpool L12 2AP	0151 228 4811	0151 228 0328
Alexandra Hospital, Mill Lane, Cheadle, Cheshire SK8 2PX*	0161 428 3656	0161 491 3867
Blackburn Royal Infirmary, Bolton Rd, Blackburn, Lancashire BB2 3LR	01254 263555	01254 294572
Booth Hall Children's Hospital, Charlestown Road, Blackley, Manchester M9 2AA	0161 795 7000	0161 741 5387
Broadgreen Hospital, Thomas Drive, Liverpool L14 3LB	0151 228 4878	0151 254 2070
BUPA Hospital, Russell Rd, Whalley Range, Manchester M16 8AJ*	0161 226 0112	0161 227 6405
Cardiothoracic Centre, Thomas Drive, Liverpool L14 3PE	0151 228 1616	0151 220 8573
Christie Hospital, Wilmslow Road, Withington, Manchester M20 4BX	0161 446 3000	0161 446 3977
Clatterbridge Centre for Oncology, Clatterbridge Road, Bebington, Wirral L63 4JY	0151 334 1155	0151 334 0882
Fazakerley Hospital, Longmoor Lane, Liverpool L9 7AL	0151 525 3622	0151 252 6086
Grosvenor Nuffield Hospital, Wrexham Road, Chester CH4 7QP	01244 680444	01244 680812
Hope Hospital, Stott Lane, Salford 6, M6 8HD	0161 789 7373	0161 787 5974
Liverpool School of Tropical Medicine, Pembroke Place, Liverpool L36 5QA	0151 708 9393	0151 708 8733
Liverpool Women's Hospital, Catherine Street, Liverpool L8 7NJ	0151 709 1000	0151 708 0636
Manchester Royal Infirmary, Oxford Road, Manchester M13 9WL	0161 276 1234	0161 272 6932
North Manchester General Hospital, Delaunays Road, Crumpsall, Manchester M8 5RB	0161 795 4567	0161 740 4450
Ormskirk & District General Hospital, Wigan Road, Ormskirk L39 2AZ	01695 577111	01695 583028
Rotherham General Hospitals, Moorgate Rd, Rotherham, S. Yorks S60 2UD	01709 820000	01709 824000
Royal Eye Hospital, Oxford Road, Manchester M13 9WH	0161 276 1234	0161 272 6618
Royal Liverpool Childrens Hospital, Eaton Rd, West Derby, Liverpool LP12 2AP	0151 228 4811	0151 228 0328
Royal Liverpool Hospital, Prescot Street, Liverpool L7 8XP	0151 706 2000	0151 706 5806
Royal Manchester Children's Hospital, Pendelbury, Manchester M27 1HA	0161 794 4696	0161 994 5929
St Mary's Hospital, Whitworth Park, Manchester M13 OJH	0161 276 1234	0161 276 6107

NORTH WEST REGION *contd*

	TEL	FAX
St Mary's Hospital for Women & Children, Hathersage Road, Manchester M13 OJH	0161 276 1234	0161 276 6107
Stepping Hill Hospital, Poplar Grove, Stockport SK2 7JE	0161 483 1010	0161 419 5003
Trafford General Hospital, Moorside Road, Davyhulme, Manchester M41 5SL	0161 748 4022	0161 746 7214
Walton Centre for Neurology & Neurosurgery, Rice Lane, Liverpool L9 1AE	0151 525 3611	0151 529 4214
Withington Hospital, West Didsbury, Manchester M20 2LR	0161 445 8111	0161 445 5631
Wrightington Hospital, Hall Lane, Wrightington, Wigan WN6 9EP	01257 252211	01257 253809
Wythenshawe Hospital, Southmoor Road, Manchester M23 9LT	0161 998 7070	0161 946 2037

NORTHERN AND YORKSHIRE REGION

	TEL	FAX
Bradford Royal Infirmary, Duckworth Lane, Bradford BD9 6RJ	01274 542200	01274 364026
BUPA Hospital, Roundhay Hall, Jackson Avenue, Leeds LS8 1NT*	0113 2693939	0113 2681340
Freeman Hospital, Freeman Road, Newcastle upon Tyne NE7 7DN	0191 284 3111	0191 213 1968
Friarage Hospital, Northallerton, North Yorkshire DL6 1JG	01609 779911	01609 777144
Hull Royal Infirmary, Anlaby Road, Hull HU3 2JZ	01482 28541	01482 674857
Leeds General Infirmary, Great George Street, Leeds LS1 3EX	0113 243 2799	0113 292 6336
Newcastle General Hospital, Westgate Road, Newcastle upon Tyne NE4 6BE	0191 273 8811	0191 272 2641
Royal Victoria Infirmary, Queen Victoria Road, Newcastle upon Tyne NE1 4LP	0191 232 5131	0191 201 0155
St James's University Hospital, Beckett Street, Leeds, West Yorkshire LS9 7TF	01132 602528	01132 426496

SOUTH AND WEST REGION

	TEL	FAX
Bristol Eye Hospital, Lower Maudlin Street, Bristol BS1 2LX	0117 923 0060	0117 928 4686
Bristol Royal Infirmary, Maudlin Street, Bristol BS2 8HW	0117 923 0000	0117 928 2000
BUPA Chalybeate Hospital, Tremona Road, Southampton SO16 6UQ*	01703 775544	01703 701160

SOUTH AND WEST REGION *contd* TEL FAX

Hospital	TEL	FAX
BUPA Glen Hospital, Redland Hill, Durdham Down, Bristol BS6 7JJ*	0117 973 2562	0117 974 3203
Derriford Hospital, Derriford Road, Plymouth PL6 8DH	01752 777111	01752 768976
Frenchay Hospital, Frenchay Park Road, Bristol BS16 1LE	0117 970 1212	0117 975 3761
Moorgreen Hospital, Botley Road, West End, Southampton SO3 3JB	01703 477165	01703 465014
Musgrove Park Hospital, Taunton TA1 5DA	01823 333444	01823 336877
Princess Anne Hospital, Coxford Road, Southampton SO16 5YA	01703 777222	01703 794143
Princess Margaret Hospital, Okus Road, Swindon SN1 4UJ	01793 536231	01793 480817
Royal Hampshire County Hospital, Romsey Road, Winchester, Hampshire SO22 5DG	01962 863535	01962 824826
Royal Hospital for Sick Children, St Michael's Hill, Bristol BS2 8BJ	0117 921 5411	0117 928 5820
Royal National Hospital for Rheumatic Diseases, Upper Borough Walls, Bath BA1 1RL	01225 465941	01225 421202
St Michael's Hospital, Southwell Street, Bristol BS2 8EG	0117 921 5411	0117 928 5820
Sarum Road Hospital, Sarum Road, Winchester SO23 5HA*	01962 844555	01962 842620
Somerset Nuffield, Staplegrove Elm, Taunton, Somerset TA2 6AN*	01823 286991	01823 338951
Southampton General Hospital, Tremona Road, Southampton S016 6YD	01703 777222	01703 783839
Western Community Hospital, Walnut Grove, Millbrook, Southampton S016 4XE	01703 475 401	01703 475402

TRENT REGION

Hospital	TEL	FAX
City General Hospital, Newcastle Road, Stoke-On-Trent ST4 6QG	01782 715444	01782 716591
Convent Hospital, 748 Mansfield Road, Woodthorpe, Nottingham NG5 3FZ*	0115 9209209	0115 9673005
Hayward Hospital, High Lane, Burslem, Stoke-on-Trent, Staffordshire ST6 7AG	01782 835 721	01782 838721
Leicester Royal Infirmary, Infirmary Square, Leicester LE1 5WW	0116 2541414	0116 2585631
Nether Edge Hospital, Sheffield S11 9EL	0114 271 1800	0114 271 1801
Northern General Hospital, Herries Road, Sheffield S5 7AU	0114 243 4343	0114 256 0472

TRENT REGION *contd*   **TEL**   **FAX**

	TEL	FAX
Park Hospital, Sherwood Lodge Drive, Burntstum Country Park, Arnold, Nottingham NG 8RX*	0115 967 0670	0115 967 0381
Royal Hallamshire Hospital, Glossop Rd, Sheffield S10 2JF	0114 271 1900	0114 271 1901
Sheffield Children's Hospital, Western Bank, Sheffield S10 2TH	0114 271 7000	0114 272 3418
University Hospital, Queen's Medica l Centre, Nottingham NG7 2UH	0115 924 9924	0115 970 9196

WEST MIDLANDS

	TEL	FAX
Alexandra Hospital (The), Woodrow Drive, Redditch, Worcestershire B98 7UB	01527 503030	01527 517432
Birmingham Children's Hospital, Ladywood Middleway, Birmingham B16 8ET	0121 454 4851	0121 456 4697
Birmingham Heartlands Hospital, Brodesley Green East, Birmingham B9 5SS	0121 766 6611	0121 773 6897
Birmingham Women's Hospital, Edgbaston, Birmingham B15 2TG	0121 472 1377	0121 627 2602
Derby City General Hospital, Uttoxeter Road, Derby DE22 2NE	01332 340131	01332 240559
Priory Hospital, Priory Road, Edgbaston, Birmingham B5 7UG *	0121 440 2323	0121 440 0804
Queen Elizabeth Hospital, Edgbaston, Birmingham B12 2TH	0121 472 1311	0121 627 2212
Royal Wolverhampton Hospital, Wolverhampton Rd, Wolverhampton WV10 0QP	01902 307999	01902 642810
Solihull Parkway Hospital, Dawson Parkway, Solihull, West Midlands*	0121 704 1451	0121 711 1080
Uffculme Clinic, Queensbridge, Birmingham B13 8BQ	0121 442 4545	0121 442 4541
Walsgrave Hospital, Clifford Bridge Road, Coventry CV2 2DX	01203 602020	01203 622197

SCOTLAND

	TEL	FAX
Aberdeen Royal Infirmary, Foresterhill, Aberdeen AB9 2ZB	01224 681818	01224 840597
City Hospital, Urquhart Road, Aberdeen AB9 8AU	01224 681818	01224 685307
City Hospital, 51 Greenbank Drive, Edinburgh EH10 5SB	0131 536 6000	0131 536 6001

SCOTLAND *contd*

	TEL	FAX
Dundee Royal, Barrack Rd, Dundee DD1 9ND	01382 660111	01382 660445
Gartnavel Royal Hospital, 1055 Great Western Road, Glasgow G12 0XH	0141 211 3600	0141 337 2408
Glasgow Nuffield Hospital, Beaconsfield Road, Glasgow G12 0PJ*	0141 334 9441	0141 339 1352
Glasgow Royal Infirmary, Glasgow G4 0SF	0141 211 4000	0141 211 4889
Edinburgh Royal Infirmary, 1 Lauriston Place, Edinburgh EH3 9YW	0131 536 1000	0131 519 5401
Ninewells Hospital, Dundee DD1 9SY	01382 660111	01382 660445
Northern General Hospital, Ferry Road, Edinburgh EH5 2DQ	01742 434343	01742 560472
Ross Hall Hospital, 221 Crookston Road, Glasgow G51*	0141 810 3151	0141 882 7439
Royal Edinburgh Hospital, Morningside, Edinburgh EH10 5HF	0131 537 6000	0131 537 6106
Royal Hospital for Sick Children, Yorkhill, Glasgow G3 8SJ	0141 201 0000	0141 201 0836
Royal Infirmary of Edinburgh, Lauriston Place, Edinburgh EH3 9YW	0131 536 1000	0131 536 1001
Southern General Hospital, 1345 Govan Road, Glasgow G51 4TF	0141 201 1100	0141 201 2999
Western General Hospital, Crewe Road, Edinburgh EH4 2XU	0131 537 1000	0131 537 1007
Western Infirmary, Glasgow G11 6NT	0141 211 2000	0141 334 0717

WALES

Morriston Hospital, Swansea, West Glamorgan SA6 6NL	01792 702222	01792 796907
Singleton Hospital, Sketty, Swansea SA2 8QA	01792 205666	01792 208647
University Hospital of Wales, Heath Park, Cardiff CF4 4XW	01222 747747	01222 743838

APPENDIX 3

GUIDE TO LETTERS AFTER DOCTORS NAMES

BCh or BChir: Bachelor of Surgery, one of the basic qualifications.

BS: Bachelor of Surgery, as above.

BSc: Bachelor of Science.

ChM: Master of Surgery.

DCH: Diploma of Child Health. Awarded in London by the Institute of Child Health, the academic unit of Great Ormond Street Hospital for Sick Children. This qualification is taken alike by physicians and surgeons who wish to do paediatric work.

DLO: Diploma in Laryngology and Otology.

DM: Doctor of Medicine, a degree requiring original research.

DMRT: Diploma in Medical Radio-therapy.

DobstRCOG: Diploma Royal College Obstetrics and Gynaecology.

DPhil: Literally, Doctor of Philosophy – doctorate in medicine, awarded for original research.

DSc: Doctor of Science.

DTM: Diploma in Tropical Medicine and Hygiene.

Ed: Edinburgh.

FACC: Fellow American College of Cardiologists.

FACS: Fellow American College of Surgery.

FFR: Fellow Faculty of Radiologists.

FRACP: Fellow Royal Australasian College of Physicians.

FRACS: Fellow Royal Australasian College of Surgeons.

FRCOG: Fellow of the Royal College of Obstetricians and Gynaecologists. Unlike the FRCP, this is awarded almost automatically to MRCOGs after several years of successful practice.

FRCOphth: Fellow for the Royal College of Ophthalmologists.

FRCP: Fellow of the Royal College of Physicians. A still higher distinction than MRCP. Until now it has been awarded selectively – capriciously, some have complained – to physicians who make a substantial contribution to medicine. A few have received it early in their careers for a prestigious breakthrough; many more as a pre-retirement gong. It is unlikely that it will be awarded on completion of two years satisfactory work, after passing the MRCP exam.

FRCPath: Fellow Royal College of Pathologists.

FRCPI: Fellow Royal College of Physicians of Ireland.

FRCPS: Fellow Royal College of Physicians and Surgeons.

FRCPsych: Fellow of the Royal College of Psychiatrists. Almost automatically awarded after several years of satisfying work.

FRCR: Fellow Royal College of Radiologists.

FRCS: Fellow of the Royal college of Surgeons. The equivalent in surgery of MRCP, earned by passing a competitive exam designed to identify those who be fit to become consultant surgeons.

FRCS Ed: Fellow Royal College of Surgeons of Edinburgh.

FRS Ed: Fellow Royal Society Edinburgh.

LMCC: Licentiate Medical Council of Canada.

LRCP and MRCS: Licentiate of the Royal College of Physicians and Member of the Royal College of Surgeons. Often a doctor who puts both MB, BS and LRCP, MRCS after his name sat for both exams because his tutor feared he might fail one – they are equivalent basic qualifications.

MB: Bachelor of Medicine.

MChir, MCh, MC: Master of Surgery. A postgraduate degree, roughly the surgical equivalent of MD, requiring original research.

MD: Doctor of Medicine, awarded for original research.

MRC: Medical Research Council.

MRCOG: Member of the Royal College of Obstetricians and Gynaecologists. This is the essential diploma for those seeking to become a consultant obstetrician and/or gynaecologist

MRCP: Member of the Royal College of Physicians. A higher diploma, possessed by a few GPs, but an essential step towards becoming a consultant physician.

MRCPsych: Member of the Royal College of Psychiatrists. The essential qualification to become a consultant psychiatrist. These days a PhD or MD as well as MPhil in psychiatry will often be acquired during the struggle to the top. Since the college is a relatively new creation older psychiatrists have already received an MRCP or, even more likely, an FRCP.

MRCS: Member of the Royal College of Surgeons. A basic qualification – an MRCS has passed half the exams required to become a houseman but not yet a GP. It is the equivalent of LRCP.

MS: Master of Surgery. A postgraduate degree, roughly the surgical equivalent of MD, requiring original research.

MSc: Master of Science. This degree is often taken by medical students who wish to pursue research for at least a part of their careers.

PhD: Another abbreviation for Doctor of Philosophy – doctorate in medicine, awarded for original research.

FRCP Ed: Fellow of the Royal College of Surgeons of Edinburgh, sometimes denoted as FRCPE.

GLOSSARY OF MEDICAL TERMS

A

Acoustic neuroma: a progressively enlarging, benign tumour, usually within the internal auditory canal. The symptoms, which vary with the size and location of the tumour, may include hearing loss, headache, disturbances of balance, facial numbness or pain, and tinnitus. It may be unilateral or bilateral. Called also acoustic neurilemoma, or schwannoma, and acoustic nerve tumour.

Adnexa: appendages, especially those of the uterus (Fallopian tubes and ovaries).

Adrenal: the adrenal glands are a pair of small organs situated at the back of the abdomen, against the upper end of the two kidneys.

Aesthetic surgery: the department of surgery which deals with procedures designed to improve the patient's appearance by plastic restoration, correction, removal of blemishes etc.

Alzheimer's disease (dementia): a progressive degenerative disease of unknown etiology. The first signs of the disease are slight memory disturbance or subtle changes in personality; there is a progressive deterioration resulting in profound dementia over a course of 5 to 10 years. Onset may occur at any age; the disease was originally described as presenile dementia, occurring in people under 65, as opposed to senile dementia, which was supposed to be a consequence of the ageing process, but there is no clinical or pathophysiological distinction between the two classes of patients. Women are affected twice as frequently as men.

Amyloidosis: a group of conditions of diverse etiologies characterised by the accumulation of proteins (amyloid) in various organs and tissues of the body such that vital function is compromised.

Aneurysm: a sac formed by the dilation of the wall of an artery, a vein, or the heart; it is filled with fluid or clotted blood, often forming a pulsating tumour.*

Angina: spasmodic, choking, or suffocative pain; now used almost exclusively to denote angina pectoris, which is caused by the shortage of oxygen in the heart muscle.

Angioplasty: a procedure for elimination of areas of narrowing in blood vessels.*

Ankylosing Spondylitis: a painful and progressive rheumatic disease of the spine. It can also affect other parts of the body especially the hip joints and the eyes. The cause is unknown and at present incurable. Anti-inflammatory drugs are prescribed to reduce the pain. Roughly 700,000 are thought to suffer from this disease but only 50–60,000 suffer severely enough to have been diagnosed.

Arrhythmias: any variation from the normal rhythm of the heartbeat; it may be an abnormality of either the rate, regularity or site of impulse origin or the sequence of activation. The term encompasses abnormal regular and irregular rhythms as well as loss of rhythm.*

Autism: a strange disorder of the mind, beginning in childhood and persisting into adulthood. Preoccupation with inner thoughts, daydreams etc...; egocentric, subjective thinking lacking objectivity and connection with reality. The self often predominates to the total exclusion of that which is not self. Sensation is normal, but there is little perception. Some autistic children are wrongly assumed to be deaf, others blind. The child is often preoccupied with some apparently meaningless repetitive action. An occasional outburst of rage may be the only sign of emotion.

Autoimmune disease: a disorder caused by a reaction of the patient's immune system against one's own body. Before birth or just after birth the body recognises every constituent of the body as its own exempting them from a defensive reaction. However if part of the body is not recognised in later life the body will attack it. The auto antibodies are associated with many diseases characterised by chronic destructive inflammation such as Crohn's disease, ulcerative colitis, glomerulnephritis, etc... Many of these conditions are incurable but can be controlled by taking drugs to suppress the reactions.

B

Balloon angioplasty: angioplasty in which a balloon catheter is inflated inside an artery, stretching the intima and leaving a ragged interior surface after deflation, which triggers a healing response and breaking up of plaque.*

Behcet's **Disease:** a chronic inflammatory disorder involving the small blood vessels, which is of unknown etiology, and is characterised by recurrent ulceration of the oral and pharyngeal mucous membranes and the genitalia, skin lesions, severe uveitis, retinal vasculitis, and optic atrophy. It frequently also involves the joints, gastrointestinal system, and central system.*

Brachial plexus: a leash of nerves with various intercommunications, arising from spinal nerves in the lower part of the neck. Its branches provide the nerves of the shoulder girdle and upper limb.

Brachytherapy: in radiotherapy, treatment with ionizing radiation whose source is applied to the surface of the body or is located a short distance from the body area being treated.*

Bronchiectasis: chronic dilatation of the bronchi marked by fetid breath and paroxysmal coughing, with the expectoration of mucopurulent matter. It may affect the tube uniformly or occur in irregular pockets, or the dilated tubes may have terminal bulbous enlargements.*

Broncoscopy: examination of the bronchi through a bronchoscope.*

Brucellosis: a generalised infection of humans caused by species of Brucella transmitted by direct or indirect contact with the natural animal reservoirs, including sheep, goats, swine, deer, and rabbits, or their infected products or tissue. Characterised by fever, sweating, weakness, malaise and weightloss.*

C

Cardiomyopathies: a general diagnostic term designating primary non-inflammatory disease of the heart muscle, often of obscure or unknown etiology.*

Carotid artery disease: disease affecting the carotid artery, the principal artery of the head.

Carpal tunnel: a fibrous bridge, the flexor retinaculum, spans the small bones at the base of the palm of the hand. The carpal tunnel is the opening between the flexor retinaculum and the bones. The flexor tendons to the fingers pass through this tunnel, enclosed in slippery synovial sheaths which prevent friction in this narrow space.

Cerebrovascular disease: disease affecting the arteries of the brain.

Chlamydia: a genus of bacteria.

Choriocarcinoma: a malignancy in the outer layer of the membrane surrounding the foetus.

Chorionic villas sampling: CVS is a method of obtaining a sample for chromosome or gene tests. It involves taking a small sample from the developing placenta at about 11 weeks of pregnancy. This can be done vaginally or abdominal, like amniocentesis. It is usually offered only to women whose babies are known to be at high risk of an abnormality. CVS may cause up to two women in a hundred to miscarry.

Cleft: a pathological fissure derived from a failure of parts to fuse during embryonic development

Coeliac disease: a disorder of the small intestine in which the assimilation of essential dietary ingredients is impaired. The mucous membrane lining the intestine does not tolerate *gliadin*, a component of the protein gluten found in wheat, barley and rye. Characteristic changes in the membrane can be seen under the microscope, and diagnosis can be confirmed by examining a fragment of it.

Colonoscopy: examination by means of a colonoscope. Called also coloscopy.*

Congenital: existing at and usually before birth; referring to conditions that are present at birth, regardless of their causation; not necessarily hereditary.

Corticosteroid: any of several hormones formed in the cortex of the adrenal glands.

Craniofacial: pertaining to the cranium and the face.*

Creutzfeldt-Jakob disease: a rare, usually fatal, transmissible spongiform encephalopathy, occurring in middle life, accompanied by progressive dementia and sometimes wasting of the muscles, tremor, athetosis, and spastic dysarthria.

Crohn's disease: a disease which affects any part of the digestive tract. Deep fissures and ulcers can occur which may cause the inflamed intestine to stick to adjacent organs or lead to infection outside the bowel wall. Suffers experience abdominal pain and diarrhea, sometimes with bleeding. Other symptoms include vomiting, abdominal swelling and general malaise. There is no known cause.

Cushing's Syndrome: disorder of body chemistry, leading to retention of salt and water. Obesity confined to the face and trunk, high blood pressure, weakening of bone and connective tissue, and sometimes diabetes and other symptoms. It is due to excessive production of steroid hormones by the cortex of the adrenal glands.

Cystic fibrosis: an uncommon hereditary defect of numerous glands, including the mucus glands of the bronchi, the sweat glands and the digestive glands. The symptoms include severe digestive disorders, difficulty with breathing and lung infections, and a tendency to heatstroke.

D

Diabetes mellitus: a chronic syndrome of impaired carbohydrate, protein and fat metabolism owing to insufficient secretion of insulin or to target tissue insulin resistance.*

Dialysis: the process of separating crystalloid and colloids in solution; it involves two distinct physical processes, diffusion and ultra filtration. The apparatus is used to take over the work of incompetent kidneys, but it may also be life saving in some types of poisoning.

Dupuytren's contracture: thickening of the fibrous lining of the palm which makes it impossible to straighten the fingers.

E

Echocardiography: a method of graphically recording the position and motion of the heart walls, the internal structures of the heart and neighbouring tissue by the echo obtained from beams of ultrasonic waves directed through the chest wall.*

Electrodiagnosis: the use of electrical devices in the diagnosis of pathologic conditions.*

Electrophysiology: the study of the mechanisms of production of electrical phenomena, particularly in the nervous system and their consequences in the living organism.*

Endocarditis: inflammation of the heart lining especially that of the heart valves. It may occur as a primary disorder or as a complication of or in association with another disease.

Endometriosis: inflammation of the endometrium; presence of fragments of mucous membrane of the same kind as the lining of the uterus in other places, e.g. in the muscle of the uterus, especially the ovaries.

Endoscope: an instrument for the examination of the interior of a hollow viscus, such as the bladder.*

Endoscopy: visual inspection of any cavity of the body by means of an endoscope.*

ERCP: endoscopic retrograde cholangiopancreatography.

F

Felty's **syndrome:** a combination of chronic (rheumatoid) arthritis, splenomegaly (enlargement of the spleen), leukopenia (reduction in white blood cells) and pigmented spots on the skin of the lower extremities.

Fistula: an abnormal passage or communication usually between two internal organs or leading from an internal organ to the surface of the body.*

G

Glioma: a tumour composed of tissue which represents neuroglia (the connective tissue of the brain) in any one of its stages of development.

Glomerulonephritis: inflamation of the capillary loops in the glomeruli of the kidney.

Guillain-Barré **Syndrome:** acute inflammation of several peripheral nerves.

H

Helicobacter pylori: a type of bacteria that causes gastritis and pyloric ulcers in humans.

Hepatitis: inflamation of the liver.

Hepatobiliary: pertaining to the liver and the bile or the bilary ducts.

Hiatus hernia: a small weakness in the diaphragm where part of the stomach protrudes.

Hirsutism: abnormal hairiness, especially an adult male pattern of hair distribution in women.*

Hodgkin's lymphoma: a form of malignant lymphoma characterised by painless progressive enlargement of the lymph nodes, spleen, and general lymphoid tissue; other symptoms may include anorexia, lassitude, weight loss and fever. It affects twice as many males as females.*

Hydatid disease: an infection, usually of the liver, caused by larval forms of tapeworms of the genus *Echinococcus*, and characterised by the development of expanding cysts.*

Hyperplasia: the abnormal multiplication or increase in the number of normal cells in normal arrangement in a tissue. Generally due to stimulation by hormones.

Hypertension: high blood pressure.

Hypospadias: a developmental anomaly in the male in which the urethra opens on the underside of the penis or the perineum.*

I

Impotence: lack of copulative power in the male due to failure to initiate an erection or to maintain an erection until ejaculation.

Inflammatory bowel disease: a general term for those inflamatory diseases of the bowel of unknown etiology, including Crohn's disease, and ulcerative colitis.

Inguinal hernia: a hernia pertaining to the groin.

Interstitial: pertaining to or situated between parts or the interspaces of a tissue.

Irritable bowel syndrome (IBS): a common complaint often described as functional bowel disorder because the function of the bowel is upset without it being diseased. It often causes pain and diarrhoea or constipation. As many people as one in five people are affected. Stress exacerbates the condition and many sufferers are advised to try and reduce the stressful elements of their life.

Ischaemic heart disease (IHD): any of a group of acute or chronic cardiac disabilities resulting from insufficient supply of oxygenated blood to the heart.*

K

Kaposi's sarcoma: an uncommon cancer-like disease of the skin with lesions resembling blood blisters.

L

Laparoscopic Cholecstectomy: Removal of the gall bladder using keyhole surgery.

Laparoscopic surgery: surgical examination by means of a laparoscope.

Leishmania: a microscopical parasite similar to that of sleeping sickness.

Leukaemia: cancer-like disease of the white blood cells.

Lymphoma: any neoplastic disorder of the lymphoid tissue.

M

Marfan's Syndrome: an inherited disorder of connective tissue which affects many organs including the skeleton, lungs, eyes, heart and blood vessels. It can affect ether man or woman of any race or ethnic origin. 5000 people in the UK have Marfan's syndrome; 75% of cases are inherited and 25% result from a spontaneous mutation. A single abnormal gene on Chromosome 15 causes the condition. The gene controls the production of fibrillin, a very fine fibre in connective tissue throughout the body.

Mastectomy: excision of the breast.

Melanoma: a tumour arising from the melanocytic system of the skin and other organs.*

Meningioma: a benign slow growing tumour of the meninges (membranes enclosing the brain and spinal cord).

Metabolic diseases: general term for diseases caused by disruption of a normal metabolic pathway (chemical changes by which foods are converted into components of the body or consumed as fuel) because of a genetically determined enzyme defect.

Myasthenia: muscular debility; any constitutional anomaly of muscle.*

Myeloma: a tumour composed of cells of the type normally found in the bone marrow.*

Myoclonus: shock-like contractions of a portion or a muscle, an entire muscle or a group of muscles, restricted to one area of the body or appearing synchronously or asynchronously in several areas.*

N

Narcolepsy: a recurrent, uncontrollable brief episodes of sleep, often associated with hypnogogic hallucinations, cataplexy, and sleep paralysis.*

Neonatal: pertaining to the first four weeks after birth.*

Nephrotic syndrome: general name for a group of diseases involving defective kidney glomeruli.*

Neuro-ophthalmology: the field of specialisation dealing with portions of the nervous system related to the eye.

Neuro-otology: the part of otology (study of ears) dealing especially with portions of the nervous system related to the eye.

Neuropathy: a functional disturbance or pathological change in the peripheral nervous system, sometimes limited to non-inflammatory lesions as opposed to those of neuritis.*

Non Hodgkin's lymphoma: a form of malignant lymphomas, the only common feature being an absence of the giant Reed-Sternberg cells characteristic of Hodgkins disease. They arise from the lymphoid components of the immune system, and present a clinical picture broadly similar to that of Hodgkin's disease except the disease is more widespread.*

O

Oncology: the study of tumours.

Osteoporosis: reduction in the amount of bone mass leading to fractures after minimal trauma.*

Otolaryngology: branch of medicine concerned with medical and surgical treatment of the head and neck, including the ears, nose and throat.*

Otology: branch of medicine which deals with the medical treatment and surgery of the ear, and its anatomy, physiology, and pathology.*

Otosclerosis: a pathological condition of the bony labyrinth of the ear, in which there is a formation of spongy bone, especially in front of and posterior to the footplate of the stapes; it may cause bony ankylosis of the stapes, resulting in conductive hearing loss.*

P

Paget's **disease:** intraductal carcinoma of the breast extending to involve the nipple and areola, characterised by eczema-like inflammatory skin changes.*

Paraneoplastic syndrome: a sympton-complex arising in a cancer-bearing patient that cannot be explained by local or distant spread of the tumour.*

Parkinson's disease: a group of neurological disorders characterised by shaking, tremors and muscular rigidity.

Peptic: pertaining to pepsin or to digestion; related to action of gastric juices.*

Peripheral nerves: cords of nerve fibres, radiating from the central nervous system and conducting impulses to and from all parts of the body.

Prolapse: the falling down or sinking of a part or viscus.*

Prostatitis: inflammation of the prostrate.

Psoriasis: a common disorder of the outer layers of the skin. The typical appearance is of thickened red blotches with a scaly surface, most often on the scalp, back and arms.

R

Refsum's **disease:** an autosomal recessive disorder of lipid metabolism.

Rhinoplasty: a plastic surgical operation on the nose, either reconstructive, restorative, or cosmetic.*

Rhinosinusitis: inflammation of the accessory sinuses of the nose.*

S

Sarcoidosis: a small focus of chronic inflammation without evidence of infection; the name implies a similarity to sarcoma (a kind of cancer) but the two are unrelated.

Sarcoma: any of a group of tumours usually arising from connective tissue; most are malignant.

Schwannoma: see Acoustic neuroma.

Schistosoma: a type of parasite or fluke; sometimes called bilharzia.

Stereotaxic: pertaining to types of brain surgery that use a system of three-dimensional coordinates to locate the site to be operated on.

Strabismus: deviation of the eye which the patient cannot overcome. The visual axes assume a position relative to each other different from that required by the physiological conditions.*

Systemic disease: one affecting a number of organs and tissues.

Systemic lupus erythematosus (SLE): a chronic, remitting, inflammatory, and multisystemic disorder of connective tissue. Acute or insidious in onset, characterised principally by involvement of the skin, joints, kidneys and seosal membranes.

T

Thrombotic disorders: pertaining to or affected with thrombosis.

Tinnitus: a noise in the ears, such as ringing, buzzing, roaring or clicking.*

U

Ulcerative colitis: this disease affects the colon and rectum: the lining of the bowel is inflamed and may be ulcerated, causing diarrhoea with mucus and blood. Other symptoms include abdominal pain and tiredness.

Uveitis: an inflammation of part of the uvea, the middle tunic of the eye, and commonly involving the other tunics.*

V

Valvuloplasty: plastic repair of a valve.

*Quoted from *Dorland's Illustrated Medical Dictionary*, edn 28, Philadelphia, W. B. Saunders Company, 1994.

INDEX OF DOCTORS' NAMES

INDEX OF CLINICAL CONDITIONS